Freedom on Trial

FREEDOM ON TRIAL

The First Post–Civil War Battle Over
Civil Rights and Voter Suppression

SCOTT FARRIS

LYONS PRESS

ESSEX, CONNECTICUT

*Dedicated to those Americans who have been abused and
killed while seeking to exercise their right to vote*

An imprint of Globe Pequot, the trade division of
The Rowman & Littlefield Publishing Group, Inc.
4501 Forbes Blvd., Ste. 200
Lanham, MD 20706
www.rowman.com

Distributed by NATIONAL BOOK NETWORK

British Library Cataloguing-in-Publication Information available

Library of Congress Control Number: 2020942269

ISBN 978-1-4930-4635-5 (hardcover: alk. paper)
ISBN 978-1-4930-6742-8 (paperback)
ISBN 978-1-4930-4636-2 (electronic)

♾™ The paper used in this publication meets the minimum requirements of American National
Standard for Information Sciences—Permanence of Paper for Printed Library Materials, ANSI/NISO
Z39.48-1992.

Contents

PREFACE

All that can save you now is your confrontation with your own history.
—JAMES BALDWIN

FREEDOM ON TRIAL, THE ALREADY VITAL AND IMPORTANT STORY OF the Great South Carolina Ku Klux Klan Trials of 150 years ago, was given an urgent new relevance by the events of the spring and summer of 2020. In the middle of a global pandemic, there were an extraordinary number of spontaneous demonstrations for racial justice aroused by the death of a Black man named George Floyd at the hands of local police in Minneapolis, Minnesota. What the tangible results of these demonstrations will be is, as of now, unknown, but the history of the Ku Klux trials offers a cautionary tale for those expecting meaningful change to happen rapidly.

Like the horrified reaction to George Floyd's death, the Ku Klux trials were another moment in American history pregnant with hope for a better future. Initially supported with great fervor by the public and our national government, the trials destroyed the Ku Klux Klan but could have achieved more. They might have been an extraordinary inflection point where American race relations could have gone in a vastly different direction, sparing this nation and many of its citizens much grief. But that opportunity was lost due to increasing public indifference, a weariness with the struggle when faced with stubborn intransigence, and the failure of institutions that did not view justice as the primary purpose of the law. The struggle for racial equality requires constancy. It is the work of generations.

Also in 2020, the global coronavirus pandemic added another layer of complexity to the ongoing concern around voter access. To a large degree, *Freedom on Trial* is about what people are willing to do to achieve political power for themselves while denying it to others. Racism was at its core, but the primary purpose of the nightly raids of the Ku Klux Klan was voter suppression as they sought to disarm African Americans and intimidate them into not exercising their newly won right to vote. Voter suppression has become far subtler over the years, but the aim is the same: the quest for political power.

The protests of 2020 also challenged how our history is remembered and memorialized. Statues honoring heroes of the Confederacy and others were pulled down from their pedestals, flags were lowered or banned, and names for streets, schools, sports teams, and much else were changed in an attempt to avoid honoring those deemed responsible for past racial injustice and division. Such changes may seem more symbolic than substantive, but how we remember our history shapes what we do in the present and expect of the future.

Freedom on Trial highlights forgotten civil rights pioneers, Black and white, whose memorialization would change our understanding of the past and thereby influence our present and future. Some of these heroes refute the axiom that we cannot judge those of the past by the morality of today, for there are always those who stand on the right side of every question, and that was as true in 1871 as it is today. This book also celebrates the devout patriotism and love of country expressed by those who certainly had the least reason to love America, the formerly enslaved. Once free, they intensely desired to fully participate in the ongoing American experiment. When new memorials are raised, it should be in their spirit, which is a love of America not just for what it has been but for what we hope it will yet be.

Finally, many white Americans in 2020 began a serious contemplation of their own personal role in ending racism in America. Some heeded the call by historian Ibram X. Kendi in his book *How to Be an Antiracist* (2019) and began a process of self-examination. This examination can go beyond the individual. In this book, I weave in the story of my own great-grandfather's crimes as a Ku Klux Klan member. One hope for this book is that it will inspire others to take a closer and harder look not only at their own behavior and attitudes, but at their own family's role in the history of racism in America. It is a humbling experience.

In an interview the brilliant writer James Baldwin gave to *Esquire* magazine in July 1968 (another tumultuous year) he said something that was a lodestar in shaping this book:

All that can save you now is your confrontation with your own history . . . which is not your past, but your present. Your history has led you to this moment, and you can only begin to change yourself by looking at what you are doing in the name of your history.

Scott Farris
July 2020

INTRODUCTION

People will not look forward to posterity who never look backward to their ancestors.

—*EDMUND BURKE*, REFLECTIONS ON THE FRENCH REVOLUTION

MY GREAT-GRANDFATHER, JOHN CLAYTON FARRIS, WAS A COMMON FARM laborer and twice-wounded Confederate army veteran from pastoral York County, South Carolina, who became a member of the Ku Klux Klan following the Civil War. This genealogical discovery is how I came to learn about the most consequential criminal trials in America history, known as the Great South Carolina Ku Klux Klan Trials. The federal crackdown that culminated in these trials, conducted from 1871 to 1873, destroyed the Ku Klux, the largest domestic terror organization our nation has ever known.* The Klan disappeared from American life for nearly a half-century until it was resurrected in a new incarnation following the release of the odious 1915 film *Birth of a Nation*, which was based on real-life characters involved in these trials.

Yet the history of these trials is not widely known, nor do they play a prominent role in most scholarly histories of Reconstruction—to the degree the history of Reconstruction is widely discussed at all. When I began working on this book, the Reconstruction era was not a topic of broad public interest. On an early visit to the new National Museum of African American History and Culture, I marveled that the full array of displays on Reconstruction might fit in a modestly sized living room. But interest in this pivotal time in American history, and what it means to us today, seems

---

*In newspapers and most written accounts from 1871, the shorthand reference to the KKK organization and its individual members was "Ku Klux," not "Klan" or "Klansman," so that is how the organization and its members will generally be referenced in this book. It also helps differentiate the Reconstruction-era Ku Klux from the twentieth-century Klan incarnations.

to be growing, partly due to the ongoing scholarship of historians such as Eric Foner and Henry Louis Gates Jr., the latter of whom developed a marvelous multipart documentary on Reconstruction for public television that aired in 2019, and also because of the new wave of protests against racial injustice that swept the United States in 2020.

With improved hindsight, we see that Reconstruction offered the opportunity for an alternate history of the United States that might have spared our nation many of the travails of racial division. It is becoming increasingly clear, as we progress toward a society where we are judged, in the words of Martin Luther King Jr., by the content of our character and not the color of our skin, that we should look more closely at the Reconstruction era for instruction as to what went right and why it went wrong.

The Great South Carolina Ku Klux Klan Trials were the high point of Reconstruction and the most concerted effort the federal government would make to secure the civil rights of African Americans—indeed, of all Americans—for a century. Eradicating the Ku Klux was a great achievement, but the tragedy of the trials is that they had the potential to be more momentous, even revolutionary.

These trials were the first great tests of the meaning of the newly adopted Fourteenth and Fifteenth Amendments to the Constitution. At issue was whether these amendments transformed the Bill of Rights, previously interpreted as only a restraint on the power of the federal government, into a guarantee of certain rights for all citizens, regardless of color or place of residence, and now made the federal government responsible for protecting those rights. As such, these trials had the potential to be one of the most dramatic inflection points in our national history, but the margin of a single vote on the Supreme Court of the United States prevented this possibility.

It had long been a family mystery why John Clayton, which is how I will generally refer to my great-grandfather in this book, rather suddenly left his home in York County and resettled in a remote area of northern Arkansas in the fall of 1871. Family gossip, which no one seemed able to either confirm or refute, was that John Clayton had killed a Black man and was fleeing justice. But John Clayton died in 1916, just a year after my own father was born. By the time I came into being decades later, there was no one alive to verify if this were true.

There were reasons for suspicion. John Clayton reportedly avoided having his photograph taken, and I have not found one that could positively be identified as being of him. One photograph some relatives thought was of John Clayton turned out instead to be an image of his cousin, John R. Faris, who lived in York County at the same time but who was the rare local white man to actively oppose the Ku Klux, earning their wrath.*

Also, until he was in his seventies and applied for a Confederate veteran's disability pension in 1909, John Clayton seemed to avoid circumstances that required interaction with government authorities. He is missing from several federal census reports, and even though he personally possessed rudimentary reading and writing skills, he declined to send his son, my grandfather William Francis Farris, to school. This left my grandfather illiterate and toiling most of his life, as his father had before him, as a poor sharecropper hardly more prosperous, and sometimes less so, than neighboring African-American families who earned their living the same, hard way while living with the added burden of racism.

A clue as to why my great-grandfather chose to live a comparatively reclusive life appeared to me when reading Foner's authoritative history, *Reconstruction: America's Unfinished Revolution* (1988). I was discomfited by Foner's observation that John Clayton's home of York County, where "nearly the entire white male population" was Ku Klux, had been a place of particularly intense violence against African Americans and their white Republican allies.[1] York was one of nine South Carolina upcountry counties where lawlessness was so widespread that President Ulysses S. Grant, to restore order and facilitate arrests, suspended the writ of habeas corpus.

This is the only time the suspension of habeas corpus has been done in the United States during peacetime—if Reconstruction can be called a time of peace, for the man who energetically led the federal government's crusade against the Ku Klux thought their actions "[amounted] to war."[2] That man was, remarkably, a former slaveowner and the first former Confederate to

---

*When my great-grandfather enlisted in the Confederate army, his surname on his enlistment papers was listed as "Faris." When he was paroled at Appomattox, his discharge papers spelled his surname as "Farris." When he put a public notice of his divorce in the newspaper, his name was listed as "Faries," as it also was when he applied for a Confederate pension in his old age. In federal indictments, his name is spelled "Ferris." How my side of the family settled on "Farris" as the preferred spelling of our name is unknown, but, unless quoting from an official document that spells his name otherwise, that is the spelling I will use for my great-grandfather in this book. As for other relatives, I will use what appears from historical records to be their most common appellation.

serve in a presidential Cabinet, US attorney general Amos T. Akerman. After conducting a fact-finding trip to South Carolina in late summer 1871, Akerman said that the crimes committed by the Ku Klux in just the South Carolina Piedmont could only be "reckoned by thousands"—and this was just during the previous twelve months and in only a relatively small portion of a single state.[3] And it was not just the number of crimes committed, but that the Ku Klux "committed some of the most heinous crimes in the history of the United States," and no one, not the elderly, the disabled, women, children—even infants and toddlers—were spared.[4]

But there was no desire for a renewed sectional conflict even though the Ku Klux uprising, particularly in the years 1870 and 1871, seemed either a continuation of the Civil War or a new rebellion against national authority. Instead, the Grant Administration chose to attack the Ku Klux in the federal courts, not on the battlefield. But there was a key role for the Army.

Just as local courts would not indict or prosecute suspected Ku Klux, neither would local law enforcement, many of whom were Ku Klux themselves, investigate or make arrests. So, federal troops were sent south as part of the crackdown on the Ku Klux, including the ironically named Company K of the US 7th Cavalry that arrived in York County under the command of Major Lewis Merrill. More thorough than most of his peers, Merrill proved to be an extraordinary detective, and his detailed investigations and reports provided the basis for most of the cases made against the Ku Klux in the Great South Carolina Ku Klux Klan Trials. Merrill's doggedness in pursuing the Ku Klux was perhaps the primary reason why, of all the locations in the South where the Ku Klux crackdown might have occurred, York County was the focal point of federal prosecutions.

When the mass arrests began, hundreds of Ku Klux turned themselves in and gave confessions (a process Merrill called "puking"), but thousands of other Southern white men, particularly those who were leaders in the Ku Klux or those accused of the most serious crimes, fled to avoid prosecution. Some two thousand men fled just from South Carolina, and two hundred of those, including my great-grandfather, were York County fugitives.[5]

Some left the country, with Canada becoming a particular haven for exiled Ku Klux. An attempt by federal agents to chloroform, kidnap, and bring to justice one of the most notorious of the York County Ku Klux leaders living in exile there, a local planter and physician named J. Rufus Bratton who was wanted for the murder of an African-American militia captain named Jim Williams, led to the first major diplomatic dispute between the United States and a newly independent Canada.

A similar desire to avoid arrest was almost certainly my great-grandfather's motivation for his rapid ride to Arkansas. It is doubtful that he fled because he was a Ku Klux leader, as he had been a private during the war and had no greater social standing after it. Instead, the seriousness of his alleged crimes was revealed in a search of the National Archives near Atlanta, where two federal indictments issued against John Clayton were located. John Clayton, his younger brother, Moses, and a dozen other Ku Klux comrades were accused of brutally assaulting and whipping two African-American men. It is also possible, confirming family legend, that John Clayton participated in even more serious crimes that convinced him of the need to take flight, but there is no official record of him participating in such a crime.

The indictments against my great-grandfather state that the purpose of the assaults was political and designed to prevent these African-American men from voting, or at least from voting for Radical Republican candidates. The adjective "Radical" was applied at the time to those Republicans who believed that African-American citizens were entitled to equal rights under the law. This label was an early clue to how long and bitter the struggle for equality would be, as it embedded in our national consciousness the idea that genuine equality, particularly social equality, is somehow an extreme, even a subversive notion.

The indictments do not provide much detail on these assaults nor John Clayton's specific role in them. If they were "typical" of the outrages committed by the Ku Klux, then John Clayton likely took his turn among his fellow conspirators beating these poor men with a whip or, more probably, a birch tree branch the diameter of a man's wrist until they were too exhausted to continue and their victims were bloody messes. One hundred lashes and more were not uncommon in these attacks.

While racism was at its core, the activities of the Ku Klux were primarily about political power. The function of the Ku Klux was to reestablish the political dominance of the white planter class that ruled the South prior to the Civil War. Returning to power, they intended to reestablish as much of the South's antebellum slave society as possible while superficially appearing to conform to the Thirteenth Amendment's ban on slavery.* They could achieve this level of power in South Carolina, where African Americans were a numeric majority, only by ensuring African Americans either voted as they were told or did not vote at all—no matter what the Constitution now said.

Whether my great-grandfather joined the Ku Klux with enthusiasm or whether he was, as many Ku Klux defendants would claim to be, coerced into joining is unknown. It is also possible that, lacking a wife (he was divorced), children, or property, he left for Arkansas simply because he wished for the chance to start life anew at the age of thirty-four and far away from the chaos and disorder brought on by the Ku Klux and then by the crackdown on the Ku Klux.

Had he stayed in South Carolina and been arrested, it is likely he would have been convicted by some of the first biracial juries in American history. It was unlikely, however, that he would have served time in prison. Despite the thousands who were arrested or turned themselves in, only sixty-five Ku Klux *from the entirety of the South* ended up serving prison sentences. Yet, despite the magnitude of the Ku Klux conspiracy, this was enough to cripple the organization, demonstrating the power of the law when it is vigorously enforced, even in limited doses.

The dismantling of the Ku Klux did not end racism or racial violence, of course. White Southerners (and plenty of Northerners) found other means to keep African Americans from enjoying the full rights of citizenship. Apathy, indifference, and bigotry would cede the South to Jim Crow soon enough, but for almost twenty years after the trials and the demise of the Ku Klux, African Americans enjoyed a modicum of civil rights that included the right (for adult males) to vote, hold office, and to serve on juries. The University of South Carolina was briefly integrated, as was public transportation and other public accommodations, and, at peak, nearly two thousand African Americans held local or state office in South Carolina during Reconstruction, and the state sent at least one African-American representative to Congress until 1900.

Jim Crow, the name given segregation backed by the force of law, ended these advances, but as bad as Jim Crow was, the Ku Klux reign of terror at the end of the Civil War was far worse. The Tuskegee Institute estimates

---

*The Thirteenth Amendment made one exception: It states that "neither slavery nor involuntary servitude" may exist "except as punishment for crime," a loophole that, over time, would cause great misery to a great many African Americans.

that nearly 3,500 African Americans were lynched from 1882 to 1968, but this was a fraction of the deaths caused by the Reconstruction-era Ku Klux. Robert Smalls, an African American who represented South Carolina in Congress for a dozen years, estimated that fifty-three thousand African Americans were murdered by whites, mostly in the South, between 1865 and 1887, his final year in Congress.[6] This is only five thousand fewer than the number of American soldiers killed in the Vietnam War. During the winter of 1870–71, African Americans in York County and many other places in South Carolina and the South were afraid to sleep in their own homes, preferring to risk pneumonia by sleeping in the woods in freezing temperatures rather than risk mutilation or death at the hands of the Ku Klux, who rode virtually every night to commit acts of terror.

The trials did not create a racial utopia, but the demise of the Ku Klux and an end to their nightly raids were a great relief to its victims. Reflecting on the brutality of the Ku Klux sixty years after the fact, an elderly African-American man, quoted in the infelicitous dialect used in the 1930s by the Federal Writers' Project, said of the Ku Klux, "What cullud person dat can't 'member dem, if he lived dat day?"[7]

President Grant's role in crushing the Ku Klux was, in the words of his biographer Ron Chernow, "the imperishable story" of his presidency.[8] Yet, Chernow also noted that this triumphal story "has been suppressed by a strange national amnesia. The Klan's ruthless reign is a dark, buried chapter in American history."[9]

If the trials have been forgotten or overlooked, it is not because of a shortage of documentation. There is a verbatim transcript of much of the Great South Carolina Ku Klux Klan Trials. This transcription, unusual for the time, was at Akerman's directive. He wanted a written record of testimony provided under oath to give proof of what was occurring in the South in hopes the nation would be moved to greater action on behalf of civil rights for African Americans. He was to be disappointed, and his own self-described obsession with the Ku Klux likely cost him his job.

Congress also authorized a special committee, the ponderously named Joint Select Committee to Inquire into the Condition of Affairs in the Late Insurrectionary States, to investigate the Ku Klux. Its hearings were conducted not only in Washington, DC, but also in seven Southern states over a six-month period. Some of the most riveting testimony was given at hearings conducted in York County, including that of Elias Hill, a severely disabled man assaulted by the Ku Klux who later concluded there was no place in America for people of African descent. He and a large group of followers emigrated to Liberia, where a few became rich and many more became disillusioned. The committee's final report covered thirteen volumes, with the three volumes devoted just to the hearings on conditions in South Carolina including nearly two thousand pages of testimony and other evidence.

There are also extensive newspaper reports, for these trials, now largely forgotten, were national news, featured on the front pages of America's leading newspapers in New York, Chicago, and elsewhere, and they were obviously of deep interest to many Southern newspapers, including York County's own surprisingly fair-minded *Yorkville Enquirer*. All this material is supplemented by letters, diaries, memoirs, and a host of official filings and reports, including those submitted to his superiors by Major Merrill.

A great deal of this material recounts some very grisly crimes. I have tried not to sensationalize or linger too long over the murders, rapes, and assaults committed by the Ku Klux, but I have deliberately personalized them. A quote usually attributed to Stalin says a single death is a tragedy, but a million deaths are a statistic. Statistics are important, but it is the stories of individuals that move us and cause deeper reflection.

The witness testimony is particularly powerful, but aside from that testimony little material is available about the African Americans who played essential roles in the destruction of the Ku Klux. Because some, though far from all, were illiterate, they left few written records behind. Not socially prominent like many of the white participants in the trials, the personal histories of the African Americans involved were of no real interest to white-controlled newspapers, or the congressional interrogators, or even the federal prosecutors entrusted with representing their interests. They were not the subject of profiles or interviews, nor were they asked on the witness stand to provide many details about their lives.

What the record does show is that, having been to a large degree the agents of their emancipation during the Civil War, African Americans were now also leaders of the resistance to protect Reconstruction. They knew that no local civil authorities would provide them with either protection or justice, and the national government was unwilling to commit more than a handful of troops. With the Ku Klux essentially a reconstituted Confederate army, African-American citizens and their allies were the front line in the battle to protect and advance the ideals of the Constitution as expanded by the Fourteenth and Fifteenth Amendments.

They did not passively accept abuse at the hands of the Ku Klux but fought back when and how they could, despite usually being badly outnumbered. To eliminate this resistance, one of the key Ku Klux goals was to disarm the Black population; how to ensure that these newly free citizens might be protected under the Second Amendment's right to bear arms became a key issue at the trials.

Self-defense was key, for every time an African American served in a state-sponsored militia to help preserve the peace, or worked as an informant for federal investigators, or testified in public at the trials or before congressional investigators, or served on the biracial juries assigned to pass judgment on known Ku Klux in a courtroom whose gallery was filled with Ku Klux, they were fully aware of the possibility—perhaps even the likelihood—of fatal retribution.

What is now clear, 150 years later, is that they took these risks in defense not only of their rights, but for the rights of all Americans who have sought fuller participation in our democracy. The Great South Carolina Ku Klux Klan Trials were about more than the guilt or innocence of those individual Ku Klux charged with awful crimes, or even achieving some measure of justice for those harmed. These trials were intended to answer two urgent and essential questions: Had the Fourteenth and Fifteenth Amendments made it so that the Bill of Rights were now rights fully guaranteed to all citizens as individuals regardless of who they were and where they lived; and was the federal government now constitutionally bound to protect those rights when the states would not?

The US attorney for South Carolina, David T. Corbin, argued that the answer to both questions was a resounding "yes," and that the Reconstruction amendments represented nothing less than a new American "revolution."[10] It fell to the Ku Klux legal "dream team" of two former US attorneys general to argue that the new amendments—and by extension, the Civil War with its more than seven hundred fifty thousand battle deaths—had barely changed American society at all.* Corbin's contention that what occurred was revolutionary would prove prophetic, but the prophecy was

---

*This figure represents the new and more accurate estimates of total military deaths during the Civil War based on the research of historian J. David Hacker first published in the December 2011 edition of *Civil War History*.

not fulfilled until the second half of the twentieth century, when the intentions of the authors of those amendments were finally ratified by the US Supreme Court.

We still do not know quite what to make of Reconstruction. It was a period of frustrated hopes and missed opportunities, of one step forward and two steps back. Reconstruction does not fit easily into the preferred American narrative of a nation always making progress toward a "more perfect Union," and to dwell on what might have been is painful, given our tortured history of race in America.

A reasonable question, one certain to be asked by some of my relatives, is why include my great-grandfather's role in this unpleasant history? Typically, as with Churchill's biography of the Duke of Marlborough, those who write about their ancestors usually select persons associated with great deeds, or at least a law-abiding existence. I do not believe in inherited guilt, but I have included my great-grandfather's role in this story because I do believe our ancestors bequeath us certain obligations. If our ancestors led exemplary lives, we hope to follow their example; if they did not, then we ought to have some ambition to make amends for their failings. Reconstruction is not a ten-year period of American history following the Civil War; rather, it is an enduring and ongoing process in which great progress has been made but more work needs to be done. This book represents a small chore committed in service to this great enterprise.

CHAPTER ONE

The dismal hour draws nigh for the meeting of our mystic circle.
—*Ku Klux Klan notice in the* Yorkville Enquirer

I

Shortly after General Robert E. Lee surrendered to General Ulysses S. Grant at Appomattox Courthouse, Virginia, two men of vastly different social standing hurriedly headed south. Both would eventually arrive in York County, South Carolina. One man was fifty-six-year-old Confederate president Jefferson Davis, whose stop in York would be brief, a way station as he fled farther south to elude Union capture, keep his government intact, and sustain what he refused to acknowledge were the terminal Confederate hopes of creating an independent nation.

The other man was my great-grandfather, twenty-eight-year-old John Clayton Farris, a property-less farm laborer who was paroled at Appomattox after serving all four years of the Civil War as a lowly private in the 5th South Carolina Infantry Regiment. For him, York County was home, a presumed final destination, where he would return to work for others, be disappointed in attempts to obtain property of his own, divorce his wife, join the Ku Klux Klan, and eventually become, as Davis was, a fugitive fleeing arrest.

Lee, rejecting suggestions the South continue to fight by switching to guerrilla warfare, agreed to surrender on April 9, 1865, but my great-grandfather and the rest of what remained of the Army of Northern Virginia did not formally lay down their arms until April 12. Grant, grateful that Lee was not prolonging the nation's agony, provided the twenty-eight thousand Confederate troops with three days of rations and said that any man who owned a horse or mule was free to take them back home.[1] It is doubtful that John Clayton owned either and so he almost certainly walked the 250 miles from Virginia back to York County, a journey that likely took two weeks or more.

There was a good chance he was barefoot, for among the many deprivations endured by Confederate soldiers by the end of the war was a lack of shoes. The Union rations long gone after a few days, his packsack likely empty, John Clayton would have had to beg, steal, or hunt for food along the way. He had made a long walk home once before, when given thirty days leave to recover from a severe bout of dysentery. Periodically having to lie down and rest, looking up at the sky he no doubt envied the birds whose flight took no account of the hills and valleys, spring mud, and swollen rivers that made the journey so slow and tiring.

The long walk certainly gave my great-grandfather time to think about his future and his hopes that it would be easier than his hardscrabble past.

A descendant of Scots-Irish immigrants who first arrived in South Carolina in the 1740s, John Clayton was one of ten children born into a poor family. The Scots-Irish, particularly, were lured to the Carolina Piedmont in the 1760s by promises of small land grants when the Cherokees were driven from their ancestral homes.[2] John Clayton's maternal grandfather reportedly owned a small plantation and a single slave named Esther, but, according to the 1850 Census, his own father, Robert M. Faries, owned little; the estimated value of his estate was a middling $320.

More troubling, in that same census, when John Clayton would have been thirteen years old, his mother, the former Mary Falls, was listed as being "insane," though by what definition or measure is unknown. Within a few years, she was committed to an asylum in Charleston, where she died in 1865. Robert Faries later remarried, but after his mother was sent away, John Clayton and four younger siblings were placed in the care of their grandmother, who had inherited the farm and the enslaved Esther on the death of her husband.

Likely first hired out while still a young teen, when the Civil War broke out John Clayton was working as a farm laborer for a family named Boleyn (also spelled "Bolin" in some records), who owned a small farm valued at eleven hundred dollars near Clover in northern York County. The 1860 Census states that my great-grandfather possessed at least basic reading and writing skills, but he owned no land and estimated his net worth as a modest $140. As will be shown later, this was less than some industrious freedmen (the name given to the emancipated) were able to earn within months of obtaining their liberty, a comparison that likely embarrassed John Clayton and fueled resentment rather than admiration of their industriousness.

There are no surviving photographs or contemporaneous descriptions of my great-grandfather, but if he was like his descendants, including the author, he was of no more than average height (perhaps less), of medium build, and possessed a ruddy complexion common to the Scots-Irish. He was handsome enough that he found a wife, a woman named Elizabeth M. Boleyn, who appears to have been his employer's younger sister. The record is unclear on when they married and whether they were married in a legal ceremony or the marriage was common law. Perhaps they married just before he went off to fight, as many young couples do during wartime, or perhaps they married shortly after he returned.

What we do know is that he and Elizabeth were involved in an unsuccessful lawsuit over property that was part of a Boleyn family inheritance so that my great-grandfather remained landless. Perhaps this failure exacerbated tensions already present in the marriage, which was childless. By the summer of 1868 the couple had split up. My great-grandfather placed a notice in the *Yorkville Enquirer* asserting that Elizabeth had left him "without any just provocation" and advised anyone "TRADING WITH OR HARBORING my wife" that he would no longer be responsible for any debts she incurred.[3] Their split would make considerably easier his decision three years later to flee South Carolina to avoid arrest by federal troops for the crimes he committed as a Ku Klux.

This notice of divorce appears to have been the only time my great-grandfather's name appeared in the local newspaper, and beyond his military service there is no evidence he enjoyed any prominence in the community. Probably no one beyond his immediate family and a few friends were aware of his return to York County in late April or early May 1865.

Jefferson Davis, on the other hand, rode into Yorkville, the county seat, on April 27 accompanied by more than two thousand troops, what was left of his Cabinet, wagons filled with government archives, and the few hundred thousand dollars in gold and silver that remained of the Confederate treasury.

Even as the Confederacy was in its death throes, he received a tumultuous welcome. "The reception in Yorkville astounded Mr. Davis," an aide recalled, and in its enthusiasm Davis said the crowd reminded him of those who welcomed him with joy to Richmond in May 1861 when that city became the Confederate capital.[4] In Yorkville, Davis spent the night in a grand, three-story plantation-style home located at 8 South Congress Street owned by Dr. James Rufus Bratton, a forty-three-year-old physician, planter, and businessman who, as a member of the most prominent and wealthy family in York County, was the antithesis of my great-grandfather in terms of social standing.

Bratton's grandfather was Revolutionary War hero Colonel William Bratton, who led the 1780 American victory in the Battle of Huck's Defeat that took place ten miles southeast of Yorkville near the Bratton plantation known as Brattonsville. By the 1840s, when it was owned by J. Rufus Bratton's father, Dr. John Simpson Bratton, Brattonsville covered more than six thousand acres and was worked by nearly 140 slaves.[5] When the elder Dr. Bratton died unexpectedly in 1843, it took six years to settle the estate among his widow and fourteen children. J. Rufus's elder brother, John S. Bratton Jr., ran the larger portion of the picturesque estate and built a new main house so splendid that the Mel Gibson film *The Patriot* (2000) was partially filmed on its grounds.[6] Brattonsville is now a living history museum.

J. Rufus also inherited a significant amount of land adjacent to the main property, as well as more than thirty slaves, but his primary occupation was as a physician, and he spent the bulk of his time at his splendid home in downtown Yorkville.* After studying medicine at the College of South Carolina, which would be renamed the University of South Carolina, and later at the University of Pennsylvania, Bratton developed a successful practice and dabbled in a number of successful business ventures. One was the purchase of the three-story redbrick Rose Hotel that was located one lot over from his home on Congress Street.

The Rose, which would be the site of a great deal of activity during the Ku Klux uprising, was considered one of the finest hotels in the South Carolina Piedmont, boasting a restaurant, a bar, and a horse-drawn shuttle

---

*Bratton's home at 8 South Congress Street was razed in 1956, though there is a state historical marker at the site where the house once stood, commemorating Davis's visit.

service to the train depot several blocks away.[7] Its elegance reflected, before the war, a level of prosperity and sophistication that led some to refer to Yorkville, which even boasted an opera house, as the "Charleston of the Upcountry."[8] In what Bratton must have certainly perceived as an indignity if not an insult, the Rose Hotel was first the headquarters of the local Radical Republican government and later was commandeered to be the headquarters of federal troops sent to quell the Ku Klux violence in York.

Like my great-grandfather, Bratton had enlisted in the 5th South Carolina Infantry on April 13, 1861, the day after the first shots of the Civil War were fired on Fort Sumter. Bratton was appointed assistant surgeon to the regiment, and the regiment mustered on the grounds of Bratton's home, where they were fed by the Bratton family before marching first to Columbia and then on to Charleston.[9]

It is likely that my great-grandfather was one of Bratton's patients during the war, both when they were in the same regiment, and possibly later when Bratton transferred out of the 5th South Carolina Infantry and was promoted to full surgeon with the Fourth Division of the Winder Hospital in Richmond, the Confederate capital. Winder was a busy place; Bratton recalled that the hospital treated nearly five thousand sick and wounded in 1862 alone.[10]

Winder was one of several hospitals where my great-grandfather received treatment. In fact, according to his service records, for nearly one-third of his time in the Confederate army, John Clayton was in hospital or otherwise recuperating from disease or the several injuries he sustained during the war. These included a head wound from a Union Minié ball received at the Battle of the Wilderness, and gunshot wounds to his right thigh, shoulder, and hand from a skirmish near Newtown, Virginia. Yet most frightening, perhaps, was the acute dysentery that led to John Clayton receiving the thirty-day pass to return home to recuperate. Disease killed nearly twice as many Confederate soldiers as battle wounds, and while Confederate records are not complete, the Union army reported that nearly fifty thousand of its soldiers died of dysentery or chronic diarrhea during the war.[11]

II

While his illness and injuries were not trifles to my great-grandfather, they likely were unremembered by Bratton if he was the attending physician for any of them as he treated many far more gruesome injuries. Bratton periodically kept a diary during and after the war and later turned his entries into a short but incomplete memoir that abruptly ends at the time he became active in the Ku Klux. Whether he stopped writing or later pages documenting his role in the Ku Klux were destroyed is unknown.

One of Bratton's most vivid recollections from his military service was of the First Battle of Manassas, the first major battle of the war, after which both sides realized the conflict would be neither short nor bloodless. With only one other physician to assist, Bratton recalled caring for more than thirty badly wounded men. "Were all that night (Sunday) to near day break busy in amputating limbs and dressing wounds. It was a gloomy weary day," he wrote."[12] The following year, 1862, Bratton, justifiably proud of his surgical skills, noted that he "performed a number of amputations this year," boasting that "all of whom got well."[13]

A tall, slender man with a firm, even imperious demeanor but a kindly face framed with a salt-and-pepper goatee, Bratton inspired confidence in those patients who were about to lose a tattered limb to his saw. That same calm determination, maintained in the most arduous of circumstances, must have terrified those whom he meant to do harm, for when he helped lead the Ku Klux in York County after the war, he could seem as merciless as a shark. Virginia Mason Bratton, who was both Bratton's niece and daughter-in-law (reflecting the often incestuous world of the planter class), recalled of her uncle/father-in-law, "He was a man of iron will and strength of purpose, but underneath an apparently cold exterior, there cowered a soul of fire, and a current of great tenderness."[14]

The burden of being an overworked physician in a losing army wore out Bratton's health. In 1864, he requested lighter duty and was sent to Georgia, which was soon invaded by Union troops commanded by General William Tecumseh Sherman. To avoid being overrun by Sherman's army, an increasingly embittered Bratton assisted in the dismantling of the Confederate hospital to which he had been assigned, a clear signal of imminent defeat that caused local residents to panic and flee. Recalling the scene of chaos, confusion, and despair, Bratton wrote in his diary, "I prayed that the day of retribution would soon come when justice long withheld should be meted out to these ruthless invaders of our Country."[15]

Virginia Mason Bratton suggests her uncle/father-in-law's feelings were deeper and darker. She later wrote, "He believes the South has been robbed and wronged," and claimed that as an old man Bratton expressed the wish that the Pilgrims had never landed at Plymouth Rock "precluding the wrongs that have been wrought." She added that he "has some hopes in some distant day that the South will rule the universe with an iron hand as did Bismarck rule Germany."[16] While it was not the universe, which seemed to turn a blind eye to the depravity that soon engulfed the South, Bratton lived long enough (he died in 1897) to see African Americans ruled once more with an iron fist, almost as in slavery times.

With no hospital to attend, Bratton was furloughed. He intended to join Confederate general Joseph Johnston's forces in North Carolina, but when he arrived in Yorkville on April 9, he learned Lee had surrendered and he stayed home. By the time of Davis's visit more than two weeks later, Bratton had had time to assess some of the cost of the Lost Cause.[17]

His elegant home would have been an obvious place for a patriotic Confederate to host his president, but it is probable that Bratton extended the invitation and it was accepted because he and Davis likely knew each other from before the war, as each was part of the relatively small class of Southern elite. If not, perhaps Bratton met Davis while working at Winder Hospital in Richmond, the Confederate capital. Whether already acquainted or not, Davis and Bratton quickly assumed an easy intimacy, for while both men were peremptory and self-righteous in their public demeanor, they were also known to be warm and charming in social situations. They reportedly spent the entire evening together conversing on the porch of Bratton's home and "bitterly reviewed what the war had done to the value of their [respective] estates."[18]

Even though, or perhaps because, he was born into a wealthy family, Bratton was exceptionally money-conscious. In his diary, he made special note of his annual income as a physician and a soldier. He began the practice of medicine with a partner but disbanded the partnership when he realized he could make more money practicing alone; he said it was a lesson to all young doctors that they should practice solo. Because he owned more than thirty slaves who would have held a collective value of at least fifteen thousand dollars, equivalent to a dozen years' income as a physician, he would later express particular outrage after emancipation that the US government never compensated him for this loss of "property."[19]

Davis, his distinguished guest, who owned more than one hundred slaves when war broke out and who fancied himself a particularly benevolent slave master, likely held a similar view. Davis had not been in good health when he assumed the presidency of the Confederacy in 1861. By 1865, the further strain of war left him "frail, gaunt, agitated, and dyspeptic."[20] In his memoir, Bratton noted that Davis was "fatigued in body and depressed in spirits, though easily aroused with his native fire; he caressed and spoke kindly to my four boys: Louis, John, Andral, and Moultrie—and when he left me in the morning and bade us good bye he observed, 'do not expect anything just or right from the Abolition Yankee. They will never grant you your rights.'"[21]

When Davis arrived at Bratton's home, a large crowd gathered to "offer their tokens of respect and sympathy," but the Confederate president declined entreaties to make a speech.[22] But when the crowd moved next door to the Rose Hotel, where other Confederate officials stayed while Davis boarded with Bratton, they were rewarded with remarks from General John C. Breckenridge, the former US vice president, 1860 presidential candidate, and final Confederate secretary of war. Addressing the crowd from the hotel's second-story portico, Breckenridge urged those below to "keep the faith."[23]

It was a simple but appropriate message for a people who lived in the region of the South that had produced some of the leading defenders of slavery, nullification, and secession: John C. Calhoun, states' rights theorist, senator, and vice president; James Henry Hammond, the South Carolina governor who coined the phrase "cotton is king"; and Congressman Preston Brooks, who nearly beat Massachusetts senator Charles Sumner to death on the Senate floor, were all raised in the South Carolina Piedmont. This heritage partially explains why York County, particularly, became such a hotbed of Ku-Kluxism.

Two days after Davis and his entourage left to flee farther south, another well-known Confederate arrived in Yorkville. General Wade Hampton, cavalry officer and South Carolina's greatest war hero, had been trying for days to catch up with Davis. Hampton had refused to personally capitulate on April 26 when Johnston surrendered the still thirty-thousand-strong Army of Tennessee, the largest Confederate army still left in the field, to General Sherman. Davis considered Johnston's surrender in the absence of a decisive military defeat an act of insubordination, and vowed he would continue the fight as long as there were men in uniform still willing to serve.[24]

Hampton was one such man. In an increasingly frantic stream of correspondence, Hampton pledged to Davis that he would lead the Confederate president and any other recalcitrant Confederate officials and troops to Texas or even Mexico to regroup with Confederate forces west of the Mississippi and continue the war. "If I do not accompany him I shall never cease to reproach myself," Hampton told Johnston, adding that he was "willing to sacrifice everything for the cause and for our Government."[25] To speed his journey and hoped-for rendezvous with Davis, and unwilling have his men accused of "outlawry," Hampton left his few remaining cavalry troops behind in North Carolina on May 1 and rode alone all night to Yorkville, only to discover Davis had left the town two days before.[26]

Before (and after) the war, Hampton was one of the wealthiest men in the South, owning twelve thousand acres of land and more than nine hundred slaves at plantations in South Carolina and Mississippi.[27] Demonstrating the flair for grand gestures that would help make him governor fifteen years later, the forty-two-year-old aristocrat, with ostentatious humility, originally enlisted in the Confederate army as a private before state officials insisted Hampton accept a commission as a colonel. During the war, he personally financed and outfitted a full Confederate "legion"—a regiment-sized combination of infantry, cavalry, and artillery totaling more than one thousand men.[28]

When Sherman's troops menaced Hampton's hometown of Columbia in early 1865, Hampton directed his wife and children to flee their town mansion and join other refugees headed to Yorkville and out of harm's way. When Hampton arrived at the Yorkville home where his family was staying and knocked on the door at 2:00 a.m., his wife, Mary, was appalled by her husband's "broken appearance," and his plans to continue what was clearly a lost fight.[29] She noted they had already lost a son, Preston, to the war, and appealed to his duty to care for his remaining family now "that their way of life had vanished."[30] Mary finally sent for General Joe Wheeler, who was also staying in Yorkville and who joined Mary in pressuring Hampton to give up the struggle. Hampton finally relented, sending a subordinate to advise Davis of his decision to stay and recuperate with his family in Yorkville, which meant this out-of-the-way hamlet was the site of the unobserved final surrender of one of the most important Confederate military commanders of the war.

As Davis did, it seems certain that Hampton would have called on Bratton while in Yorkville. As fellow Carolinians of means and education, their paths had likely crossed dozens of times, and the Ku Klux uprising would bind them together for another fifteen years. Bratton's elder brother, John, became one of Hampton's closest political advisors; Hampton would later help secure legal representation for Bratton and other Ku Klux defendants, and when he became governor, Hampton aggressively sought amnesty for J. Rufus Bratton so he could return to South Carolina from his six-year exile in Canada.[31]

Davis, meanwhile, was captured by Union troops ten days later in Irwindale, Georgia. He was to have been tried for treason before a biracial jury until he was pardoned by President Andrew Johnson in 1868.

III

Despite this final flurry of activity, Yorkville and York County had not been the site of any major engagements during the war.* There had been a Union cavalry raid that resulted in the burning of a railroad bridge northeast of nearby Rock Hill, but Sherman's army had come no closer than Columbia, eighty miles to the southeast, which was burned to the ground under still disputed circumstances. York had been spared outward signs of physical devastation, but the people of the county had suffered greatly. Of the four thousand York County men who enlisted in the Confederate army, more than eight hundred were killed, reportedly giving York the highest combat death rate of any county in South Carolina.[32]

This devotion to the Confederate cause does not mean that York was a place of vast plantations as existed in the South Carolina Low Country around Charleston. York and the Carolina Piedmont had been primarily settled in the mid- to late eighteenth century by poor, uneducated, Protestant (mostly Presbyterian) Scots-Irish immigrants, such as the Brattons and Farrises. Except for a very few large plantations like Brattonsville, most

---

*Yorkville residents voted in 1915 to shorten the town's name to "York."

farms were small or medium-size. By the time of the war, beyond a local gold mine, York had no industry. A green land of rolling hills and ravines, much of the county was (and is) heavily forested, a perfect place for armed men to move stealthily about, or to hide from just such men.

With a long growing season, cotton did thrive in York's reddish sand and clay loam soil, and so the subsistence farming that dominated local agriculture during the first century of European settlement was replaced with the South's great cash crop, King Cotton, especially once the Kings Mountain Railroad reached Yorkville in 1852. By then, York was producing four million pounds of cotton per year, the largest amount of any county in the South Carolina upcountry. Also, unlike the Low Country, where African Americans represented a significant majority of the population, York's population after the war of twenty-four thousand residents was nearly evenly split between whites and Blacks.* This even split would lead to a hotly contested struggle for political power once African Americans were able to exercise the right to vote.[33]

With a population of nearly two thousand, Yorkville was the largest town in York County, though it would soon be surpassed by nearby Rock Hill when that town became a rail hub while Yorkville remained an end-of-the-line stop for the small Kings Mountain Railroad. Yorkville possessed the county courthouse, a charming downtown, several large Protestant churches, and streets lined with elegant Georgian and Greek Revival homes. Arriving in Yorkville to report on the Ku Klux outrages in 1871, a reporter for the *New York Tribune* condescendingly found Yorkville to be "a pretty village, as Southern villages go . . . [with] several handsome houses, standing in the midst of shrubbery, clipped in stiff, geometrical forms, such as one sees in the gardens of old French chateaux—half a dozen churches, a girls' seminary, a military school for boys, and a large and exceptionally well printed and edited weekly newspaper."[34] The newspaper was the *Yorkville Enquirer*, which had to suspend publication for several months after the war because of a lack of supplies.

A lack of ink and newsprint was hardly the only deprivation experienced by the South after the war. Many cities, such as Columbia, lay in ruins; a quarter-million Confederate soldiers had died during the war and

---

*African Americans composed nearly 60 percent of South Carolina's overall population, or more than four hundred thousand of the state's seven hundred thousand residents in the 1870 Census.

at least as many had suffered wounds, some crippling; and the emancipation of four million former slaves meant the South had lost two-thirds of its assessed (white) wealth.* Not since the fall of the Roman Empire, white Southerners believed, "had an entire people lost so much."[35]

In fact, white Southerners thought their peculiar fate was worse than the fall of Rome. A mammoth Democratic Party rally held in Yorkville on August 29, 1868, in preparation for the upcoming presidential election between Grant and New York governor Horatio Seymour, drew two thousand whites and even two hundred African Americans, whom the *Enquirer* lauded for ignoring "the slavish orders of the [Union] Leagues" by coming out "to hear the other side of the question." The main rally speaker was Colonel John P. Thomas, who had led cadets from the South Carolina Military Academy (later known as The Citadel) into battle. "History records the atrocities of Ghengis [*sic*] Khan, the Great Conqueror, and of Attila, the Scourge of the World," said Thomas, a professor of literature and history, "but it has been reserved for modern radicalism to improve upon these barbarities, and subject a conquered people to the dominion of their former slaves."[36]

Many Southern whites, mirroring the feelings of African Americans who considered emigrating to Liberia before and after the war, now yearned to leave the United States and start anew elsewhere. Hampton reported that he was regularly approached and asked during these first months of peace to organize a colony outside the United States to which white Southerners could flee the hated Union.† Hampton said he had received so many such entreaties that he could not respond to them all individually, and so in August 1865 prepared an open letter published in several state newspapers, including the *Yorkville Enquirer*.

"The desire to leave a country which has been reduced to such a deplorable condition as ours, and whose future has so little of hope, is doubtless

---

*Seldom emphasized is that thirty-six thousand African-American troops, at least half of whom hailed from the Southern states, had died during the war fighting for the Union.

†Thousands of Southerners did emigrate south following the war, including an estimated four thousand "Confederados" who went to Brazil and whose descendants still reside there. Even more went to Mexico, actively encouraged to do so by the Emperor Maximillian, but after Maximillian was deposed by forces under the command of Benito Juárez in 1867, Southern emigrants found titles to their lands were no longer honored, and most returned to the United States. (See: Dawsey and Dawsey, eds., *The Confederados*, and Rolle, *The Lost Cause*.)

as wide spread as it is natural," Hampton wrote. "But I doubt the propriety of this expatriation of so many of our best men." Southern efforts would be better focused, Hampton said, on reestablishing law and order, rebuilding the cities and towns then in ruins, and restoring the state's commercial and agricultural economy. Hampton pledged to devote his own energies to these goals, while adding that he would continue to gather "all information which would be desirable in establishment of a colony in case we should be ultimately be forced [*sic*] to leave the country."[37]

Bratton was not one of those who desired to emigrate, but he found the postwar world required a great adjustment in behavior and expectations that he and other wealthy whites considered humiliating. For generations, planters had convinced themselves that slavery was more than moral, it was a positive good, and that the master-slave relationship was benevolent and agreeable to all concerned. It was "beyond their understanding that the Blacks did not plan to continue to stay in their place and behave like slaves."[38] They felt betrayed by their former property—and they were still extraordinarily reliant on Black labor.

With emancipation, labor became an acute problem as freedmen and women left the plantations where they had been enslaved to seek and be reunited with loved ones who had been sold elsewhere during slavery. Many wished to farm on their own or seek new kinds of jobs. Some just wished to know the joy of being free to go wherever they chose. Virtually none desired to work for those who had held them in bondage. "They will almost starve and go naked before they will work for a white man, if they can get a patch of ground to live on and get from under his control," wrote one planter of African Americans, oblivious that his observation soundly contradicted the widespread white belief that Blacks were indolent and dependent upon whites for their survival.[39]

An imperious aristocrat by nature, Bratton thrived on control, but now he found that he had to work almost daily in his fields himself to get his crops in because so many of his former slaves had departed. The result was poor. Bratton's first cotton crop after the war yielded four bales. He killed his last hog on the day before Christmas 1865, and was distraught when one of his former slaves, a man named Bill, accidentally caused a fire that burned down Bratton's gin house. Abandoning the pretentious paternalistic concern planters claimed to hold for those they held in bondage, Bratton now told those freedmen still working on his plantation to "go their way with their freedom either in peace or misery"; he did not care which.[40]

Bratton had difficulty adjusting to the idea that freedmen, being free, could now express ideas contrary to his own. Even though a freedman had stayed on with Bratton during the worst of times to work the plantation, Bratton decided to send away "Bob & his family . . . on account of his radical politics."[41] Bratton would later tell a congressional investigating committee that he had no problem with African Americans voting, provided they voted how he and other leading whites told them to.

The South had seceded on the gamble that its massive cotton crop (it met 75 percent of the world's demand before the war) would compel European nations to support its quest for independence. Instead, because the Union naval blockade prevented exports, the South had simply ceded the global cotton market to competitors in Egypt and elsewhere. Cotton seed was now, after the war, scarce and cotton prices were low. With cotton dethroned, the *Yorkville Enquirer* suggested that York would need to return "to the old system of cultivation," meaning subsistence farming. The good news was, the *Enquirer* noted in the summer of 1865, that while the wheat crop was "almost a failure . . . vegetation, generally, is flourishing." The corn crop provided the largest yield the county had seen in years, while fruit trees were "breaking down under their unusual burden," although, the *Enquirer* said, the fruit was not much good because of recent wet weather. There would be no starvation, but simply not dying would not be enough to get York, or the South, back on its feet. The imperative, the *Enquirer* opined, was "that a market may be made, that our people may have some sort of currency to operate with."[42]

The lack of money in circulation in York and throughout the South meant a lack of business prospects, which meant that ambitious young men had few avenues in which to channel their energy. This was a key reason a half dozen young Confederate veterans in Pulaski, Tennessee, located four hundred miles west of Yorkville, decided in the spring of 1866 to form a social club with a curious name that quickly captured the imagination of the South: the Ku Klux Klan. According to one of the founding members of the Ku Klux, Captain John Lester:

When the war ended in 1865, the young men of Pulaski . . . returned home and passed through a period of enforced inactivity. In some respects, it was more trying than the ordeal of war which lay behind them. The reaction which followed the excitement of army scenes and service was intense. There was nothing to relieve it. They could not engage at once in business or professional pursuits. Their business habits were broken up. None had capital with which to conduct agricultural pursuits or to engage in mercantile enterprises. And this restlessness was made more intense by the total lack of the amusements and social diversions which prevail wherever society is in a normal condition.[43]

IV

How the group chose the name Ku Klux Klan has been the subject of speculation never fully clarified by Lester or the group's other founders. Historian Allen W. Trelease, who developed the first genuinely scholarly history of the Reconstruction-era Ku Klux, is probably correct that the inspiration was a popular Southern college fraternity, Kuklos Adelphon, which had originated at the University of North Carolina in 1812 and would likely have been known to the several founding Ku Klux members who were college graduates.[44] "Ku Klux" was a bastardization of "kuklos," which is the Greek word for "circle." "Klan" was likely added for its alliterative quality and to reflect the clannish heritage of the Scots-Irish founders. The elaborate and often silly initiation and other rituals were also likely inspired by those used by Kuklos Adelphon and most college fraternities, while the titles adopted for Ku Klux leaders, such as grand cyclops for the president and grand magi for the vice president, had a Masonic tone, another organization that would have been well known to members, who were also often Masons.

Lester insisted the name was "utterly meaningless," but had an air of the "mysterious," which turned out to be critical to its growth.[45] As historian Stanley Horn noted, had the group instead adopted plausible alternatives such as "the Merry Six" or the "Pulaski Social Club," the Ku Klux might never have expanded beyond its original six members and the name Ku Klux Klan would be absent from American history.[46]

Initially, the activities of the Ku Klux in Pulaski consisted of little more than picnics and an occasional parade with members marching in garish costumes they had made and personalized themselves. Just being in costume and unrecognizable seemed amusing enough for members at first. Unlike the revived twentieth-century Klan, which was a merchandising scheme as well as a political movement, there was no "uniform" of a white robe topped by a pointed hat that was ordered from a central supplier. The only guidelines for original Ku Klux attire were that each member had to make and wear a gown or robe of sufficient length to cover their entire body, a mask to cover their face, and a high hat, usually made of cardboard, to make them appear taller than they were. The fabric of the gowns was often calico, while the hats were adorned with spangles and stars; later, when the Ku Klux wanted to seem more menacing, they adorned their hats with horns and antlers.[47]

For the first year and more after its founding, the Ku Klux remained an obscure local phenomenon; it did not even merit a mention in the local Pulaski newspaper until March 1867, and there is no record of the Ku Klux engaging in violence or having any political purpose through most of 1867.[48] The first recorded instance of violence being perpetrated by men in Ku Klux garb was in December 1867, when a white man was killed and a Black man beaten by men in the disguise of the Ku Klux.[49] A few weeks later, on Christmas Day 1867, in Columbia, Tennessee, the appearance of a group of horsemen in Ku Klux garb was enough to break up a boisterous freedmen's celebration that was annoying whites. The conservative Nashville *Republican Banner* newspaper praised the Ku Klux for preventing a "race riot" by the sheer force of their presence, beginning the legend widely repeated in Southern newspapers that the Ku Klux stood as "a force for law and order."[50]

But the real emerging purpose of the Ku Klux was not maintaining law and order, nor was it to uphold traditional moral values or even to protest supposed corruption in the Reconstruction governments of the Southern states. As one historian of South Carolina has pointed out, "it is difficult to find the connection between corruption in Columbia and the whipping of a Black family one hundred miles away." While Ku Klux might occasionally whip thieves, drunkards, or adulterers, the primary purpose of the organization was political power, and its evolution from social fraternity to terrorist organization coincided with the realization that white Democrats were no longer in control in the South.* Republicans, with their new

---

*For several years after the war, many white Southerners, especially those who had been members of the Whig Party before the war, resisted identifying themselves as Democrats, and preferred to be known as members of the "Conservative" party. (See: Woodward, *Origins of the New South, 1877–1913*.)

African-American constituents, now had the upper hand in political organization. The entry of the Ku Klux in South Carolina in the spring of 1868 occurred "immediately after the failure of the whites to defeat the new state constitution" that had been authored primarily by African Americans and white Republicans.[51]

There is a legend that former Confederate cavalry commander and onetime slave trader General Nathan Bedford Forrest, who was named grand wizard when he joined the Ku Klux in either 1867 or 1868, personally directed the group's expansion throughout the South. This is generally untrue. Forrest was always coy about the extent of his involvement with the Ku Klux, but it appears he was primarily a figurehead who enjoyed the prestige of being perceived as the leader of a popular counterinsurgency.[52]

It would, in fact, be a matter of considerable debate over just how organized and centralized the Ku Klux was. The Ku Klux constitution suggested there was a hierarchy led by the grand wizard in Nashville, but the Ku Klux was generally a loose confederation of groups inspired by the original club in Tennessee, though these groups, drawing on their wartime experience, would prove capable of collectively organizing and launching operations that crossed state lines.[53]

The expansion of the Ku Klux was more organic than planned, and it was Southern newspaper editors more than anyone else who played the "primary role" in expanding the Ku Klux or at least in inspiring imitators.[54] Editors found murders and assaults committed by mysterious men in garish disguises good copy, but as key figures in the political establishment in the South, they were especially enthusiastic if the purpose of the Ku Klux was to keep African Americans in their place and hated Radical Republicans out of office. Articles about Ku Klux activities and atrocities were reprinted by newspapers throughout the South, and it was not coincidental that 1868, a presidential election year, saw a "phenomenal expansion" of the Ku Klux as a violent, politically oriented uprising throughout the South.[55]

The Ku Klux found especially fertile ground in York County, where the first public notice of the Ku Klux was in the pages of the *Yorkville Enquirer*, which would often combine condemnation of Ku Klux violence with an occasional wink in its direction. In its April 2, 1868, edition there appeared a notice on the advertisements page under the heading "K.K.K." with this cryptic message:

The dismal hour draws nigh for the meeting of our mystic circle. The Shrouded Knight will come with pick and spade; the Grand Chaplain will come with the ritual of the dead. The grave yawneth, the lightnings flash athwart the heavens, the thunders roll, but the Past Grand Knight of the Sepulcher will recoil not.

This notice, or whatever it was, was signed, "By order of the Great Grand Centaur, SULEYMAN, G.G.S."[56]

Enquirer editor Lewis Grist professed to be mystified by the notice's origin or meaning, saying he had received it and the payment to place it in the paper anonymously through the mail. Given Grist's position in the community, it is extraordinarily unlikely that he was unaware of who was involved in introducing the Ku Klux into York. He claimed "no good" could come from the presence of "that singularly secret and doubly mysterious and hideous organization known as the 'Ku-Klux-Klan,' which is so rapidly spreading over the country."[57] But a week later, he slyly reprinted an article from the *Memphis Ledger* that insisted the Ku Klux was nonviolent and devoted only to "the maintenance of order and good government."[58] Neither objective would soon be present in York County.

Some believe York County was the first place in South Carolina where the Ku Klux organized. If true, this was likely due, at least in part, to the population being nearly evenly divided among Black and white, which meant there would be a hard-fought battle for political control. Conservative whites used to being in control intended to use every means at their disposal to regain and retain that control. Origin stories suggest that York men who had traveled to Tennessee learned of the group and were inspired to form a chapter back home. Other accounts suggest a klan in nearby Chester County included some York residents who were then authorized to form a klan of their own. A man named J. D. McConnell insisted he was initiated into the first Ku Klux in York in early 1868 by Dr. J. Rufus Bratton and Major James W. Avery, who would for the next several years be considered the primary leaders of the Ku Klux in York County.[59]

Who formed the first klan in York is perhaps irrelevant. What is remarkable is how rapidly it grew and how it came to dominate York County. Credible estimates are that 80 percent of the county's adult white male population was Ku Klux.[60] York County may have been an outlier, but the membership numbers there make plausible Forrest's claim that the Ku Klux had a half-million members throughout the South.[61]

"In no Southern county did the Klan organize more fully or take over more completely," historian Trelease wrote, adding that York was "in a state of near-anarchy which no one dared to combat."[62] The Ku Klux ability to act with total impunity in York, committing some of the most atrocious of crimes, meant that "the county received more national publicity and national attention than any other in the South," local historian the Reverend Jerry West concluded.[63] Another local historian said the Ku Klux in York represented nothing less than "a second civil war."[64] Southerners vehemently denied the Ku Klux was a second rebellion against the national government—but if not an army, the Ku Klux was indisputably the largest domestic terror organization in American history.

The Ku Klux evocation of war was partly because two-thirds of the Ku Klux were Confederate veterans; one-third were too young to have served.[65] Individual klans were organized much as army companies had been, where residents of the same general locale enlisted and served together. The klans were often led by the same men who had been the members' superior officers in the military, and so members were used to taking orders from these men. The military ethos of a "band of brothers" created in wartime was now perverted in service to the Ku Klux's code of secrecy. Further, four years' battle-hardened experience in discipline and group cohesion made these men exceptionally dangerous. Law enforcement and poorly trained citizen militias were totally inadequate to put down the Ku Klux; it would become clear that only an opposing military force could do that.

There is no record of when or why my great-grandfather joined the Ku Klux. Given the participation of so many of his former comrades in arms, peer pressure was certainly a significant factor. But it is also worth noting that what John Clayton and others did as part of the Ku Klux was not a radical departure from their former lives. What they did by choice as Ku Klux they had been *required* to do by law before the war.

From the early eighteenth century until emancipation, state law in South Carolina and all the slave states required that every adult white male regularly ride in nightly slave patrols to prevent insurrections of the enslaved and to capture runaway bondsmen. Even the poorest of whites who had never and would never own a slave were still bound to protect not only the community, but also the property of the planter class and thereby Southern society.

These patrols, which critics have suggested influenced the development of modern law enforcement, had the right to stop and question any African-American person they came across, to demand proof that he or she had permission to travel at night, and to whip any who did not—or even to whip those who did. Most able-bodied men, such as my great-grandfather, were required to serve on a slave patrol several times each month. The patrols existed not simply to maintain order but also to demoralize African Americans with the reminder that the South was for them one very large prison from which they could not escape, and within which every white Southerner played the role of jailer. There were multiple motives for Ku Klux behavior, including political advantage or just sport, but at its most base the Ku Klux sought to "reassert psychological dominance over the freedmen . . . just as patrols had done in the prewar period."[66]

Social reformer and Indiana congressman Robert Dale Owens, who was part of a federal commission charged with determining how to help African Americans transition from bondage to freedom, noted that "a certain element of barbarism" is present in any society that practices slavery.[67] For his entire life, John Clayton had been, as had his peers, inured to brutality against African Americans. Perhaps, before the war as part of a slave patrol, he had already engaged in violence against African Americans. There is no record one way or the other. But emancipation had in some ways exacerbated the savagery Southern whites had always exercised against African Americans. During slavery, owners had a financial stake in the general well-being of their property, which occasionally tempered brutality in the service of the master's economic self-interest. Emancipation eliminated this modest protection. Republican politician Carl Schurz, who toured the South at President Johnson's request, reported that the disturbing new attitude of whites toward freedmen and women was that "the blacks at large belong to the whites at large."[68]

As with Dr. Bratton, who turned out his former slaves when they expressed independence of thought, the planters who might once have moderated violence toward African Americans as their valuable property now seemed to have a special enmity toward freedmen and women. Before the war—and afterward—white Southerners had convinced themselves that the bond of master to slave was familial and so, astonishingly, felt genuinely betrayed that their former property embraced freedom and felt no debt of loyalty toward their former masters.

In a hierarchical and patriarchal society like the Old South, men like John Clayton looked to men like Bratton for guidance as to what was proper behavior, and the behavior advised by men like Bratton was brutish and savage. This does not absolve John Clayton and his fellows of culpability and approbation for what they did, but the notion that respectable men of the South were a force for order and incapable of barbarity, while the Ku Klux was exclusively the work of the underclass like my great-grandfather, is a lie, one even accepted by legendary scholar W. E. B. Du Bois, the first African American to earn a PhD from Harvard University.

Du Bois demonstrated how widespread and ingrained eugenics had become by the 1920s and 1930s when he authored his masterwork *Black Reconstruction in America* by blaming the "lynchings and mob law . . . murders and cruelty" that plagued Southern African Americans after the war on the disappearance of the planter class because they had "merged their blood" with poor whites and disappeared as a class.[69] In truth, Ku Klux tended to be a higher social order than the typical Southerner—more likely to have been slaveowners before the war, more likely to head a family, usually having a net worth two to three times that of a typical Southerner, and many had college degrees.[70]

Toward the end of the Ku Klux trials, a number of York County men very similar in age and background to my great-grandfather made brief statements as they were sentenced for their involvement in the Ku Klux. Perhaps John Clayton would have echoed their sentiments had he stayed to face the consequences of his actions, or perhaps not. Many of those who went before the bar insisted they had been reluctant Ku Klux recruits. Some claimed they feared they would be whipped, as their African-American victims were whipped, if they refused to join.

A man named William Shearer captured the combined forces of fear and peer when he said, "Well, everybody else was in, and I didn't exactly feel safe without I belonged to it."[71] Others said their choice to join the Ku Klux was affirmed by the knowledge that the most respectable men in the county, including their former Confederate commanders, belonged. As they faced time in a federal prison, they wished these respectable men had provided a better example. Said a Ku Klux named William F. Ramsey, "It seems to me that men who had good learning and knowledge ought to have teached us better."[72] But these men of good learning and knowledge were themselves inclined to commit the most heinous and appalling of crimes.

CHAPTER TWO

We ask for no special privileges or peculiar favors, we ask only for even-handed Justice.

—STATEMENT OF PURPOSE, ADOPTED BY THE COLORED
PEOPLE'S CONVENTION OF THE STATE OF SOUTH CAROLINA, 1865

I

JIM WILLIAMS, A UNION ARMY VETERAN AND MILITIA CAPTAIN, WAS THE most feared African-American man in York County, which explains the horrific way in which he was lynched by a large party of Ku Klux personally led by Dr. J. Rufus Bratton. Williams's sin, as US Attorney David T. Corbin later summarized it, was that he was "a pretty independent negro . . . [and] was called, consequently, a pretty bad boy."[1] Local whites would insist after his murder that Williams had repeatedly threatened to kill the white population "from the cradle to the grave," although those who later testified under oath acknowledged they had not personally heard Williams make such a threat, and one of the Ku Klux who participated in the lynching later said the alleged threats had no bearing on their decision to kill Williams.[2]

Louis F. Post, a stenographer assigned to assist Major Lewis Merrill in his investigation of Ku Klux crimes (and who later was employed to transcribe the Great South Carolina Ku Klux Klan Trials), said all the testimony he heard indicated that the "martyred" Williams "was the kind of man whose memory South Carolina white men would honor had he been white . . . a self-respecting, brave, and law-abiding man, of whom his white neighbors might well have been proud as a citizen of their own rearing risen from slavery to leadership."[3]

But Williams did not inspire pride or admiration among neighboring whites, only loathing. He had refused Ku Klux demands that he disarm his militia, and he was militant in demanding that he and his fellow freedmen and women be left alone by the Ku Klux. According to Milus Smith Carroll, a Ku Klux who said he participated in the lynching, Williams's "downfall" (an odd construction for the murder of a formerly enslaved person) was a speech Williams gave in Yorkville on March 6, 1871, a sales day in town. "Late in the afternoon," Carroll said, "he (Williams) mounted his mule and rode down to Rose's Hotel, which was headquarters for the radical party, and delivered his speech in which he boasted that if ever the KKK came into his country very few, if any, of them would return to their homes. In less than two hours thereafter, plans were perfected to raid his place that night."[4]

Williams's defiant assertion of equality was intolerable to the many white Southerners who continued to insist the result of the Civil War had not fundamentally changed their society. As Wade Hampton told a congressional subcommittee investigating Ku Klux atrocities, the "natural consequences of the war" were limited to "the abolition of slavery, the impossibility of peaceful secession, and the recognition of the supremacy of the United States Constitution."[5] If the North insisted on more, Hampton said, then the South had been deceived at Appomattox when the generous terms Grant offered Lee suggested that rapprochement not reconstruction would shape the postwar culture.

Hampton was correct that the war had not ended on terms well understood by both sides. Since the Union had never acknowledged the Confederacy as a separate nation, there had been no treaty to end the war and clearly define the peace. Nor were any terms immediately forthcoming. In the first months after the surrender of the Confederate armies, the South, still in shock from defeat, might have grudgingly accepted almost any changes demanded by the victorious North. But the North was preoccupied, first by the shock of Lincoln's assassination and then by the power struggle between the Republican-controlled Congress and President Andrew Johnson, a Tennessean and unionist who had never left the Democratic Party and who sympathized with the South. Into this political vacuum, former Confederates simply resumed their control of state governments whose authority was backed by armed white militias still "uniformed in Confederate gray."[6] Slavery was acknowledged to be theoretically abolished, but these neo-Confederate governments began passing a series of laws, known as "Black Codes," that were intended to create a labor system that would be "back to near as slavery as possible."[7] The South had lost the war, but was rapidly winning the peace.

South Carolina's Black Codes, like those in other Southern states, barred African Americans from most professions to force them to continue working only as plantation laborers who, by these laws, were to toil from sunrise to sundown. Laborers were required by law to sign contracts that prohibited them from seeking other employment, and no African American could leave a plantation or entertain guests without the permission of their employer. If an African American was stopped and unable to produce proof that they were employed under a contract, they could be arrested for "vagrancy," an offense defined with extraordinary breadth, which was punishable by floggings and forced labor—as was any crime involving an "insult" to a white person, another offense defined with considerable scope. Most egregious of all, since it evoked one of the worst aspects of slavery— the separation of families—African-American children, even those in loving two-parent homes, could randomly be declared "orphans" and placed in uncompensated "apprenticeships."[8]

Stunned by this perceived Southern defiance, the Republican-controlled Congress finally found its Radical footing. In 1867 it outlawed any military organization that was not part of the regular federal army, namely the white militias, and replaced the neo-Confederate state governments with Republican-led Reconstruction governments that included large numbers of African-American legislators and other officials. In South Carolina, the new governor was a former Ohio physician and Union general named Robert K. Scott, who first came to South Carolina to run the Freedmen's Bureau. The Black Codes were repealed and new civil rights laws approved, but the question was how to enforce those laws. Reliance on state or local law enforcement was hopeless, as most white lawmen (and many of their constituents) were Ku Klux. While Congress had, with its militia ban, implied that the Army was now responsible for maintaining order, Major General Henry W. Halleck, commander of the Division of the South, refused to intervene on grounds the military should not interfere in civil affairs. As one historian noted, "State Republicans had to build a law enforcement system practically from scratch."[9]

There had been a great deal of violence around the 1868 election, which was carried by Republicans in South Carolina, but violence in 1870, with

white Democrats determined to regain control of state and local governments, was far more intense. Hundreds of whippings and a dozen murders
of African Americans, just in York County alone, led most African Americans to sleep outside in the woods rather in their homes for fear of a Ku
Klux raid. Scott and the Republican-dominated legislature's solution to this
intensifying violence was provocative, but they had few options.

Realizing the ban on militias now put Republican state governments
at risk, Congress repealed the prohibition, and in March 1869 legislation
was passed in South Carolina to create state militias open to both white
and Black males between the ages of eighteen and forty-five, but virtually
no whites would agree to serve with Blacks. Former Confederate officers
volunteered to form all-white militias of former veterans, and Scott initially
approved their formation until African Americans strongly protested, making the reasonable argument that if Scott proposed to "arm the white K.K.s
to operate against them" then it was better to have no state militia at all.[10]

One of the few whites who would serve with African Americans was
John R. Faris, first cousin of my great-grandfather, who was elected captain of a mostly Black militia near Kings Mountain in York County and
who earned the Ku Klux's deep enmity for doing so.* Faris had served in
the Confederate army with "Campbell's Rifles" in the 12th South Carolina Infantry Regiment. It is not clear why he took a different path than
most of his relatives and became a Republican after the war, but possibly
he was part of a branch of the family who were Presbyterian Covenanters,
ultraorthodox Presbyterians who considered slavery "an evil of enormous
magnitude."[11]

If Faris was anti-slavery, his reformist inclinations did not extend to
social equality with African Americans. During the 1870 election campaign,
he hosted a delegation of Republican officials canvassing York County that
included a Black state representative named John Mead. Worried about too
close an association between Mead and his family, Faris, after consulting
with his wife, set "a long table" for dinner and placed Representative Mead
at the far end. Later, aware that none of the whites were willing to share
a bed with Mead, even though one of those officials acknowledged Mead

---

*As noted earlier, my ancestors spelled our family name in many different ways. In each case, I used the
spelling preferred by that branch of the family.

"was the most honorable man of the old delegation, white or colored," Faris fixed "a bed on the floor," which Mead graciously and "readily accepted."[12]

Black Carolinians "greeted the formation of the militia with unbridled enthusiasm," and, urged on by African-American women desperate for protection of their homes and family, nearly one hundred thousand African-American men had enrolled in militias organized throughout the state by the fall of 1870.[13] Those involved took great delight in being part of a force to protect their community. There was no standard uniform, so each militia developed its own and they were often quite colorful, some red, others white or yellow, often with epaulettes, and some adorned with ribbons and feathers.[14]

Unfortunately, Scott secured only about eleven thousand rifles, enough to arm about 10 percent of the militia members. At least another thousand weapons might have been purchased except that the Scott-appointed state inspector general took a one-dollar kickback on every ten-dollar gun purchased by the state; "he called it a commission."[15]

Even though they were sparsely armed—and many were left to drill while carrying sticks and brooms—even a single armed African American, let alone one hundred thousand, played to the greatest of all Southern white fears. Having spent two and a half centuries fretting over slave insurrections, a literal army of armed Blacks was deemed intolerable. Yet, when push would come to shove, the Black militias and their inadequate weaponry posed little threat to white supremacy. While a considerable number of African-American men had joined the Union army, most African-American militia members had no military training. By contrast, two-thirds of the Ku Klux were experienced Confederate veterans who were, according to Major Lewis Merrill, receiving funding and arms from sympathizers in the North, particularly from New York.[16] Reflecting on this inequitable conflict, a state constable asked, "Does [Scott] think a lot of ignorant colored men with clumsy muskets in their hands can catch a squad of experienced soldiers on blooded horses?"[17]

II

But one African American who did have military experience was Williams, which is likely why he was elected captain of his militia. There are gaps in records and memories of ancestors, but Williams probably escaped bondage sometime in 1864, though possibly earlier. According to the recollection of family members, Williams had committed some infraction while working on the plantation owned by J. Rufus Bratton's brother, John S. Bratton Jr., and he ran away rather than submit to a flogging.[18]

From overhearing the conversations of whites, slaves were remarkably well informed on a host of issues, so perhaps Williams was aware that a Union regiment of African-American troops had been formed and was then stationed at Beaufort on the South Carolina coast. That regiment was initially known as the 1st South Carolina Volunteer Infantry Regiment (Colored), and it was the first authorized regiment of African-American soldiers in the Civil War and also the first regiment made up solely of those formerly enslaved. The more heralded 54th Massachusetts Infantry Regiment, featured in the movie *Glory* (1989), was mustered several months after the 1st South Carolina and was composed primarily of free-born Blacks.

If he headed for Beaufort, the closest place to York County where he might have joined the Union army, Williams had to make an extraordinarily dangerous two-hundred-mile journey while avoiding capture or death. The regimental commander, Colonel Thomas Wentworth Higginson, an abolitionist from Massachusetts, marveled at the risks African Americans took to escape slavery and join the Union cause. In his memoirs, Higginson wrote of an elderly African-American man named Miller who received a diabolical five hundred lashes when he was caught trying to escape from a Savannah-area plantation, and also of an African-American woman named Fanny Wright whose baby was shot dead in her arms while she was in a boat escaping to a Union-held island off the Carolina mainland.[19]

By the time Williams joined the regiment in 1864, it had been reorganized and renamed the 33rd United States Colored Infantry Regiment. Records from this period, especially for African-American troops, can be murky and incomplete. A house fire later destroyed Williams's army papers, and his widow, Rosa, could not recollect in which regiment her husband had served. Jim Williams was also a common name, which makes it difficult to say with absolute certainty where and how the Jim Williams of this story served.

But there are records that a Private Jim Williams served in the 33rd Colored Regiment and that he worked as a teamster. We know from testimony given later at the Ku Klux trials that Williams had the background to be assigned work as a teamster, for he had been responsible for driving and maintaining the carriage of his master while enslaved. The 33rd Colored was also subsumed under the command of General William Tecumseh Sherman, and after the war Williams relished emphasizing that he had served under Sherman, the commander most feared and hated in the South. Given that a number of white witnesses during the Ku Klux trials reported hearing Williams's boast, it appears to have had the desired effect of presenting Williams as a man not to be trifled with.

In truth, Williams likely did not see active combat. The Union's top general, Ulysses S. Grant, was a strong advocate of enlisting African Americans in the Union cause and liberally involved Black soldiers under his command in combat. But Sherman actively resisted enlisting Black troops, even once ignoring a direct order from Lincoln to do so, and would only use African-American soldiers under his command in logistical support roles.[20]

This does not mean that Williams was not well trained as a soldier, nor was he spared the horror of war. All who served saw that war was, in Sherman's words, "all hell."

Susie King Taylor, the wife of a soldier, served the 33rd Colored as a "laundress," a euphemism for her being the first Black nurse in the Union army—a role for which she received no pay despite having won the admiration of Clara Barton, founder of the American Red Cross.

Observing the Union siege of Charleston, Taylor noted "the many skulls lying about. . . . They were a gruesome sight, those fleshless heads and grinning jaws, but by this time I had become accustomed to worse things and did not feel as I might have earlier in my camp life."[21] Taylor, who was literate and taught soldiers in the 33rd how to read and write, also observed the hatred the Black troops inspired in Southern whites, even when these troops tried to prevent the burning of Charleston in the chaos that followed the Confederate abandonment of the city:

> For three or four days the men fought the fire, saving the property and effects of the people, yet these white men and women could not tolerate our black Union soldiers, for many of them had formerly been their slaves; and although these brave men risked life and limb to assist them in their distress, men and even women would sneer and molest them whenever they met them.[22]

In contrast to Sherman's self-acknowledged bigotry, Higginson, a Unitarian minister who had been an ardent supporter of violent anti-slavery fanatic John Brown and an early mentor to the shy and eccentric poet Emily Dickinson, expressed admiration at how his soldiers, all former slaves, constantly confounded his expectations.* He said he discovered that African Americans were as intelligent and as courageous as whites, and more stoic in the face of pain or adversity. He found particularly absurd the widely held notion, North and South, that Blacks were inherently lazy and would work only under the threat of the lash. In his diary he wrote:

> *Last night, after a hard day's work (our guns and the remainder of our tents being just issued) an order came from Beaufort that we should be ready in the evening to unload a steamboat's cargo of [ten thousand feet of] boards, being some of those captured by them a few weeks since, and assigned for their use. I wondered if the men would grumble at the night-work; but the steamboat arrived by seven, and it was bright moonlight when they went at it. Never have I seen such a jolly scene of labor. Tugging these wet and heavy boards over a bridge of boats ashore, then across the slimy beach at low tide, then up a steep bank, and all in one great uproar of merriment for two hours. Running most of the time . . . pouring great courses of ridicule on the heads of all shirkers . . . all this without any urging or any promised reward."*[23]

Higginson was further surprised by the depth and sincerity of his men's Christian faith and their apparent patriotism for a nation where they had been enslaved. He put down in writing the many hauntingly beautiful spirituals all the men seemed to know, even though Southern law had prevented African Americans from gathering for a church service except in the company of their masters.† He was also brought to tears during a ceremony to note the Emancipation Proclamation taking effect on January 1, 1863,

---

*Higginson was one of the so-called "Secret Six" who helped Brown plan and finance his 1859 raid on the federal armory at Harpers Ferry as a precursor to a planned slave revolt. Higginson corresponded with Dickinson over twenty years, offered editorial advice, and then, along with Mabel Loomis Todd, published the first collection of Dickinson's poems in 1890, four years after the poet's death.
†In the movie *Glory*, several of the prayers uttered in the scene around the campfire on the night before the 54th Massachusetts mounts the assault on Fort Wagner are taken verbatim from prayers that Higginson heard his troops proclaim and which he recorded in his diary.

when a collection of African-American men and women spontaneously began singing:

> My country tis of thee
> Sweet land of liberty
> Of thee I sing!

"I never saw anything so electric," Higginson wrote. "It made all other words cheap; it seemed the choked voice of a race at last unloosed."[24]

The African-American soldiers clearly looked forward to participating in American democracy once they had won their freedom, and they demonstrated that they had followed politics even while enslaved. There were many nights, Higginson said, when the men would step up on the tops of barrels and take turns delivering speeches to their comrades on a host of topics. Their political sophistication was evident in the speech of one soldier, Corporal Prince Lambkin, whom Higginson said had predicted civil war since the rise of the Republican Party and the presidential campaign of John C. Frémont. Lambkin gave "a very intelligent account" of that campaign, full of historical references, and noted that the slaves on the Florida plantation where he had been held had followed the news closely enough that they refused to work on the day Lincoln assumed the presidency on March 4, 1861, "expecting their freedom to date from that day."[25] Another group of former slaves from Georgetown, South Carolina, reported they had all been brutally whipped for singing in celebration the day Lincoln was elected.[26]

Williams was one of some one hundred eighty thousand African-American men who fought for the Union army and whose participation had been decisive in ensuring a Union victory.* By the end of the war, one in four active Union troops was African-American, and most military historians now agree with Major Martin Delany,† the highest-ranking

---

*Another twenty thousand African Americans served in the Union navy. In addition to providing nearly two hundred thousand soldiers and sailors for the Union war effort, also key to Union victory were another half-million slaves who had left their owners during the war, depriving the South of considerable manpower, while hundreds of thousands more who remained behind did what they could to thwart the Confederate war effort as spies, saboteurs, and providers of provisions for liberating Union troops.

†Delany, considered the first advocate of Black nationalism, was born free in what is now West Virginia and was one of the first four African-American men admitted to Harvard Medical School until the white students successfully petitioned for their removal. He also coedited *The North Star* with friend Frederick Douglass, and advocated for Black emigration to Africa before a late-life change of heart led him to become a Democrat who campaigned for Wade Hampton in the 1876 South Carolina gubernatorial race.

African-American officer during the war, who told an African-American audience, "Do you know that if it was not for the black men this war never would have been brought to a close with success to the Union, and the liberty of your race if it had not been for the Negro?"[27]

Proud of his own contribution to the war and the emancipation of himself, his family, and his people, and politically awakened, Williams was also well aware of the disparity between his militia and the Ku Klux, who were disciplined veterans of four years of often intense combat. Closing this gap was a key reason he drilled his militia regularly, although not nearly so relentlessly as asserted by local whites.

In seeking to justify Williams's murder as an act of self-defense by the white community, Ku Klux attorney and former US attorney general Henry Stanbery later asserted that Williams was "constantly drilling them as if he were preparing them for war."[28] In truth, according to Andy Tims, who served as clerk for Williams's militia company, the militia sometimes drilled as often as every Saturday evening, but usually only every other week.[29] Williams's company was one of the fortunate militias to be issued a compliment of nearly one hundred Enfield breech-loading rifles in August 1870, but they were provided so little ammunition that, Tims said, they could fire "never more than two or three rounds" during any target practice.[30]

"Doubtless Captain Williams enjoyed parading his company, just as white men do," wrote Post, Merrill's stenographer. "Doubtless he felt the pride of authority, just as white men do; doubtless his spirit rose erect with a sense of official responsibility, military at that, just as the spirits of white men do." And if he had refused to disarm, Post said, "Is not that a tribute to his personal courage and official competency? Surely it may be better taken as evidence of his sense of responsibility and the courage of it than of a wantonly evil purpose."[31]

York County whites knew that Williams intended no evil purpose, or so said one of the Ku Klux who participated in Williams's lynching, but that did not make the presence of armed African Americans any more tolerable to whites, and the Ku Klux raids had been particularly focused on completely disarming African Americans.[32]

On February 11, 1871, Williams was part of a group of African Americans who met with a delegation of whites at a small crossroads establishment called Tate's Store in the Clay Hill section of York County. The meeting had been organized by a charismatic local African-American leader and preacher named Elias Hill who had hopes of reducing tensions between neighboring whites and Blacks, but who was so disabled that he did not attend the meeting himself.

It was already known that Governor Scott was debating whether to disband all militias dominated by African-American membership to appease whites and avert further bloodshed. Williams agreed at the meeting that he would collect his militia's guns and store them in a "secure place," but he said he would accede to their demand that he disband his militia and return its guns to the state only if he received a direct order to do so from Scott, as well as far stronger assurances that the Ku Klux would refrain from their nightly raids.[33]

The whites present made no such assurances, and the very next day, February 12, a race riot broke out in nearby Union County in which eight African-American men were taken from the county jail and murdered by a group of some five hundred to seven hundred Ku Klux "in black gowns, with masks fitting tight to their faces."[34]

Williams was at a loss at what to do. He traveled to Columbia and learned that Scott did intend to disarm the African-American militias. They had served their purpose in countering white violence during the 1870 election and in ensuring a high Black turnout for Republican candidates, but Scott now worried he had gone too far in provoking the white population. Williams was furious that Scott and the Republican legislators "had not done what they had promised."[35]

For weeks, Williams teetered between surrender and continued resistance. He hoped to somehow assure whites that "he didn't intend to hurt them," and thought militia commanders who were turning in their weapons were "cowards."[36] Yet members of his own militia, exhausted by the nightly Ku Klux raids, believed they should disarm if it would appease whites and reduce tensions. Two white men later testified that Williams had confided in them a week before his murder that he intended to turn his militia's weapons back to the state and resign as its captain.[37] But then he had a final change of heart and decided to take his stand that March 6 afternoon in Yorkville on the steps of the Rose Hotel.

III

The murder of Williams was sensational enough that it was still fodder for the curious fifty years later when Milus Carroll was asked by the *Yorkville*

Enquirer to reminisce on his participation in the crime as if the "famous raid" were the anniversary of a great battle. Carroll unashamedly admitted that Williams's alleged threats, if he had made them at all, were not taken "with especial seriousness," nor were they the reason he was killed. "The trouble here was that whites had become nervous and impatient because of the constant drilling and parading of the militia company under Williams, and the loose, irresponsible talk of the negroes . . . we had stood as much as we could," Carroll said.[38]

After hearing of Williams's defiant speech, Bratton and fellow York County Ku Klux leader Major James W. Avery sent word to at least five separate klans to converge that night in a muster area known as the Briar Patch along Howells Ferry Road five miles west of Yorkville. Carroll said he counted eighty-four Ku Klux riders who answered the call. Another Ku Klux named Andrew Kirkpatrick recalled that most of the men were dressed in red and white gowns with black "capes that came down over their heads," some ornamented with horns. Blankets had also been placed over the Ku Klux's horses to help conceal their owners' identities.[39] The Ku Klux intended to disarm every member of Williams's militia company that they could find, though it had already been decided that Williams was to be hung whether he cooperated or not.[40] There was no doubt who was in charge. "Bratton was at the head of the party; he was riding in front," a Ku Klux named John Caldwell later testified.[41]

The size of the raiding party and the fear he engendered in the white community suggests that Williams must have been an imposing man. If so, it was by force of personality because, according to his wife, Rosa, and his aunt, Kate Hanna, he was only five and a half feet tall and stocky in build. He weighed 180 pounds and had come back a "heap fatter" from his time in the Union army, suggesting even army rations provided considerably more calories than a slave's diet. The exact date of his birth is unrecorded, but census records and his family's recollection suggest that Williams was about forty years old at the time of the Ku Klux raid. He was of mixed-race heritage, and Williams's aunt said his skin was the color of "ginger cake."[42]

When the eighty-four Ku Klux came within a quarter-mile of Williams's home, Bratton ordered the group to halt and selected a dozen men to go on with him to find Williams while the rest of the Ku Klux stayed behind with the horses. It was an area of thick forest and underbrush where even a large party of horsemen could move about unheard, and Williams's house was located in "an old piney thicket on the side of a hill."[43] Williams was well acquainted with his attackers, particularly Bratton. Rosa Williams had been owned by J. Rufus's older brother, John S. Bratton Jr., and she and Jim lived with four of their children in a small house along Love Creek just a few miles south of John Bratton's home. Williams himself had been hired out to John Bratton before running away to join the Union army.[44]

Before arriving at Williams's house, the Ku Klux had stopped at the homes of several members of Williams's militia, Carroll said. "But few of the militiamen were home; but in most cases their women handed the guns out the doors, and we had no trouble."[45] It was about 2:00 a.m. the morning after Williams had made his allegedly provocative speech in Yorkville when he and Rosa heard the Ku Klux outside their door.

Williams removed a loose floorboard and dropped down to hide under the house.[46] Seconds later, following a hard knock on the door, Bratton and the other Ku Klux burst into the cabin. Rosa tried to stay calm as she told Bratton that her husband was not home, "that he had gone away without telling where he was going."[47] But then Bratton noticed the loose floorboard. "He might be under there," he told his fellow conspirators. "Sure enough," Carroll would later recall, "there was Jim crouched down under the floor."[48]

Williams was yanked from his hiding place, Bratton placed a rope around his neck, and Williams was ordered to hand over all guns in his possession, particularly the rifles his militia had been issued by the State of South Carolina. Williams insisted the rifles were not and had never been in his personal possession, and Rosa later testified that her husband willingly gave the Ku Klux the only two guns he personally owned.[49]

Bratton and his fellow Ku Klux then led Williams out of the house by a rope. Rosa followed, pleading for her husband's life. Bratton told her to go back inside, shut the door, and to put their children to bed, the youngest of whom was an infant girl. "I shut the door, but didn't go to bed," Rosa would later testify, ensuring this small act of defiance was noted in the court record. "I looked out of the crack after them until they got under the shadows of the trees. I couldn't see them then."[50]

About two hundred yards from the Williams home, one of the Ku Klux, perhaps Bratton, spied a tall tree with sturdy limbs extending straight out from the trunk "and suggested that that was the place to finish the job."[51] Williams, with a noose around his neck, was forced at gunpoint to climb up the tree and onto a limb about ten or twelve feet off the ground while the Ku Klux tied the other end of the rope to the limb.

A man accustomed to being immediately and unquestionably obeyed, particularly by African Americans, Bratton ordered Williams to jump to his death, a directive Williams understandably refused. A Ku Klux named Bob Caldwell then climbed the tree and gave Williams a shove, but as Williams fell he grasped the limb with his free hands and held on for his life. Caldwell then crawled out on the limb, pulled out a hunting knife, and hacked and cut at Williams's fingers until Williams was forced to release his grip and drop. According to a Ku Klux who was there, "He died cursing, pleading, and praying all in one breath."[52]

Before they left, Bratton and his fellow conspirators, perhaps channeling the Roman soldiers at Golgotha who had placed a mocking sign on Christ's cross labeling him "King of the Jews," pinned a note on Williams's shirt that ridiculed his pride in command and his commitment to training and drilling his militia. It read: "Jim Williams on his big muster."[53] Identification of the handwriting on the note was later used to determine who should be charged with Williams's murder, and Major Merrill would advise his superiors that "one of them is one of the leading men of this county," meaning Bratton.[54]

The Ku Klux who had remained with the horses for the half hour it had taken Bratton's group to lynch Williams reported that they had heard distant and disturbing sounds of screaming and crying, "something like a woman in distress."[55] When the lynching party returned, Bratton said nothing except to order the men to "mount your horses." When one of the Ku Klux, John Caldwell, asked where Williams was, Bratton replied, "He is in hell, I expect."[56]

Then Bratton, with an air of insouciance that disturbed even some of his fellow Ku Klux, pulled out his pocket watch and said evenly, "We have no time to spare; we have to call on one or two more." Bratton then promised the men as soon as they were done, they would stop at his brother John's plantation for refreshments: "crackers, cheese, and . . . bottles of whiskey."[57] Bratton's promise of an early-morning picnic disturbed James Neil, who as part of the lynching party had witnessed Williams's frantic attempts to live. "Some men," Neil muttered under his breath to a fellow Ku Klux, "are powerfully hard-hearted."[58]

After raiding several more African-American homes, the Ku Klux "found an abundant lunch waiting" at Brattonsville. Upon arrival, the Ku Klux waved the guns they had seized, and Carroll insisted the raids had yielded twenty-three militia rifles.[59] Later, during the trials, other Ku Klux insisted the raids had only yielded a random assortment of perhaps twelve to fifteen guns, including pistols and squirrel guns.[60]

As the sun rose and the Ku Klux were enjoying their picnic just a few miles away, Rosa went to look for her husband. She ran into an elderly man who told her that her husband's body had been found and was still hanging from the tree. Because as many as ten African-American homes had been raided by the Ku Klux that night, the community was in a high state of agitation, and word of the lynching spread quickly. When the coroner arrived at the scene, he found some seventy African Americans, including members of Williams's militia company, surrounding the hanging body and making threats of revenge.[61]

When Williams's body was cut down, it was taken nearby to Brattonsville and placed inside the home known as the Brick House, which doubled as a general store on the main floor with the second story serving as the home of Napoleon Bratton, the younger brother of Rufus and John. Napoleon Bratton later boasted that he stood on the second-story porch of his home with a repeating rifle and dared distressed members of Williams's militia to approach.[62]

A hastily assembled coroner's jury, which included some of the Ku Klux involved in Williams's murder, returned "the standard verdict of death by persons unknown."[63] Avery and several other suspected Ku Klux were arrested the next day by federal troops under the command of Captain John Christopher, but they were soon released and not charged.[64] The federal government had not yet asserted authority, and local officials, most of whom were also Ku Klux, had no interest in investigating Ku Klux crimes.

While angry Blacks milled outside the Brick House, curious whites were nowhere to be seen as they chose to stay out of sight for the next several days. Even the Brattons were afraid, worried that "they were going to be killed that night . . . and very much alarmed."[65] Following the Ku Klux picnic of whiskey, ham, and crackers, the extended Bratton family, including women and children, gathered at the main house at Brattonsville, owned by the family matriarch, Harriett Bratton. They then sent word to Avery to send a host of Ku Klux to come and help guard the house. Avery dispatched fifteen to twenty men to keep an anxious watch, but, with Williams dead, no other leader emerged to organize the African-American militia into action.[66] In fact, a young lieutenant in the militia, perhaps worried he would soon suffer the same fate as befell his captain, allegedly went to Avery and urged him to take possession of fifteen to twenty militia rifles in the lieutenant's possession.[67]

Before his body was placed in a plain wooden coffin, Jim Williams was lovingly clothed by family and friends in the blue Union army suit that he had worn with pride during and after the war.[68] Williams, who had fought to win and then maintain his freedom and his rights as a citizen, was then lowered into a grave at Brattonsville, the family home of his murderer, in a cemetery that had, before the war, been reserved for the plantation's slaves, and which, following a local Revolutionary War skirmish called the Battle of Huck's Defeat, was the site of a mass grave for those who died fighting to oppose American independence.* It was a grim metaphor for the fate of the hopes and dreams African Americans had held dear upon emancipation.

IV

Williams's expectations of what freedom would mean were very much in line with those of most African Americans. First on the list was the chance to reclaim their identity. As a slave, Williams had been called Jim Rainey, which followed the custom of slaves generally being given the surname of their masters as his last owner was named Rainey. But Williams knew that the name of his biological father was Peter Williams, and when he joined the Union army he enlisted under the name Jim Williams, not Jim Rainey.

When Williams was born in York County, he and his mother, named Rittie, belonged to a man named James Lowry. This is according to an army pension application filed by Rosa Williams twenty years after her husband's murder. At a relatively young age, Williams was presented as a wedding gift

---

*According to Historic Brattonsville historians, the cemetery for slaves there was initially the site of a mass grave for the roughly thirty loyalists killed during the Battle of Huck's Defeat. Turning the site into a slave cemetery was another way to dishonor those Tories who had fought and died for the cause of remaining British subjects.

from Lowry to his daughter, Mary, when she married a man named Quay Donivan who lived in nearby Chester County. Years later, to settle some debts, Donivan sold Williams to Samuel Rainey Sr., brother to J. Rufus Bratton's mother, who in turn gave Williams to his son, Samuel Rainey Jr., son-in-law to John S. Bratton Jr.[69]

Like many African Americans out of bondage, Williams wanted a normal family life, and not to have himself or family members traded and sold like livestock. Before he met Rosa, family members believe Williams had become partners with a woman named Hannah, who was enslaved by the Bratton family but who died, as did their baby, in childbirth. Williams then fathered a boy named Gil with a woman named Ollie who was later "sold and taken away somewhere." Rosa had also known heartache. A fellow slave named Green Bratton, with whom she had two children named Henry and Lula, abandoned her for another woman, though she and Bratton remained on friendly terms for the rest of her life; he even filed an affidavit to help her secure an army pension as the widow of a Union veteran. Perhaps seeking a mother for his own young son and desiring to help Rosa raise hers, Williams married the former Rosa McKnight in April 1857 at Brattonsville in a small ceremony witnessed by other slaves and presided over by a preacher named John Harris. Slave marriages had no legal standing in the South, but Rosa insisted that all accepted that the couple were husband and wife.[70] Together, they had a son, James Jr., and a girl named Patience.

Rosa worked as a cook for the Brattons, while Williams's duties at the Rainey plantation included driving his master's carriage when needed. This facility with horses helped prepare Williams for his future military duties as a teamster. Slaveowners had convinced themselves that the master-slave relationship inspired mutual loyalty, and Samuel Rainey's widow, Julia (he had died in 1866), later insisted her husband had treated Williams "very kindly, retaining all the old family."[71] True or not, Williams had no desire to remain a slave, a condition no kindness would make tolerable.

Contrary to white fears, Williams's commander in the army, Higginson, said he always found it remarkable that the African Americans in his regiment expressed no desire for revenge against their former masters. "Two things chiefly surprised me in their feeling toward their former masters," Higginson wrote, "the absence of affection and the absence of revenge."

Some of the African-American soldiers acknowledged their masters had been kind but still saw them as "natural enemies," Higginson said. "It was not the individuals, but the ownership, of which they complained."[72]

Williams's own absence of malice was literally testified to during the Ku Klux trials by Julia Rainey, who noted that when Williams returned from the war he ended up living barely two miles from the Rainey plantation where he had been enslaved. Despite Rainey's testimony that Williams was "disturbing the neighborhood generally" through alleged threats of violence against whites, she admitted that Williams was still "at liberty to enter my kitchen at any time to see the old family servants; there was always a great deal of politeness between us . . . for two months before his death, I suppose he averaged twice a week in my kitchen."[73]

What Rainey and most whites still could not bring themselves to understand, or perhaps because it was not in the economic and social interest of whites to do so, was that the recently freed African Americans did not wish to subjugate whites as they had been subjugated; they simply wished to be left alone. They sought no retribution. They did not lust to intermarry or aspire to socialize with whites. Most sought only to do what normal people did, but which had been denied them in slavery: the opportunities to legalize marriages, reunite families that had been scattered by slave sales, worship in their own churches, and build schools so their children might be educated and aspire to a better life.

Higginson was awed by how desperately his troops wished to learn to read and write. "Their love of the spelling-book is perfectly inexhaustible— they stumbling on by themselves, or the blind leading the blind, with the same pathetic patience which they carry into everything," he said."[74] The desire for education for themselves and their families continued unabated after the war. According to the 1870 federal census—the only census that would ever list Williams as a free man—Williams's adopted eight-year-old son, Henry (who was the son of Green Bratton), was able to read and write. Possibly, he was a pupil of the extraordinary Elias Hill, who traveled around the county to give lessons; if not, he likely attended a school organized by the Freedmen's Bureau.

The Bureau of Freedmen, Refugees and Abandoned Lands has been aptly described as "America's first attempt at a comprehensive social-welfare agency."[75] The Freedmen's Bureau was always badly understaffed and never had more than nine hundred agents working throughout the South. Yet it still did heroic work, building schools and hospitals, providing legal services, and feeding the hungry, including poor whites. In fact, despite its mission to help freedmen, in some localities "more whites than blacks received Bureau aid."[76] Reporting on one region where 80 percent of Bureau aid went to whites, Whitelaw Reid observed, "A stranger might have concluded that it was the white race that was going to prove unable to take care of itself, instead of the emancipated slaves."[77]

The bureau's efforts to establish schools in the South, which, unlike New England, did not have a history of established public education, was supplemented by appropriations from state governments under Radical Republican control. But more important and more impressive was the amount of money African Americans themselves dedicated to the construction and operation of schools. In the five years after emancipation, despite being generally impoverished, and despite the notion they would forever be wards of the government, African Americans raised among themselves more than a million dollars to build schools and hire teachers, the opening of each school an occasion for "joy incomparable."[78] Despite aiding poor whites as well as Blacks, the Freedmen's Bureau ceased operations in 1872 due to Northern indifference.

The modest nature of the aspirations of emancipated African Americans can be gathered by a statement of purpose adopted by a convention of freedmen who gathered at the Zion Church in Charleston in 1865 to oppose the newly adopted Black Codes:

> *Lifted up by the providence of God, we ask for no special privileges or peculiar favors, we ask only for even-handed Justice, or for the removal of such positive obstructions and disabilities as past, and the recent legislators have seen fit to throw in our way and heap upon us. . . . We simply desire that we shall be recognized as men; that we have no obstructions placed in our way; that the same laws which govern white men shall direct colored men; that we have the right of trial by a jury of our peers . . . that we be dealt with as others in equity and justice.*[79]

Real justice ought to have meant that African Americans received grants of land that they had earned through a quarter-millennium of sweat equity, and for a brief moment toward the end of the war it appeared that a land redistribution program that would have radically altered Southern society might be instituted. In January 1865, his army having occupied Georgia and preparing to move into South Carolina, Sherman was urged by Secretary of War Edwin Stanton to transfer ownership of lands confiscated along the Georgia and South Carolina coasts to African Americans. Sherman was no reformer and had no interest in the future of African Americans, but he was anxious to relieve himself of the responsibility for caring for the thousands of African Americans who were flocking to his army for sustenance and protection. Sherman's Field Order No. 15 declared that African-American families each be given title to forty acres of land and directed the army to loan African Americans mules as needed, which was the origin of the rumor that rapidly flew across the South that the federal government would soon provide every African-American family with "forty acres and a mule."[80] By June, some forty thousand African Americans had settled on four hundred thousand acres of land included under Sherman's order.

Union general Oliver O. Howard, who, unlike Sherman, *was* a reformer and deeply dedicated to African-American rights, sought to follow Sherman's lead after he was appointed the first head of the Freedmen's Bureau. In June, Howard, who would go on to help found the Washington, DC, university that bears his name, directed his agents to transfer ownership of land under bureau control to African Americans in forty-acre lots. But shortly after assuming office upon Lincoln's assassination, President Johnson ordered that all lands seized by the federal government during the war be restored to their former Confederate owners.

Howard initially ignored Johnson's order, asserting the president could not supersede the congressional legislation that created the Freedmen's Bureau and that had granted the bureau land to be sold to the newly freed slaves. But Johnson insisted Howard follow his orders, and so Howard had the unhappy task of traveling to South Carolina and advising those African Americans who had been working the lands provided under Sherman's order that they would have to abandon what they had believed were their lawful new homes. Speaking to one gathering of two thousand angry freedmen, Howard said he feared violence might erupt until "a sweet-voiced negro woman" began singing, "Nobody Knows the Trouble I've Seen," which quieted the crowd, though most in attendance still angrily shouted "never" and "can't do it" when Howard pleaded with them to "become reconciled to their old masters."[81]

Of course, some industrious African Americans earned and saved enough money to buy property; Elias Hill was able to purchase forty acres in Clay Hill. In some instances, whites rewarded African Americans for their service with a small grant of land. The Brattons reportedly gave Green Bratton, Rosa Williams's first husband, ten acres near the Mount Zion Church near Brattonsville on which he developed a small vegetable farm and store.[82]

During the Ku Klux trials, an African-American man named John Thomasson testified that his wife, whose name was not given, had been bequeathed property by her former mistress in return for Mrs. Thomasson staying to care for her after emancipation. But after the woman died and Thomasson and his wife took legal possession of the property, they were repeatedly harassed by the Ku Klux, who heard that Thomasson was allegedly influential in the Black community.

During the first and second Ku Klux raids, Thomasson said he was told to never vote again or "they would send me to hell." On a third raid, the Ku Klux set about destroying the couple's possessions, including a treasured clock, as well as all their glassware and the home's glass windows. Discovering a bottle of ink that was a sign Thomasson was literate, the Ku Klux made him swallow the entire contents, and then warned he had three days to leave York County or "we'll know what to do with you." The specific nature of the threat was unrecorded for, according to the trial transcript, Thomasson "here related a matter too indecent for publication." Thomasson left immediately, but when he and his wife returned two weeks later in hopes of retrieving a few small items they had left behind in their haste to leave, the Ku Klux raided again, firing shots randomly into the house with one bullet coming within three inches of his wife's head. Having fled to Tennessee, Thomasson said his wife died a few months later. "They scared her to death," Thomasson said of the Ku Klux, adding that he had to abandon the property that was legally his and which was, presumably, appropriated by a member of the Ku Klux.[83]

The refusal of whites to allow African Americans to accumulate wealth or property to prevent them from becoming self-sufficient, but instead remain dependent upon white employers, was one of the many injustices that caused Williams to seethe with anger. Said a man who knew of Williams's fury, "The Government—Yankees, as he called them—had promised him forty acres of land, and they hadn't given it to him, and he said that if war had to take place he would have a whole plantation."[84] Instead, he was buried in a plantation's slave cemetery. Such injustice forced others, including the charismatic Elias Hill, to conclude that Blacks might never find a true home in America.

CHAPTER THREE

Don't you pray against Ku Klux, but pray that God may forgive Ku Klux.
—ELIAS HILL RECOUNTING WHAT HE WAS TOLD BY HIS ASSAILANTS

I

FORMER SLAVE ELIAS HILL WAS AN AUTODIDACT, A SELF-TAUGHT preacher and teacher and "the most remarkable man in South Carolina," said a Philadelphia journalist who found Hill's intellect and eloquence all the more extraordinary because either polio or muscular dystrophy had left Hill unable to walk, crawl, or feed himself without assistance.[1] The horrific beating Hill received from the York County Ku Klux in May 1871 was, therefore, a remarkably repugnant crime, even measured against the hundreds and thousands of murders, rapes, beatings, and whippings committed by the Ku Klux in the years following the Civil War. Hill's beating was such a cruel and appalling act that Ku Klux sympathizers were embarrassed by it, and the whipping of Hill became a turning point in the federal government's previously tepid efforts to put down the Ku Klux.

Hill's case never went to trial, but he was able to tell the story of his beating to a congressional committee chaired by Pennsylvania senator John Scott that convened on July 25, 1871, at the elegant Rose Hotel in Yorkville to gather testimony on the Ku Klux atrocities that seemed especially prevalent in York County. Hill was carried into the room on a special chair borne by two of his nephews and used a small "pry stick" to adjust his posture when necessary.

Committee members were unnerved by the sight of the fifty-two-year-old Hill with his many afflictions. Those who met Hill always struggled to use the proper similes to describe his appearance. One had said Hill's legs "resemble the talons of a large bird more than anything else."[2] Another said

Hill's arms and legs were "small as those of a child, and drawn up around his body like handles to a vase."[3]

As Hill took his place before the committee, Congressman Job Stevenson, a Republican from Ohio who himself looked like Abraham Lincoln's twin, marveled aloud that Hill's legs were "about the size of a man's wrist."[4] The subcommittee's lone Democrat, Congressman Philadelph Van Trump, also of Ohio, who spent most of his time during the hearings sympathizing with the Ku Klux when not denying the group's existence, assessed Hill's appearance and expressed disbelief "that such a pitiful man as you had been whipped," staggered that anyone could be heartless enough to assault such a deformed man.[5]

But those who knew Hill understood why he inspired fear among those committed to keeping African Americans in a condition akin to slavery. While he could not even crawl, he was still a leader that others would follow, for he was locally prominent in three areas important to the newly free: education, religion, and politics.

Once observers stopped gawking at his contorted body, their focus shifted upward. Upon his shrunken shoulders, they saw Hill's "massive intellectual head . . . and [his] intelligent, eagle-like expression."[6] When he spoke, they became transfixed by his euphonious voice, which was also extraordinarily powerful. Thomas Summer Simpson, who had lived under the care of Hill's mother, Dorcas, and who was fifteen years old when Hill was assaulted, could still recall more than fifty years later how Hill "had such a powerful voice he could be heard a long distance when preaching." This was remarkable because another of Hill's afflictions was that his jaws were drawn so tight that he could barely open his mouth, and could only be fed through an opening in his mouth where two teeth had been removed.[7]

The members of Congress sat transfixed as Hill, in a calm and mellifluous voice, provided a lengthy description of his assault in the early hours of May 6, 1871, when he heard the sound of barking dogs and snorting horses and knew immediately who and what was afoot. "As I had often laid awake listening for such persons, for they had been all through the neighborhood, and disturbed all men and many women, I supposed that it was them," Hill said. Listening to the ruckus but unable to move, Hill heard the Ku Klux go first to his brother's home next door and abuse his sister-in-law as they demanded to know where Hill was.[8]

"I could not understand what they said, for they were talking in an outlandish and unnatural tone, which I heard they generally used at a negro's house," Hill said. He heard the Ku Klux repeatedly whip his sister-in-law until she finally pointed to Hill's cabin and said, "Yon is his house." When a Ku Klux burst through Hill's door and yelled, "Who's here," Hill, knowing his likely fate, did his best to reply flatly, "I am here. [The Klansman] shouted for joy, as it seemed, 'Here he is! Here he is! We have found him!'"[9]

Throwing off Hill's bedclothes, two Ku Klux grabbed his shriveled arms, yanked him out of bed, and carried him into the yard, throwing him to the ground next to a small boy, Hill's nephew, who had also been rousted from his brother's home. They demanded that Hill identify who was responsible for a recent spate of fires that had burned white-owned cotton gin houses. "I told them it was not me; I could not burn houses; it was unreasonable to ask me," he said, referencing his crippled condition. "Then they hit me with their fists, and said I did it, I ordered it. They went on asking me didn't I tell black men to ravish all the white women? No, I answered them." A half dozen Ku Klux took turns striking Hill as he laid helplessly on the cold ground. He was unable to recognize his attackers, as "they all had disguises on," flowing robes and hoods with fabric horns attached.[10]

Next, the Ku Klux demanded to see the correspondence Hill had been maintaining with Republican congressman A. S. Wallace, a particular enemy of the local KKK, with whom Hill had made inquiries about the American Colonization Society and what opportunities were still available for African Americans to emigrate to Liberia. Hill said he would show the Ku Klux where the congressman's letters were filed among his papers if they would take him back into the house. "Never expect to go back," a Ku Klux snarled. "Tell us where the letters are."[11]

As the Ku Klux stormed into Hill's cabin, Hill emphasized to the committee that he was heartbroken to hear his treasured clock, a rare symbol of middle-class status for African Americans, shatter as it fell to the ground. One of the Ku Klux in the yard still standing guard over Hill called out, 'Don't break any private property, gentlemen, if you please; we have got him we came for, and that's all we want."[12]

The Ku Klux then grabbed Hill by his withered legs and dragged him across the yard and laid him there, nearly naked in the cool night, while they rifled through his belongings, confident that Hill would not be going anywhere. At this point, Hill urged his young nephew to run and seek help while Hill remained shivering in the dark for a half hour while all six Ku Klux searched the cabin for the letters from Wallace. Finally finding Hill's correspondence with Congressman Wallace, the Ku Klux burned the letters in Hill's fireplace, but continued to peruse a small account book Hill used to keep the financial records of the church and school that he operated.

Returning to the yard, the Ku Klux asked Hill if he was afraid. "They pointed pistols at me all around my head once or twice, as if they were going to shoot me, telling me they were going to kill me, wasn't I ready to die? And willing to die?" Hill said. "I told them I was not exactly ready, that I would rather live." That Hill could maintain his composure and control his fear infuriated the Ku Klux. One harshly grabbed Hill's drawn-up leg, causing him to moan in pain. "God damn it, hush!" the Ku Klux yelled. He then pulled out a horsewhip and ordered Hill to raise up his shirt. "I reckon he struck me eight cuts right on the hip bone," Hill recalled. "It was almost the only place he could hit my body, my legs are so short—all my limbs drawn up and withered away with pain." Another Ku Klux took a strap and buckled it around Hill's neck, saying, "Let's take him to the river and drown him."[13]

"I was somewhat afraid," Hill said, "but one said not to kill me."[14] This Ku Klux, who was later identified as a man named Tom Simril, made Hill an offer.[15] If he would agree to place a card in the *Yorkville Enquirer* that announced he would never vote Republican again, Hill could live. Two of Hill's nephews, June Moore and Solomon Hill (the ones who had carried him into the Rose Hotel for his congressional testimony), had already been prevailed upon to do just that after earlier Ku Klux raids on their homes. Hill pleaded that he did not have the money to purchase such an advertisement and was told to borrow some. He was then asked if he would quit preaching. Wishing neither to lie nor die, Hill said, "I told them I did not know. I said that to save my life." The Ku Klux also then made the comparatively odd demand that Hill cancel his subscription to a Republican newspaper he received from Charleston. With this final directive, the Ku Klux then ordered his sister-in-law to come and pick Hill up and carry him back to bed, whipping her with a strap as she did so.[16]

Gathering around Hill's bed as his sister-in-law laid him down, the Ku Klux made one last surreal demand: They ordered Hill to pray for them.

"I tried to pray," Hill said, "[And] they said, 'Don't you pray against Ku Klux, but pray that God may forgive Ku Klux. . . . Pray that God may bless and save us.'" Chilled and still terrified, Hill tried to stammer out a proper prayer, but the Ku Klux "said that would do very well" and all but one left quietly. The remaining Ku Klux, perhaps unnerved or even impressed by Hill's strength of character during the ordeal, returned Hill's accounts book. "Here's that little book," he said, forgetting to disguise his voice, but speaking "in his common, plain voice, then he went out."[17]

Less impressed, a pugnacious and scowling Congressman Van Trump tried to bait Hill into acknowledging that his beating had been justified. Were not Hill's sermons, he demanded, simply political screeds in favor of the Republican Party and rants against injustices perpetrated by whites? "No, sir," Hill replied. "I preach the Gospel, repentance toward God, and faith in our Lord Jesus Christ."[18] Unpersuaded, Van Trump pressed Hill to confess his grievances. "You do not feel very kindly toward the white race?" he stated more than asked. Hill replied, "I am afraid of them now. . . . I have good-will, love and affection for them, but I fear them."[19]

Hill had, in fact, lost faith that whites would ever agree to live in peace with African Americans. He told the subcommittee that if there were not federal troops present (a regiment of the US 7th Cavalry had been stationed in Yorkville since March and troops were housed at the Rose Hotel), he would not have testified. "I would not then have come up here to report for anything in the world, for I would have expected to have been killed tonight if I had."[20]

Hill had already gambled with his life when he filed a report of his beating with the cavalry regiment's commander, Major Lewis Merrill. He had not met Merrill and likely heard that Merrill had, upon his arrival, adopted a friendly attitude toward the white establishment in Yorkville in the belief that reports of Ku Klux outrages had been greatly exaggerated. Hill challenged Merrill to investigate his report and to confirm what was "known by all that know me," which included the fact that Hill was perhaps "the worst afflicted person known on earth still living." He also begged Merrill to be discreet, "as many of my color have been killed for reporting what was done to them by K.K.K." Hill had plans and was not anxious to "be sacrificed for the truth."[21]

II

Those plans were to return to Africa, where, Hill said, his father had been born. When and where in Africa we do not know, but it is possible Hill's father had been a recent arrival to the United States. The Constitution theoretically banned the international slave trade in 1808, but it continued to flourish in South Carolina and much of the South until the outbreak of the Civil War; one of the most active international slave traders in South Carolina was a close relative of Governor James Henry Hammond.[22] Deplorable (and illegal) as it was, the continued importation of slaves from West Africa provided a constant stream of living reminders of the native lands of the ancestors of African Americans.

Hill's mother, Dorcas, on the other hand, was a light-skinned mulatto who may have been the daughter of her master, Revolutionary War hero Colonel William D. Hill, who fought at the Battle of Kings Mountain. Elias was born in 1819 and was perfectly healthy as a young child. At the age of seven, however, Hill contracted what he called "rheumatism" but which was more likely polio or muscular dystrophy, and his condition progressively worsened with age. Sometime around 1840, when Elias was about twenty-one, Hill's father had somehow earned and saved enough money to purchase his freedom from the Hill estate for $150. He then raised enough money to buy Dorcas's freedom, too, but there was a catch: "He could not get her without taking me," Hill said, "as I was a cripple," and therefore considered worthless to his owners. "They compelled him in the contract to take me when he bought his wife, who was my mother."[23]

Hill's frail body held a powerful mind. It had been illegal in South Carolina since 1740 to teach slaves to write; schools for even free Blacks were banned in 1834. But out of pity or perhaps because they considered Elias a freakish mascot, white children occasionally stopped by the Hill cabin after school and either deliberately or inadvertently taught Hill the alphabet.* From these meager beginnings, Hill became "so much of a scholar as I am."[24] The primary reading material available to him was the Bible, and Hill "became deeply impressed with its teachings, and early began the preaching of the

---

*One of the children may have been his master's youngest son, Daniel Harvey Hill, who would later become notorious as the Confederate general who mislaid General Robert E. Lee's battle plans so that they fell into Union hands and helped foil Lee's 1862 invasion of Maryland at the Battle of Antietam. It was enough of a victory for the Union that it gave President Lincoln the confidence to issue the Emancipation Proclamation, which took effect January 1, 1863.

gospel."[25] The Bible's influence on Hill's self-instruction is evident in his penmanship (he could grasp a pen only "with all his fingers knotted in a bunch around it"), as he began each paragraph of his writings with a large capital letter as he would have seen in printings of a King James Bible or psalters.[26]

Whatever preaching Hill did before the Civil War, he did in secret. While slaves might be allowed to join their masters at church (seated in a segregated balcony, of course), it had been illegal in South Carolina since 1800 for African Americans to assemble in groups, including in a Black-led church or any gathering that involved any form of "mental instruction."[27] An exception was made in South Carolina's largest city. Although free Blacks accounted for barely 2 percent of South Carolina's overall African-American population, in Charleston there were enough free Blacks that churches and fraternal organizations were generally tolerated. The number of free Blacks in the Piedmont of northwestern South Carolina, on the other hand, numbered only in the dozens.[28]

It is not clear that Hill and his family were even truly free, despite having purchased their freedom, for South Carolina outlawed manumission in 1820. The only way around the ban was to get a special exemption from the state legislature, and the Hills do not appear to have obtained such an exemption.[29] This left them in a legal no-man's land with the potential of being re-enslaved if they were ever caught without papers verifying they had purchased themselves out of bondage. So they lived off the beaten path in the then remote Clay Hill district, a dozen miles northeast of Yorkville, hoping to avoid interaction with whites as much as possible.*

After the war, Hill remained at Clay Hill, "among the gullies and ravines and rooted in the red clay soil of York County where Allison's Creek emptied into the Catawba River."[30] Under the Black Codes enacted at the end of the Civil War, African Americans could only enter professions by paying a license fee that was usually prohibitively expensive, but somehow (likely through donations from parishioners) Hill acquired the state license that allowed him to preach. He also raised funds to construct a wood-framed church near his log cabin home that he named the Sardis Baptist Church. Sardis was the capital of Lydia and one of the great cities

---

*The place where Hill is believed to have resided alongside his church and school is now under the water of Lake Wylie, a reservoir along the Catawba River constructed to prevent flooding in Rock Hill. The lake is ringed by lakefront homes belonging to those who commute to nearby Charlotte or Rock Hill.

of the ancient world, whose early Christian church had become moribund. In Revelation 3:2, Saint John is directed to write a letter to the church at Sardis with the injunction, "Wake up, and strengthen the things that remain, which were about to die; for I have not found your deeds completed in the sight of My God."

By all accounts, Hill was a powerful and riveting speaker. As noted earlier, those who heard him speak were mesmerized by what a *Philadelphia Press* reporter called his "clear, sonorous voice."[31] Another white observer said, "He had a voice of unusual power and sweetness," adding that "in intellect he has few superiors, and in piety and Christian graces, and in powers of persuasion, few equals."[32]

Near the Sardis Baptist Church, Hill also had a small wood-frame school constructed where he could teach children and adults alike. He was long remembered "as the only colored teacher in that section of the country" at that time, and he also rode a ten-mile circuit throughout this northern part of York County to both teach and preach.[33]

It was not an easy journey. Unable to walk or stand, Hill was placed in an armchair, cushioned with a quilt and comforter, that was then placed in the bed of a spring wagon from where he preached or taught. If he needed to go somewhere the wagon could not, his nephews or other strong young men carried him about in his chair, just as he was carried into the Rose Hotel to provide his congressional testimony. Hill's lessons were likely basic as he helped the newly freed and their children to finally obtain the elementary education they had been denied for a quarter-millennium, but his insights could also be profound. "In all York County, its legal and medical professions included, there are not a dozen better-informed men than old Elias, nor one with a stronger intellect," the *Philadelphia Press* reporter asserted.[34]

And so, despite his self-described "hideous deformity of a body," Hill was "a leader among his people. Educated, eloquent . . . he has impressed them with a superstitious reverence, and is implicitly followed and obeyed," said a white journalist.[35] This exaggeration says more about the racial bias of a journalist who still saw most Blacks as docile primitives than any Svengali-like powers held by Hill, but given that he was already a community leader in education and religion, it was natural that he was also tapped to become a local political leader as president of the Clay Hill chapter of the Union League. It was in this role that he particularly drew the ire of the Ku Klux.

III

The Union League was begun during the Civil War in the North as a middle-class patriotic club, but afterward it became the chief political voice for the freedmen and women. It was the primary venue for organizing political support for the Republican Party in the South, but became much more encompassing—beyond even the services provided by the Tammany political machine in New York.

Union League chapters in the South provided a political education for its members, who were primarily African Americans, though there were also whites-only and even a few mixed-race chapters. Members heard debates on the great issues of the day and recruited candidates for office. The League chapters also helped raise money to build schools and churches and provide emergency funds to care for the sick. League leaders provided legal and financial advice to members and mediated disputes, while the League even occasionally operated as a labor union, organizing work stoppages to protest low wages or the unfair division of crops between landowners and workers or sharecroppers. League chapters petitioned law enforcement to arrest white criminals and to allow African Americans to serve on juries. Absent action by civil authorities, League members sometimes acted as sheriffs, enforcing the code of law.[36]

Ku Klux defenders would claim that their organization was identical in purpose to the Union League and was, in fact, a reaction to the League, whom they accused, not without evidence, of trying to intimidate, sometimes by force, any African American who might support the Democratic Party. The Union League did keep its membership secret and usually met at night, primarily to accommodate members who worked during the day. The League had its own oaths, passcodes, and initiation rites that included prayer and renditions of patriotic songs such as "Rally Around the Flag, Boys," usually sung with such gusto that one initiate said it "almost made the hair stand on my head."[37]

But the Union League had no paramilitary role. In 1870, two years *after* the Ku Klux organized in South Carolina, Republican governor Robert Scott ordered the creation of state militias to help keep order. Given

Democratic opposition to the Scott administration, most whites refused to serve in the militias unless they were segregated. Scott flirted with allowing all-white militias, but then dropped the idea in the face of criticism from African Americans, his key political constituency. Whites sometimes referred to the League and the mostly Black state militias interchangeably, but the militias were not part of the League. The League, however, took the lead in recruiting members and helping organize what became primarily African-American state militias. Even though the Ku Klux predated the formation of these militias, Southern whites justified the crimes of the Ku Klux as acts of preemptive self-defense.

The true trigger for the explosion of violence in 1870 was the elections that were held in October that year. Reeling from the Democratic Party's losses in the 1868 election, and aware that African Americans represented roughly 60 percent of South Carolina's voting population, white conservatives, reluctant to use the Democratic name, organized themselves as the Union Reform party and superficially tried to rally Black voters and disaffected white Republicans embarrassed by the corruption of the Scott administration and its allies. The Union Reform party even nominated a handful of Black candidates for local offices.

The ploy was a failure. Too many white conservatives found it humiliating and refused to support a ticket that even superficially treated African Americans as political equals. It is estimated that more than half of eligible white voters declined to participate in the election. African-American voters, meanwhile, were not fooled by a Union Reform party platform that offered them little more than "ballyhoo and barbecue."[38] Even a Union Reform leader candidly admitted the idea of a fusion ticket was a ploy intended to "overturn our negro governments and re-establish white supremacy."[39]

While the white vote was depressed, African-American turnout was suppressed.

There was no secret ballot in 1870 in South Carolina or most anywhere else.* In full view of anyone who wished to observe, voters dropped colored pieces of paper into containers to signify which party they supported. White employers threatened to fire any employee who voted Republican. In the Piedmont, particularly, there were multiple shootings and whippings of African Americans before the election and armed Ku Klux blocked Black

---

*The secret ballot was not widely adopted in the United States until the 1880s.

voters from several polling places. More violence was promised to any African American who defied the Ku Klux and still voted Republican.[40] White Republicans were not immune to threats and violence and, if anything, their supposed treason to their race seemed to enrage white conservatives even more than the idea of Black voters. One official reported that Ku Klux and their supporters had put out the word pre-election that "they would begin by killing all the damned *white* Republicans first."[41]

To counter these tactics, Scott accelerated the formation of the primarily Black militias so that by the fall of 1870 there were nearly one hundred thousand members. African-American women promoted enrollment, with some refusing to perform household chores "or have sexual relations if their husbands did not join."[42] The militias used beatings and other means of intimidation to prevent African Americans inclined to support the Union Reform ticket from voting. African Americans were recruited from North Carolina to cross the state line and cast fraudulent ballots, and there were other frauds committed, such as individuals casting multiple ballots.[43]

Scott won reelection with more than 60 percent of the vote, Republicans maintained huge majorities in the state legislature, and South Carolina's entire congressional delegation was Republican, which now included three African Americans: Joseph Rainey, who had been elected in a special election prior to October; the half-Jewish Robert C. De Large; and English-born Robert Elliott. The Piedmont, which was where Ku Klux violence had been the most intense and where African Americans were not in a majority, was the only part of the state carried by Union Reform candidate Richard Carpenter, a Republican originally from Vermont.

Conservative whites seethed with anger at the election results and, in November, the Ku Klux began a sustained campaign of terror that remains to this day "the most violent period in South Carolina's history since the Civil War."[44] The day after the election, a race riot started by armed whites killed nine African Americans in Laurens County, southwest of York. In York County, the Ku Klux committed two particularly brutal murders that were intended to send a message to the entire Black community.

At about midnight on December 2, a large group of fifty to seventy-five Ku Klux surrounded the home of a man named Thomas Roundtree, whom the Ku Klux had labeled a "bad Negro." They began firing into Roundtree's house until he jumped out of a window and tried to run away, partly to draw fire away from the home where his wife and children were inside. He was shot down before he had gone ten yards, and then a Ku Klux dismounted from his horse and slit Roundtree's throat from ear to ear. When Roundtree's body was examined, it had thirty bullet wounds. At around the same time, another African-American man, Tim Black, who lived near Rock Hill, was murdered. His body had eighteen bullet wounds and his throat was also cut. Roundtree's widow, Harriett Roundtree, identified several of those involved in the murder of her husband and they were arrested, but a former legislator and Ku Klux leader named William C. Black organized the defense for the accused and produced false alibis that freed them all. Mrs. Roundtree and her children, on the other hand, were then driven from their home.[45]

There was little use appealing to civil authorities for help. Most white sheriffs and judges were Ku Klux, and those that were Republican were being murdered. In Union County, Ku Klux murdered a Republican justice of the peace, which led hundreds of African Americans to flee the county. In every upcountry county African Americans were afraid to stay in their homes. Said Elias Hill, "All our colored people that could walk, males and females, and many children, staid out during that winter and spring."[46]

They laid outside at night in all types of weather, as rain, snow, and freezing temperatures were less fearsome than the Ku Klux. A few found shelter. "We didn't stay home," recalled Eliza Hill White, Elias Hill's grand-niece who recalled that when she was no more than ten years old the Ku Klux had marked her father for death. "We would leave at sundown every night, walk over a mile and slept that fall in the house of some white people, the Farises"—presumably John R. Faris, my great-grandfather's cousin, who let frightened African Americans, particularly armed members of his militia company, sleep on his property.[47]

When conditions outside were too frightful, African-American men still slept outside and left their families at home, hoping the Ku Klux raiders would not bother their wives and children once they learned the man of the house was not at home. It was a hope that was regularly shattered and left fathers and husbands anguished by the rape and beating of wives and daughters. Wishing, perhaps needing, to strike back in some way, a handful of African Americans set fires to white-owned buildings, especially cotton gin houses so important to their nemeses' livelihood. This only infuriated whites all the more and gave the Ku Klux further pretext, if any was needed, to commit even more violence.

In Columbia, Governor Scott vacillated about what to do. Now that his own reelection had been secured, he fretted that the state militias were doing more to incite violence than end it. He ordered militias in Laurens County to return their arms to the state. He contemplated disarming other militias to further appease white sentiment. Yet, at the same time, he declared martial law in Laurens, Union, Newberry, and Spartanburg Counties but had no means to enforce it. African-American legislators were threatening Scott with impeachment for not forming and deploying more militia; Congressman Elliott went so far as to accuse Scott of being "criminally guilty" for not doing more to end the Ku Klux outrages. Lacking an adequate state police or military force, Scott was under heavy pressure to ask for federal troops, a request he had so far put off in the belief it could reignite the Civil War.[48]

IV

Elias Hill was unwilling to wait and see what Governor Scott or President Grant could or would do; he intended to seek peace locally. In early 1871, Hill solicited a meeting with local whites to broker a truce he hoped would "pacify the neighborhood." He hoped the two sides could reach a compromise that would end Ku Klux outrages and the retaliatory arsons, and that such an agreement between white and Black neighbors in the Clay Hill precinct would include a pact of mutual aid.[49]

On February 11, 1871, a group of African Americans met with a delegation of whites at a small crossroads establishment in Clay Hill called Tate's Store. Hill did not make the trip but sent as his personal representative his nephew, June Moore. Among the group of whites was Dr. J. Rufus Bratton, who continued to publicly tout himself as a champion of African Americans while still operating as one of York County's Ku Klux leaders. Also attending was local militia captain Jim Williams.[50]

The group drafted a joint statement published in the *Yorkville Enquirer* that included the surprising acknowledgment by whites that the arsons which caused so much consternation were retaliation for outrages against African Americans. But the statement did not call out the Ku Klux by name and instead condemned all "acts of lawlessness committed at night by disguised persons, and we most positively condemn all such outrages, no matter by whom committed."[51]

There was also a pledge to assist law enforcement in bringing offenders to justice, though a postscript pinned the blame for the troubles on the Union League. "The opinion having been freely expressed in the meeting that there was a probability of the outrages continuing while the Union League kept up its organization, the members of the League present pledged themselves to hold no more secret political meetings at night." The *Yorkville Enquirer* opined that ending secret nighttime meetings was not enough; the Union League should disband. "We are fully persuaded that the best means they [the African-American community] could adopt to get rid of the 'Ku-Klux' danger would be to disband their own secret organization, and thereby remove the pretext for one in opposition to it."[52]

While not present at Tate's Store and unable to gauge the sincerity of the participants, Elias Hill was led to believe that the whites who attended had "pledged themselves . . . to protect the colored people in case of outrage and that they would come to their assistance, and use their influence in keeping it from that side of the creek which is our neighborhood especially."[53]

If the whites at the meeting did agree to a common defense, Hill learned when his own beating occurred that they had not meant it. While lying on the ground as the Ku Klux ransacked his home, Hill had dispatched his young nephew to the house of a nearby white neighbor, James L. Bigger, "asking him to come to our relief; but he refused to come . . . the next day he was heard to say that he had known of their coming, that he knew they were coming," but he had declined to warn Hill. A dispirited Hill told the congressional committee that he knew of at least a half dozen white neighbors who had foreknowledge that he was to be subjected to a Ku Klux raid and provided no warning. Rather, "every one that spoke at all rejoiced" to hear that Hill and other African Americans raided by the Ku Klux that night "were whipped, and telling all the causes and reasons—all this they did, their pledge to the contrary.* This is why we do not now take their pledges as good in every case."[54]

Congressman Van Trump demanded Hill offer proof that his neighbors had rejoiced in the beating of "such a pitiful man." Hill replied, "If you knew

---

*Before Hill was attacked, the same group of Ku Klux had raided another half dozen African-American homes, providing similar whippings, burning down one man's house, and raping another man's wife.

a man was going to be whipped and beaten, would you not try to hinder it?" Van Trump acknowledged that he would. Hill said his neighbors knew he was to be whipped and did nothing. "That is the reason why we think they rather rejoiced than were sorry." Van Trump sneered that Hill "had a pretty active brain for a colored man," and then tried to place Hill at risk of reprisal from these very same neighbors, several of whom were Ku Klux, by demanding that Hill name those who knew he was to be beaten. Hill, who had been threatened by a local planter even before he testified, asked to be excused from doing so, but Van Trump insisted. Hill lowered his voice to a "hoarse whisper," as if softly spoken words might not make it into the official record, and listed a half dozen names, including E. A. Farris, another cousin of my great-grandfather.[55]

On February 10, the day before the meeting at Tate's Store, the Ku Klux for the second time raided the home of John R. Faris, the cousin who still captained a mostly African-American state militia company. In the earlier raid, the Ku Klux had shot up John R.'s home, though fortunately no one was injured. This time, forty to fifty Ku Klux arrived at his home at 1:00 a.m. and demanded all the guns in his possession. The number of guns seized by the Ku Klux was "variously stated at from seven to twenty-seven in number," according to a *Yorkville Enquirer* account of the incident, which suggested that Faris was storing some of his militia's weapons. Once again, no one was injured, but Faris was rattled and likely threatened with further violence. When he came into Yorkville the following Monday, he refused to discuss the incident and left for Columbia, presumably to report the assault to Governor Scott. His visit may have had some impact, for on the day Faris arrived in Columbia, Scott finally wrote to President Grant, asking for federal intervention.[56]

V

Hill no longer cared what a white-led government might do. Despite the congressional investigation, the presence of federal troops, and the upcoming Ku Klux trials, Hill did not believe peace could be had. "[F]or certain of us, we have lost hope entirely since the whites pledged themselves at the meeting at the forks of the road three miles from where I live, and then broke all those pledges, those whites who professed to be our friends." Hill told the congressional committee that he and most of his congregation intended to migrate to Liberia.[57]

The first American slaves were brought to Jamestown in 1619, exactly two hundred years before Hill's birth, which meant that by 1871 some African Americans could trace their heritage in America back a quarter of a millennium, which predates the American roots of those whose ancestors arrived in Massachusetts on the *Mayflower* in 1620. But Ku Klux violence, and despair that they would ever be accepted as full citizens in the land of their birth, led "hundreds of thousands" of Southern Blacks to consider leaving the South following emancipation—just as Southern whites had asked Wade Hampton to lead them out of the United States following their defeat in the war.[58]

While some African Americans did do as some former Confederates did and moved to Mexico, many more considered moving to Haiti, the only nation in the Western Hemisphere with a Black-led government, or points even farther south. Others looked west to Kansas, Texas, and Oklahoma. Hill, who said he "loved the United States, which he cherished as his own native land," had considered moving to the West, but he read newspapers and saw that the Ku Klux was active throughout the South along the route they would travel, and knew that Blacks were not warmly welcomed on the frontier.[59] Oregon, for example, did not repeal its constitutional ban on African Americans and mixed-race persons from living in or even entering the state until 1922 and did not formally ratify the Fifteenth Amendment, which banned racial discrimination in voting, until 1959.[60]

It was Africa that captured the imagination of many African Americans, even though they had never seen the land of *some* of their ancestors, for many were mixed race, the result of white-on-Black rape. Hill concluded that Liberia provided "greater encouragement and hope of finding peaceful living and free school and rich land than in any place in the United States that I have read of."[61] Perhaps he also chose Liberia, in part, because his father had been born in Africa and had perhaps regaled his son with tales of life there. Africa, quite logically, had a strong pull for many African Americans. "The colored man never is and never can be really free until he sets his foot on the soil of his forefathers," said Scott Mason, a member of Hill's congregation.[62]

Self-styled racial moderates in antebellum America had long advocated "recolonizing" African Americans "back" to Africa. The American Colonization Society (ACS), formed in 1816 and first led by George Washington's nephew, Bushrod Washington, helped fifteen thousand free Blacks move to what was initially considered an American colony until Liberia became an independent nation in 1847. Abraham Lincoln continued to advocate for voluntary colonization until 1863. The ACS continued its works after the war, as many Americans, North and South, were skeptical the United States could be a peaceful multiracial country. But many, perhaps most, African Americans deeply opposed emigration. "We Negroes love our country," said the formerly enslaved civil rights activist Frederick Douglass. He called emigration "a disheartening surrender" to racism, and added it was logistically impossible anyway. To move four million African Americans to Africa would be "as vain as to bail out the ocean."[63]

Aware of Hill's planned expedition and others like it, a convention of African-American delegates from the eleven former Confederate states met in Columbia in October 1871, weeks before the Hill group's departure, and adopted a resolution that condemned emigration as a scheme "emanating from a few unscrupulous and irresponsible men, enemies to the colored race."[64]

In fact, emigration was unpopular even among "enemies to the colored race." While some whites wished African Americans to simply disappear, now that they were no longer valuable property, white planters did not wish to lose cheap Black labor. In fact, planters often refused to purchase the cotton crops of African-American renters if they believed the money would be used to finance emigration.[65] Southern Republicans, Black and white, also did not want to lose any of their core base of supporters, and African Americans who wished to remain Americans, and who were already badly outnumbered in the South, especially did not want to see some of their most talented, ambitious, and prosperous neighbors depart, which would make the tasks ahead even more difficult to achieve.

Hill's Sardis Church congregation did indeed include some of the most prosperous African Americans in the area. "The entire number is made up of some of the most industrious negroes in that section of the county," the *Yorkville Enquirer* reported, "many of whom, since their emancipation, have shown themselves to be thrifty and energetic, and not a few of them had accumulated money."[66] While only 5 percent of African Americans in South Carolina had assets, nearly a quarter of those in Hill's party headed for Liberia did. It was this financial independence that allowed Hill's group to emigrate when so many African Americans who wished to do so could not. In the decade after the Civil War, while perhaps hundreds of thousands of African Americans considered it, only thirty-one hundred actually emigrated to Liberia.[67]

But a statistic more important to Hill's followers than assets owned was that of the thirty-one households headed to Liberia, twenty-one had already been victimized by the Ku Klux Klan. As Hill told the congressional subcommittee, "We do not believe it possible, from the past history and present aspect of affairs, for our people to live in this country peaceably, and educate and elevate their children to that degree which they desire."[68]

On November 1, 1871, three months after his congressional testimony and with the Great South Carolina Ku Klux Klan Trials scheduled to begin within weeks in federal court in Columbia, Hill and 167 followers left Yorkville. They almost did not get out of York County. The American Colonization Society reneged on a promise to pay for the group's train fare from Rock Hill to the port at Norfolk, Virginia. Hill and his company had to come up with nine hundred dollars in cash on the spot at the Rock Hill railroad station.[69] Fortunately, the congregation was well fixed financially. One of Elias Hill's several nephews, Frances Johnson Hill, had reportedly saved a remarkable three thousand dollars to pay for his migration.[70]

Nearly ninety years later, Frances Hill's daughter, Eliza Hill White, recalled how the group left Norfolk for Liberia aboard a black-hulled, double-decked, three-mast barque named the *Edith Rose*. The voyage took thirty-eight days, and while not at all comparable to the horrifying voyages their ancestors had made as human cargo on ships going in the opposite direction, the journey had its challenges. Two children died along the way (there were also two births), and the ocean waves became so boisterous that passengers had to be strapped in their beds. "After dark, I remember we were scared to death and couldn't speak," Eliza White recalled in an interview conducted on her one hundredth birthday. "The sailing vessel would rise high as this house and go down with the big waves."[71]

Hill and 244 fellow emigrants (the additional numbers coming from other communities in the South) arrived in Monrovia, Liberia's capital, on December 16. In January, the *Yorkville Enquirer* published a letter from Hill that assured African Americans who had remained behind that they would receive a warm welcome if they chose to emigrate as well. He told them that he had held church the day after their arrival, choosing as the text for his sermon Romans 10:1: "Brethren, my heart's desire and prayer to God for Israel is that they might be saved."[72]

In his letter home, Hill painted a fetching portrait of a "flourishing" Monrovia, which he described as being "clothed with green, and rich with fruit trees laden with delicious fruit—oranges, lemons, pineapples, the cassada [cassava], eddoes, melons, sweet potatoes, and coffee." He noted land was plentiful and available, and was particularly enthused to learn two hundred acres had been set aside as the site of a future college.[73] He did not mention that Liberia was in a political crisis that was on the verge of erupting into civil war.

But if a reminder was needed as to why the Clay Hill emigrants had left South Carolina in the first place and were willing to gamble on an uncertain future in Liberia, on the same page as Hill's letter was another article noting that the still Republican-controlled South Carolina legislature was advancing a bill to provide a small pension for the ever-increasing number of those left widowed and orphaned by Ku Klux violence in the South Carolina Piedmont. Widows were to get six dollars per month and each orphan four dollars per month, with the program funded by a small increase in the property tax in nine upcountry counties where the bulk of the Ku Klux violence in the state was occurring.

Some of the Clay Hill company would greatly prosper in Liberia. Two of Hill's nephews, June Moore and Solomon Hill, became wealthy coffee and cocoa planters and lived in homes and enjoyed a lifestyle eerily reminiscent of those of Southern planters. Solomon Hill wrote home to York County that after only three years in Liberia, he already owned two thousand coffee trees and was "better satisfied than I ever was since emancipation, and am worth more than ever before."[74]

Moore and Solomon Hill created a joint venture that by the 1880s was doing one hundred thousand dollars in business annually, and Hill's brick and stucco mansion was so sumptuous it eventually became home to the United States diplomatic legation. Their prosperity may have come at a moral cost, however, as it was rumored the two men were some of the many successful American-born immigrants who used coerced native labor to work their plantations.[75]

When he first arrived in Monrovia, Elias Hill had already noted with disgust that American emigrants to Liberia treated the local natives with "selfishness, disrespect, inhumanity and oppression." While recent American arrivals "live and delight in luxury and ease," he saw them force natives to work at hard labor for low wages while ill fed and poorly clothed. "Shame and disgrace on the mean, wealthy and respected people of the city!" Hill railed.[76]

Hill did not live long enough to try to effect any reforms. The Clay Hill contingent had settled twenty miles into the interior, and Hill contracted malaria within days of their arrival at the community of Arthington. Hill was unconscious for the better part of two months before dying on March 28, 1872.

He was not alone. The mortality rate from malaria among American immigrants to Liberia generally was 20 percent, and the Clay Hill party fared worse than most. By May, a third of those who had traveled to Liberia with Hill had died, and some survivors began returning to York County less than a year after they had departed. Of the 167 men, women, and children who had emigrated from Clay Hill, forty-seven died within months of arriving in Liberia. Of the 120 survivors, at least thirty-six would return to South Carolina.[77]

Eliza White said her family was one of the first returnees; her father found life in Africa just too different from the life he knew in the United States.[78] June Moore opined that disease was not the real cause of the South Carolinians' deaths. "They did not die so much from Sickness," he said, as from "Wanting to go back to the States."[79]

These emigrants learned what the millions of African Americans who never contemplated emigration already knew: While their ancestors had come from Africa, and they had held on to a portion of their African heritage through food, music, stories, and forms of worship, and while many of their white countrymen might despise them, they were no longer Africans but Americans, and as American as the descendants of immigrants from any European nation.

But what did it mean to be an American? That was the question that would dominate the Great South Carolina Ku Klux Klan Trials. The Fourteenth Amendment had declared that those four million formerly enslaved were now citizens and entitled to all the "privileges and immunities" this entailed. But there was no broad agreement on what those privileges and immunities entailed for Blacks *or* for whites. Since they were adopted, the guarantees in the Bill of Rights had never been thought to apply to individuals; had that now changed?

When the trials began in Columbia as Elias Hill and his followers were traversing the Atlantic, the cases selected were ones that the prosecution and defense each hoped would define the meanings of the newly ratified amendments to the Constitution. These debates over constitutional law would involve some of the finest legal minds in the country, including three US attorneys general. Those working for the Ku Klux would argue that amendments had changed virtually nothing, while the prosecution argued they were nothing less than a second American revolution.

Chapter Four

They take all kindness on the part of the Government as evidence of timidity, and hence are emboldened to lawlessness by it.
— US ATTORNEY GENERAL AMOS T. AKERMAN

I

THE UNITED STATES CONSTITUTION AS DRAFTED IN PHILADELPHIA IN 1787 declares that all American citizens are entitled to certain "privileges and immunities," but it does not spell out what those privileges and immunities are, nor does it even provide a clear definition of who is an American citizen. Before the Civil War, this hardly mattered. People viewed themselves first as citizens of the states where they resided and secondarily as citizens of the United States.[1] The Civil War changed that thinking. Before the war, the United States was referred to in the plural, as in "the United States are," while after the war the preferred conjugation was "the United States is."[2] America had been thought of as a collection of largely autonomous states; now it was considered a single nation.

Abraham Lincoln, not unexpectedly, played a significant role in this change of thinking, particularly through his masterful Gettysburg Address. Building an extraordinarily layered argument in the spare 272 words he uttered on November 19, 1863, while dedicating the cemetery at the Gettysburg battlefield, Lincoln was, in the words of historian Garry Wills, "correcting the Constitution itself without overthrowing it."[3] Lincoln did this by arguing that the Constitution could only be correctly interpreted if read through the lens of the Declaration of Independence, which Lincoln noted predated the Constitution and the states, and which therefore took precedence over both.

Lincoln went so far as to offer a proof that this was so. He provided a precise date for the founding of the nation—"four score and seven years ago"—which, counting back from 1863, was 1776 when the Declaration was signed, not 1787 when the Constitution was drafted or 1789 when it became effective. Lincoln had long believed, as he stated in his first inaugural address, that "the Union is much older than the Constitution."[4] Even the Constitution acknowledges as much. The Constitution's preamble states that the intent is not to form a union from scratch, but "to form a more perfect union" out of one that was already in existence.

Lincoln also makes clear that the real driving force behind the Constitution was not a collection of states balancing interests and making political and moral compromises; rather the impetus for both the Declaration and the Constitution was "the people," and that the Civil War had been about whether a "government of the people, by the people, for the people, shall not perish from the earth." We are not thirteen or thirty-five or fifty individual states, but one nation whose original founding document, the Declaration, Lincoln declared at Gettysburg, is "dedicated to the proposition that all men are created equal."

The Constitution may not repeat the words "equal" or "equality" (nor does it ever explicitly mention the enslaved*), but that did not mean that equality is not integral to the Constitution. What Lincoln argued is that the Constitution had to be considered in concert with the Declaration, an old testament and a new testament, as it were, of a single national bible of canonical scripture.

Even today, there are many self-described constitutional "originalists" who find Lincoln's proposition a radical notion, and Lincoln had plenty of critics at the time he made his Gettysburg Address. Those critics understood that what Lincoln was advocating represented something close to a second revolution even if, as Wills noted, he was correcting rather than overthrowing old concepts.

The *Chicago Times* was among the many who accused Lincoln of betraying the Constitution he had sworn an oath to defend, and claimed he dishonored those Union soldiers who had died in its defense. "How dare he, then," the *Times* howled, "standing on their graves, misstate the cause

---

*In referencing the enslaved, the Constitution refers to them as "other Persons" for the purpose of the census and "such Persons" in levying a per-head taxation on imported slaves and a (rarely enforced) ban on the importation of slaves after 1808.

for which they died, and libel the statesmen who founded the government? They were men possessing too much self-respect to declare that negroes were their equals, or were entitled to equal privileges."[5]

But those who found Lincoln's words reasoned and inspiring also realized that, powerful as they might be, they were only words in a persuasive speech, not a binding statute. They might influence opinion, but they held no force of law. Further, the man who uttered those words and who might have pushed to have these thoughts enshrined in law had been murdered in April 1865 and was replaced as president by a man, Andrew Johnson, who held considerably different views on the Union and deep sympathy for the South. A majority of whites in that region—and plenty in the North as well—had embraced Wade Hampton's view that the war had changed hardly a thing. Secession was illegal and slavery was (theoretically) no more, thanks to the recent ratification of the Thirteenth Amendment. In the view of men like Johnson and Hampton, the three-quarters of a million deaths in this brutal family quarrel left everything else almost as exactly as it had always been.

Those who thought the war should have achieved more than this were especially startled when they read headlines such as the one that appeared in the November 14, 1865, *New York Tribune* that said, "South Carolina Re-establishing Slavery." A *Tribune* correspondent reported that the new Black Codes being instituted by a South Carolina legislature filled with former Confederates contained "almost every incident [associated with] Slavery," and supplied "abundant illustrations of the perils still impending over both the negro and the Union, under State Governments which shall be at liberty to disregard everything but the technical requirements of the amended Constitution."[6*]

For many Republicans in Congress, this audaciousness seemed nothing less than a continuation of the rebellion. With Johnson in the White House endorsing this brazenness, these Republicans became convinced that only further amendments to the Constitution could ensure that the aims of the war—or at least their aims—were truly and finally accomplished.

---

*The *Tribune* is referring to the Thirteenth Amendment, which abolished slavery and involuntary servitude except as punishment for a crime—a loophole the South would soon exploit. The Thirteenth Amendment had been approved by Congress on January 31, 1865, and was ratified by enough states for inclusion in the Constitution in December 1865.

One of these Republicans was Ohio congressman John Bingham, who would become the primary author of the Fourteenth Amendment and whose twin aims were to leave no doubt that African Americans were American citizens, and to define what the privileges and immunities of national citizenship were. At minimum, Bingham argued, the Bill of Rights, or at least the first eight of them, should be nationalized so they would apply to every American citizen, including African Americans.

II

Since their adoption in 1789 as the first ten amendments to the Constitution, the Bill of Rights had been judicially interpreted not as rights guaranteed to individuals, but restrictions on the power of the federal government. State governments remained free to ignore the Bill of Rights as they saw fit. Chief Justice John Marshall wrote in the court's 1833 decision in *Barron v. Baltimore* that if the framers of the Constitution had wanted the Bill of Rights to also restrain action by states, they would have added the phrase "no state shall" in outlining the general prohibitions.[7]

Armed with Marshall's opinion and terrified by an 1831 slave revolt led by Nat Turner that killed sixty whites in Virginia and which was blamed on abolitionist agitation, the South in the 1830s began to radically restrict free speech and a free press. There were no repercussions since states, as the Supreme Court had just ruled, were not bound by the First Amendment or the following seven either.

Southern states made it a felony punishable by imprisonment to produce or possess anti-slavery literature or even to speak against slavery in private conversation. With the acquiescence of the North and the federal government that was then under the Democratic administrations of Andrew Jackson and then Martin Van Buren, postmasters in the South were allowed to seize and destroy any abolitionist materials sent through the mails.* To ensure African Americans would not comprehend any material that might still slip through this ban and incite rebellion, laws were passed that made it a crime to teach African Americans to read or write. Under pressure from

---

*In the late 1830s, anti-abolitionist violence was actually more prevalent in the North than the South because that is where most abolitionists lived. Mobs broke up abolitionist meetings, looted abolitionists' homes, and assaulted abolitionist advocates, murdering abolitionist editor Elijah Lovejoy in Alton, Illinois, in 1837. (Curtis, "Curious History of Attempts to Suppress Antislavery Speech, Press, and Petition in 1835–37," 800–802)

the South, which many in the North decried as yet another example of the political and institutional dominance of the "Slave Power," Congress refused to receive anti-slavery petitions sent by citizens to prevent public debate in Congress over slavery, and also to ensure that no anti-slavery sentiment appeared in any official government publication.[8]

This government-sponsored censorship had great consequences in developing the Southern mindset, which had increasingly become convinced, absent access to any argument to the contrary, that those of African descent were biologically inferior and that slavery was not a necessary evil but a positive good for both races. President Johnson sent Union general Carl Schurz, a German émigré and Republican Party leader, on a fact-finding tour of the South in the summer of 1865 and then tried to suppress Schurz's report because of its unflattering description of conditions there. Schurz had observed, for example, that "One of the greatest drawbacks under which the southern people are laboring is, that for fifty years they have been in no sympathetic communion with the progressive ideas of the times."[9] The state-sanctioned prohibitions on any public discourse around slavery meant that my great-grandfather and his peers in the Ku Klux had likely never heard any serious critique of slavery before the war.

Bingham had long been a particularly vocal critic of how the South had protected the institution of slavery from criticism and inspection by infringing on the rights of free speech and a free press, and by providing no recourse to challenge such restrictions. The right "to know; to argue and to utter, according to conscience . . . is the rock on which [the] Constitution rests," he said.[10] Before the Fourteenth Amendment was considered, Congress had approved legislation extending the Freedmen's Bureau as well as the Civil Rights Act of 1866. The latter declared African Americans to be citizens and granted them some basic civil rights, such as the ability to enter into contracts, file lawsuits, and appear as witnesses in court. Congress overrode Johnson's veto of the legislation, but the wrangling over the measure convinced Bingham that only a constitutional amendment would ensure that Congress had the authority to approve and enforce civil rights legislation.

Echoing Lincoln's belief that the Union was the creation of a single entity, "the people," and was not a collective of states, Bingham said his goal in drafting the Fourteenth Amendment was to expressly state what the Constitution previously did not:

> *What is that? It is the power in the people, the whole people of the United States, by express authority of the Constitution to do that by congressional enactment which hitherto they have not had the power to do, and have never even attempted to do; that is, to protect by national law the privileges and immunities of all the citizens of the Republic and the inborn rights of every person within its jurisdiction whenever the same shall be abridged or denied by the unconstitutional acts of any State.*[11]

Bingham denied the proposed amendment infringed on the rights of states because "no state ever had the right, under the forms of law or otherwise, to deny to any freeman the equal protection of the laws or to abridge the privileges and immunities of any citizen of the Republic, although many of them have assumed and exercised the power, and that without remedy."[12]

During debate, Bingham and other supporters, such as Michigan senator Jacob Howard, clearly stated that their intention in drafting the Fourteenth Amendment was to ensure that states could not infringe on the rights of individuals that were "guaranteed and secured" by the first eight amendments in the Bill of Rights.[13]

But if Bingham and other supporters believed their intent was clear, the actual wording of the Fourteenth Amendment was maddeningly vague as the result of the type of political compromise necessary in almost everything, but especially to forge a change to the original Constitution. Section 1 of the amendment reads:

> *All persons born or naturalized in the United States, and subject to the jurisdiction thereof, are citizens of the United States and of the state wherein they reside. No state shall make or enforce any law which shall abridge the privileges or immunities of citizens of the United States; nor shall any state deprive any person of life, liberty, or property, without due process of law; nor deny to any person within its jurisdiction the equal protection of the laws.*

The Ku Klux trials would try to bring clarity to these inexplicit words, but even the mildest of interpretations was too much for President Johnson, who futilely sought authority to block the amendment, and then campaigned against it in an effort to rally Southern support behind his expected 1868 presidential campaign. But a race riot in Memphis, encouraged and abetted by state and local officials (the state attorney general personally handed out firearms to white rioters), and directed by the mostly Irish-American police force, killed forty-six African Americans. It was one of several incidents that convinced more than two-thirds of Congress that a constitutional change was necessary to protect the interests of the freedmen and women.

Pennsylvania congressman Thaddeus Stevens, leader of the Radical Republicans in the House, acknowledged the proposed amendment fell short of his own aspirations to create a nation where "no distinction would be tolerated in this purified Republic but what arose from merit and conduct." But Stevens said he would support a less-bold step because "I live among men and not among angels," and Congress needed to act before the Southern states were readmitted to the Union and Congress was "flooded by rebels and rebel sympathizers" who would never vote to approve such an amendment.[14]

Congress approved the Fourteenth Amendment overwhelmingly, but on a strict party-line vote, and the amendment was then sent to the states for ratification. When Republicans won even larger congressional majorities in the 1866 elections, white Southern moderates urged their states to ratify the Fourteenth Amendment to avoid antagonizing congressional Republicans further. Former Confederates still in control of Southern state governments refused while knowing that it would invite harsher Reconstruction terms. It was more honorable, they said, if those terms were "imposed and not voluntarily accepted."[15] A half dozen of the former Confederate states rejected ratification, and then Congress made ratification a condition for a state's readmission into the Union. When, on July 9, 1868, South Carolina became the twenty-eighth state to ratify, the Fourteenth Amendment officially became part of the Constitution.

III

The Fourteenth Amendment was written in five sections with five purposes. The first section was the most revolutionary and so potentially far-reaching that, while it fell short of the aspirations of the most ardent egalitarians such as Stevens, others viewed it as practically a "second American Constitution, the 'new birth of freedom,' for which Lincoln had prayed at Gettysburg."[16] This section declared that any person, with no reference to race, who was born or naturalized in the United States and subject to its jurisdiction was a citizen. Further, no state can pass any law that abridges a citizen's right to enjoy the privileges and immunities of American citizenship or that deprives any person of the right to due process and equal protection under the law. Creating the concept of national citizenship was "a radical repudiation" of the theory of state sovereignty.[17] The previous preeminence of state citizenship was what led Robert E. Lee to side with the Confederacy because he felt more loyal to Virginia than the Union.

The Fourteenth Amendment did not guarantee the right to vote, but its second section provided a penalty of lost representation in Congress for any state that denied the vote to any males over the age of twenty-one. Likewise, the Fifteenth Amendment, certified for inclusion in the Constitution two years later, on March 30, 1870, also did *not* guarantee a right to vote but stated only that no one could be denied the vote on the basis of "race, color, or previous condition of servitude." States could still establish other qualifications and conditions for voting, usually obstacles to doing so, but only if these conditions were not explicitly based on race. In the 150 years since, states, particularly in the South, have repeatedly devised techniques to suppress the vote of African Americans and others, but by means that they hope do not appear overtly racial.*

Suffragettes were deeply angered that both amendments provided protection only for men and did not expressly include women as either citizens or potential voters. The amendments split the previously aligned movements that had advocated for equal rights for women and for all African Americans. Elizabeth Cady Stanton adopted particularly racist language in condemning the Fourteenth and Fifteenth Amendments, saying it was outrageous that an ignorant "Sambo" would be allowed to vote while an educated white woman would not.[18] States could still grant women the right to vote, and several Western territories and states did during the nineteenth

---

*Longtime Georgia US senator Walter F. George, who served in the Senate from 1922 to 1957, said, "We have been very careful to obey the letter of the Federal Constitution, but we have been very diligent in violating the spirit of such amendments and such statutes as would have a Negro to believe himself equal of a white man." (Tindall, *Emergence of the New South*, 161)

century, including Wyoming, Colorado, and Utah, but there was no federal penalty for states that did not. Stanton also made the point that excluding women from citizenship and the vote doubly disadvantaged Black women, a problem that prosecutors in the Ku Klux trials acknowledged and sought to redress.*

The third section of the Fourteenth Amendment asserted the United States would not assume or pay any debt incurred by the Confederate states, which was a considerable blow to the Southern economy (as was the refusal to compensate slaveowners for their emancipated "property"). The fourth section said anyone who had taken an oath to defend the Constitution while assuming a public office before the war, but who had participated in the rebellion, could no longer hold public office, although there was a provision to allow Congress to waive this restriction. The Fourteenth Amendment's fifth and final section granted Congress the power to pass legislation to enforce the amendments.

IV

Enforcement legislation, however, was delayed as the Republican-dominated Congress was preoccupied with its impeachment of President Johnson, so further major efforts to address Reconstruction had to wait until Ulysses S. Grant was elected president in 1868. A central theme of the campaign was what to do about continued resistance to acknowledging and respecting the rights of freedmen and women of the South. In one Thomas Nast cartoon, Grant was depicted riding a white horse covered in a banner that read "Union" and "Equal Rights" while thrusting a sword into his opponent, New York governor Horatio Seymour, who sat astride a black horse that was branded with the initials "K.K.K."[19]

In a contest that was closer than might have been expected given his status as a war hero, Grant defeated Seymour by three hundred thousand votes in an election in which an estimated five hundred thousand African Americans cast ballots, with the overwhelming majority of those votes going to Grant. Grant carried five Southern states, but by such small margins that it was clear African-American votes had made the difference in

---

*The response of Frederick Douglass, an advocate of women's suffrage, argued for the primacy of guaranteeing the vote to Black men by saying, "When women, because they are women . . . are dragged from their homes and hung from lamp-posts . . . then they will have an urgency to obtain the ballot equal to our own." (Blight, *Frederick Douglass*, 491)

his victory. Grant failed to carry Georgia and Louisiana because Democrats successfully used violence and intimidation to keep African Americans from the polls.[20] That lesson was not lost on either the Ku Klux or the Republicans in Congress.

Grant's father was an abolitionist but his in-laws owned a number of slaves, and Grant benefited from the labor of several slaves loaned to his wife by her parents. His in-laws refused to turn over title to the slaves for fear Grant would emancipate any under his control. This Grant did for the only slave he ever owned, a thirty-five-year-old man named William Jones, who may have been a gift. Grant manumitted Jones in 1859, less than a year after acquiring ownership, which was all the more admirable because Grant was in dire financial straits at the time and might have received as much as one thousand dollars had he sold Jones.[21]

During the war, Grant had been among the most progressive Union commanders when it came to using Black troops. In the first major engagement of the war to feature African-American troops, at Milliken's Bend in Louisiana on June 7, 1863, one thousand Black troops fended off a furious attack by two thousand Confederate troops from Texas who flew black flags to indicate they would give no quarter to any Black troops who surrendered. Grant declared the African-American troops "most gallant" and for the rest of the war became an ardent advocate for recruiting as many Black soldiers as possible.[22] He also refused Confederate requests for prisoner exchanges unless African-American soldiers were included, which Robert E. Lee refused to do, describing Black soldiers as "this species of property."[23]

Grant even experimented with a land redistribution program at the expense of Confederate president Jefferson Davis's family. During the siege of Vicksburg, Grant seized the plantation belonging to Davis's brother, Joseph, in order to create what he hoped would be "a Negro paradise." Freedmen and women leased the land from the government and made the land pay by selling rations, mules, and tools to the Army. Within two years, this community had built a school, a church, and an infirmary and was earning an annual profit of sixteen thousand dollars.[24]

Grant had made a quick two-week tour of the South after the war and was initially hoodwinked into thinking the South was adapting to the idea that African Americans were now free. But as head of the Army, he continued to receive disturbing and distressing reports of atrocities that included the murder of thousands of African Americans in Louisiana alone.

Well before congressional discussions about a proposed Fourteenth Amendment, Grant issued a general order that all laws must be evenly applied without regard to race, and in 1867, before the rise of the Ku Klux, he recommended that Texas be placed under martial law as a warning to all the Southern states that wanton violence against Blacks would not be tolerated. Grant, likely unaware at the time there was a place called York County, South Carolina, noted that white militancy was greatest in those areas of the South least touched by the war. These areas "are much less disposed to accept the situation in good faith than those portions which have been literally overrun by fire and sword," he reported.[25]

By the time Grant was nearing the end of his first year as president, he was again hopeful and buoyed by the recent ratifications of both the Fourteenth and Fifteenth Amendments. He considered final ratification of the latter in March 1870 "as the realization of the Declaration of Independence." He was so convinced the work of securing civil rights for African Americans was nearly complete that, drawing on the magnanimity he displayed at Appomattox, he considered both a general amnesty and a full pardon for all Confederates who had participated in the rebellion. But as he continued to receive "many complaints about outrages" perpetrated by the Ku Klux and others throughout the South, he had a change of heart. "So long as the state of society in those districts is such as to call for military aid and to preserve order," he said, "it would be useless to recommend to Congress the removal of disabilities."[26]

On May 31, 1870, exactly two months after the Fifteenth Amendment was ratified, Grant signed the Enforcement Act of 1869 into law. It would be the first of three enforcement acts Congress would approve in less than a year to give teeth to the new constitutional amendments. Criminal cases under federal jurisdiction had previously been limited to crimes against the nation, such as treason, or crimes outside state jurisdiction, such as piracy on the high seas. So-called common crimes such as murder, theft, and assault had always been prosecuted in state courts, but the few attempts by state prosecutors to bring Ku Klux to justice for these crimes were stymied by the refusal of local law enforcement to investigate the crimes, or white juries to indict or convict for these crimes.

Therefore, this first enforcement act created a new set of federal crimes that involved violating the civil rights of another citizen. This type of crime had never previously existed, and that it would be tried in federal, not state, courts underscored the theory behind the Fourteenth Amendment that the federal government, not the states, was now the guarantor of an individual's civil rights.

Under this first enforcement act, it became a federal crime to bribe or intimidate voters. (There were also provisions on voting fraud aimed at the Northern urban political machines.) It was now a federal crime to conspire with others to deprive a citizen not just of the right to vote, but of "any right or privilege granted or secured to him by the Constitution or the laws of the United States." It was a crime to ride in disguise upon public highways at night, and the act included a provision that no one could serve as a juror in trials of those accused of violating the Enforcement Act without swearing under oath that they were not a member of any group or conspiracy whose intent was to prevent citizens from voting. The act also empowered the United States military to enforce the law.

For those found guilty of the crime of violating another's civil rights, one section of the Enforcement Act stated the maximum penalty was ten years in prison and a five-thousand-dollar fine. But a separate section of the act said prosecutors could seek and judges could impose additional penalties based on the type of crime that was committed while seeking to deny someone's civil rights. For example, if a Ku Klux committed murder to prevent someone from voting, then they could be subject to the same penalty given someone convicted of murder, i.e., death or life imprisonment, even though they had not been convicted of murder per se, but of violating another's civil rights. To obtain that type of penalty, federal prosecutors would have to prove a murder had been committed, yet murder was still considered a common crime under state jurisdiction. The Ku Klux trials would have to sort out whether this complicated—critics would have used the term "convoluted"—provision was constitutional.

V

Harsh penalties are meaningless if there is neither the means nor the intent to enforce a law. Grant's first attorney general was Ebenezer Rockwood Hoar, a longtime member of the Massachusetts Supreme Court and a naturally cautious and conservative man. Hoar was reluctant to have the federal government prosecute cases related to racial violence in the South, despite growing pressure to act to stem the rising tide of violence there.[27] The end result was that the initial effect of the Enforcement Act was "wholly negligible."[28]

But Hoar was not in office long. He opposed one of Grant's pet projects, the annexation of Santo Domingo, which Grant thought not only offered abundant natural resources and potential naval stations, but was also a place where several hundred thousand emancipated slaves might emigrate and find peace while reducing racial conflict in the South. Grant made a bargain whereby Southern Republicans agreed to support annexing Santo Domingo in return for Hoar's resignation and his replacement with a Southerner committed to the cause of civil rights for African Americans.

Hoar's replacement was Amos. T. Akerman, a former slaveowner who was the first former Confederate to serve in a presidential Cabinet and whose career is a rebuke to those who argue we cannot judge those of the past by the morality of today; some things are always right or always wrong, and there are always those, like Akerman, who know the difference.

No attorney general in American history, historian William S. McFeely wrote, "has been more vigorous in the prosecution of cases designed to protect the lives and rights of black Americans" than Akerman.[29] McFeely made that assessment in the 1980s, but even though the United States has since had African-American attorneys general, his assessment of Akerman may remain true. Certainly, no attorney general before or since pursued the cause of equal rights for African Americans at greater risk to his own personal safety or that of his family.

Throughout his prosecution of the Ku Klux, Akerman kept his wife and young children at their home in Cartersville, Georgia, where they were socially shunned and once assailed by a mob intent on burning down their house. After he was mysteriously dismissed by Grant while the Ku Klux trials were still ongoing, Akerman bravely returned home to Georgia and remained there, simultaneously hated and admired, farming and practicing law until his death in 1880.

Akerman avoided at least one purported attempt on his life when he went to a local stable to retrieve his horse to find that the poor animal had been shaved and painted with stripes to resemble a zebra. In front of a crowd that had gathered to gauge his reaction, Akerman only amiably said the horse could not be his, as he had left no such animal and therefore could not accept the one offered, and he returned to his hotel. Later, he was told the Ku Klux had planned to ambush him on the road, and the markings painted on the horse were intended to make him easy to identify.[30]

At the time of his appointment as attorney general, Akerman was unknown outside Georgia and had no national profile. The *New York Times* asserted in one headline that there was "Universal Surprise at the Choice," while another headline asked, "Who Is Mr. Akerman?"[31] He was, McFeely wrote, "as obscure a man as any who has held an important cabinet post."[32] Akerman was tall and slender, balding and sporting a pencil-thin mustache. Scrupulously neat and dignified, Akerman was also affable and approachable, though his most notable feature was the intense gaze that emanated from his deep-set eyes and which gave him the countenance of someone "of learning and disposition to deep meditation."[33]

Though he came to love the South, Akerman was not a native Southerner. He was born in 1821 on a farm near Portsmouth, New Hampshire, the ninth of twelve children in the family of Benjamin and Olive Akerman. His father was "public-spirited . . . with a larger share of modern ways of thinking than was accepted by his contemporaries," Akerman said.[34] Both his parents valued hard work and education, and were "zealous in religion," holding their children to "a strict practice and to [an] orthodox creed" that Akerman retained throughout his life and passed on to his own children.[35]*

Akerman's mother died when he was fourteen and his father lost the family farm when he was sixteen, but the family insisted he continue his studies at the Phillips Exeter Academy. He was a student of such promise that two classmates and his grandmother lent him the money needed to attend Dartmouth College. There he participated in the debating society, was elected Phi Beta Kappa, helped edit the campus literary magazine, and gave a commencement address titled "The English Poets as Advocates of Liberty."[36] Just as at Phillips Exeter, his Dartmouth instructors expected great things, but Akerman was not personally ambitious, which was in some ways oddly crucial to his later success.

After graduation in 1842, anxious to repay his debts to his classmates and grandmother, Akerman went south to teach, a not atypical choice for educated New Englanders of the time, who found the South exotic and

---

*Akerman would father seven sons; two became lawyers, two college professors, and one a doctor.

planters willing to pay good salaries for the instruction of their children. There was no public education system in the antebellum South, though some planters did invite the children of poorer neighbors to participate in and benefit from instruction. But in the prewar years, Southerners were less literate than their fellow citizens in the North, where a robust public education system had been established decades earlier.

For the next four years, Akerman taught and tutored the children of several families in North and South Carolina, but soon reached the conclusion that teaching was not his vocation. He lamented that he was frequently losing his temper with his "dull students," and in 1846 he took a teaching job in Savannah that would also allow him to simultaneously study the law with the family patriarch, Judge J. McPherson Berrien, who had served as US attorney general under President Andrew Jackson.[37]

Admitted to the bar in 1850, Akerman briefly practiced in Peoria, Illinois, where a sister lived, but he missed the Southern climate and culture and returned to Georgia, where he purchased a farm north of Atlanta in Habersham County (where he had summered with the Berrien family) and practiced law in nearby Elberton. Already comparatively late in life to be starting a profession, the growth of Akerman's law practice was further stunted by his preference for farming over the practice of law.

A friend who had known Akerman since his school days chastised Akerman for falling short of expectations that he would enjoy a stellar career in politics. In a return letter, Akerman modestly asserted that perhaps he had been "overrated" at Dartmouth, and as for politics, he said, "Any man with tolerable capacity can make a political figure if he will only set himself perseveringly to work and become reckless of means."[38]

But Akerman did not avoid politics altogether. A Whig until the war, Akerman had opposed the war with Mexico and the annexation of Texas and was suspect of military men entering politics. He was perturbed that the cost of war allowed political leaders to avoid expenditures on programs of benefit to citizens "on pretence [sic] that the Treasury is too empty." He disdained what he believed was the phony patriotism of slogans such as "our country, right or wrong," saying, "A true patriot is one who would blame and disown the faults of his country as those of a private friend." And he could be cynical about America's founding myths. "The Declaration of Independence will always have an historical interest, though as an exposition of our country's political doctrines it has long been value-less," he wrote in his diary. "We do not believe that all men are created equal; and other truths propounded in that document as fundamental, have been first disregarded in practice and finally disavowed in theory."[39]

A Union man and an admirer, as Lincoln was, of Kentucky senator Henry Clay, Akerman opposed secession, but he also opposed abolition, believing Africans were better off in America where they could be elevated by contact with "a superior race."[40] By the time the Civil War came, Akerman's correspondence suggests he owned nearly a dozen slaves. But given that he was now forty years old, opposed secession, and abhorred war and violence—"A gun is not a bewitching thing to me," he said—he did not join the Confederate army in the immediate aftermath of Fort Sumter. He did later enlist in the Georgia Home Guard, but was not ordered into active duty as a supply officer until Sherman's troops entered the state in the spring of 1864. Just before he left for the front, he married twenty-three-year-old Martha Rebecca Galloway, a schoolteacher who would bear Akerman's seven sons and actively support him in his efforts to dismantle the Ku Klux.

Years after the war, Akerman claimed he had supported the Confederate cause only "reluctantly," and justified doing so on the grounds that the North had abandoned Southern unionists. As a transplanted Northerner, Akerman believed Southerners had underestimated the North. Southerners believed the reluctance of Northern congressmen to fight duels with their Southern colleagues betrayed softness.* The Southern disposition to link honor with private vengeance, Akerman said, ignores "that those who leave it to the law to avenge their wrongs are from that very disposition the more efficient soldiers when the law calls them to the field."[41]

Akerman was initially stunned by the superficial peacefulness of the peace. Like many Southerners, he anticipated a race war as slaves sought retribution for the wrongs they had suffered. "I had no conception that slavery could be abolished as easily and safely as was actually done," he

---

*Historian Joanne Freeman has documented more than seventy incidents of violence in Congress between 1830 and 1860, with most, she said, instigated by Southern congressmen "who had long been bullying their way to power with threats, insults, and violence." The one fatal congressional duel held in 1838, however, ironically led to the death of a Northern congressman sympathetic to Southern slave interests, Jonathan Cilley of Maine, who was shot by Kentucky congressman William Graves, an anti-Jacksonian Whig. A Northern broadside that criticized the Southern dueling culture said: "They call it *honor*, but we think/It cannot be denied/By any but a heathen/'Tis vanity and pride." (Freeman, *Field of Blood*, xv, 104)

said.[42] For his part, Akerman believed that Confederate ideology had been defeated when the Confederate army was. The doctrine of states' rights and "the subjugation of one race by the other as an appurtenance of slavery . . . should go to the grave in which slavery had been buried."[43] Many other Southern whites felt differently, but Akerman dismissed them as those who "consulted the past rather than the future, were moved in politics by resentment rather then [sic] by reason, and so got where they now are. Fruitless strivings against the inevitable is the sum of their labors."[44] Had Akerman understood in 1867 how deeply rooted racial prejudice was, he said, he might have stayed out of politics altogether.

But after the war, with the Whigs no longer in existence, Akerman, who had never been a Democrat, joined the Republican Party and was selected to participate as a delegate to the convention charged with developing a new Georgia constitution. News reports that stated he was "the principal framer" of the new constitution were an exaggeration, but he actively engaged in convention debates, and the final product reflected most of his new values. It incorporated the Bill of Rights, granted African Americans citizenship, and declared the US Constitution the supreme law of the land.

The following year, Akerman was a presidential elector and campaigned vigorously for Grant in the 1868 election. His reward was appointment as US attorney for Georgia, but he could not take the required "test oath," as he had, in fact, served in the Confederate army, and so did not take office until December 1869, when Congress finally relieved him of that obligation. Six months later, Grant named Akerman to replace Hoar.

VI

Akerman was the first head of the newly formed United States Department of Justice, which Congress established on July 1, 1870. Previously, the position of attorney general had been considered part-time, with many attorneys general continuing their private practice while serving. They did not run a department nor, until the Civil War, did they even supervise the US attorneys or marshals assigned to the several federal judicial districts. Instead, they served the role of today's White House legal counsel, offering legal and political advice to the president only. When the government needed attorneys for trials or other matters, they contracted with outside counsel, a practice that was often quite expensive. By using in-house counsel, Congress hoped to save one million dollars per year, even as Congress also expected a significant increase in the federal court workload due to the Enforcement Acts.[45] Even so, they had no conception of how large that workload would be once Akerman focused his attention on the Ku Klux.

Partly out of symbolism, Akerman housed the Department of Justice offices in the new Freedmen's Savings and Trust Company building located on Pennsylvania Avenue next to Lafayette Square, where the new US Treasury Department Annex is now situated.* Akerman's obscurity in the North had made his confirmation relatively easy despite his Confederate background, and because he pleased congressional Republicans with his stated commitment to supporting and enforcing the Fourteenth and Fifteenth Amendments.

Back in Georgia, a few newspapers expressed hope that Akerman's appointment meant that Grant was softening his views on Reconstruction. But a newspaper whose editors knew Akerman well understood that his appointment meant the opposite. The *Macon* (GA) *Journal and Intelligencer* predicted Akerman would mean trouble for the region he had adopted as his home. "He is cold-blooded, calculating, persistent, energetic, and tireless, and hates the South and Southern people most cordially," the *Journal and Intelligencer* opined, "all of which traits, it appears to us, are likely to be very acceptable in the chief law officer for the present administration."

*The story of the Freedmen's Savings and Trust Company is one of the sadder stories of Reconstruction, given its generations-long ramifications. The bank was established in 1865 specifically to give African-American Union soldiers and other freedmen and women a place to deposit the first money most of them had ever been able to earn (though some whites in areas without alternative banks were also depositors). While a separate entity, the Freedmen's Bureau aggressively marketed the bank, explaining to freedmen and women, for example, that if they set aside just ten cents per day for deposit in an account bearing 6 percent interest they would accumulate $489.31 in just ten years. Depositors were given the false impression deposits were federally insured. Instead, the bank was improperly established and mismanaged. There was no requirement bank trustees be depositors, and many were therefore disengaged from their oversight duty. Some used their position to secure insider loans. Some were crooks. A white clergyman who worked for the bank, Philip D. Cory, was convicted of embezzling ten thousand dollars from its Atlanta branch. He was the only person ever convicted for improprieties related to the bank, but was pardoned when he promised to make restitution; he was later appointed an Indian agent in the West. Under the sway of notorious speculators, such as Jay Cooke, the bank issued loans at lower rates than they paid depositors, and the 6 percent interest rate paid on savings was too high to be sustainable. The bank was already in poor financial shape when the Panic of 1873 sounded its death knell. When the bank closed in 1874, it had a grand total of thirty-two thousand dollars in assets, while more than sixty thousand depositors lost a total of three million dollars. Congress refused to intervene. Black wealth that might have afforded social mobility and upon which future generations might have built was wiped out, and the failure of the Freedmen's bank created a lasting distrust of financial institutions within the African-American community for generations. (Fleming, *The Freedmen's Savings Bank*)

The newspaper accused Akerman of betraying the region that had "raised him out of the dust of obscurity" by turning on the cause he himself had supported during the war. "No Radical in Georgia or anywhere else at the South, in our knowledge, has wagged a more venomous tongue against the cause now lost, and its honest supporters."[46]Akerman made no apologies for his change of heart, and was surprised that more Southerners did not share his revulsion at the crimes of the Ku Klux.*

Grant understood that Ku Klux intimidation of African-American voters in Alabama and Georgia had thwarted the will of the majority in the 1870 elections, a fact he noted in his annual message to Congress on December 5.[47] Meanwhile, Ku Klux violence in the South Carolina Piedmont had reached a fever pitch, leading to Governor Scott's appeal for federal troops in mid-February 1871. Grant read one of Scott's "horrifying" reports aloud to his Cabinet in late February and began the process of securing federal troops for South Carolina, swearing they would stay there "during the remainder of his administration," if necessary.[48]

While the administration already had considerable authority under the first two Enforcement Acts to address the situation, Grant and congressional leaders agreed the situation was serious enough that a special session was called in March 1871 to pass a third Enforcement Act that gave the president authority to suspend habeas corpus and declare martial law as he saw fit. Democrats complained that "Kaiser Grant" was assuming dictatorial powers to ensure Republican political dominance in the South, and even Grant's old friend and comrade Sherman charged that the law championed by Grant was a misuse of the military.[49] These objections were for naught, and the newest enforcement bill, which became known as the Ku Klux Klan Act, became law on April 20, 1871.

Akerman had been an enthusiastic backer of the legislation and had helped Grant lobby Congress on its behalf. To those who thought the

---

*One former Confederate as repulsed by Southern attitudes as Akerman was General James Longstreet, a South Carolina native, whom Lee had called his "Old War Horse." Like Akerman, Longstreet supported civil rights for African Americans, even leading African-American militia and others in trying to rebuff an 1874 attack on the Louisiana state Capitol by eight thousand armed members of the White League, an offshoot of the Ku Klux Klan, who were unhappy with election results. Longstreet also dismissed claims by those promulgating the theory of the Lost Cause that the Civil War had been about states' rights, replying incredulously, "I never heard of any other cause of the quarrel than slavery." In retaliation, Lost Cause advocates have engaged in a century-and-a-half-long campaign to besmirch Longstreet's military reputation. (Chernow, *Grant*, 857)

law went too far, Akerman said, "It is my individual opinion that nothing is more idle than to attempt to conciliate by kindness that portion of the southern people who are still malcontent. They take all kindness on the part of the Government as evidence of timidity, and hence are emboldened to lawlessness by it."[50] Having lived in the South the previous thirty years, Akerman understood the passions behind the Ku Klux violence and how they were an extension of the recent conflict. The Ku Klux outrages "amount to war," Akerman said, "and cannot be effectively crushed under any other theory."[51] But this was an unusual kind of war and would need an unusual type of soldier. Fortunately, just such a soldier was extraordinarily prepared for the coming battle.

CHAPTER FIVE

I never conceived of such a state of social disorganization being possible in any civilized community as exists in this county now.
—Major Lewis Merrill on York County, South Carolina

I

IF MAJOR LEWIS MERRILL OF THE 7TH CAVALRY HAD NOT BEEN AVAILABLE for duty in the federal campaign against the Ku Klux, this entire episode in American history would have played out very differently. Merrill was "just the man for the work" of combatting the Ku Klux, said Attorney General Akerman, who was delighted to have a man on the ground with such a unique set of relevant skills and experiences.[1]

Merrill had spent much of his military career specializing in the very personalized type of combat known as guerrilla warfare and did so primarily on the American frontier "where clear lines of battle did not exist and an officer learned to exercise sound judgment in resolving conflicts with little oversight or direction."[2] Further, hailing as he did from a family of attorneys and serving in the Army as a judge advocate in military court, Merrill possessed a shrewd legal acumen; in the campaign against the Ku Klux, he would also demonstrate a natural ability for interrogation and detection.

Merrill graduated from West Point in 1855, ranked twentieth in a class of thirty-four. One of his first assignments as a young lieutenant was to help keep order in "Bleeding Kansas." Pro- and anti-slavery militia forces there were locked in a violent struggle for political dominance that featured such atrocities as the sacking of the town of Lawrence by pro-slavery forces, and retaliation meted out by abolitionist John Brown and his sons that involved hacking five pro-slavery settlers to death with broadswords at Pottawatomie Creek. North and South, men, including several from York County, were recruited to go to Kansas under the pretense of being settlers when, in fact, they intended to fight rather than farm.* Like the Ku Klux fifteen years later, it was a conflict where people were not always who they appeared to be.

In 1858, Merrill was sent to the Utah Territory under the command of future Confederate general Albert Sidney Johnston to help put down a rebellion against federal authority by the Church of Jesus Christ of Latter-Day Saints, more popularly known as the Mormons. Here, Merrill further confronted those who pursued nefarious deeds in disguise, for the rebellion included the massacre of 120 members of a California-bound wagon train by the church's Nauvoo Legion while in costume masquerading as Native Americans.[3]

When the Civil War broke out, Merrill was sent to the border state of Missouri, where Union and Confederate supporters were near evenly matched and irregular fighting dominated that theater of the war. Armies there were not dressed in distinctive uniforms, neatly facing each other on an open battlefield where honor and gallantry were rewarded. Rather, the fighting in Missouri featured deceit and chicanery. Combat was often intimate, pitting neighbor against neighbor, which made it all the more savage, with little distinction made between military and civilian targets. That two of the most active bushwhackers were the future outlaws Frank and Jesse James suggests how wantonly bloody the fighting in Missouri often was.

Merrill was granted permission to organize an eight-hundred-man volunteer Union cavalry unit that became known colloquially as "Merrill's Horse." Merrill was promoted to the rank of colonel, and he and his unit were charged with clearing northeast Missouri of rebel forces.† In a preface to his work in York County, one of Merrill's strategies was to arrest hundreds of Confederate sympathizers and then release them only after they had sworn an oath of loyalty to the Union, a strategy that Merrill acknowledged had negligible impact. "I cannot point to one single instance in which they have faithfully kept their promise," he ruefully reported.[4]

---

*In 1856, as part of a broad campaign throughout South Carolina and the South, York County residents raised fourteen hundred dollars to send seven local men to Kansas and establish residency so they could vote in favor of legalizing slavery in the Kansas Territory. (Pettus, "York County Men in Bloody Kansas," 6–7).

†Merrill's troops later fought in Arkansas, where he was wounded during the Union capture of Little Rock. This led to his promotion to (brevet) brigadier general. When the war ended and the Army was again stocked primarily with career soldiers, a readjustment of rank was required and Merrill obtained the "permanent" rank of major.

Merrill was the commanding officer during a notorious incident at Palmyra, Missouri, where ten Confederate guerrillas, who had already been sentenced to death for some "particularly gruesome" murders of noncombatants, were executed ahead of schedule in retaliation for the abduction and murder of a seventy-year-old pro-Union man.[5] This caused such a stir that Lincoln summoned Merrill to Washington for a report of the incident. Merrill took personal responsibility for ordering the accelerated executions, which he said had the desired effect of largely pacifying that portion of Missouri. But he told Lincoln defensively that he had taken the action only because he received no response to his telegraphed requests for instruction from his superiors. According to Merrill, Lincoln placed a hand on his shoulder and said, "Remember, young man, there are some things which should be done which it would not do for superiors to order done."[6]

Despite this lengthy and intimate acquaintance with the dark side of human behavior, Merrill admitted that he was still not fully prepared for the level of Ku Klux terror he encountered in York County. Before he arrived in Yorkville at the head of, ironically, Company K of the 7th Cavalry, Merrill said, "I fully believed that the stories in circulation were enormous exaggerations, and that the newspaper stories were incredible." When he reported for duty, his commanding officer, the Yale-educated attorney and sleepy-eyed General Alfred Terry, commander of the Department of the South, set him straight: "When you get to South Carolina you will find that the half has not been told you."[7]

Federal troops were necessary to put down the Ku Klux because civil governments had lost authority in the South, particularly in South Carolina. Reconstruction governments might hold majorities in the Southern state capitals, but their laws were not enforced by local law enforcement, which was either ineffective, intimidated by Ku Klux, sympathetic to Ku Klux, or Ku Klux themselves. Justice, at least for African Americans and white Radicals, did not exist.

An African-American man named William Wright learned how true this was in October 1869, when, in what was one of the first Ku Klux outrages in York County, he was whipped and beaten by a dozen Ku Klux and his house was burned to the ground for the alleged offense of living with a white woman. Wright recognized one of his assailants as Elijah Ross Sepaugh and swore out a complaint against him. A jury acquitted Sepaugh, who then swore out a complaint against Wright, alleging perjury. Wright, the victim in the case, was the one convicted and sentenced to prison.[8]

South Carolina governor Robert Scott did not know what to do, paralyzed by fear that whatever he did would lead to further and greater violence. Republican members of his legislature (many of whom were afraid to return home to their constituents for fear of being murdered) pressured the governor to deploy the state militias to put down the Ku Klux. South Carolina whites, meanwhile, insisted that the overwhelmingly African-American militias had provoked the violence simply by their existence. Bowing to this extortive argument, Scott decided that deploying the militias would not end the violence, but would instead antagonize whites to greater mayhem and brutality. "Such a remedy would be as bad as the disease," Scott concluded. Calling out the militias would also be an admission there was no viable civil government in South Carolina and that South Carolina was "in a condition of social anarchy."[9] Which it was. Republican members of South Carolina's congressional delegation told Grant that South Carolina's state government was "powerless to preserve law and order."[10]

But Scott was playing a double game. To placate whites, Scott began taking steps early in 1871 to disarm the mostly Black state militias that had been established just a year before, leaving the African-American community nearly defenseless. At the same time, with the accurate expectation that this effort at white appeasement would have little to no impact, he was aggressively seeking federal intervention, begging Grant to send in federal troops to restore order.

No longer euphoric about the progress of racial conciliation, Grant was deeply moved by reports from Scott and others regarding the thousands of African Americans who were afraid to sleep in their homes at night for fear of a Ku Klux raid. Grant was outraged by reports of mass murder, including an incident in Union County, South Carolina, where a force of hundreds of Ku Klux lynched fourteen members of an African-American militia company. Grant initially vowed to send two full regiments just to South Carolina, but instead, wary, much as Governor Scott was, of provoking the South too much, he sent a far smaller number of troops, sixteen companies, or roughly half what two full regiments would have been—and this was reinforcement not just for South Carolina but for the entire South.[11]

These additional deployments increased the number of federal troops in South Carolina from four hundred to about one thousand. South Carolina's population was more than seven hundred thousand. Even with the new deployments, in 1871 fewer than four thousand federal troops were stationed throughout the South, a region of eleven million people. A few Southern states had almost no federal troops. Only sixty federal soldiers were stationed in Arkansas in 1871.[12] And yet, these few numbers of troops would have an enormous impact on Ku Klux activity.

Despite his resolve to maintain federal troops in the South for as long as it took to pacify the Ku Klux, Grant clearly was avoiding a military solution to the problem. There were practical reasons for this. Just as Scott feared deploying the state militia might exacerbate the violence rather than temper it, Grant had no interest in engaging in the type of guerrilla war with the South he had tried so hard to avoid with his generous terms at Appomattox. However much Ku Klux activity might have seemed a resumption or even an extension of the rebellion that led to the Civil War, the Grant Administration planned to treat the Ku Klux not as an insurrectionary army but as criminals. This was a gamble, for as legal scholar Robert Kaczorowski has written, the chance of "complete success would probably have been greater if Congress and the President had recognized Klan terrorism as rebellion and used the military to quash it. Legal officers instead were directed to put down insurrection through judicial process."[13]

Grant was following the precedent set by George Washington in how he handled Shays' Rebellion in Massachusetts (a method that President Eisenhower would also use to handle Southern resistance to court-ordered school integration nearly a century afterward in Little Rock, Arkansas). Grant wished to use federal troops only as an auxiliary force to temporarily restore order and provide time for civil authorities to regroup and reassert their authority. It was true that even a small number of federal troops could have an outsized influence on local affairs. The Confederate veterans who were the bulk of the Ku Klux membership were well aware of the fighting ability of federal troops and were not anxious to engage them. As one US attorney working in the South noted, "The Ku Klux never fire on United States soldiers, but they do not hesitate to shoot . . . (U.S.) Marshals whenever an opportunity is presented."[14]

It was unknown, of course, whether civil authorities in the South might ever gain enough genuine control to ensure peace and justice for African

Americans—or if they would ever have the desire to do so. But given that the alternative to treating the Ku Klux as criminals was engaging in a military campaign that might reignite civil conflict, an option that had essentially no public support in the North, there was little dissent within the administration for the path Grant was charting, and there was considerable hopefulness that it might prove to be effective. General Terry ended up embracing this policy and neatly encapsulated the theory behind it: "If in a single state [the Ku Klux] could be suppressed, and in that State *exemplary* punishment meted out to some of the most prominent criminals, I think that a fatal blow would be given to it everywhere."[15]

II

Acting as an arm of federal law enforcement was an unfamiliar role for most military commanders in the field, and so federal troops in some states were not particularly effective in tamping down Ku Klux violence. But when Terry reached his conclusion that a vigorous enforcement of the law, even in a single locale, might achieve what otherwise would require thousands of troops to accomplish, it was because he had begun to receive a series of reports from Merrill that showed what a motivated commander might accomplish when committed to the task at hand.

"I know of few, if any officers of the Army, who are so well qualified for duty of the peculiar nature of that in which Major Merrill has been engaged as he," Terry wrote. "To a general aptitude for and a considerable knowledge of the law, he adds great general intelligence and sagacity. With these couple natural energy and a zeal which is only limited by sound discretion." Terry had great confidence in Merrill's integrity, and so even though Merrill was reporting acts of cruelty that seemed to defy belief or any notion of human decency, Terry vouched for the accuracy of his reports because Merrill was "an officer of great intelligence, and I think that the utmost confidence may be placed in his representations."[16]

Given his previous military experiences in Kansas, Utah, and Missouri, Merrill understood what he was being asked to do. Further, coming from a family of lawyers while having served as a judge adjutant general himself, he had legal acuity and an intuitive understanding of how his work would support the anticipated trials and judicial process. While York County was clearly an epicenter of Ku Klux activity in the South, York received national attention and became the focus of federal Ku Klux prosecutions largely because of Merrill's unique qualifications for the mission and his zeal for justice. His skill and diligence would uncover the type of solid evidence needed to draft credible indictments against members of the Ku Klux.

As the member of Grant's Cabinet most committed (by far) to stamping out the Ku Klux and promoting racial justice, Akerman echoed Terry's judgment of Merrill and realized he had found the man on the scene who could put national policy into action. Merrill, Akerman gushed, was "resolute, collected, bold and prudent, with a good legal head, very discriminating between truth and falsehood, very indignant at wrong, and yet master of his indignation; the safer because incredulous at the outset, and, therefore, disposed to scrutinize reports the more keenly."[17] Merrill's presence in York County, as much as any other factor, would lead Akerman to conclude that York was the natural place to focus federal efforts to dismantle the Ku Klux, with the hope shared by General Terry that such efforts would be a sobering example to Ku Klux throughout the South.

A New York newspaper reporter who interviewed Merrill described the cavalryman as having "the head, face, and spectacles of a German professor, and the frame of an athlete."[18] The description captured Merrill's dual character, which could be "tediously didactic" yet also "boundlessly energetic."[19] This blend of the active and academic can likely be attributed to his family of origin.

Born in 1834 in New Berlin, Pennsylvania, Merrill's father, James Merrill, was an attorney who had studied law under Radical Republican congressional leader Thaddeus Stevens, and joined his mentor in advocating for African-American equality. This included the elder Merrill advocating for African-American suffrage when he was a delegate to Pennsylvania's 1838 constitutional convention. Two of Merrill's brothers were also attorneys. But Merrill's ancestors also included some highly regarded soldiers. Both his grandfather and great-grandfather had served with distinction in the Revolutionary War. So, while some believed Merrill had "inherited his father's keen legal mind," Merrill decided to pursue a career in the military instead.[20]

When the Civil War ended, Merrill was assigned to a variety of posts on the western frontier and continued a role he had often filled during the war, which was serving as a judge advocate. His work in military law continued when he was assigned in 1868 to the newly formed 7th Cavalry. That work, plus his family background, led Merrill to concede that "I am more familiar with legal points than officers generally are."[21]

Yet Merrill was hardly infallible. While stationed with the 7th in New Mexico, Merrill became embroiled in a dispute that would provide fodder for his later critics. Merrill had been tasked with prosecuting one Captain Samuel B. Lauffer, an officer in the Quartermaster Department accused of filing a false affidavit regarding the theft of an Army mule. To pass time during lulls in Lauffer's trial, Merrill, even though he was the prosecutor, gambled in games of cards with Lauffer, who was the defendant, as well as other officers. Merrill won a considerable amount of money from Lauffer, who was able to pay only a portion of his gambling debt before he was acquitted at his court-martial. The two men then went their separate ways.

Merrill was transferred to Kansas, where he unwisely pressed Lauffer to pay the remainder of his gambling debt. Lauffer, however, realized he had a way to evade his debt. Lauffer told Merrill that he had since learned that it had been "illegal and improper" for the men to play cards for stakes while Merrill was the prosecutor in Lauffer's court-martial. Not only did Lauffer not intend to pay Merrill the outstanding debt, he insisted that Merrill return the two hundred dollars Lauffer had already paid him. To put Merrill in an even more precarious position, Lauffer told fellow officers that the money he paid Merrill was not a gambling debt at all, but a bribe Merrill had accepted in return for deliberately botching Lauffer's prosecution.[22]

One of Merrill's superior officers in the 7th Cavalry, Lieutenant Colonel George Armstrong Custer, who in a half dozen years would lead his troops to annihilation at the Battle of the Little Big Horn, asked Lauffer for copies of his correspondence with Merrill. Custer then allegedly made Lauffer's allegations known to others in the Army, perhaps in retaliation for Merrill having successfully prosecuted a friend of Custer's in a separate case.[23]

Hearing that Custer and Lauffer were slandering his reputation, Merrill demanded Custer convene an inquiry to clear his name, but both Custer and Lauffer refused to file a formal complaint. Custer instead forwarded Merrill's letter to General Terry, who concluded Lauffer's charges were without merit. General William Tecumseh Sherman also weighed in, noting that he was "personally acquainted with Major Merrill and believe he possesses the confidence of the army generally, and can hardly suppose there can be any truth in this story." The matter died there, and Merrill's career advanced at the time, although Ku Klux sympathizers would use this episode later to tar Merrill's reputation and delay future promotions.[24]

Merrill was stationed at Fort Leavenworth when word came that he was to lead the troops of Company K to Yorkville. It was a long, slow journey by train, and Merrill's were not the first federal troops to arrive in Yorkville. An infantry company had been dispatched in late February, though their arrival was delayed when the Ku Klux sabotaged the Kings Mountain Railroad, the small line whose terminus was Yorkville. Only a few rail ties had been torn up and were easily repaired, but the overnight delay provided the Ku Klux with the time they desired to raid the Rose Hotel office of Republican York County treasurer Edward M. Rose before federal troops could impede their plan.

The Ku Klux had accused Rose of inciting local Blacks to set fire to white property, a charge Rose denied. At one o'clock in the morning on February 27, about twenty Ku Klux broke into the hotel with the intention of hanging Rose, but the treasurer jumped out a window and ran, escaping injury despite his estimate that the Ku Klux fired more than one hundred shots in his direction as he fled. Rose kept going and left the county. According to the Ku Klux, Rose absconded to Canada with twelve thousand dollars in county funds; Rose countered that it was the Ku Klux who had robbed the county treasury of one thousand dollars during the raid.[25] Dr. J. Rufus Bratton, whose house was less than fifty yards from the hotel, would later claim he had not bothered to rise from bed to hear what the fuss was about.

Aware of this previous incident with incoming federal troops, Merrill chose to make a statement with his arrival in Yorkville. He and the ninety troops under his command disembarked at the Chester, South Carolina, rail station and, to avoid any new sabotage of local rail lines, rode by horseback the remaining twenty-two miles into Yorkville, loudly arriving at about nine o'clock at night on March 26, 1871—less than three weeks after the lynching of Jim Williams.[26]

Locals greeting Merrill assured him his presence and those of his troops was welcome, but unnecessary. A delegation of community leaders, led by Bratton, met with Merrill immediately after his arrival to offer warm greetings and assure him that reports of local violence were grossly exaggerated. Further, the violence was the result of a few vigilantes, they told Merrill, and no such group as the Ku Klux actually existed. "They all assured me that the state of affairs in the county was bettering rapidly and that there was every prospect now for permanent quiet," Merrill reported.[27]

Even so, they offered to circulate a pledge that would be signed by leading citizens of the county and published as an open letter in the local paper that would condemn all violence and pledge support for law and order. This open letter was reprinted multiple times in the *Yorkville Enquirer*, each time with a set of different names listed, until more than three hundred local men had attached their name to the pledge. Several of the signatories would later be arrested and charged with participating in Ku Klux outrages.[28]

Merrill later learned that there had been great debate about whether to sign this pledge, but the argument that prevailed was that "not signing would look suspicious and the paper amounted to nothing anyway."[29] Merrill further learned that those signing the paper had consulted legal counsel, who assured them that they could not be arrested for any crimes committed before Congress had approved the Ku Klux Klan Act on April 20. This would prove to be not necessarily true and was a major point of debate at trial. Meanwhile, Merrill and his wife, Anna, who had arrived in Yorkville along with the wives of several officers, were graciously entertained in the homes of the town's leading citizens. Merrill reciprocated this goodwill and, at least initially, was considered by locals to be "a gentleman and good soldier."[30]

Concurrent with signing the open letter, the leading citizens of York had ordered a temporary halt to Ku Klux raiding in hopes that Merrill and all the federal troops would speedily withdraw if there were no new incidents that would justify them remaining.

Merrill was initially fooled. While he knew such a thing as the Ku Klux did exist, and involved "much greater numbers than is commonly supposed," including some of the leading citizens who had been assuring him there was no such organization, he was also pleased that he had "heard of no instance or lawlessness occurring during his first several weeks in Yorkville."[31] He was "fully impressed with the notion" that the past acts of violence reported in the newspapers represented nothing more than "a few occasional cases that might be regarded rather as vigilance committee matters than anything else." From his cordial conversations with local leaders he thought "there was every probability" that with their cooperation there would soon be a "speedy termination" of even these supposedly rare acts of violence.[32]

Then Merrill learned of the beating of Elias Hill.

III

In the days after his brutal whipping, while still recovering from his substantial injuries, the afflicted Hill made out a report of his assault and had it delivered to Merrill. After detailing the outrages he had suffered, Hill added this postscript: "As many of my color have been killed for reporting what was done to them by K.K.K., I, the above signed and reported, beseech the authorities, through which this may pass and be executed, not to make known or expose his name, lest he be sacrificed for the truth."[33]

It now occurred to Merrill, the son of an abolitionist, that he had been hearing only one side of affairs in York County, and that from those whites who had a vested interest in obfuscating the truth. With Hill's admonition in hand, Merrill now set out to discover the whole truth. It disturbed him greatly. "I am now of opinion that I never conceived of such a state of social disorganization being possible in any civilized community as exists in this county now," he said.[34]

Merrill said it was clear that the Ku Klux felt no genuine fear of punishment. "It is idle to attempt anything through the local civil authorities," he complained, "and even if I could persuade myself that it would be advisable to try it, it would be impossible to bring the negroes to the point of testifying before local tribunals." Merrill related the story of one African-American man who had been brought in to testify at a coroner's inquest regarding the murder of a man named Alex Leech. The witness refused to testify and Merrill asked whether the coroner had done anything to induce him to tell what he knew. "No," the man told Merrill, the coroner "only laughed and the white men standing about the room nudged each other and laughed." Merrill later corroborated the man's story and noted with disgust that the coroner never bothered to "elicit one single fact in regard to the murderer" even though a modest effort "would have easily traced the crime to its author."[35]

Such incidents deterred African Americans from seeking redress from local authorities, which gave local whites the false impression that African Americans had become resigned to the idea that freedom for them meant nothing more than living as semi-slaves. "These white people are fully convinced that because the negroes do not show any signs of resistance they are completely cowed," Merrill wrote in one of his earliest reports to General Terry. "This is far from the truth—they are very patient and still hopeful that something may be done by the authorities to stop these outrages and secure them peaceful lives."[36] But even Merrill was surprised at how willing local African Americans were to risk their lives to assist in the investigations.

As word spread that Merrill was now sincerely and actively investigating Ku Klux crimes, "many a Negro found his way into Major Merrill's office with a gruesome story," wrote Louis Post, who had been assigned to work as a stenographer for Merrill as he took down information from victims and (later) confessions from the accused.[37] Merrill rejected charges from Ku Klux sympathizers that most of these stories had been made up by African Americans in search of attention and status. Merrill said he believed most of what the African Americans told him was true. "Their temper, I think, from the conversation I have had with the negroes generally, is to ask that justice may be done them, and they may be secured in quiet lives," he said.[38]

Merrill asked Elias Hill to act as an informant regarding Ku Klux outrages in the Clay Hill area and to provide "full reports of these outrages." Merrill believed these reports implicitly, noting that even local whites considered Hill "a man of very pure character and excellent sense." Hill was already preoccupied with his plans for emigration to Liberia and so was unable to do all that Merrill asked. But Merrill credited Hill, "because he had a very great influence among the negroes," with convincing many African Americans to cooperate with the investigation. They did so at great risk, Merrill noted. "In almost every instance of outrage they have been threatened with death if any statement was made by them in regard to it. They were threatened with death in many instances if they simply told the fact that it had been done."[39]

Merrill said he did not accept every report of Ku Klux outrages as truth, nor did he trust every African American who came to him with information. He had learned to rely on a half dozen "special negro agents" in whom he believed he could confide and whom he asked to watch Ku Klux leaders and report on their movements or plans for raids so that "I might possibly catch them in the act."[40] Merrill never revealed the names of these African Americans, but in one of his reports to General Terry he relayed the story of one key African-American informant who actually rode with the Ku Klux on raids against fellow African Americans.

There were a number of African Americans in York County and elsewhere who publicly expressed support for the Democratic Party, and who sometimes spoke on behalf of Democratic candidates at mixed-race rallies.

An enormous Democratic rally in Yorkville prior to the 1868 presidential election, for example, drew two thousand white Democrats and "one or two hundred colored people," the *Yorkville Enquirer* said, "who, ignoring the lavish orders of the (Union) League, had come out to hear the other side of the question."[41] *Enquirer* editor Lewis Grist later offered this supposed witticism where he stated, "We are not only in favor of negroes voting, but also are in favor of *showing them how to vote*."[42]

Those African Americans who took a political position at odds with the prevailing sentiment of the local African-American community also risked their well-being, for several African-American Democrats reported they had been the targets of intimidation and sometimes violent retribution, including severe beatings, from Union League members.[43]

But taking a contrary political view opposite the majority of the Black community is one thing; concurring with the actions of the Ku Klux to the point of joining in raids on fellow African Americans is another. Yet some did. An African-American man named Hampton Avery assisted the Ku Klux in a raid on the home of an elderly African-American couple named Abram and Emeline Brumfield in which the Ku Klux placed a noose around the neck of another elderly African American named Sam Sturgis and pretended they were going to hang him.[44]

Avery and the handful of other African Americans who rode with the Ku Klux likely did so for a variety of reasons. Some were certainly coerced into participating either because the Ku Klux needed a guide to the homes of their African-American targets or simply because the Ku Klux were determined to demonstrate white dominance by forcing African Americans to commit violence against other African Americans. Others may have thought cooperation with the Ku Klux would spare them from being the object of violence themselves or, more cynically, may have even hoped to secure employment or other benefits by ingratiating themselves with the dominant white community.

The man who rode with the Ku Klux and later became one of Merrill's best and most reliable "special negro agents" was a local farmer who told Merrill he was initially "compelled" to accompany the Ku Klux on raids. The man, Merrill reported, participated on "8 or 9 occasions . . . giving as a reason for doing so that it was only by this means that he could live at home and secure his crop." The man's cooperation won the confidence of the Ku

Klux, who then "freely discussed their acts and places in his presence," Merrill reported. Tormented by what he had seen and what he had participated in, the man was relieved that he could now unburden himself to Merrill and help bring the Ku Klux to justice for their atrocities. "Through him I have important information in regard to past outrages," Merrill said.[45]

Having heard the Ku Klux share their stories and having ridden with them himself, Merrill's informant was certainly aware that if the Ku Klux learned of his cooperation with authorities, he would meet a fate similar to that of Charles Good, another local African American who sought to help authorities track down the Ku Klux responsible for the raids.

Good was a local blacksmith known to have voted the Radical Republican ticket, and for that offense he was so badly whipped by Ku Klux that he could not work for almost a week.[46] Good, however, vowed that he would not change his politics and announced he could identify his attackers. He was murdered by the Ku Klux several weeks later. Even one of his assailants seemed to admire Good's courage, noting, "He was determined—didn't seem to care who knew his political principles."[47] Rather than admire a man of principle, the Ku Klux ensured that Good suffered an agonizing death. According to witnesses, Good was tied to a tree with his own suspenders, and was then shot in the face with buckshot and left to die a slow death.[48]

But a woman whose husband and brother were among the Ku Klux who participated in Good's murder later said that it was not his politics that led to Good's death. Lucy Zipporah Smith Howell said that Good was killed because he had become "obnoxious" to the Ku Klux for trying to help authorities identify who was participating in the Ku Klux raids. Good was a favored local blacksmith who, Howell said, surreptitiously put special markings on the shoes he placed on horses and mules owned by his white customers "so that the mules and horses could be identified by the shoe markings as they traveled over the country." Speaking to the *Yorkville Enquirer* a half-century after Good's murder, Howell, who gaily acknowledged that she had enjoyed sewing Ku Klux disguises for her husband and brother, knew enough details of Good's murder and how the Ku Klux disposed of Good's body in the Broad River (by weighing it down with two plowshares and then driving stakes through it to secure it to the river bottom) to suggest her account of the motive behind Good's murder is credible. In the same interview, she expressed pride that she knew so much about Ku

Klux activities that she was eventually required to take the Ku Klux oath of secrecy, even though the order refused to accept women members.[49]

IV

Merrill was outraged by reports of such atrocities. "It requires great patience and self-control, to keep ones [sic] hand off these infamous cowards," he fumed.[50] Frustrated that President Grant had not yet exercised the extraordinary powers granted him under the Ku Klux Klan Act, Merrill telegraphed General Terry on May 25, two weeks after he learned of the beating of Elias Hill, to request permission to arrest large numbers of suspected Ku Klux anyway and hold them until trial could be arranged. Unbeknownst to Merrill, the telegraph operator was Ku Klux. Before Merrill could receive a reply to his message, local Ku Klux leaders, who were increasingly astonished to learn how much Merrill knew about their organization and its activities, were already aware of his request and debating how to respond.[51]

Among the options discussed and discarded was an armed assault on the federal troops' camp, which cooler heads realized would only definitively confirm the existence of the Ku Klux and invite more federal intervention. A small group of renegade Ku Klux, however, were intent on carrying out a small raid where they would fire shots into the federal camp in hopes of frightening Merrill and goading some of his men to desert. Informants, perhaps African-American or perhaps disgruntled Ku Klux, advised Merrill of the plan. Merrill then made it widely known that he was aware of the plot and claimed to know which Ku Klux were involved. Several prominent citizens, including Bratton, immediately went to Merrill and volunteered to stop the attack, but Merrill noted they were less interested in the welfare of the troops and instead expressed "a very strong desire to know the name of my informant." Merrill declined to name names, but said the incident underscored his belief that community leaders could stop the violence any time they chose, if that had been their inclination. "In all my conversations with people, I have been met constantly with the palliative remark in regard to these outrages—conceding that they are wrong and all that—almost always the conversation has contained the substance of this remark: 'But you cannot but acknowledge that they have done some good,'" Merrill noted with disgust, "as if lawless violence could ever do anything but harm."[52]

This game of cat and mouse between Merrill and the Ku Klux continued. Determined to learn who was informing to Merrill and whether there was a traitor in their midst, the Ku Klux broke into Merrill's office and stole some of his notes. Merrill then prepared a phony memo and left it lying in his office in an attempt to identify the party who was burglarizing his office, which he did.[53] The Ku Klux had its own small victories; Merrill lamented that the Ku Klux had, in fact, successfully coaxed more than a dozen of his troops into deserting.[54]

Not yet given the green light to make arrests, Merrill decided to use his time in Yorkville to prepare the cases he hoped would one day be made against the York County Ku Klux in a court of law. Aware that many African Americans were still afraid to sleep in their homes, Merrill announced that the federal Army camp on the edge of Yorkville would serve as a refuge for any who needed it. Those who took Merrill up on his offer were then quietly interviewed away from prying eyes and ears while Merrill took copious notes. The information did not always come from African Americans. Several Ku Klux, perhaps ashamed of their past activities or believing the Ku Klux was doomed, also began to cooperate. Merrill dubbed them "pukers."[55]

From these various sources of information, Merrill had detailed information on how the Ku Klux was structured. At the county level, the Ku Klux was organized by divisions that were composed of smaller squads of twenty or fewer. Merrill detailed the Ku Klux's initiation oath and its secret signals that allowed members to identify fellow Klansmen. This included the use of special whistles, and Merrill displayed his thoroughness in his reports by writing out the calls on a musical staff. Even though York County was a comparatively small place, he noted how the Ku Klux went to great lengths to avoid the use of names and to hide the identity of the organization's leaders. Members were assigned numbers, and that was how they were to refer to each other during raids.

Merrill's report was consistent with other reports of how the Ku Klux operated. A white man named Samuel Poinier told congressional investigators that when Ku Klux had collared their intended victim the Klansmen "would stand in a row, and the leader would call out 'Number one!' when 'number one' would step up and strike the victim one blow; then 'number two' would be called and so on. In one instance, it went as high as a hundred,

I believe. Each man steps up and strikes the victim. I suppose the object is to implicate them all alike."[56]

According to Merrill, each Ku Klux was required to provide their own horse and make their own disguise, which they wore on every raid. Merrill was convinced, however, that members were being provided arms purchased with money "supplied . . . from abroad," by which he meant New York and other Northern cities where anti-Black sentiment was strong.[57] The *New York Herald* would also assert that "the Ku Klux in South Carolina have been largely furnished with arms from Northern sources . . . especially of New York."[58]

Many Ku Klux, Merrill began to learn, claimed to have been forced or intimidated into joining. A new initiate, he said, was ordered to commit "some minor act of lawlessness until he is fully committed." If the initiate performed this directive well, he was included in more serious crimes; if not, he was excluded from the group's full confidence. He also concluded, "Beyond doubt the object of the organization in this vicinity is to terrify the negroes into obeying the whites in voting or to compel them to stay away from the polls." To achieve this level of control, the Ku Klux deliberately targeted "the more active and intelligent of the Negroes who have influence with their own color," and used violence to either drive them out of the area or, failing that, to kill them. The same fate awaited any white man who chose to "affiliate with the negroes politically," Merrill said.[59]

To expand his sources of information, Merrill obtained a "moderate sum" of money from Governor Scott that Merrill used to hire local detectives and to bribe turncoat Ku Klux willing to "supply all the missing links in my chain of evidence."[60] Akerman sought to duplicate this strategy more broadly by enlisting the newly created US Secret Service in developing an espionage program against Ku Klux throughout the South. The Department of Justice had no investigative branch of its own—the antecedent to the FBI was not established until 1908—so Akerman provided fifty thousand dollars in Justice Department funding to allow the Secret Service to recruit spies and infiltrate the Ku Klux. Akerman then left it to the discretion of the new head of the Secret Service, Hiram C. Whitley, to determine where to send his agents.[61]

Whitley was an interesting choice to serve as the federal government spymaster in the campaign against the Ku Klux. He was an unapologetic racist who, in his memoirs published in 1894, said it was "fallacious" to believe that African Americans, in their "superstition and simplicity," could ever "cope with white men."[62] Before the war, he had posed as an anti-slavery zealot in Kansas to capture runaway slaves and return them to their owners for a bounty. During the war, Whitley briefly commanded a regiment of free-born African Americans where his use of torture to "discipline" troops nearly led to a mutiny, and the regiment was soon disbanded.[63]

After the war, Whitley worked for the Internal Revenue Service, tracking down bootleggers. In that capacity, he earned a reputation as a skilled detective and was asked by the government to investigate one of the earliest Ku Klux crimes to gain national attention, the 1868 murder of Georgia Republican politician George W. Ashburn, who was leading the charge for racial equality and who had an African-American wife. His success in that case led directly to Whitley being named head of the Secret Service, which had been created in 1865.

Within two weeks of his meeting with Akerman, Whitley had sent three men to the South. These and other agents who followed typically pretended to be "pedlars, itinerant businessmen, or recently arrived immigrants" to try to infiltrate the Ku Klux.[64] To ensure secrecy, Whitley did not tell agents about other agents to preserve their cover identities. It worked so well that on one occasion, two Secret Service agents infiltrated the same Ku Klux den and each believed the other to be actual Ku Klux.[65]

A limited budget meant that Whitley seldom had more than a dozen agents in the field. While the Secret Service collected valuable information in several states—and just the idea of government infiltrators helped further demoralize the Ku Klux—the Secret Service was not a factor in suppressing the Ku Klux in South Carolina, where it had difficulty penetrating Klan dens. But it did not need to, as Merrill had done an outstanding job, collecting information on some eleven murders and six hundred whippings and other outrages that had occurred just in York County.[66] This was the type of information that Congress was seeking as it undertook one of the largest investigations in its history.

Chapter Six

*If ever our people were earnest in anything it is to teach the negro his
duty to be quiet and passive and attend to his duty.*
—Dr. J. Rufus Bratton, testifying before the Joint
Select Committee to Inquire into the Condition of
Affairs in the Late Insurrectionary States

I

Still seeking conciliation with his former Confederacy adversaries, Grant
seemed to hope the mere passage of the Ku Klux Klan Act in April 1871
would persuade the Ku Klux to disband voluntarily. Beyond the few hundred troops he had already dispatched to the South, Grant was reluctant to
do more militarily to antagonize the South. So, even though the act granted
him the extraordinary power to suspend habeas corpus, Grant did no more
immediately after its passage than issue a toothless proclamation that called
on citizens to obey the new law and officials to enforce it. As if to under-
score his hope that goodwill would triumph, Grant then went on summer
vacation to Long Branch, New Jersey.[1]

Congress now took the lead in investigating the Ku Klux by establishing the Joint Select Committee to Inquire into the Condition of Affairs
in the Late Insurrectionary States. Pennsylvania Republican senator John
Scott was selected chairman of what would become "one of the largest
investigations in Congressional history up to that time."[2] When the committee's investigation was completed, its thirteen-volume report contained
some seven thousand pages of witness testimony and evidence, including
the two thousand pages just on South Carolina.

The committee convened in Washington in May and continued to
meet, except for a month's break in summer, into the fall. In June and July,

a three-member subcommittee chaired by Scott and also comprising Ohio congressmen Job Stevenson, a Republican, and Philadelph Van Trump, a Democrat, traveled to South Carolina to take testimony in the field in the state where the Ku Klux seemed to reign supreme. The subcommittee heard witnesses in Spartanburg, Union, and Columbia before ending its field hearings in Yorkville, where there was nearly a riot and a gunfight involving committee members.

In the fall, subcommittees would also hold hearings in Alabama, Florida, Georgia, Mississippi, North Carolina, and Tennessee. Very little evidence was gathered from Arkansas, Louisiana, Texas, or Virginia, and Kentucky, despite a high level of Ku Klux activity there, was not included because it had not been part of the Confederate insurrection.

The committee and subcommittees had both Republican and Democratic members, and any member had authority to call witnesses and cross-examine all those who appeared. In their selection of witnesses, questions, and statements, Democratic members worked to minimize the Ku Klux conspiracy and focus instead on the supposed corruption and incompetence of the Reconstruction Republican governments. Republicans, meanwhile, did their best to coax African Americans victimized by the Ku Klux to testify, a task made difficult because such witnesses were then exposed to retribution from the Ku Klux. As one of the foremost chroniclers of the history of the Ku Klux noted, "Some few Negroes were subsequently raided by the Ku Klux . . . as a result of evidence they had given."[3]

In an attempt to get some Ku Klux to fess up to outrages they had participated in, witnesses who testified were granted immunity from prosecution. Even so, some prospective witnesses refused to testify when summoned. James W. Avery, the acknowledged head of the Ku Klux in York County, fled to Canada to avoid appearing before the subcommittee. More typically, suspected Ku Klux agreed to appear but told only as much of the truth as was convenient, preferring instead to plead ignorance or a faulty memory, or simply commit perjury.

Confederate general Nathan Bedford Forrest testified during a hearing held in Nashville, but Forrest remained coy about his relationship to the Ku Klux. Despite his role as the first and only grand wizard of the Ku Klux, historians still debate whether this title was primarily honorary or whether Forrest wielded real power within the organization.

Forrest himself could not decide what his role was—or had been. He told the committee that while the Ku Klux had once existed, he had ordered it to disband two years before. At its height, Forrest boasted, it had had hundreds of thousands of members, and in 1867 and 1868 he had been receiving fifty to one hundred letters per day from people in the South, inquiring about the Ku Klux. But Forrest also claimed he counseled all who wrote to avoid committing acts of violence.[4] He later admitted to friends that he had engaged in "some gentlemanly lying" while testifying.[5] But what were lies and what was truth was difficult to parse.

Another witness who did more than some gentlemanly lying was Dr. J. Rufus Bratton. Unlike Avery, Bratton, York County's other Ku Klux leader, agreed to testify when the congressional committee convened in the Rose Hotel in Yorkville in late July. Bratton appeared before the committee only an hour before Elias Hill was to appear and give his riveting account of the brutal beating he had received at the hands of the Ku Klux. Asked if he knew Hill, Bratton brushed the question aside: "Only by appearance, I know him when I see him."[6] But as to the attack on Hill or any alleged outrages committed by the Ku Klux, Bratton insisted he had no "personal knowledge" of any acts of violence in York County. "I merely hear rumors and reports," he said.[7]

Questioned specifically about the lynching of Jim Williams, which he had personally led, Bratton pretended he could not remember Williams's name nor the date when he was killed. "I have no knowledge of that fact . . . no man has said, 'I did it' or 'he did,'" Bratton said. "I know nothing about it as to who hung him." Asked if he had conducted the coroner's inquest as a leading local physician, Bratton said he had been away on "other business." He added that "generally in these cases in the country they take the nearest physician," without noting the inquest was held at his younger brother's home while he and the rest of the family were in hiding at his mother's house located just a hundred yards away.[8]

As for alleged whippings of African Americans, Bratton said he had made inquiries and doubted even fifteen African Americans in total had received whippings in the previous year (a figure that was, in fact, nearly equal to the number of African Americans who had been whipped by Ku Klux led by Bratton just on the night Williams was lynched). Bratton said African Americans were filing false reports of beatings with Major Merrill because "a great many of these people dislike to work, and if they can get the protection of the State or the United States to relieve them from work they will do it."[9]

Chairman Scott expressed surprise that Bratton denied being aware even of the Ku Klux assault on the Rose Hotel, when Ku Klux allegedly fired more than one hundred shots in the direction of fleeing county treasurer Ed Rose—an incident that occurred within fifty yards of his home. Bratton airily responded that he had no interest in investigating that or any commotion. "I make it a rule not to get up for these disturbances," he said, inadvertently acknowledging that such disturbances had become a regular occurrence in York County.[10]

Bratton disputed whether there was such an organization as the Ku Klux Klan. A few local white men might have banded together for self-protection against fires being set by disgruntled African Americans, he conceded, but as far as he knew there was no organization, by any name, created to interfere with the rights of African Americans. "I do not know of any cases where a darkey has been interfered with at the polls," he said, but he candidly admitted that he and the majority of whites in York County opposed allowing African Americans to hold Union League or other mass meetings because "when they attend in large numbers they create confusions and annoyance."[11]

Five minutes after asserting he had no knowledge of the Ku Klux and was unaware of any acts of violence in York County, Bratton boasted that he had "often" condemned Ku Klux violence, and said he had advised local whites that "it is not the remedy for our disease." Asked if this meant that he now acknowledged there was such a group as the Ku Klux, Bratton caught himself and repeated his earlier denial, "I do not know of any organization of that kind . . . I am no member of the Ku-Klux, and know nothing of their proceedings."[12] But if there were such an organization, he could not help adding, "every good, honest man ought to sanction it . . . if the motive be to keep down dishonesty and rascality, and place honest and virtuous men in power."[13]

Bratton assured the congressmen that they were wasting their time investigating outrages in York County when local whites felt nothing but kindly toward African Americans. "I tell you the feeling, the honest purpose of the people of this county and State, so far as I know, are in favor of the negro," Bratton said. "They do not wish to take away one particle of the rights of the negro, civil, moral, religious or political." That being said, Bratton said his advice to African Americans was to "have as little to do with politics as possible," but if they insisted on voting they should do so only as directed by more intelligent white men.[14] "I mean simply this," Bratton said, "that the honest, intelligent white people are the only persons in the county capable of ruling it."[15] He added an ominous note. "If ever our people were earnest in anything it is to teach the negro his duty to be quiet and passive and attend to his duty," Bratton said.[16]

Wade Hampton had appeared before the subcommittee several days earlier while it was taking testimony in Columbia. Unlike Bratton, Hampton acknowledged that "outrages" had been committed against African Americans and white Republicans, but insisted that these were not acts of rebellion or hostility toward the national government. "I think it is solely the spasmodic efforts of people to throw off the incubus of this local government," Hampton said.[17]

Hampton then spent a considerable amount of his time expressing white resentment toward the tax policies of the Republican Reconstruction governments, complete with spreadsheets and supporting documents. Hampton asserted that it was the Radical state government that was the proximate cause of white violence because its policies were "a daily and hourly annoyance, a grief and vexation."[18] Hampton expressed incredulity that where South Carolinians had paid only three hundred fifty thousand dollars in taxes in 1860, in 1868 the Republican Reconstruction government in Columbia had levied and spent $2.2 million—a more than 600 percent increase. The implication was that if South Carolina's state government could operate on three hundred fifty thousand dollars in 1860, then the additional $1.8 million being spent now must be almost exclusively due to graft.[19]

Chairman Scott, however, asked if it were not true that at least a million dollars of the state budget was devoted to retiring state debt incurred during the prosecution of the war on behalf of the Confederacy. Hampton admitted he did not know the details of the budget or what was included in the $2.2 million in state expenditures, but members of the Radical government could have easily outlined what these expenditures were intended to do, for they were fundamentally altering what South Carolina citizens might expect from their state and local governments.

South Carolina state senator Jonathan Jasper Wright was a free-born Black from Pennsylvania—the first African American to be admitted to the bar in that state—who came to South Carolina first to teach and then to serve as a legal advisor with the Freedmen's Bureau; he later became a state supreme court justice. "This is a progressive age," Wright said, and government should "do those things for the public good which the public good requires."[20] Wright and his cohorts were unapologetically trying to make South Carolina and the South more like New England and the Midwest.

The Radicals established the first public school system in South Carolina, increased funding for the state hospital and asylum, and devoted funds toward internal improvements such as roads, canals, and railroads to spur development of commerce. South Carolina also took the notable and unique step of setting up a state commission to purchase underutilized land for resale to families seeking to purchase small plots. By 1876, some fourteen thousand African-American families and some whites obtained homesteads until the program was ended—when Hampton became governor.[21]

Before the war, most state revenue was generated by a per-head tax on slaves and high fees for state permits and professional licenses. The ambitious agenda pursued by the Radical Reconstruction governments required a new source of revenue, and so the South Carolina legislature, and others throughout the South, began taxing property. An ad valorem tax had long been established in the North as the primary source of state and local revenues, whereas in South Carolina public schools were funded by the poll taxes. Republican legislators hoped property taxes would also encourage large property owners to sell off land that was not in production so that African Americans and others hungry for land to farm might purchase these properties. Unfortunately for those who desired this outcome, little property changed hands.

Hampton rejected the idea that the Radical Republican agenda represented progress; he considered it tyranny. Hampton portrayed the plight of land-owning Southern whites as even more grievous than that of American colonists on the eve of the Revolution, for in South Carolina "we had not only taxation without representation but representation without taxation."[22] Hampton said it was outrageous that so many state officials, because they owned little or no property, paid little or no property taxes, yet they set tax policy for others. As perhaps the largest landowner in the South, Hampton believed only men of property ought to have a hand in public affairs. He opposed universal suffrage and believed that the only African Americans who should vote were those with "proper qualifications as to property and intelligence."[23]

Meanwhile, Hampton said, men of property like himself, who felt they lacked representation because their favored candidates had failed to win election, struggled to pay their tax bills after having been "the subjects of the most tremendous confiscation that had ever taken place in the world," meaning both the uncompensated liberation of their slaves and, he said, valuables lost to looting Union troops.[24] Hampton and other slaveowners had been genuinely astounded that the federal government made no effort to compensate them for the emancipation of their slaves. Given that Hampton owned nine hundred slaves when the Civil War broke out, this was an extraordinary loss of wealth, while his ownership of some twelve thousand acres of land meant that his annual tax bill was substantial.[25] Hampton made no mention of reparations to the formerly enslaved for their generations of uncompensated labor.

Time did not alter Hampton's opposition to Radical Republican policies, even when they had little or nothing to do with race. When he became governor of South Carolina in 1877, Hampton would drastically reduce property taxes, cut state funding for the state hospital and asylum, and close the public schools so "education went back into the hands of private academies and military and denominational schools, as had been the case during the antebellum period."[26]

II

Hampton's complaints about being gouged by high taxes seemed small and petty when compared to the testimony provided to the subcommittee in Yorkville by African-American witnesses who had literally lost pieces of flesh to the Ku Klux. Hampton Hicklin (who may very well have been named for the prominent South Carolina family) was an African-American farmer whom the Ku Klux had targeted for voting the Radical ticket. On the first Ku Klux raid, Hicklin came home in time to see from a place of hiding a group of Ku Klux tear down his new chimney, kill all his poultry, destroy all the breakable possessions in his home, and whip his wife when she refused to tell the Ku Klux where her husband was. As the Ku Klux were leaving, Hicklin hid in some nearby bushes and was able to identify several of the men as they went by on their way to whip several of Hicklin's neighbors. The next day, Hicklin went into Yorkville to seek Sheriff R. H. Glenn's assistance in the belief that Glenn was not sympathetic to the Ku Klux—a view Major Merrill also held at the time. But the Ku Klux learned Hicklin had gone to the sheriff and returned for a second raid. Dragging Hicklin from his bed, they tied his hands "and whipped me and whipped me until they cut me all to pieces," Hicklin said. They then took him far away from his home and whipped him some more. "They whipped me so I couldn't travel. I was two days crawling thirteen miles [home]," Hicklin told the congressmen.[27]

As he did with most African-American witnesses, Democratic committee member Van Trump of Ohio attempted to trap Hicklin in inconsistencies that would call into question Hicklin's truthfulness. Van Trump pressed Hicklin to describe in detail the shades of gray of the mules he recognized, asked how he could tell whites from Blacks solely by the appearance of their hair, and how Hicklin could identify one of his attackers because he was missing an arm when, Van Trump said, there must be dozens of Confederate veterans in the area who had lost arms in the war. "I have lived here eighteen years, and I know every citizen around there," Hicklin replied.[28] Van Trump's questioning was so picayune that Hicklin could not suppress a laugh. "What amuses you so?" an indignant Van Trump asked. "I just consider that you thought I didn't know these men, and want to trap me up on that. I know them as well as you can make figures on that paper," Hicklin replied.[29]

A twenty-year-old African-American woman named Martha Garrison said the Ku Klux came to her house to confiscate any guns her husband or father had. The two men managed to escape, and while the Ku Klux found no guns they still ransacked Garrison's home and broke her dishes and everything else she owned that was breakable. The Ku Klux returned the next night and accused Garrison of reporting what they had done the night before, a charge Garrison denied. Three Ku Klux held Garrison's arms and legs while four others took turns beating her with "a bundle of hickories as big as my wrist," and then one struck her on the head with the butt of a gun. Garrison's face was so swollen she could not see out of one eye "for a long time," and her injuries were still visible to the committee members five months after the attack.[30]

There were still prospective witnesses filling the "stairs, halls and porches" of the Rose Hotel, hoping for a chance to be heard, when the committee adjourned.[31] The last African-American witness to offer testimony to the subcommittee in South Carolina was seventy-seven-year-old Andrew Cathcart, who had purchased his freedom from slavery around 1850 and acquired a small farm located seven miles north of Yorkville on the road to Charlotte. Cathcart, who intended to join Elias Hill in emigrating to Liberia, testified how the Ku Klux came to his home and forced him to destroy his rifle while they repeatedly slapped his face and ransacked his house. The Ku Klux stole every penny he had: $31.40. They then struck him with the butt of a gun with such force that "I thought it would burst my head open," Cathcart said, adding that he spit up blood for two months after the assault. They then marched Cathcart to a building where his daughter and another woman taught school. The Ku Klux spent fifteen to thirty minutes, by Cathcart's estimation, trying to tear down the building until one yelled, "Burn it up." The Ku Klux set a fire under the building and rode away, but Cathcart, despite hardly being able to walk, crawled under the schoolhouse and put out the fire, saving the school.[32]

Before the African-American witnesses appeared, Merrill had also testified. In addition to providing an overview of the hundreds of whippings that had been reported to him, Merrill supplied details on nearly seventy other outrages committed by the Ku Klux, including several of the most notorious murders, such as that of Tom Roundtree and Alexander Leech. He focused particularly on Ku Klux abuse of women and children, including a young girl identified as the daughter of Abraham Webb who "was whipped and made to dance" and a boy named Sylvester Barron who was "beaten with clubs and pistols."[33]

Merrill's testimony left Congressman Van Trump unmoved, and he demanded to know Merrill's political leanings. "I am an officer in the army bred up in a school which taught me that officers of the army were not proper persons to mix in politics," Merrill replied. Van Trump continued to push, and Merrill ultimately admitted that, given his background, he leaned Republican in his views, but insisted he was not partisan "at all."[34]

Also unmoved was the *Yorkville Enquirer*, which ridiculed the hearings as the work of "the sub-outrage committee." The *Enquirer* gave prominent placement to a statement signed by "several citizens" that strongly insinuated that Merrill had bribed witnesses to provide false testimony, and claimed that the subcommittee had received much erroneous information from a Ku Klux quisling named William K. Owens, described as a "bad character" who should have obtained no one's confidence. Owens did not testify, but fled York County in fear of his life.[35]

To provide "a Republican stand-point," the *Enquirer* also reprinted an article from the *Washington Chronicle* that noted that the situation in South Carolina was so awful that "in many neighborhoods nearly every negro man and Republican white man had slept in the woods for months every night." The *Chronicle* added that the "bitter spirit" present among the people of York County was evident in an incident that had occurred when the subcommittee members were dining at the Rose Hotel during their first night in Yorkville. According to the *Chronicle*, the supper nearly turned into a gunfight when local Republican congressman Alexander S. Wallace pulled out a revolver to protect himself from a local critic.[36]

The *Enquirer* provided its own, less dramatic account. In that version, Wallace, who was so despised by local Democrats that he feared for his safety while home and spent most of his time as a virtual refugee in Washington, DC, had joined the Republican members of the committee for dinner. A man named James H. Barry, who had been a major in the Confederate army and was described as "a regular boarder at the hotel," seated himself opposite Wallace. Other reports stated that the inebriated Barry initially contemplated pouring hot coffee on Wallace, but instead he suddenly threw a pitcher of cream that missed Wallace and drenched Congressman Job Stevenson instead. Wallace, Stevenson, and other diners rose from their chairs in great excitement and "thrust their hands into their pockets," presumably to draw out weapons. Instead, to the relief of those present, they instead pulled out handkerchiefs to wipe away the cream from Stevenson's face and coat. Barry, who later sent his apologies to Stevenson, was ushered out of the hotel and charged with assault. The *Enquirer*'s editor, Lewis Grist, opined that he was "satisfied that Barry intended no disrespect to the members of the Congressional Committee."[37] If disrespect was intended toward the despised Wallace, who because of the incident endured the nickname "Buttermilk" Wallace for the rest of his career, it was of no consequence to Grist or any other local Democrat.

If that had been the end of the evening, it would have remained a mildly amusing anecdote, but if the dinner had not been eventful enough, there was real bloodshed later. African-American musicians had gathered as a band outside the hotel to serenade the congressional visitors. A large crowd gathered, including African Americans who wished to support the work of the subcommittee, young whites who came to heckle the committee members and their African-American supporters, and a few souls who came just to enjoy the music.

One of the town constables, William H. Snyder, who was Ku Klux, tried to clear the sidewalks, primarily of the Black band. When one of the musicians, Tom Johnson, was slow to obey Snyder's order, Snyder attempted to arrest him. Johnson resisted, and Snyder drew his pistol and fired five shots into Johnson, who the *Enquirer* referred to as a "belligerent darkey," wounding him in the face, shoulder, hand, arm and back—each shot taking effect, but not inflicting dangerous wounds."[38]

African Americans believed that Snyder and other whites were hoping to start a riot "in which they would be slaughtered." Merrill, who was also dining with the subcommittee members in the Rose Hotel, rushed outside to defuse the situation. Merrill urged the African Americans to disperse and go home and prevailed upon Yorkville's mayor to convince whites in the crowd to do the same.[39] The next day the committee began its four days of hearings in Yorkville without further incident, but always with the threat of violence hanging in the air.

III

On March 1, 1871, the week before the lynching of Jim Williams and three weeks before Merrill's arrival in Yorkville, John Clayton Farris, my great-grandfather, joined with a dozen other Ku Klux, including his younger brother, Moses P. Farris, to whip a Chester County resident named Wilson Robbins, a thirty-eight-year-old African-American farm laborer and father of five children aged three to sixteen. The federal indictment issued against John Clayton and his cohorts provides few details of the assault, including John Clayton's exact role. Based on notes scribbled on the indictment, Robbins told federal authorities that my great-grandfather and the other Ku Klux whipped him "because he voted the Radical ticket."[40]

Nearly three months later, on May 20, while York County's leading residents were urging the Ku Klux to lay low to convince Merrill his presence was unneeded, John Clayton joined a half dozen other Ku Klux in York County to whip an African-American man named Giles Good. As with Robbins, no details of the assault are provided, but the indictment against my great-grandfather said he and his co-conspirators were engaging in these beatings with the intent of "unlawfully hindering, preventing and restraining divers [*sic*] Male citizens of the United States of African descent, above the age of 21 years . . . from exercising the right and privilege of voting."[41]

Good, a thirty-six-year-old farmer who sixteen years later would be lynched by a York County mob in retaliation for his alleged role in the murder of a twelve-year-old boy, was reportedly "a negro of much influence among his fellows."[42] He was known to wear a blue Yankee overcoat, though it is not clear whether he was a Union army veteran.* Good was, however, such a passionate Republican that he allegedly once helped plot the murder of a fellow African American who had joined "the Democratic club."[43]

John Clayton never stood trial for his alleged crimes. Even though these assaults occurred in early 1871, the indictments against him were not actually issued until April 1, 1872, by which time my great-grandfather was long gone. He had fled to Arkansas in mid-October 1871, just as Merrill and his troops began making mass arrests of suspected Ku Klux. John Clayton settled in northern Arkansas in Baxter County, where an older sister, Eliza Jane Thacker, already lived. He may also have been aware that the federal marshal for Arkansas had become notorious for refusing to serve warrants on fugitive Ku Klux, even those whom federal prosecutors alleged were "covered all over with blood."[44]

It is also possible if, as some other Ku Klux rank and file claimed they had contemplated, John Clayton had determined to quit the Ku Klux, then northern Arkansas was a good choice for a new home. The Ku Klux had

---

*Articles published by the *Yorkville Enquirer* at the time of his lynching claim Good was the leader of a criminal organization that the *Enquirer* called, with no irony, "a secret clan." ("The Broad River Horror," *Yorkville Enquirer*, December 15, 1886, 2) A boy named John Lee Good (no relation to his assailant) was allegedly killed by four of Good's compatriots after the boy came upon the men stealing cotton from his father's farm. Good, who had a long rap sheet, was also arrested as the alleged head of the conspiracy. While officials moved the five defendants twice to avoid vigilante justice, when they men were returned to Yorkville in April 1887 to stand trial, a mob stormed the county jail, seized the suspects, and lynched all five from a large oak tree located a half mile from the jail, letting them strangle to death. ("The Story of the Lynching," *Yorkville Enquirer*, April 13, 1887, 2) One of the physicians who participated in the inquest into the lynching was Dr. R. Andral Bratton, son of Dr. J. Rufus Bratton. ("The Gallows," *Yorkville Enquirer*, April 16, 1885, 2)

already been largely subdued by the time he arrived there. Former Arkansas governor Powell Clayton, a Quaker from Pennsylvania, had essentially waged war on the Ku Klux in 1868–69. He declared martial law in ten southern and eastern Arkansas counties and dispatched a sympathetic state militia composed of African Americans and scalawags (in segregated units) to arrest scores of Ku Klux, of whom three were executed by state military tribunals.[45]

Had John Clayton stayed in York County to face trial in federal court, he stood a likely chance of being convicted. Notes on his indictment in the handwriting of US Attorney David Corbin state that one of his fellow Ku Klux accomplices, John Meeks, had agreed to testify for the prosecution, and Meeks claimed he could specifically identify John Clayton and his brother, Moses, as having participated in the assault on Robbins. According to Corbin's notes, there were another half dozen witnesses prepared to testify for the prosecution in that case, and five witnesses who were prepared to testify against him regarding the assault on Good.[46]

As a peon, not a Ku Klux leader, whose case never came to trial, my great-grandfather's case was indicative of several aspects of the federal crackdown on the Ku Klux, which finally began once President Grant returned from summering in New Jersey.

Returning to Washington in August, Grant conferred with Senator Scott, who reported on his committee's work and provided additional detail to what Grant had already read in the newspapers or received in reports from Attorney General Akerman. It was clear conditions in the South for African Americans and their white allies remained alarming and the criminality so widespread that "if all known violators were arrested, the jails would be filled and the court calendars taxed."[47] Unsurprisingly, simply passing the Ku Klux Klan Act had not disbanded the Ku Klux; if the law was to have an effect, it would have to be enforced.

Grant had no desire to be considered a military despot or to resume the recently ended conflict on even a small scale. Before he declared any part of the South in rebellion and used the extraordinary power of suspending habeas corpus in peacetime, he wished to be sure he had no better alternative. So, he sent Akerman to North and South Carolina on a fact-finding mission.

Before Akerman departed, he received several unhelpful suggestions. Republican congressman Benjamin Butler, who had been a primary author of the Ku Klux Klan Act, proposed that the Department of Justice should offer a general amnesty to any Ku Klux who turned themselves in. Akerman replied that such a proclamation would be unwise and ineffective "until the scoundrels get more extensively alarmed."[48] Another Republican official, demonstrating how little those in the North understood what was happening in the South or why, asked if the Ku Klux might dissolve if the government reduced the whiskey tax. Given that the Ku Klux Klan was not a society of moonshiners but "the most atrocious organization the civilized part of the world has ever known," Akerman responded that stronger measures were likely necessary:[49]

> *A portion of our southern population hate the northerners from the old grudge, hate the government of the United States because they understand it emphatically to represent northern sentiment; and hate the negro because he has ceased to be a slave and has been promoted to be a citizen and voter, and hate those of the southern whites who are looked upon as in political friendship with the north, with the United States government and with the negro. These persons commit the violence that disturbs many parts of the South. Undoubtedly the judgment of the great body of our people condemns this behavior, but they take no active measures to suppress it.[50]*

As a Georgian, Akerman understood this depth of feeling in the South. Compromise or appeasement were not options likely to generate results.

In North Carolina, federal officials had already issued indictments against nearly one hundred Ku Klux, but the courts were moving slowly. Akerman was undaunted. "If you cannot convict, you, at least, can expose, and ultimately such exposure will make the community ashamed of shielding the crime," he told one of his prosecutors.[51] Despite prosecutions moving at a snail's pace, Akerman was pleased to hear even these modest efforts were impacting the Ku Klux and those who supported them. A local official begged Akerman to ease the prosecutions that had barely begun "lest there be starvation, because so many of the outlaw class are hiding in the woods for fear of arrest."[52] Akerman doubted starvation was in the offing and instead had already caught a glimpse of what was possible when there was "an energetic, but at the same time, strictly just and lawful exercise of power."[53]

But South Carolina, at least in the upcountry, posed a far greater challenge, although there, too, Ku Klux feared the arrests they expected were coming soon. In his testimony before the congressional committee in Yorkville in late July, Elias Hill noted with barely concealed pleasure how the mere sight of a federal soldier frightened the Ku Klux. "Just let a man in a Yankee uniform go out there, and not one in fifty of our white neighbors but will run," Hill said. "What makes them run but guilt—conscious guilt?"[54] Before federal troops arrived in York County, Hill said, "all our colored people that could walk, males and females, and many young children, staid out during last winter and spring. Now the white men, the young men and boys, from fifteen to the gray-headed, are out, some by night and hunting by day, an excuse that if a summons should come for them they would be absent. Some in my neighborhood have fled the state, and others are ready to go."[55]

Historian Richard Zuczek has argued that Ku Klux activity was already waning in the South Carolina Piedmont and additional federal intervention was unnecessary if the goal was to restore order. Zuczek has suggested that Grant and Akerman were instead so angered by what had been exposed regarding past outrages that they decided the Ku Klux had to be "punished and, if possible, destroyed."[56] But Akerman at the time was skeptical that the South Carolina government was capable of controlling the Ku Klux, and local governments were unwilling to do so. While there were fewer outrages occurring in the summer of 1871, this was primarily due to the presence of federal troops and the unwelcome national attention focused on the Ku Klux phenomenon. Akerman did not believe the temporary lull in Ku Klux activity would last and agreed with Merrill that the outrages would resume on the same previous scale the minute federal troops were withdrawn.

Akerman also made no apologies for not only the desire but the need for punitive measures so South Carolina and the South did not return to the previous state of near-anarchy. "Ultimately, these measures will promote the peace and prosperity of the South. The present medicine is harsh, but needed to overcome the disease," he said.[57]

Reviewing Merrill's findings, and those of the congressional committee while also conducting his own inquiries, Akerman concluded that at least two-thirds of adult white males in nine upcountry counties in South Carolina were still Ku Klux and the remaining third were sympathetic to the Ku Klux. As far as he could ascertain, Akerman told Grant, this part of South Carolina remained in a state of "rebellion," and he therefore recommended the extraordinary step authorized by the Ku Klux Act of suspending the right of habeas corpus in these counties.[58]

Grant was traveling in New England and also occupied with directing federal aid in the aftermath of the Great Chicago Fire that had occurred on October 7. But on October 12, he issued a proclamation drafted by Akerman that gave Ku Klux members in York and eight other upcountry South Carolina counties five days to disband and surrender all their weapons, ammunition, disguises, and anything else used in their assaults on the constitutional rights of "certain portions and classes of people." When there was, expectedly, "no noticeable response" to the proclamation, another proclamation was issued October 17 that formally suspended the right of habeas corpus in those counties. Because Akerman was still in South Carolina, Solicitor General Benjamin Bristow handled this proclamation, but complained to future Supreme Court justice John Marshall Harlan that "I don't like the precedent." Bristow shared Secretary of State Hamilton Fish's irritation at Akerman's fixation on destroying the Ku Klux, and had already begun the machinations he hoped would allow him to replace Akerman as attorney general.[59]

IV

Ku Klux worried about arrest and prosecution had been jittery all summer and into the early fall. Grant's warning proclamation on October 12 was like uncorking a bottle whose contents were under extreme pressure. Akerman had directed Merrill to focus enforcement on those community leaders active in the Ku Klux as the surest way to break the conspiracy's back. But when federal troops assisted by US marshals were dispatched to make mass arrests five days later, Merrill discovered that many if not most of the suspected Ku Klux leaders had fled the state, "leaving their poor followers and ignorant dupes to stand sponsors for the crimes of which they had been the chief authors and instigators."[60]

Some Ku Klux leaders went to Texas, others to Pennsylvania, while the two ringleaders in the lynching of Jim Williams, J. Rufus Bratton and James W. Avery, made their way to Canada. The government would later attempt to retrieve them for trial by drugging, kidnapping, and spiriting them across the international border, sparking the first diplomatic dispute between the United States and the newly independent Dominion of Canada.[61]

Leaderless, the Ku Klux rank and file who were now rounded up by federal troops were "bewildered and demoralized," Merrill noted.[62] Of course, some rank and file, like my great-grandfather, fled too. Perhaps two thousand suspected Ku Klux fled South Carolina.[63] In York County alone, more than two hundred Ku Klux are thought to have fled, with devastating consequences to the community.[64] Between those who fled and those who were arrested, "virtually every family" in York County was affected.[65]

York and all the counties where habeas corpus had been suspended were in a tizzy. Mary Davis Brown, a lifelong York County resident and farm wife who lived a few miles northwest of Yorkville, wrote in her diary that word of Grant's proclamation had caused such "Great excitement" that Sunday services at the Beersheba Presbyterian Church that she attended had been canceled. "We have no preachen [sic] to day," she wrote on October 15. Men were racing out of the county and out of state before the federal troops came looking for them. The next day she noted a local storekeeper was distraught because "his clerks all gone and such excitement that he is not selling. He is boxen [sic] up some of his goods and sending them back." Brown began listing the men she knew, many of them relatives, neighbors, or fellow parishioners, who were leaving "fore [sic] parts unknown. . . . It was hard to see them leave. We don't know whether ever to return."[66]

On October 17, Merrill and his troops began making mass arrests, targeting community events, like shucking parties, where they might find many suspects all in one place. Church services resumed the following Sunday "but verry [sic] few out," Mary Brown noted. "The yanks is going in every direction gathering up and putting in jail," she wrote, adding that the federal troops were now searching houses one by one, seeking suspected Ku Klux. It was a calamity that seemed to shake Brown's faith in God. "Enabel [sic] me to say thy will be done," she wrote. She was so distressed that she failed to make another entry in her diary for another three weeks.[67]

Later critics, particularly John S. Reynolds of the so-called "Dunning School" of historians who wrote particularly sympathetic studies of the Ku Klux after the turn of the century, would claim that Merrill made many false arrests, used excessive force, and raided the homes of Ku Klux at night in a deliberate attempt to frighten women and children.* Though what Reynolds seemed to find most objectionable was that the arrests were made with the assistance and "in the presence of Negroes."[68] In truth, most arrests were made in daytime and, despite the large number of persons arrested, there were "few

---

*These historians were named for Columbia University professor William Archibald Dunning, a native of New Jersey, who mentored a number of young Southern scholars and actively encouraged their interpretation of Reconstruction as a massive failure due to what Dunning (and his protégés) believed was the obvious racial inferiority of African Americans.

instances—five or six perhaps—of mistaken identity" where the wrong man was arrested because his name was identical to that of the man being sought. These mistakes, one newspaper asserted, were "promptly corrected."[69]

There was also only one instance when a suspect was killed during arrest. That occurred the following spring, in April 1872, when Minor Parris, a Ku Klux indicted in connection with the murder of a freedman, was shot while trying to flee in a boat on the Broad River. Parris, who allegedly had sworn he would never be arrested, ignored multiple orders to halt and turn back. Soldiers fired a volley from two hundred yards away and a bullet struck Parris in his hip. As he lingered near death, Parris was asked why he had not obeyed the order to halt and replied that he did not think the soldiers would shoot, suggesting that the Ku Klux themselves had not considered the federal troops to be particularly aggressive in carrying out these arrests.[70]

The arrests had a tremendous impact on York County. A reporter from New York City who came to Yorkville after the arrests began in earnest noted that Yorkville seemed like a city under siege:

> As I walked up the long street from the depot to the hotel, the place had the look of a town in war time recently captured by an invading army. There were soldiers everywhere. An infantry camp of clean, white tents, arranged in regular rows, with the alleys between prettily shaded with arbors of green boughs, stood in an oak grove near the station. A squad of cavalry rode by; blue coats strode up and down the street and lounged about the doors of the stores, in which there seemed to be much talk and little traffic. Groups of countrymen in gray homespun stood upon the street corners and in the Court-House yard, engaged in low and excited talk. Other men who appeared, by their dress, villagers, could be seen through the open doors of lawyers' and doctors' offices, or standing in knots of three or four upon the sidewalks, absorbed in conversation on the one topic of the arrests. Everybody but the negroes and soldiers had the look of excitement and despondency always observable in the inhabitants of a conquered town, and the people I met eyed me suspiciously, as if they feared I might have come to empty some new vial of Government wrath upon their devoted heads.[71]

Many suspected Ku Klux who decided not to flee believed they could simply hide until Merrill and the federal government gave up and went away. John Clayton's younger brother, Moses Pinkney Farris, who was also indicted for the assault on Wilson Robbins, chose not to accompany his brother to Arkansas. Why is unknown. Perhaps they were simply not that close, as John Clayton was nine years older than Moses. Moses may have also had more reason to stay. Whereas John Clayton had separated from his wife a few years earlier and seemed to have nothing holding him in York, Moses would soon marry a local woman named Rachel Robbins.

It is unclear what, if any, association existed between Rachel Robbins and Wilson Robbins. Perhaps, given that slaves often were assigned the surname of their owners and kept them even after emancipation, Wilson was owned by a relative of Rachel's, but that is speculation. But what stands out repeatedly in the white-on-Black violence of the Ku Klux era is how often the assailants and those who were assaulted knew each other intimately, reflecting the personal betrayal that so chagrined Elias Hill.

Moses and several comrades avoided arrest by hiding out for nearly a year until arrests of suspected Ku Klux ended. Moses and his friends would sleep away from their homes at night, and in the daytime would stay in the hills in western Chester County and observe "the Yankee troops search around in the valley below them." Ku Klux sympathizers ensured the men were fed and occasionally able to sleep in a soft, warm bed, though such a respite nearly led to Moses's capture. One night, Moses and a man named E. L. Gaston were staying at a home that had a potato cellar accessible by raising some of the floor planks. When federal troops surrounded the house, Moses, "being a small man," successfully crawled into the cellar and hid, while Gaston, "being a large man," could not get through the opening into the cellar and was arrested. Moses never was arrested and spent no time in custody, but essentially wasted a year of his life.[72]

But most rank-and-file Ku Klux did not flee, and most of those who tried to hide were found. Some got tired of hiding in the woods and were discovered when they went home to see their families. Others were reported by African Americans who kept "a vigilant watch for the raiders who are especially wanted at headquarters, and [they] will frequently walk 20 miles by night to announce the discovery of the hiding place of some chief of a Klan, and to pilot a squad of Cavalry back to capture him."[73]

In the first week following the suspension of habeas corpus, nearly eighty men were arrested and confined in the York County jail. Most were

told Merrill, "my little boy is still living, but the doctor says he will die before morning. I want to go back." Merrill asked the man when he would return. "Tomorrow sundown," the Ku Klux replied. The man, making another twenty-eight-mile round-trip journey, returned as scheduled, reported his son had died, and that he had been able to bury the boy before returning to Yorkville. "To appreciate the profound impression which this incident made upon me," Post said, "one must believe that both these men supposed, as I did, that the prisoner had come back to be hanged."[84] It was a rare tale of grace before the sordidness of the Ku Klux crimes were exposed at trial.

CHAPTER SEVEN

*I fear that we will not be able to control the court, tempers run very high,
and the populace is unsettled.*

—FEDERAL JUDGE HUGH LENNOX BOND

I

It was a whimsical beginning to what were to be, given their role in
destroying the Ku Klux Klan, the most consequential criminal trials in
American history. On August 2, 1871, a Wednesday, federal circuit clerk
of court Daniel Horlbeck went into the streets of Columbia and selected,
apparently at random, "a small colored boy" to accompany him back to the
courthouse.[1] Arrests of suspected Ku Klux would not begin for another
ten weeks, but in anticipation of the heavy caseload expected for the
court's fall and winter term, the "rubicund" Horlbeck, as the *Charleston
Daily News* described him, was beginning the process of selecting juries
for the upcoming trials.[2]

Horlbeck led the boy, hopefully with parental permission, to his office.
There, in the presence of Chief Deputy US Marshal Edward Butts and in
accordance with an old Carolinian custom, the boy was instructed to draw
names of prospective jurors from a jury box. The boy's name and age were
not recorded, but by practice under the old custom he would have been less
than ten years old, his youthful innocence a symbol of the supposed impar-
tiality of justice. The box held the names of roughly two hundred men from
throughout South Carolina who had been randomly chosen from voter rolls.
The boy had drawn a few names when Butts was called away, meaning no
one from the marshal's office was present as the boy continued to pull names
from the box. Butts's absence during the remainder of the selection process
would become a point of contention at trial.

But if using a child to select jurors was an old custom, what was not traditional, and perhaps why Horlbeck specifically selected a young African-American boy to do the drawing, was that the jury box contained the names not only of white men but also of Black men who were now also voters. The Great South Carolina Ku Klux Klan Trials would be among the first trials in American history to include African-American jurors, and were the extraordinarily rare trials where African Americans would make up the majority of the selected juries.

African Americans had been excluded from jury service—North as well as South—since the nation's founding. While scholars say it is possible an African American may have sat on a few local juries during the early days of the Republic, the first documented instance of an African American sitting on a jury anywhere in the United States did not occur until 1860 in Massachusetts. Even in the half dozen Northern states that did not expressly prohibit African-American men from voting (jurors, then and now, are chosen from voter rolls), "custom and prejudice" prevented them from serving.[3]

Nor could African Americans testify in court. The depth of antipathy to allowing African Americans in the courtroom in any capacity other than as a criminal defendant can be ascertained from this 1846 Ohio Supreme Court decision that affirmed the exclusion of Blacks from being witnesses at trial:

> *No matter how pure the character, yet, if the color is not right, the man cannot testify. The truth shall not be received from a black man, to settle a controversy where a white man is a party. Let a man be a Christian or an infidel; let him be Turk, Jew, or Mahometan; let him be of good character or bad; even let him be sunk to the lowest depths of degradation; he may be a witness in our courts if he is not black.*[4]

Proponents and opponents alike understood Black participation in the justice system was central to African Americans achieving civil equality, but opponents feared it would also lead to political equality or, the greatest horror of all, social equality. When he vetoed the Civil Rights Bill of 1866, which sought to define national citizenship and enshrine the right of African Americans to testify in court, President Andrew Johnson said if Congress could allow that, then at some future date Congress could "also declare who, without regard to color or race, shall have the right to sit as a juror or as a judge, to hold any office, and, finally, to vote."[5] Republican advocates of Blacks serving on juries, keen not to go too far in bucking the convention of race, insisted this would never happen.

Critics of the right of African Americans to testify or serve as jurors predicted it would lead quite directly to something much more radical and abhorrent: intermarriage. When he learned that Massachusetts had allowed two African-American men to serve on a jury in 1860, an Indiana congressman expressed incredulity that any state

> would allow a white man to be accused of a crime by a negro; to be arrested on the affidavit of a negro, by a negro officer; to be prosecuted by a negro lawyer; testified against by a negro witness; tried before a negro judge; convicted before a negro jury; and executed by a negro executioner; and either one of these negroes might become the husband of his widow or his daughter![6]

A leading congressional opponent of Black jurors was Maryland senator Reverdy Johnson, a former US attorney general who, following the death of Daniel Webster, was widely regarded as "the leading American lawyer" and expert on constitutional law.[7] In 1867, as Congress debated a bill that would allow African Americans to serve on juries in the District of Columbia, Johnson said, "[T]he question for the Senate to decide is whether we are willing to have ourselves tried by a jury of black men for the most part just emerged from slavery, without the capacity absolutely necessary to a faithful and intelligent discharge of that duty." Johnson shuddered to think of white men being subjected to a judgment "pronounced by twelve ignorant black men."[8]

Johnson's fears were now realized. No longer in the Senate but still the most prominent defense attorney in the country, he was hired to defend the Ku Klux during the trials in Columbia. There he would admit to being completely discomfited by addressing the first Black jurors he had seen in his lengthy legal career.

It was Wade Hampton's idea to hire Johnson and another former US attorney general, Henry Stanbery of Ohio, to defend the Ku Klux at trial. Aware that few advocates could speak with more authority, Hampton had secured Johnson's services once before, when he needed to defend his military reputation. General William Tecumseh Sherman had charged that Hampton was primarily responsible for setting the fire that eventually burned most of Hampton's hometown of Columbia to the ground. Sherman claimed Hampton had committed the "folly" of ordering cotton stored in the city set on fire, lest it fall into Yankee hands. Hampton claimed he had actually countermanded an order to set the cotton on fire and, already despondent that he had been unable to save his home city, was enraged by Sherman's accusation that he had accidentally destroyed it.[9] In the spring of 1866, with South Carolina still without representation in the US Senate, Hampton asked Johnson to read and enter into the congressional record a letter Hampton wrote, rebutting Sherman's charges, which Johnson did, while requesting a congressional inquiry that never occurred.

In securing the services of two former attorneys general, who were reputedly the two highest-paid defense attorneys in the nation, Hampton was seeking representation in two courts: the federal court in Columbia and the national court of public opinion. Hampton worried that a former Confederate arguing the case might make it appear the South had not accepted the result of the war, remained in a state of rebellion, and was actively encouraging acts of barbarism against freedmen and women. If that was the message from the trials, then there would be no loosening of federal control over Southern affairs, and all hopes of redemption would be lost before they had even begun.

Hampton believed the Ku Klux defense would be better argued and better received by the American public if those asserting there was no reign of terror in the South were Northern men whose loyalty to the Union was undisputed. On October 22, 1871, with mass arrests of suspected Ku Klux continuing and trials of the accused scheduled to begin the following month, Hampton wrote a letter to a political confidant, former South Carolina congressman Armistead Burt, and proposed that they quickly raise money to hire Northern lawyers to defend the Ku Klux, as "they would have more weight than our own advocates & could speak more freely."[10]

During his testimony in July before the congressional committee investigating the Ku Klux, Hampton insisted he had never heard of the Ku Klux Klan and had condemned outrages perpetrated against African Americans. But now he was outraged by the continued presence in the South of federal troops, small as that number was. He still deeply believed in states' rights and, as he told the congressional committee, considered all federal civil rights legislation unconstitutional.

"I apprehend for our unfortunate people greater trials and wrongs than they have yet suffered, from the Ku Klux laws," Hampton told Burt. "God only knows what the end will be, but I can only see sorrow & suffering ahead for them."[11] If the arguments formulated by Akerman and others prevailed, America generally and Southern culture specifically would be radically altered. It was time, Hampton said, "that there should be some concert in action among us in relation to political affairs."[12]

Hampton and Burt estimated that fifteen thousand dollars would be needed to procure the finest men, and directed Democratic Party leaders in each county to raise a specific sum to achieve that goal. The fundraising campaign fell short, raising only ten thousand dollars (roughly a quarter-million in 2019 dollars), but it was enough to secure the services of Johnson and Stanbery, a legal "dream team" for the nineteenth century.[13]

II

Johnson was born in Annapolis, Maryland, in 1796, when George Washington was still president. By 1871, he was one the nation's most famous attorneys and an éminence grise in the nation's capital, the proverbial Washington "wise man." His father had been an esteemed lawyer, state legislator, and state attorney general in Maryland, and Johnson, a veteran of the War of 1812, first studied the law under his father. Shortly after starting his practice, Johnson became the protégé of a Maryland lawyer twenty years his senior named Roger Taney, the future chief justice of the US Supreme Court. Taney would render his most infamous decision in a case involving a slave named Dred Scott, in which Johnson argued for the slaveowner and Taney wrote the majority opinion that African Americans had no rights and were not citizens of the United States.

An alumnus of St. John's College in Annapolis, Johnson was urbane, courteous, and cheerful and known for his "quickness of mind [and] his remarkable memory." While he had a "deep and impressive voice," Johnson was not physically imposing.[14] He was solidly built and of medium height with a distinctive high forehead. "[T]he dome of his head was [his] most striking feature," an admirer said, "so lofty, so symmetrically rounded, that it seemed to tower above all others, as the dome of St. Peter's minimizes all other designs."[15]

But what was more important than his profile in setting Johnson apart from his peers, a colleague said, was his "untiring, persistent preparation for the trial of causes committed to his professional care."[16] He was such a skilled attorney that by age thirty-five, he was already earning eleven thousand dollars annually, an astonishing sum for the time. Johnson remained one of the nation's most renowned attorneys even after a shooting accident cost him his sight in his left eye in 1842. Not long afterward, he began to suffer from what appears to have been macular degeneration in his right eye, making it so that, a colleague said, "he could not walk the streets, or even a room with furniture in it, without the guiding assistance of someone, and was not able to recognize features at all." Friends and associates read cases, correspondence, and newspapers aloud to him, and he had long ago memorized important legal and constitutional commentaries, but his blindness required that he rely on his memory rather than notes when arguing a case.[17]

A great admirer of Henry Clay, as was Lincoln (and Amos Akerman), Johnson was first elected to the Senate in 1845. In Washington he shared a house with legendary South Carolina senator and former vice president John C. Calhoun, part of the famed Senate triumvirate that included Clay and Webster. Johnson said Calhoun enjoyed practicing his theories of states' rights on Johnson, but while Calhoun was a strong advocate of nullification (Johnson was not), Johnson later quoted Calhoun as stating that secession was a much different matter, being unconstitutional and nothing less than a "revolution" against the national government.[18]

Johnson left the Senate in 1849 to become President Zachary Taylor's attorney general until Taylor's death in 1850, when he resumed his lucrative private practice. In two cases involving the protection of the McCormick reaper patent, Johnson was co-counsel with Lincoln in one, and with Thaddeus Stevens in the other. Johnson's own views on slavery were nuanced to the point of incoherence. He called slavery "a great evil," but questioned whether it was constitutionally permissible to abolish it. Other times he suggested the master-slave relationship was "in some respects mutually advantageous."[19] He eventually landed on the "popular sovereignty" theory of Stephen Douglas in which white voters would decide whether slavery was permissible in their states and territories or not.

In his most notorious case, Johnson handled pro bono the appeal of the slaveowner in the case of Dred Scott, a slave who sued for his freedom because his owner, an Army surgeon, had taken him to live for an extended period of time in several free states and territories. Scott had attempted to purchase his freedom from his master's widow, but she refused and so he sued for his emancipation in 1846 on the grounds that his time living in free states made him free.

Eleven years later, the US Supreme Court, in a 7–2 opinion written by Johnson's mentor and friend, the then eighty-year-old Taney ruled that slavery was protected by the Constitution, which therefore meant that the Missouri Compromise that banned slavery north of the 36th parallel was unconstitutional. African Americans, the court continued, were not and could never be citizens of the United States, and they therefore had no standing to sue in a federal court nor were they entitled to any rights of citizenship. Blacks were so inferior to whites, Taney wrote, "that they had no rights which the white man was bound to respect." Taney said this could be verified because so many signers of the Declaration of Independence owned slaves and therefore could not have believed African Americans were included under the creed that "all men are created equal."[20]

During the two oral arguments conducted by the Supreme Court in the case, Johnson laid out the "southern view of our Constitution" in a "forcible presentation" that was so close in theory and wording to the rationale used in the majority opinion that critics charged Johnson had used his personal friendship with Taney to influence the court's decision.[21] In truth, while Taney had freed his own slaves, the chief justice was a passionate defender of the Southern institution and needed no prodding from Johnson to reach the opinion he authored.[22]

Taney had hoped his opinion would be the end of the anti-slavery movement and the Republican Party; instead, it helped precipitate the Civil War and the destruction of the Southern society he so admired. Even as *Dred Scott* became known as the most egregious Supreme Court decision in American history, Johnson continued to defend Taney from criticism, saying on Taney's death in 1864, "We knew him to be humane, to be charitable, to be a Christian gentleman."[23] Johnson had been one of the Senate's most vocal opponents of the anti-immigrant Know-Nothing movement in large part because his friend Taney was a Roman Catholic.

Lincoln was a strong critic of the *Dred Scott* decision, which along with his anger at Douglas's Kansas-Nebraska Act had lured him back into politics.

But in 1861, at Lincoln's request, Johnson wrote a legal brief defending the new president's right to suspend the writ of habeas corpus. Johnson said a president has a constitutional duty to carry out the laws and suppress revolt. In the brief, Johnson wrote that while "the power to declare war is vested solely in Congress, the conduct of the war is solely with the President." Having written the brief, Johnson then devoted much of his energies during the war, usually free of charge, to obtaining the release of people he believed had been wrongfully detained when habeas corpus was suspended.[24]

Johnson returned to the Senate in 1862, where he favored raising Black federal troops and agreed service to the Union should win a slave his freedom, but he argued freedom for the slave-turned-veteran's family would still have to be purchased from their owner. Johnson also opposed the Emancipation Proclamation, but later modified his views and voted in favor of the Thirteenth Amendment. He supported mass pardons for Southerners, except those who served at the highest levels of the Confederacy, whom he believed should be executed. By 1864 he had soured on Lincoln and decided that his onetime co-counsel was unfit for the presidency. He later defended the only female conspirator charged in Lincoln's assassination, Mary Surratt, because he objected to the conspirators being tried by a military tribunal when they, particularly Surratt, were not subject to military law.

On civil rights for African Americans, Johnson's views evolved very modestly. He believed former slaves were not competent to participate in civil life, but said some free-born Blacks might be capable of serving on juries. He opposed Black suffrage, arguing voting was a privilege not a right, but said African Americans might elevate themselves over several generations to a point where they might finally qualify for the vote. Social equality, of course, was out of the question. Oregon senator George Williams, who served with Johnson in the Senate and would later become Grant's third attorney general, said, "I had an impression of Mr. Johnson that he was not a man of very strong convictions and that he could speak with equal readiness and facility upon one side of a question, as upon the other, and that he was not very particular as to which side he espoused."[25]

The ability to present a dispassionate defense steeped in constitutional precedent, rather than an ideological screed that might fan Northern resentment and inspire additional federal intervention, was exactly what Hampton was looking for in the defense of the Ku Klux. Johnson's co-counsel in defending the Ku Klux, Stanbery, was also not an ideologue, but unlike Johnson he was "in no sense a politician" but rather "simply, plainly, a logical, clean-cut, close lawyer." Like Johnson, he was known for his thorough preparation for every case and for legal briefs that were "rare specimens of logic, perspicuity and force."[26] Also like Johnson, and which also made him either an odd or the perfect choice to defend the Ku Klux, Stanbery had professed anti-slavery views before the war.

Stanbery was born in New York City in 1803, but his father, a physician, moved the family to Zanesville, Ohio, in 1814. Known as a "studious boy," Stanbery entered Washington College in Pennsylvania at the age of twelve and graduated at sixteen. He then studied law under future Ohio US senator Thomas Ewing Sr., who had also served as secretary of the treasury under Presidents William Henry Harrison and Zachary Taylor.[27] Ewing was also the foster father of Union general William Tecumseh Sherman and also later his father-in-law when Sherman married Ewing's daughter, Ellen.

A Whig like his mentor, Stanbery was the first elected state attorney general of Ohio, and he opposed the expansion of slavery into the western territories. When the Whig Party dissolved over the issue of slavery in the 1850s, Stanbery became a Republican and an admirer of Lincoln. "His appearance was admirable," an observer said of Stanbery, "tall, straight, with a mild and impressive voice, courteous and dignified manner, and sound physique."[28] A reserved, but not unfriendly man, he commanded thousands of dollars in fees and became wealthy through the quality of his work rather than the force of his personality. A fellow attorney said that Stanbery did not possess any "marked characteristics," and meant it as a compliment.[29]

In 1866, President Andrew Johnson nominated Stanbery—then one of the nation's most prominent attorneys—to the US Supreme Court, but the already antagonistic Republican-led Senate refused to confirm the appointment. Johnson then named Stanbery as his attorney general, a post Stanbery held for barely a year before he resigned to lead Johnson's defense in the president's impeachment trial that occurred in the Senate over thirty-seven days in March, April, and May of 1868.

Stanbery, however, was in ill health during the Senate trial and did not speak but submitted his arguments to the senators in writing, leaving oral arguments to other members of the president's defense team. Those seeking to remove Johnson from office fell one short of the two-thirds vote necessary for conviction. Johnson renominated Stanbery to serve as attorney general once more, but a vindictive Republican Senate majority would not even consider the appointment, "more as a rebuke to the Executive than as an expression of unfriendliness to the nominee." But Stanbery, who considered himself a personal friend of Johnson's, took the rebuke personally and after the trial "his sympathies were with the Democratic party."[30] He was largely done with politics and returned to practice law in Cincinnati, from where he was summoned by Hampton.

III

Akerman was not intimidated by Hampton's strategy of securing nationally renowned attorneys to handle the Ku Klux defense. "Skillful lawyers residing on the spot can generally match men of eminence from a distance," he wrote, "the very fact of sending off for celebrated counsel often striking the jury as evidence of a cause inherently weak."[31] While he had briefly participated in an earlier Ku Klux trial in North Carolina, Akerman was too busy managing the Department of Justice and Ku Klux trials throughout the South to contemplate handling any courtroom duties in Columbia himself. He was also extremely confident in the abilities of his man "on the spot," US Attorney David T. Corbin.

The thirty-eight-year-old Corbin had asked for Akerman's help and with good reason. Already under stress from the death of his oldest son the year before, Corbin was overwhelmed with work. He had spent weeks in York County, conferring with Major Lewis Merrill and interviewing victims and potential witnesses himself. Preparing the scores of indictments, most written out in longhand without the help of a secretary, was an arduous task, made more so because Corbin was working in "uncharted constitutional territory." He was charging men with crimes that had not previously existed and which were created under statutes that were often unclear and sometimes provided contradictory direction.[32]

Corbin then had to prepare his arguments and questions for witnesses, all while under the pressure of knowing the trials would receive national attention, that opposing counsel included two of the most experienced and renowned attorneys in America, and that he could also be the victim of Ku Klux violence as retribution. To take some of the pressure off Corbin, Akerman secured the assistance of South Carolina attorney general Daniel H. Chamberlain, another transplanted Northerner.

The term "carpetbagger" is an epithet in American politics, meaning, as William Safire defines it in his *Political Dictionary*, "a man on the make."[33] During Reconstruction, it specifically meant a Northern man who had come South after the war to "take advantage of the Negro vote, gain election to office, and get rich by plundering the Southern people."[34] There were certainly grifters and shysters who came to the South to make money off the misfortune of those who had been part of the former Confederacy. But a large number of those pejoratively labeled "carpetbaggers" by Southern (and Northern) critics, including Corbin and Chamberlain, went South with much the same ideals possessed by Peace Corps volunteers a century later; they desired to help a people in need.

Northern transplants were initially welcomed in the South immediately after the war. They brought badly needed capital and helped inflate land values, which helped get more than a few planters out of debt. While the term was inspired by the image of a man so untethered to a community that he could fit all his worldly possessions in a carpetbag, a large number of so-called carpetbaggers were professionals, including lawyers, teachers, doctors, and newspaper editors. Many were Union army veterans who had served in the South and either enjoyed the country, the climate, and the culture, or they desired to help rebuild what they had first helped to destroy. As for possessing political aspirations, "nearly all" carpetbaggers arrived in the South before 1867 and thus before African-American men were granted the vote. Absent Black suffrage, the chance of a transplanted Northern Republican achieving political office in the South was "remote," so this seems an unlikely motivation for their relocation.[35]

While both men ended up in politics, neither Corbin or Chamberlain had initially come to South Carolina to make money or to seek office. They were Union veterans who had come to South Carolina for more altruistic reasons. This would not save either man from being savaged by critics of the time and later by historians whose agenda was to portray Reconstruction as a wicked conspiracy against a helpless but noble South.

"Dunning School" historian John S. Reynolds's *Reconstruction in South Carolina* was published in 1905, the height of the Jim Crow era and the same year Thomas Dixon's novel *The Clansman* was also published. Adopting the twee tone that Southern intellectuals of the period seemed to think conveyed chivalry, Reynolds lashed out at Corbin, claiming he:

> used his place as United States Attorney as a means of persecution in order to swell his fees—that he had helped to pack the juries in the Kuklux [sic] trials . . . that in those trials he had taken advantage of his office to insult a clergyman and speak disrespectfully to a lady . . . [and] that he was without one aspiration of a gentleman and never rose to the plane of reputable lawyer.[36]

The clergyman and the "lady" whom Corbin allegedly insulted had been charged with witness tampering and intimidation, as will be discussed in a later chapter.

It is debatable whether Corbin, despite Reynolds's assertions, felt any genuine hostility toward the South, given that it was his adopted home, but if he did he had fair reason.

Corbin was raised in Vermont, where he taught school and worked as a farm laborer to pay his way through Dartmouth College. Corbin had just begun practicing law when the war broke out. Enlisting as a private in the 3rd Vermont Volunteer Infantry Regiment, Corbin rose to the rank of captain and, at the Battle of Savage's Station in June 1862, was badly wounded and captured as a prisoner of war. He was sent to the Confederacy's infamous Libby Prison in Richmond, where he came close to dying until he was released in a prisoner exchange in the fall of 1862.

Honorably discharged, Corbin soon became restless to help the war effort and reenlisted in the Veteran Reserve Corps, which had been established for partially disabled soldiers who could still perform light duty. Corbin spent most of his time assigned to the judge advocate general. After the war's end, in the fall of 1865, he was ordered to report to Charleston, South Carolina, and work for the Freedmen's Bureau where he held Provost Court for Charleston and the nearby Sea Islands. He resigned his commission in 1867 and was immediately appointed US attorney for South Carolina by President Andrew Johnson. In 1868, he was also elected to a four-year term in the State Senate.[37]

While serving in the South Carolina Legislature, Corbin was considered by his peers as "one of the most conservative and fair of the Republican

Party."[38] He had wavy chestnut hair, a high hairline, and dark brown eyes that always seemed fixed in an intense and determined gaze. He was committed to destroying the Ku Klux, recognizing that efforts to pursue the conspiracy in state courts had been a "lamentable failure." In a letter to Akerman, Corbin expressed his philosophy that "the purpose of the U.S. Government is to secure every citizen his life, liberty, and property, and to protect them in their enjoyment." He was disgusted that civic leaders, including "many doctors and ministers of the gospel," were active in the Ku Klux. "They had the outside of gentlemen, but were found to have the inside of savages." He also seemed undaunted by his opposing counsel, passing on to Akerman the gossip that the seventy-five-year-old and nearly blind Johnson planned to use the Ku Klux trials in order to make a "go for the presidency."[39]

Corbin's notice of the political ambitions of others may have reflected his own aspirations. The *Charleston Daily News* noted that Corbin had secured several offices of public trust and speculated that "Major Corbin, finding his rather numerous duties as city attorney, district attorney, phosphate president, leader of the Senate and codifier of the laws" had arranged for Attorney General Chamberlain to conduct the prosecution on a day-to-day basis while Corbin attended to his duties in the State Senate.[40] While it had been Akerman who recruited Chamberlain's assistance, the state attorney general's presence did not free Corbin to attend to his other duties. The Ku Klux trials represented far too much work. Both men were in court together virtually every day of the trials, but the thirty-six-year-old Chamberlain was an invaluable addition to the prosecution team.

Unlike Johnson and Stanbery, who came from prominent families, Chamberlain's hardscrabble life was similar to Corbin's. The ninth of ten children in a Massachusetts farming family, Chamberlain was a gifted student who had to work his way through school. At seventeen, he taught school while working on the family farm but could still afford only a portion of one year at the Phillips Academy in Andover. At twenty-one, Chamberlain enrolled in Worcester High School, located twenty miles from his family's home and then one of the few public secondary schools in the United States. The school was free, but room and board were not. Chamberlain's admiring teachers were so anxious that he remain in school that he was made a part-time teacher. He worked and saved, but when the time came to enter Yale as a much-older-than-average freshman, he still had to borrow funds from his high school instructors, college professors, "and other generous and admiring friends."[41]

As a youth, Chamberlain had made a point of traveling to listen to the leading orators of the day, particularly abolitionists such as Charles Sumner, Henry Wilson, William Lloyd Garrison, and Wendell Phillips. Debate was the primary competitive collegiate sport of the day, and Chamberlain became Yale's finest debater, receiving a medal for excellence in oratory. Having also received top honors in English composition and a reputation as the "ablest politician on the campus," Yale's president wrote a letter of recommendation that described Chamberlain as "a born leader of men." Entering Harvard Law School in 1862, Chamberlain felt guilt at not enlisting in the Union army, but he owed his patrons nearly two thousand dollars for his Yale education and concluded he could not hope to repay his debts unless he earned his law degree. But by his second year, he knew he had to enlist or else "years hence I shall be ashamed to have it known that for any reason I did not bear a hand in this life-or-death struggle for the Union and for Freedom." He then borrowed even more money to purchase enough life insurance to pay off his creditors, should he be killed.[42]

One of his professors interceded with Massachusetts governor John Andrew to obtain a commission for Chamberlain as a lieutenant in the 5th Massachusetts Cavalry, a Black regiment. Chamberlain served primarily as an adjutant, keeping records, including for the regiment's final leader, Colonel Charles Francis Adams Jr., the historian and grandson and great-grandson of presidents. Chamberlain never saw combat, though he did see fallen Richmond at the end of the war.

Briefly stationed in the West along the Rio Grande, Chamberlain returned to Massachusetts after being mustered out of the service, but then headed south again, this time to South Carolina because of the death of one of his Yale classmates, James P. Blake. Blake had gone to the South Carolina Sea Islands after the war to serve as a teacher for and missionary to the freedmen and women, but he drowned in a boating accident. Blake's father asked Chamberlain to recover his son's body and settle his affairs. Blake's body, Chamberlain discovered, had washed out to sea and was never found, but after settling his friend's affairs he decided to stay, seduced by the "sensuous allure" of South Carolina's subtropical climate and the opportunity to make money and pay off his debts as a cotton planter.[43]

Chamberlain rented a plantation on Wadmalaw Island near Charleston, which placed him further in debt and proved to be a poor business decision. With cotton prices low, he did no better than break even. He was, however, selected as a delegate to the South Carolina constitutional convention of 1868, where he won admiration for his ability to explain complex legal and constitutional issues clearly and concisely. Of the 124 delegates to the convention, seventy-three were African American, yet for all the convention's progressive aims, white delegates sat in front of the meeting room and Blacks still sat in the back.[44]

The convention developed a remarkably forward-thinking constitution that embraced racial, political, and civil equality, expanded rights for women (including allowing a divorce without the old requirement of a legislative decree of approval), protected debtors through a homestead exemption, and established a previously nonexistent statewide public school system. The convention nominated a slate of candidates for the various state offices. The only African American nominated was Francis Cardozo as secretary of state. Chamberlain was nominated and then elected state attorney general, while another transplanted Northerner, General Robert Scott of Ohio, who had been running the Freedmen's Bureau in the state, was selected governor. Chamberlain had not finished law school and had never tried a case, but he was now the state government's top attorney. This admirer of abolitionists who had been an officer in a Black army regiment was also fully committed to the protection of African-American rights.

IV

Just as opposing legal counsel provided contrast between the aging Democratic lions Johnson and Stanbery and the young Republican Turks Corbin and Chamberlain, so, too, were those charged with arbitrating the Ku Klux trials dissimilar in temperament and philosophy—for the Ku Klux cases were presided over by not one but two judges sharing the bench. They were Radical Republican Judge Hugh Lennox Bond of Maryland, who was circuit judge for the Fourth Federal District, and Democrat and former slave-owner George Seabrook Bryan, who was the federal district court judge for South Carolina.

The Judiciary Act of 1869 had expanded the federal judiciary, setting the number of Supreme Court justices at nine (what it remains today), and creating nine new independent circuit court judges, one for each of the nation's nine circuit districts.* These circuit judges had the same powers and jurisdiction as Supreme Court justices and were intended to significantly reduce the time Supreme Court justices spent riding the circuits. The circuit judges held court with local federal district court judges as a means to reduce the alleged parochialism and partiality of local federal court judges.[45]

Between the two judges, Bond was the younger man but the more dominant personality during the trials, although each had demonstrated strong judicial independence and personal courage during their careers. Bryan, sixty-two when the Ku Klux trials began, was described as "elderly and faint-hearted," but he was younger than both Johnson and Stanbery and had a stellar career as a jurist.[46]

Bryan's father had been a Charleston merchant, but his grandfather had been a judge on the Pennsylvania Supreme Court and a delegate to the first colonial congress held in 1765 in New York City to protest the Stamp Act. Perhaps it was that heritage that made Bryan a strong Union man, for he was known before the Civil War as "one of the chief anti-secession leaders in South Carolina."[47] He had also been a Whig and a close personal friend of Henry Clay before the Whigs dissolved, which led to him eventually joining the Democratic Party.

Bryan's prewar anti-secession views made him a logical choice to be the first federal judge appointed in South Carolina after the war, a position he would hold for twenty years. As a federal judge, Bryan first gained national attention by demanding that Carolinians no longer be tried under military law but in open court. Bryan granted several writs of habeas corpus, but the local federal military commander, the colorful and controversial General Daniel Sickles of New York, refused to comply with the writs.† Bryan held Sickles in contempt, but Sickles refused to submit to arrest. Bryan appealed to President Johnson to enforce a lawful judicial decree. The matter was kicked to the Supreme Court, which sided with Bryan, ending martial law throughout the South.[48]

---

*Circuit riding and the circuit courts themselves were abolished in 1911, with much of their authority transferred to the US district courts.

†Sickles, born into a wealthy New York family, was involved in a host of scandals during his life, most notably the murder of his wife's alleged lover, the son of Francis Scott Key, a crime for which Sickles escaped punishment by being the first person to ever assert "temporary insanity" as a defense in an American courtroom.

Bryan was also the first judge in the South to refuse to administer the "test oath" to attorneys who sought to practice before the federal bar. The test oath meant that before attorneys could practice before the federal bar, they had to first swear that they had not served as officers in the Confederacy. As observers noted, this would have disqualified ninety-nine out of a hundred attorneys licensed to practice in South Carolina. Once again, the Supreme Court upheld Bryan's decision, which ended the test oath requirement for attorneys throughout the South.[49]

Despite Bryan's history of judicial independence, Bond concluded that he would need to take the lead in overseeing the Ku Klux trials. Before Bond arrived on the scene, Bryan had presided alone over several trials of suspected Ku Klux in Greenville, South Carolina, in August and September, but the juries refused to convict, a fact Bond blamed on Bryan's failure to "give the firm direction necessary to bring a successful prosecution."[50] Bond noted correctly that Bryan's past independence had been in defense of the South against federal intrusion, but in the Ku Klux trials he was under the sway of local opinion.

Wade Hampton himself had written Bryan before the trials to advise how important it was that he join Bond in presiding over the trials in Columbia. The pressure on Bryan to make rulings that would obstruct prosecution of the Ku Klux continued throughout the trials. "The democrats have got hold of him," Bond said of Bryan in a letter to his wife. "[They] visit him in crowds & persuade him to be a stick between our legs at every step." Bond charged, without much evidence, that "they have stuffed him full of the idea that the Democrats will make him Gov[ernor] if he differ with me." Bond became aggressive with his colleague, writing to his wife that "I went to him (Bryan) the other day & frightened him half to death. I stormed at him and told him . . . he had better not keep the court sitting doing nothing but posing about the smallest matter in the world day after day."[51]

Bond was not alone in his criticism of Bryan. Louis F. Post not only worked as a clerk for Merrill and as a court reporter, he also moonlighted as an anonymous correspondent for the *New York Tribune*. In an article published December 18, 1871, Post first ridiculed the sixty-year-old Bryan as a mediocre self-published poet, a "Carolina Dogberry," before providing this assessment of his judicial demeanor:*

---

*In Shakespeare's *Much Ado About Nothing*, Dogberry is a comical character, a pretentious and self-important night watchman given to malapropisms when he attempts to sound more sophisticated than he is.

It may be disrespectful to criticize the behavior of a judge, and bad taste to speak harshly of an old man, but if there are exceptional cases, he certainly is one. Judge Bryan, on the Bench, is weak, vacillating, ignorant, and old-womanish; and it may not be amiss to add that he is far from being always courteous to his presiding brother, and his whole bearing as associate Justice is marked by bad taste to the highest degree.[52]

If Post found Bryan discourteous to Bond, it is doubtful Bond noticed, for Bond reveled in his combative personality, a trait he may have first acquired fighting for food and attention as one of fifteen children in a family headed by a clergyman and physician who helped establish Baltimore's first medical school. But Bond, born in 1828, spent most of his childhood in New York City, where he graduated from the University of the City of New York (now called New York University) before returning to Baltimore to read and practice law. In 1860, at the age of thirty-two, he was appointed judge of the Baltimore Criminal Court.

Bond, who held strong anti-slavery views, joined the nativist American Party (more popularly known as the "Know-Nothings") before becoming a member of the anti-secession Union Party, given that the Republican Party was politically toxic in Maryland, a slave state. When war broke out, Southern sympathy was particularly high in Baltimore, but that did not dissuade Bond from striking down a city ordinance that banned city residents from flying the American flag. He also charged a grand jury to indict for murder city residents and Confederate sympathizers who, on April 19, 1861, ambushed and rioted against Union troops making their way through the city on their way to defend Washington, DC. The violence left four soldiers and twelve civilians dead and were the first deaths directly related to the Civil War. Admirers called him "fearless," but critics sent him death threats addressed to the "black-hearted, nigger-loving son of a bitch."[53]

With the Union Party in power, Maryland emancipated its eighty thousand slaves in 1864, but after the war the party split between a conservative faction, whose members rejoined the Democratic Party, and Radicals, who became Republicans. Bond was the Republican nominee for governor in 1866, but he was badly trounced, and Republicans did not win a single seat in the state house of delegates that year.

Bond instead advanced the interests of African Americans through philanthropy and his position on the bench. As in the South, Maryland under Democratic Party rule after the war instituted Black Codes. Bond was able to dismantle one particularly obnoxious statute that allowed planters to have Black children, including those with intact two-parent families, assigned to them as unpaid "apprentices" to do manual labor. A quirk in Maryland law allowed Bond to hear writs of habeas corpus from petitioners anywhere in the state. For these re-enslaved children, Bond issued dozens of writs, "invariably" releasing the children to their parents. His efforts attracted the attention of US Supreme Court chief justice Salmon P. Chase, who was doing circuit duty in Baltimore, and who declared the apprenticeship laws unconstitutional.[54]

While Maryland's schools were not legally segregated, in practice Black children were not permitted to attend public schools. But Bond, a devout Methodist, believed Christians had a duty to help educate African Americans. He was active in an association dedicated to building and staffing schools for African Americans. In the association's first year of existence in 1865, the group opened twenty-five schools that served three thousand pupils; two years later, there were eighty schools established to teach Black children. Despite these efforts to elevate the status of African Americans, Bond believed "blacks to be inherently inferior to whites, [but] he also believed that the races shared a common humanity that required equality of citizenship without roiling the prevailing social system."[55] This concern for African Americans did not extend to support for social welfare programs, which Bond said "tends to idleness."[56] Nor did he contemplate anything approaching social equality, saying, "To make a man equal before the law does not make it obligatory for me to eat, sleep or drink with him."[57]

As he now prepared to preside over the Ku Klux trials, Bond was aware of the enormity of the task at hand. Of his Carolina hosts he said, "It will take a moral Ajax to wrest from these people the accumulated prejudice of two centuries and make them believe in the common brotherhood of man."[58] Aware of how deep such prejudices ran, Bond worried about the combustible nature of local opinion and confided to his wife, "I fear that we will not be able to control the court, tempers run very high, and the populace is unsettled."[59]

CHAPTER EIGHT

The Constitution of the United States is on trial.
—THE CHARLESTON DAILY COURIER

I

In its November 27, 1871, Monday edition, the *Charleston Daily Courier* left no doubt as to their view of the importance of the trials set to begin that day in Columbia. "The Constitution of the United States is on trial," the newspaper trumpeted. "In the history of this country no questions more important have ever arisen or been presented to a judicial tribunal for adjudication than are those which will arise in the trials now to take place."[1]

The size of the courtroom gallery and the prominence of many of its members, including Wade Hampton, who sat at the defense table, testified to the historic nature of the trials, but the setting and the initial arguments made the occasion seem less momentous.

With Columbia still rebuilding from the fire that destroyed most of the central city in 1865, a new federal courthouse and post office was still under construction. The Ku Klux trials instead opened in the ballroom of the Nickerson House Hotel. The Nickerson, with its distinctive seventy-foot-high bell tower, was not the poshest hotel in Columbia, and until a few years before had not been a hotel at all; it had housed the Columbia Female College.* On the ballroom stage, an impromptu bench had been placed where Bond and Bryan sat. Flanking the judges' bench, also up on

---

*Several weeks later, the trials were relocated to the more elegant surroundings of the library room of the State Capitol.

the stage, were tables where reporters from local and national newspapers, including from New York and Chicago, took copious notes, another sign of the significance of the occasion.

Centered below the stage, the tables reserved for opposing counsel and the officers of the court were arranged in the shape of a T. On one side sat Corbin, Chamberlain, Major Merrill, and others assisting with the prosecution. Chamberlain's involvement in the prosecution had not been widely known beforehand, and his appearance caused a stir in the room. On the opposite side of the table were the defense counsel: Johnson and Stanbery, several local attorneys who were assisting in the defense, and their patron, Hampton, and Hampton's son.

A variety of other court officials sat wherever they could find room. This included Johnson's son, Louis, who was, ironically, the US marshal for South Carolina, his deputies, the bailiff, and others who, in the flowery description of the *Charleston Daily News* correspondent, "disposed themselves in negligent but not ungraceful attitudes upon the steps of the stage." On each side of the room were chairs arranged in double rows for the prospective jurors—one side for the soon-to-be-empaneled grand jury, the other for the petit juries who would hear the trials. Along the sides of the room and further back were chairs for the large audience. Whites and African Americans sat on different sides of the room; the juries would be integrated, but the galleries remained segregated.[2]

If the crowd expected the fireworks to begin immediately, they were disappointed.

While great constitutional issues were at stake and grisly details of criminal behavior were soon to be detailed, the court first had to address controversy over jury selection. The night before the trials were to begin, Bond wrote to his wife that because of the process that had involved the African-American boy, "the jury has been drawn all wrong" and he expected the process would have to start again. Not only would this delay the proceedings by weeks, Bond worried the issue would allow critics to allege the government was seeking "packed juries."[3]

But even before that issue could be addressed, after the court was gaveled into session, "two tedious hours" were occupied by calling the names of prospective jurors whose names had been pulled from the jury box nearly three months before by the boy.[4] After thirty names had been called, Corbin rose and challenged the jury selection process, worried that any impropriety would provide an opening for the Ku Klux to appeal any convictions. Corbin did not object to having the jury names drawn by the boy, which he acknowledged was "an old custom sanctioned previously by this state," but federal procedure required that not only the clerk of court but also a US marshal be present when the names were drawn. Chief Deputy Marshal Edward P. Butts was initially present when the boy began drawing names but was then called away; Horlbeck, however, did not stop the selection process to wait for Butts's return.[5]

Johnson, surprisingly so, since it did close one possible avenue of appeal for his clients, offered to waive any objections to the process by which prospective jurors had been selected, and so Corbin withdrew his challenge. Johnson, however, had another complaint. The problem was that the initial draw had simply not provided enough prospective jurors to fill the grand jury and the several petit (trial) juries that would be necessary to handle the several cases before the court. Of the scores of names drawn by the small boy back in August, only thirty people had answered the call to jury service—eight for the grand jury and twenty-two for the petit juries—and most of them were African-American.[6]

Whites whose names were drawn had generally refused to answer the call when contacted for jury duty. Some whites whose names were drawn disapproved of the trials and boycotted. Others were fearful of Ku Klux retribution were they to serve on juries that would at the least expose Ku Klux crimes and those involved, even if no conviction was obtained. But the biggest obstacle to white participation was federal law.

The Enforcement Acts of 1871, known as "The Ku Klux Klan Acts," required every juror in a federal civil rights trial to take an oath that they were not and had never been members of the Ku Klux or of any conspiracy that went "in disguise upon any public highway . . . for the purpose, either directly or indirectly, of depriving any person, or any class of persons, of the equal protection of the laws, or of equal privileges or immunities under the law."[7] This was a quandary for thousands of potential white jurors who were Ku Klux: Respond that you could not serve on a federal jury because you were or had been Ku Klux and there was the possibility of arrest and prosecution for being part of the conspiracy; lie under oath and insist you were not Ku Klux and, if discovered, you were exposed to the possibility of being prosecuted for perjury.

As the court weighed what to do to secure more jurors, Johnson challenged the idea that prospective jurors should come from all across South Carolina. He said jurors should instead come only from the Western District of South Carolina where all the defendants resided so they could truly be tried by a jury of their peers. The threat of juror intimidation was not openly articulated, but it is clear Johnson hoped that jurors from western South Carolina would be more likely to acquit defendants who lived nearby, since the accused might, along with family and friends, seek retribution against jurors who voted to convict. Corbin countered that the trial was being conducted by the Fourth Circuit Court of the United States, which encompassed all of South Carolina, and Bond concurred with Corbin's reasoning. He gave the US marshal forty-eight hours to summon more prospective jurors from all across South Carolina, and when the court reconvened there were enough jurors to empanel a grand jury.[8]

Once again, most whites refused to answer the call, and so most jurors who participated in the trials were Black, including fifteen of the twenty-one grand jurors, although the foreman was white. The pool for the trial juries was two-thirds Black, meaning that every jury in the Ku Klux trials was majority Black, and in several cases eleven of the twelve jurors were African-American. Even though two-thirds of the grand jury were African Americans who would have understood the strain under which witnesses testified, Bond still charged them to "exercise great patience. Many of the witnesses are laboring under a great deal of unusual excitement, many of them are ignorant people not accustomed to appearing in Courts, and it is absolutely necessary that you should bear with them patiently."[9]

Southern (and many Northern) newspapers were considerably less patient and kind regarding African-American participation in the trials. A trial in which a majority of the jurors were Black was a "farce ... being acted in the United States Court under the name of a trial," the *Charleston Daily Courier* opined, neglecting to mention that the lack of white participation in the juries was largely by choice. Southern newspapers also sneered at Black witnesses brought to Columbia to testify, ignoring that African-American witnesses were risking their lives to testify against men already on trial for assaulting, raping, and murdering African Americans. The *Daily Courier* called the witnesses "lazy and idle looking negroes" anxious to be "paid and clothed at government expense," adding in a later editorial that African-American witnesses would "swear to anything" in return for the two dollars per day they were paid to be in Columbia.[10]

While Southern (and many Northern) newspapers heaped scorn on the Black jurors, deriding them, as they also did Black legislators, Black officials, and Blacks of any station, as lazy and ignorant, African Americans called to jury service took their duties seriously. And, if not for the color of their skin, most would have instead been labeled pillars of their communities. Many, according to the 1870 federal census, were literate and owned property.

Juror Ephraim Johnson, who lived in Georgetown and was about sixty years old, worked as a drayman and owned land valued at six hundred dollars. Committed to education, Johnson later became an ordained Methodist minister, and two of his children, according to 1880 Census records, became schoolteachers. Joseph Keene, who was also about sixty and listed as a "mulatto" in the 1870 Census, was a particularly prosperous farmer. He owned real estate valued at fifteen hundred dollars and personal property valued at five hundred dollars. Andrew Curtis was one of the younger jurors at age twenty-nine, and owned a much smaller farm, valued at five hundred dollars. He supplemented his income by working at a Columbia cotton mill, but he, his wife, and seven-year-old daughter were all literate. Joseph Taylor, fifty, was a farm laborer who owned no land, and his wife, Eliza, was a washerwoman, but both could read and write and had enrolled their daughter, India, in school, while a second child, Alexander, was also literate. Some of the jurors were illiterate, such as Henry Daniel, of Columbia, but the thirty-year-old Daniel, who was single, lived with his parents, and worked as a farm laborer, was also a Union army veteran, having served in Company E of the 2nd Regiment, Colored Light Artillery.

The jurors only got to speak publicly during the voir dire process, but they demonstrated a sober approach to their impending duties. January

Simpson, a seventy-year-old farmer who lived near Columbia, was asked if he had any preconceived notions of the defendants' guilt or innocence, and replied, "I cannot tell anything until I've heard the evidence."[11] Likewise, when John H. Pugh was asked if he had already formed an opinion in the case, he replied, "I could not, because I have no knowledge of it."[12] Not all jurors were accepted, including Pugh. E. C. Rainey was rejected because he had recently served on a jury in a case where Bond was the presiding judge. Stanbery had no objection to Pugh from the defense side, but Corbin used one of his preemptory challenges to ask Pugh to "stand aside" for reasons he did not articulate.

Despite the often-complex instructions provided by Bond regarding complicated constitutional questions, there was no recorded incident of misbehavior by any juror during the trials, nor did anything involving the juries become the basis for appeal. While unpopular with whites, African Americans began regularly serving on juries until the advent of Jim Crow laws in the 1890s, and even some critics in the South acknowledged it had not negatively impacted the justice system. An editor of the *Houston Telegraph*, a newspaper whose acknowledged "sympathies are not with the newly enfranchised citizen," reported before the Ku Klux trials that "[t]he experiment of negro jurors . . . has been tried in this country, and I am glad to say that, while humiliating, it has been attended with no serious results."[13]

II

When a half dozen Ku Klux burst into Amzi Rainey's home on the night of March 22, 1871, he climbed into the loft of his cabin and hid in a box, but the Ku Klux were beating his wife and threatening to kill her if he did not come out, so he did. At that point, one of his younger daughters, who was about ten years old, came out of a back room and begged the Ku Klux, "Don't kill my pappy; please don't kill my pappy!" One of the Ku Klux shoved her back and said, "You go back in the room, you God damned little bitch; I will blow your brains out!" He then pointed and fired his pistol, striking the little girl in the forehead. The ball glanced off her head, but the wound, while spurting large amounts of blood, was not mortal.[14]

The blood seemed to excite the Ku Klux like a frenzy of sharks, and they began randomly firing their weapons throughout Rainey's house—Rainey guessed he heard about fifteen shots—before they set his clothes on fire and then, laughing uproariously, yelled at him to "put out that fire," or else he would burn up and "go to hell." His injured daughter's cupped hands were now full of blood, which she threw to the floor as the Ku Klux dragged her father outside and about 150 yards from the house. There he was surrounded by an estimated twenty-five Ku Klux who seemed intent on killing him. But one of the Ku Klux leaders said, "Let's talk a little to him first," and asked Rainey how he had voted in the past election. "I told them I voted the Radical ticket," Rainey said, recognizing such a candid admission might prove fatal. The Ku Klux leader told Rainey to raise his right hand and swear that he would never vote Republican again and he could live. Rainey took this oath and was allowed to run back to his home as the Ku Klux pelted him with rocks "about the size of my fist," Rainey said. When he got back to his home, he discovered several Ku Klux had stayed behind to rape his fifteen-year-old daughter in the presence of his wife and a half dozen of his younger children.[15]

The nauseating assault on Rainey and his family, including the shooting of a young child, was the case that led to the first indictments issued by the just-empaneled grand jury. A few weeks before court convened, Akerman noted that Major Merrill had already secured confessions from 250 alleged Ku Klux just in York County. Reading Merrill's reports, Akerman could only shake his head in despair. In a letter to General Terry, Akerman wrote:

I doubt from the beginning of the world until now, a community, nominally civilized, has been so fully under the domination of systematic and organized depravity. If the people of the North really understood it, there would be an outbreak of indignation unparalleled since April, 1861. To those, however, who have not been there, or are in a similar state of society, the truth is incredible; but if half of it comes forth, and is credited, the country will sustain all that has been done, and will insist that Congress shall furnish, and that the Executive shall apply remedies still more energetic. . . . I feel greatly saddened by this business. It has revealed a perversion of moral sentiment among Southern whites which bodes ill to that part of the country for this generation. Without a thorough moral renovation, society there for many years will be—I can hardly bring myself to say savage, but certainly far from Christian.[16]

Those 250 confessions plus Merrill's investigations had yielded an extraordinary amount of information on a host of crimes involving hundreds more suspected Ku Klux who had not confessed. The problem was that the federal justice system had nowhere near the resources to prosecute all these cases, even if confined to just South Carolina. Akerman had initially urged Corbin to focus prosecution on Ku Klux leaders or men of standing in the community as a lesson to other Ku Klux, but with so many prominent members of the Ku Klux having fled to avoid prosecution, the focus now shifted to those cases most likely to result in convictions and those most likely to resolve the constitutional issues at play.

Under Akerman's direction, Corbin and Chamberlain sought cases that provided the opportunity for the broadest possible interpretation of the Fourteenth and Fifteenth Amendments and the accompanying Enforcement Acts. Without judicial interpretation, these new amendments were a collection of words without definition. The Fourteenth Amendment referenced the "privileges and immunities" of citizenship when there was no constitutional definition and no national consensus of what those privileges and immunities were. Also open to interpretation was the degree to which federal law now superseded what had traditionally been state prerogatives.

In selecting the Rainey case as the first of the several expected trials, Corbin believed he had found a case perfect for the prosecution's goals. Corbin reported to Akerman that Rainey was a "most respectable mulatto," who had "always maintained an excellent character."[17] Given that Rainey could have caused no other offense, it seemed clear to Corbin that the only reason Rainey was attacked and his family terrorized was that he had voted Republican and was a vocal supporter of the hated local Republican congressman Alexander "Buttermilk" Wallace. The political purpose of the raid was evident by the Ku Klux's insistence that Rainey take an oath to never vote Republican again. Rainey's good character, the cruelty exhibited, and the clear political motivation behind the attack, Corbin thought, made this an excellent first case to bring to trial and possibly have it certified to the US Supreme Court for a ruling on those constitutional questions requiring resolution. For the assault on Rainey and his family, the grand jury issued an eleven-count indictment against seven alleged Ku Klux: Allen Crosby, Sherod Childers, Banks Kell, Evans Murphy, Hezekiah Porter, Sylvanus Hemphill, and William Montgomery.

But before any witnesses could take the stand to provide riveting and graphic testimony, Johnson and Stanbery moved to quash all eleven counts of the indictment, which led to a robust debate over what federal crimes had been committed in the raid on the Rainey family.

Corbin was among those who believed the Fourteenth Amendment had radically altered the relationship between the national and state governments. He believed that the Fourteenth Amendment changed the Bill of Rights from a negative restriction on federal power into a positive conveyance of civil rights ("privileges and immunities") now enjoyed by all citizens individually, and which the federal government was now duty-bound to protect when the states would not. Corbin was particularly hopeful that the courts would agree these rights went beyond the right of African-American men to vote, because otherwise African-American women and children, often the victims of some of the most heinous Ku Klux crimes, would be beyond federal protection because they had no right to vote.

The eleven-count indictment filed by Corbin therefore did not limit the charges to the Ku Klux denying Rainey his right to vote, but also with violating his constitutional rights under the Fourth Amendment to be free of unreasonable search and seizures. The indictments also tied this denial of Rainey's civil rights to a variety of common crimes such as assault, burglary, and breaking and entering—crimes that would typically be prosecuted in state courts.[18]

Corbin acknowledged he was experimenting and conceded the novelty of "setting up Constitutional rights in an indictment." But, he wrote Akerman, the more he studied the new amendments "the more I am convinced that the citizens of the Country generally may appeal to it under the legislation of Congress, and many a poor man in the South will rejoice that it is so."[19]

But Corbin acknowledged that a successful prosecution of the Ku Klux would be "a very difficult matter."[20] He would have to prove that the attacks on Rainey and other Ku Klux targets were not random acts of violence that would fall under state jurisdiction for prosecution (which state authorities had repeatedly declined to do), but rather these attacks were made for the "special intent" of using violence as a tool to intentionally deny another person their lawful civil rights.

III

As Ku Klux counsel, Johnson and Stanbery argued that the Fourteenth Amendment had not changed the federal system at all, nor had the Fifteenth Amendment conferred a right to vote. Several counts of the indictments referenced the "right of suffrage," but Stanbery asserted there is no federally guaranteed right to vote and few federally guaranteed rights. Period.

Rights emanate from the states, not the national government, Stanbery said, adding "there are very few rights that I can go to a Federal tribunal to vindicate."[21] Under the Constitution, Stanbery said, states, not the federal government, set voting requirements, and states have wide latitude to do so around such qualifications as age, literacy, ownership of property, and gender. The Wyoming Territory, for example, had just two years earlier granted the vote to women, "the softer sex," Stanbery noted with amazement. The Fifteenth Amendment had only ensured that these qualifications had to be equally applied and could not vary based on the race of the potential voter. "All that Congress has done is to say that where a white man can vote, a black man, who has equal qualifications, shall vote," Stanbery argued.[22]

Stanbery then questioned how an assault that occurred on March 22, 1871, could deny Rainey the right to vote in an election that would not be held until November 1872. A right "is not property or a chattel that can be seized and converted to another's use," Stanbery said. "The *power* to vote is another thing, but I am now speaking of the right," he said.[23] Certainly, a person could be prevented from voting, Stanbery said, but that would require the person being restrained from voting on the specific date of the election. The prosecution could not possibly prove that an assault that occurred in March was intended to govern the action of an individual in November of the following year, Stanbery said. In fact, Stanbery argued, there was no evidence that the Ku Klux beat Rainey and shot and raped his daughters just "so that he could not vote."[24]

Stanbery also objected to the indictments' references to burglary and breaking and entering, since the federal government had no authority to prosecute these types of crimes. The only exception would be if a federal officer was assaulted while exercising their official duties, he said, but that was not the case in the assault on Rainey and his family. The only crimes specifically mentioned in the Constitution that are under federal jurisdiction, Stanbery noted, are treason, counterfeiting, and piracy—none of which applied in these cases.[25]

Contrary to Corbin's belief that the Fourteenth Amendment had dramatically transformed the American constitutional system, Stanbery countered that it had done no more than declare that anyone born in the United States or who was naturalized was a citizen. That was it. He glibly summarized the three Reconstruction amendments—the Thirteenth, Fourteenth, and Fifteenth—as follows: "In the first place, slavery was abolished; then, they [former slaves] were made citizens of the United States. Finally, that [Fifteenth] amendment provides that there shall be no discrimination against any citizens of the United States because of their color or previous condition."[26] Corbin was wrong, Stanbery said: As the Supreme Court had ruled repeatedly before the war, the Bill of Rights was still limited to being only a restriction on federal power. All individual rights were guaranteed by the states. "Great God!" he exclaimed. "Have we forgotten altogether that we are citizens of States, and that we have States to protect us?"[27]

But the Southern states, including South Carolina, were not protecting the rights of many of its citizens, Corbin countered. In South Carolina, no protection under civil authority was being provided for a majority of its citizens, as 60 percent of the state's residents were African-American. Stanbery's argument represented the Constitution as it was, Corbin said, not the Constitution as it emerged from "the revolution we have recently had," referencing both the Civil War and the adoption of the three new constitutional amendments.[28]

Where the Founding Fathers had worried about the national government encroaching on individual rights, the Fourteenth Amendment recognized that it was now the states who were encroaching on the civil rights of citizens, Corbin said. Sometimes, as in the adoption of the noxious Black Codes, these states were denying equal protection of the law through state power. But in other instances, the states were denying equal protection of the law through "inaction" by refusing to protect its citizens from outrages, such as those perpetrated by the Ku Klux, or to prosecute those responsible for those outrages. While this was a sin of omission rather than commission, the result was the same, Corbin said: African Americans and whites voting Republican were being denied the ability to freely exercise their rights as citizens.[29]

The court could no longer only interpret the Constitution "as it was given to us in early days," Corbin said; rather, constitutional interpretation now needed to take into account "the history of the country, and in light of recent events, and with reference to the purpose which Congress and the people of the United States had in passing the Fourteenth and Fifteenth amendments."[30] Corbin could not help but note that Johnson, while still senator from Maryland, had voted in favor of the Fourteenth Amendment. "I would like to have known then, and would like to know now, what he meant by it."[31]

Corbin challenged Stanbery's notion that the right to vote could only be interfered with on election day. "The right . . . to vote is a continuing right—one that exists at all times, and is liable to be exercised at any and all times, as occasion requires," Corbin said. "It is the source of power. It is a right that exists in citizens; and to intimidate a person to prevent him from voting at any time between elections is a conspiracy."[32]

Chamberlain joined in the rebuttal to Stanbery by emphasizing that the seven defendants in the assault on Rainey were not being charged with burglary or assault, but that these actions were the tools used by the Ku Klux conspiracy to prevent Rainey from voting. That this was the Ku Klux's intent in raiding Rainey's home was evident from the facts, Chamberlain argued:

They break violently into his house, that they smite down his wife, and next ravish his daughter, and then fell him to the floor, that then they drag him forth upon the public highway, and, when the controversy rages high whether he shall be hung or simply whipped, they tell him that if he will hold up his right hand and swear before God that he will never again exercise his own free choice in the matter of suffrage, his life shall be spared.[33]

What complicated the issue was that Congress, in approving the Enforcement Acts, had developed a convoluted alternative system for determining what penalty should be imposed on those convicted of trying to deny a citizen the exercise of their rights. One section of the Enforcement Acts devoted to penalties was straightforward: Convictions could result in a prison term of up to ten years and a fine not to exceed five thousand dollars. But Congress also provided an alternative where the sentence could be equal to the penalty typically assessed for whatever crime was used in that conspiracy. In other words, if a Ku Klux was found guilty of denying a person their civil rights by beating that person, then the penalty could be the same as was typical for assault and battery. If the Ku Klux murdered a person to prevent them from exercising their rights, then the penalty could be life imprisonment or death. Corbin admitted this was an odd construct, but said, "Congress has a right to measure the punishment in any way it pleases, and it has adopted that mode. I admit it is inconvenient—excessively so [and] I would very much prefer that Congress had done it differently; but what has the Court to do with that?"[34]

IV

Responding to Corbin's question of what he believed the Fourteenth Amendment meant when he voted to ratify it in the US Senate, Johnson first noted he had also voted in favor of the Thirteenth Amendment to abolish slavery, curiously adding, "How it will turn out—how it has turned out—is a matter upon which differences of opinion exist."[35] As to the Fourteenth Amendment, Johnson insisted that while the amendment confirmed African Americans were citizens, the only right it conveyed to African Americans was the right to sue in the federal courts. It certainly did not grant African Americans the right to vote, or it would have said so. Had Congress tried to take the right to regulate suffrage from the states, "it would never have been adopted by the people of the United States," Johnson said.[36]

Just the opposite had occurred, Johnson said. The Fourteenth Amendment does not ban states from excluding African Americans from voting, but only outlines a severe penalty for doing so through the loss of proportional representation in Congress. In other words, a state that specifically denied African Americans the right to vote would not be allowed to include African Americans in their census population counts when congressional representation was being considered. Because African Americans composed 60 percent of South Carolina's population, denying African Americans the right to vote would cause South Carolina to lose 60 percent of its seats in the US House. While the Fifteenth Amendment does prevent states from denying the vote based on race, Johnson said the point was that the Fourteenth Amendment conceded the power to regulate voting lies with the states so violations of voting law should be handled at the state, not federal, level.[37]

Johnson expressed amazement that the men who assaulted Rainey on March 22 could be charged under a law that did not take effect until April 20. Corbin and Chamberlain responded that the men were being charged for being part of an ongoing conspiracy—the Ku Klux. "Oh, say my brothers, you are to punish it, because conspiracy is always a continuing act," Johnson said. "Then, I suppose it goes on still. I suppose, therefore, that any man who is alleged to have been initiated into the conspiracy two years ago, or one year ago, or ten years ago, might be now, and punished at all times. Once a criminal, he is forever a criminal!"[38]

Johnson also attacked the strange way that Congress had structured the punishment for violating the Enforcement Acts. Since common law crimes such as assault or breaking and entering could only be prosecuted in state courts, the federal crime established by the acts was denying another person their civil rights. But instead of simply mandating a set penalty of prison time and/or a fine for denying someone their civil rights, the punishment was supposed to match the state penalty for the common law crime that was committed in the course of denying the civil right. This bizarre construct, Johnson said, meant that the prosecution would need to first prove a burglary or murder had occurred and then also prove that the motive behind the crime was to deny a person their civil rights in order for the case to fall under federal jurisdiction.[39]

If the indictments were not struck down, Johnson said the court would have to give juries in these cases this instruction: "We ask you, gentlemen, when you render your verdict, to find, substantially, two verdicts—'Guilty of violating the Act of Congress,' and 'guilty of having committed a crime punishable by the laws of South Carolina.'" But if South Carolina had jurisdiction over a crime, then that preempted federal jurisdiction. It was nonsensical, Johnson said, for Corbin and Chamberlain to assert that federal prosecution for a violation of the Enforcement Acts did not preempt South Carolina from exercising its own authority to prosecute the same offense as a common law crime within its jurisdiction. What if, Johnson asked, "the offense alleged to have been committed in the perpetration of the conspiracy was murder, and the man who is charged with having committed that capital offense is hung, the Courts of South Carolina could hang him again[?] If that is what they mean, why I deny it. They have not the lives of a cat. . . . A man is not to be tried and punished twice for the same offense."[40]

After this lengthy peroration, Johnson pleaded exhaustion and asked the courts if he might say just "a few more words"—and then spent another thirty minutes challenging Grant's authority to suspend habeas corpus, a power previously only used during wartime:

> *The war is not over, it seems. Are we in a state of rebellion now? Or does it rage within the limits of South Carolina? They say there was an organization within the State of South Carolina which looked to depriving some citizens of the State of the rights secured to them by the Constitution. I have regretted it. But is that rebellion? Why, in that sense, every crime that is perpetrated is a rebellion.*[41]

Despite the significant constitutional questions raised, Judges Bond and Bryan rendered their decision on the motion to quash the indictments the following morning. Bond said both judges were "embarrassed" to rule after so little deliberation, but the backlog of cases meant expedience was necessary. "The fact that so many persons are now in confinement upon these charges, and that so many witnesses are in attendance upon the Court, at great personal expense, makes it necessary that we should not delay longer," he said.[42] His haste prevented Bond from formulating a thoughtful basis for his decision; he failed to even mention how the Fourteenth Amendment might have altered the federal government's authority to enforce civil rights.

Bond was struggling to balance his desire to see African Americans protected from Ku Klux outrages while staying true to his generally conservative and traditionalist constitutional beliefs. He and Bryan agreed to uphold two of the eleven counts in the indictments, agreed to quash six of the counts, and were divided in opinion as whether to quash the remaining three counts. The judges upheld the first and eleventh counts of the indictments. One count referenced that Rainey had been attacked particularly because of his support of Congressman Wallace. The federal government clearly had jurisdiction over elections for federal office, so this count should stand, Bond said. Bond also rejected Stanbery's argument that the only time a person may interfere with another's right to vote is on election day and upheld another count that charged the defendants with trying to impede Rainey's right to vote. "A man may be so effectually intimidated weeks before an election that he would not dare go within a mile of the polls, and all the mischief the Act is intended to remedy would flourish," Bond said.[43]

Of the half dozen counts that were quashed, Bond and Bryan agreed several were so vaguely written "the defendants could not possibly know, from its language, with what offense they were charged." They also rejected Corbin's argument that private individuals could violate the Fourth Amendment right of a person to be free from an unreasonable search and seizure. The Fourth Amendment applied only to government action, not private individuals breaking into a home. The right of a person to be secure in their home is not derived from the Constitution, they ruled, but from common law, and so was a violation for the state, not federal, courts to hear.[44]

Bond acknowledged that he was willing to proceed on those counts that referenced ordinary crimes, such as burglary, as the measure for how to determine the proper punishment for a civil rights violation, telling his wife in a letter, "Whether this case ought to be tried in the U.S. Courts or the State tribunals is a legitimate matter for arguments."[45] Judge Bryan, however, thought otherwise and would not allow those counts to proceed.

It was an unsatisfying ruling all around. Corbin had already complained that Congress, in both the constitutional amendments and the Enforcement Acts, had used such "indefinite" language that it left "the Court, the attorney, and the people to grope around to find out what they mean. But it is the policy of Congress, not 'my policy,'" he said, and he could only do his best to ascertain what Congress meant.[46] On the plus side, the narrowness of the court's ruling simplified the indictment process going forward so that Corbin and Chamberlain "could attend to the prosecution."[47]

Still, even though the assault on Rainey had not yielded the case on which larger constitutional issues might be settled, Bond—and even Bryan—had found a way to prosecute the Ku Klux in federal court. It was instructive, though, that Bond had not allowed the prosecution of the Ku Klux to go forward because of the new constitutional amendments, but because he believed the federal government had always had jurisdiction over federal elections. This would set the parameters for the trials to follow, which were much more limited than Akerman and his team of prosecutors would have hoped.

Crosby and his six comrades never went to trial for their raid on Rainey. Given the narrow scope of the indictments, it was a case that neither the prosecution nor the defense wanted to see certified to the US Supreme Court. For both the defense and the prosecution, resolving the constitutional issues at play took precedence over justice for the victims or determining the guilt or innocence of the accused. The defense reached a bargain with the prosecution. Those charged with assaulting Rainey would plead guilty to the two remaining counts if the next case, which involved the murder of Jim Williams, would be certified to the Supreme Court.

How Crosby and the other defendants felt about this arrangement is not recorded, but each of the men charged with assaulting Rainey received sentences of eighteen months in prison and fines of one hundred dollars in return for their guilty pleas, as Bond and Bryan, having already quashed those indictments that referenced common law crimes, simply ignored the convoluted alternative sentencing methodology that had been the subject of so much debate.

The defendants were quizzed before sentencing, and a theme emerged that would continue throughout the following trials: Those who appeared in court insisted they had been coerced into joining the Ku Klux or had joined while not understanding what the Ku Klux was about, and while they admitted that they had joined a raid or two, they would not admit to actively participating in any of the whippings or other more serious crimes. After a fourth consecutive defendant insisted he had only "staid with the horses" while others committed the actual violence against Rainey and his family, Bond sighed and asked what appeared to be a rhetorical question: "It turns out that those who happen to be indicted didn't do anything, and all those that haven't been caught, did the whipping?"[48]

Given the horrific nature of the crimes committed against Rainey, his wife, and daughters, the sentences seem light, but Crosby, Childers, et al., were small fish, mostly young men, semiliterate at best, and clearly not leaders of the Ku Klux. The prosecution hoped for a bigger catch in the next trial, which involved two of York County's most prominent citizens, the particularly heinous lynching of Williams, and whether that murder was a violation of Williams's Second Amendment right to bear arms.

CHAPTER NINE

The right to bear arms is not a right given by the Constitution of the United States.

—*Ku Klux legal counsel Reverdy Johnson*

I

Protecting the rights to vote, testify in court, and serve on juries were all necessary to ensure African Americans could exercise their new full rights of citizenship, but the most important of all the Bill of Rights as far as the freedmen and women were concerned was the Second Amendment right to own firearms. Without weapons, African Americans could not defend their homes from Ku Klux predations and guarantee their own or their family's safety. What was an African American to do when a Ku Klux invaded his home and assaulted him and his family, asked Missouri senator Charles Drake while Congress debated the first Enforcement Act. "Throw a pillow at him instead of a bullet?"[1]

"If there is any right that is dear to the citizen, it is the right to keep and bear arms, and it was secured to the citizens of the United States on the adoption of the amendments to the Constitution," Corbin said, referencing his belief that the Fourteenth Amendment meant that the Bill of Rights no longer simply limited the power of the federal government, but instead expressly guaranteed those rights to individuals citizens.[2] Further, Corbin was still trying to find a way by which the federal government could intervene to protect African-American women and children, who did not have the right to vote and who would need other protections under the law beyond the Fifteenth Amendment protection from racial discrimination in voting.

The case on which Corbin planned to defend his theory of a new federal guarantee of the Second Amendment was the lynching of Jim Williams. He had drawn up two sets of indictments for two separate groups of alleged perpetrators, numbering more than thirty persons in all. Among those included in the first indictment were Major James W. Avery and Dr. James Rufus Bratton, the two alleged York County leaders of the Ku Klux who had masterminded and directed Williams's murder back in March. Avery and Bratton, however, had fled South Carolina months before and were unavailable to stand trial—for the time being.

Given that the key defendants were not present to stand trial, an agreement was reached between prosecutors and defense counsel and blessed by Bond and Bryan whereby the case against Avery and Bratton was certified directly to the US Supreme Court in hopes that the high court would address two questions: Was the Second Amendment now a federally secured right because of the Fourteenth Amendment, and was using common law crimes as the measure of punishment in civil rights cases constitutional?[3]

To help achieve clarity on the issue of punishment, the indictment against Avery and Bratton included the charge that Avery, Bratton, and others had committed murder to deprive Williams of his civil rights. This meant that if convicted under the Enforcement Acts, Avery, Bratton, and their co-conspirators could face the death penalty, even though the actual crime charged was violating Williams's civil rights. The Supreme Court was in no rush to address either question—and never would take up the case against Avery and Bratton.

Meanwhile, realizing it might take months to obtain guidance from the Supreme Court, the court in Columbia pressed ahead with the prosecution of another Ku Klux alleged to have participated in Williams's murder, Robert Hayes Mitchell.

Unlike his Ku Klux leaders, Mitchell had not fled South Carolina but was ready to stand trial. He had been selected to go first more or less at random from the more than two dozen defendants in custody who were alleged to have participated in the raid in which Williams was lynched. One count of the indictment charged that Mitchell participated in the murder to deprive Williams of his Second Amendment right to keep and bear arms. While the prewar interpretation of the Second Amendment meant that Congress could not interfere with the right to bear arms, Corbin argued that the Fourteenth Amendment now made the right to keep and bear arms one of the "privileges and immunities" of citizenship that was also protected from state action—or in the case of South Carolina's inability to stop the Ku Klux from seizing the guns of African Americans, from state inaction.[4]

Stanbery rose to object to that count of the indictment. He argued that Bond and Bryan had already ruled that the Fourteenth Amendment had not transformed the Bill of Rights into a set of guarantees of individual rights when they ruled that the Fourth Amendment's protection against unreasonable search and seizure did not apply to Ku Klux raids on the grounds that the Ku Klux were operating as private citizens, not a government authority. Corbin appealed to Bond and Bryan to reconsider whether "the Fourteenth Amendment changes all that theory" because the right of African Americans to bear arms was so important to their safety and freedom that "we propose to fight for it to the last."[5]

Stanbery countered that the Constitution was not the source of the right to keep and bear arms. That right preceded the Constitution and was a natural right that existed under common law, he said. The Second Amendment simply directs the federal government not to interfere with this natural right, Stanbery said. As a common law right, the right to keep and bear arms was, therefore, a right that should be protected by the states, Stanbery said, and it was not, in an argument not likely to resonate with modern gun rights advocates, a right included under the privileges and immunities of national citizenship.[6]

Corbin countered that there had never been a common law right to own firearms. He noted that in England, the source of American common law, Protestants had been disarmed during the reign of their last Catholic king, James II, and then, after James was deposed by the Glorious Revolution, only Protestants were guaranteed the right to own weapons. The Second Amendment to the American Constitution, Corbin argued, represented "the first time in the history of the world" in which citizens were guaranteed the right to keep and bear arms and such a right had never been "guaranteed or granted before." This meant that it had to be part of the privileges of being an American citizen. Further, Corbin said, many of the guns seized by the Ku Klux, and the target of their raid on Williams, were guns provided to state-authorized militias, one of which Williams was a captain. If African Americans could not be protected from the seizure of guns issued by the authority of the state government, then the Ku Klux Enforcement Acts "mean nothing," Corbin said.[7]

Johnson joined Stanbery in urging Bond and Bryan to follow the precedent they had set with their earlier ruling, which was that the Fourteenth Amendment had not guaranteed an individual protection under the Fourth Amendment. Following that precedent, they had to rule the Fourteenth Amendment similarly did not offer Second Amendment protection "for they stand upon the same footing." Johnson, the nation's acknowledged expert on constitutional law, said, "So, my brother tells us that the right to bear arms is a right of the citizen. . . . What does the Constitution of the United States say about bearing arms? Nothing. What does the Fourteenth Amendment say upon the same subject? Nothing."[8]

Johnson said the formation of state militias proved his point. The state had provided arms to African Americans who joined the militias, but had refused to provide guns for whites-only militias even though the Ku Klux Enforcement Acts stated the law should make no distinction based upon race. With Black militias armed, and white militias not sanctioned, "does that not place the white man in a worse situation than the black man?" Johnson asked, ignoring that there had been no intention to form segregated Black and white militias; this segregation was the result of most whites refusing to serve in a biracial militia.[9]

Referencing allegations that Williams had made threats against the white community, Johnson argued that if a Black militia was behaving in a manner so that "terror fills the whole region," then the state would clearly have the right to disarm the military company. "I think there can be no doubt of that," he said. And if that were so, then this was evidence that "the right to bear arms is not a right given by the Constitution of the United States; but exists under the local law of the State." The right to bear arms was one of "a thousand rights which may be restrained in part, modified in part, or annulled; but whether they are to be restrained, modified or annulled, depends upon the inquiry: does the public safety demand it?" Public safety required that the right to bear arms be modified, Johnson said, coming to the crux of the matter for white Americans still terrified of retribution from African Americans for their past enslavement. "In the name of justice and humanity, in the name of those rights for which our fathers fought, you cannot subject the white man to the absolute and uncontrolled dominion of an armed force of a colored race," Johnson railed.[10]

Bond ought to have been sympathetic to the idea of ensuring African Americans were protected in their right to bear arms. In 1866, at a rally in Baltimore, Bond had told a crowd of African Americans that the right to bear arms in order to defend one's person, family, and home was one of the fundamental tenets of liberty. Such a right had been included "in every declaration of rights, in every constitution in every free State," he said. It was "the palladium of citizenship" and "the ultimate guarantee" that an individual's rights would be protected. To deprive any person of such a right, Bond had said, "is to make him a subject and not a citizen."[11]

Yet, despite this previously expressed passion, Bond announced that the court was not ready to rule on the Second Amendment question and asked Corbin if the government was ready to proceed with another indictment. Corbin issued a final appeal to the bench. Seizing their firearms in order to leave African Americans defenseless was "one of the principal things in connection with this [Ku Klux] conspiracy," he said. "It was systematically done." Disarming African Americans was key to preventing them from voting, Corbin said, and every indictment he had prepared included the charge that the Ku Klux defendants had conspired to interfere with the Second Amendment rights of African Americans. "All the cases returned by the grand jury have that count," Corbin said, "and we will never abandon it until we are obliged to."[12]

II

Corbin's resolve lasted only until the next morning. Bond announced the court was still not ready to rule on the question of whether the Fourteenth Amendment guaranteed individuals the right to bear arms under the Second Amendment. An exasperated Corbin gave a heavy sigh and told Bond and Bryan that "we will tear up the indictment to pieces and withdraw that count." It had been more than two weeks since the court convened, and while four Ku Klux had pled guilty and been sentenced for the assault on Amzi Rainey, not a single Ku Klux had yet stood trial. "We are determined to go to trial on something," Corbin said, and so the court agreed to proceed with jury selection while Corbin hurriedly drew up new indictments against Robert Hayes Mitchell and ten other alleged co-conspirators in the murder of Jim Williams: Sylvanus Shearer, William Shearer, Hugh Shearer, James Shearer, Henry Warlick, Eli Ross Stewart, Josiah Martin, Hugh Kell, James

Neal, and Milus Carroll, the last being the Ku Klux who later wrote a short memoir recounting his role in Williams's murder.[13]

In his opening statement to a jury of one white and eleven African-American men, Corbin said he would begin by first proving, once and for all, that the Ku Klux Klan did exist, and that the acts of violence committed were not perpetrated by random criminals but were part of a broad general conspiracy. It was "an organization, perfect in all its details, armed and disguised . . . [and] bound together by a terrible oath," Corbin said, his voice rising to a crescendo as he quoted from the Ku Klux constitution, "the penalty for breaking of which was declared to be the doom of a traitor—death! death!! death!!!"[14]

Corbin then demonstrated that the profane and the mundane can coexist by producing a copy of the KKK constitution and bylaws that had been recovered from the home of a suspected Ku Klux leader, Samuel G. "Squire" Brown.* In addition to blood oaths, included within the constitution were directions on how individual klan leaders (a "Cyclops" and a "Scribe") should keep the minutes of meetings and what fine should be levied for missing a meeting (thirty cents), as well as four "sacredly binding obligations":

1. We are on the side of justice, humanity, and constitutional liberty, as bequeathed to us in its purity by our forefathers.

2. We oppose and reject the principles of the Radical party.

3. We pledge mutual aid to each other in sickness, distress and pecuniary embarrassment.

4. Female friends, widows and their households shall ever be special objects of our regard and protection.

"Persons of color" were, of course, prohibited from being members, as were women. The white men who were members were told each was responsible to "provide himself with a pistol, Ku Klux gown, and signal instrument [i.e., a whistle]."[15]

---

*"Squire" is an informal term of respect for someone of high social standing who is also usually a large landowner.

Any Ku Klux disclosing any of this information or anything regarding the activities of the Ku Klux would, as Corbin noted, "suffer death," but any Ku Klux condemned to death had the right to appeal for a pardon from "the Great Grand Cyclops of Nashville, Tennessee," suggesting that the group, while perhaps loosely connected in some ways, did possess a hierarchy and an overarching purpose.[16]

Kirkland Gunn, a professional photographer and Ku Klux who "puked," appeared as a prosecution witness and was asked how the Ku Klux intended to achieve its objective. "Well, sir, that is known, I think; but the way I was told that they were going to carry this into effect was by killing off the white Radicals, and by whipping and intimidating the negroes, so as to keep them from voting for any men who held Radical offices." Stanbery then rose to note that while the Ku Klux constitution opposed Radical principles, it said nothing about preventing anyone from voting.[17]

To further confirm the Ku Klux was a South-wide conspiracy unified in purpose, Gunn testified that he had been sent to visit "Ku Klux brethren" in Catoosa and Whitfield Counties in Georgia to raise money for the Ku Klux in South Carolina. "For what purpose?" Corbin asked. "For paying lawyers' fees, and paying witnesses to go to Court," Gunn replied. In a stage whisper loud enough for all to hear, Johnson said, "I hope they raised it," with Stanbery adding sotto voce, "That is encouraging." Corbin turned to opposing counsel and said, "I should think that would be comforting information to you."[18]

The next Ku Klux who appeared as a witness for the prosecution was Charles W. Foster, a grocery and liquor store owner, who said that he joined the KKK so they would not interfere with his liquor business. He said the purpose of the Ku Klux was to "put down radicalism—put down Union Leagues, &c." Stanbery again rose to object that the Ku Klux constitution said no such thing and advocated no criminal behavior. "It is a paper that, apparently, is innocent—that contains no criminal agreement," Stanbery said, adding that taking the Ku Klux oath did not mean a person was part of a criminal conspiracy just "because somebody else put a criminal interpretation upon it." He had belonged to many societies that had constitutions and bylaws, Stanbery said. "Can I be made a criminal because some other member in that society had a criminal intent?"[19]

Judge Bond, however, wryly noted that the "difficulty" with Stanbery's analogy was that while the preamble of the Ku Klux constitution sounded as benign as that developed for any "charitable association . . . there is a clause which punishes anybody with death who shall disclose any of its purposes; and in order to execute these charitable objects, men are required to go in disguise. It does not look much like a charitable organization, and the question asks this witness to explain the meaning of that paper as his Klan understood it."[20]

To conceal its primarily political purpose, Foster said Ku Klux would sometimes find obscure reasons to "correct" the behavior of African Americans. He said he and twenty other men whipped an elderly Black man named Presley Holmes so badly that he cried and his shirt stuck to the blood on his back because Holmes had expressed the desire to be buried in a cemetery that had been reserved for whites only. They beat another man named Jerry Thompson because he had allegedly threatened to kick an "old soldier's hind parts," but Foster acknowledged the real reason for the assault was that Thompson was a member of the Union League. This was the same raid where the blacksmith Charles Good was whipped so badly that even Foster called it "very severe" because Good was a Union League leader and possibly an informant to federal authorities.[21]

Yet another Ku Klux witness for the prosecution, Osmond Gunthorpe, agreed that the Ku Klux's aims, for all its unrestrained violence, were coldly rational. Gunthorpe said he had joined the Ku Klux when it was first formed because "I thought it was an organization for the protection of each other," but stopped actively participating when "I found it to be a political organization, to try to control the elections for the Democratic Party."[22]

Sensing an opening, Stanbery rose to ask Gunthorpe why he felt the need to join an organization designed for self-defense. "What was the apprehended danger?" Stanbery asked. "There was general talk that there was a danger of the negroes rising," Gunthorpe said, but added, "I only heard talk; I never was alarmed."[23]

III

Finally, believing they had established the truth of the existence of the Ku Klux and that its primary purpose was achieving white political dominance, Corbin and Chamberlain began to focus on the facts of the crime at hand, the lynching of Jim Williams. Andy Tims had been the company clerk in the militia Williams commanded. Tims said he had been acquainted with Williams for nearly twenty years, but knew very little about the man. But he had a vivid recollection of the night Williams was murdered because before they lynched Williams, the Ku Klux raided Tims's home, too.

At what Tims estimated to be about 2:00 a.m. on March 7, three disguised men rode up to his house "cussing and swearing a great deal." The men shouted, "Here we come—we are the Ku Klux. Here we come right from hell." Tims said he was prepared to open the door, but the Ku Klux broke down the door before he could do so. The men grabbed Tims and demanded "your guns." Tims gave them the only gun he had, and then the Ku Klux demanded to know where Williams lived. "We want to see your captain tonight," the men told Tims, and they rode away in the direction that Tims had pointed.[24]

Tims cut through the woods, hoping to warn Williams the Ku Klux were on the way. En route, he ran into two other men, Henry Haynes and Andrew Bratton, who had heard the ruckus at Tims's house, and they joined him in the sprint toward Williams's cabin. When they arrived, they saw a distraught Rosa Williams sitting in the doorway, but Bond upheld Stanbery's objection and refused to let Tims tell the court what Mrs. Williams said to him.

Following the tracks left by a large party of Ku Klux, Tims, Haynes, and Bratton continued to search for Williams. There had been multiple Ku Klux raids that night, and a large number of African Americans, many of them members of Williams's company, were out as well, aware that the Ku Klux had planned to raid their captain. Finally, sometime between 9:00 and 10:00 a.m., Tims said they came upon a field where "we saw Williams hanging on a tree. . . . His toes were just touching the pine leaves." On his chest was pinned the note: "Jim Williams on his big muster."[25]

The group left Williams untouched as Tims raced to Yorkville to retrieve the coroner. Only when they all returned several hours later was Williams's body let down and taken to Napoleon Bratton's home and store, where an inquest was hastily organized and held. The pro forma verdict of "death by persons unknown" was issued.

On cross-examination, the Ku Klux attorneys asked Tims no questions about Williams's murder, but instead pressed Tims to tell the type and number of guns issued to Williams's militia company and whether Williams and his men had made threats to the local white population. Tims said the company had been issued Enfield breech-loading rifles, but so little ammunition that some members had none with which to practice. Tims insisted that he had never heard Williams order any of the company to burn the homes of white people, nor did he ever hear Williams threaten to "kill from the cradle to the grave," though he had heard white people insist that Williams had done so. Tims also said he had been a poll manager at McConnellsville, where both he and Williams had voted the previous fall unmolested.[26]

Stanbery took over the cross-examination and continued to press Tims about how the militia had obtained its guns and why there were no white militias similarly armed. Corbin objected to Tims being asked questions he was not qualified to answer. "If the court please, there is no end to this testimony." Bond also chastised Stanbery, asking how it was relevant to Williams's alleged murder that an African-American militia had been formed *after* the Ku Klux had organized. Stanbery replied that Williams's murder had nothing to do with a conspiracy to prevent African Americans from voting. "We want to show that there was a totally different intent from that of preventing voting," Stanbery said, "that the cause of the hanging of Rainey [Stanbery would not use Williams's name but instead the name of his former master] was owing to the negroes having been armed, and to the threatenings made by Rainey, the captain of the company. We expect to show that he was a very dangerous man."[27]

On the night Williams was murdered, the Ku Klux also attacked several other African Americans. Jurors heard testimony from Gadsden Steel, whose home was raided shortly before Williams was hanged. Steel said the Ku Klux pulled him from his bed and pistol-whipped him while demanding that he give up his guns and show them where Williams lived. Steel told the Ku Klux he had no guns and had never been a part of Williams's militia company, but admitted he had voted for the Radical ticket. "There, God damn you," a Ku Klux snarled. "I'll kill you for that." But another Ku Klux, who was only called "Number Six" by his fellow klansmen, intervened. Butting Steel in the chest with two-foot horns attached to his cap, this klansman told Steel he could live if he would tell which African Americans possessed guns and then guide the Ku Klux to Williams's home.[28]

Steel insisted that he had heard most of Williams's militia had relinquished their guns, but a Ku Klux named John Caldwell later testified that a terrified Steel had told the Ku Klux that Williams might still have "twelve

THE RESULT OF THE FIFTEENTH AMENDMENT,
And the Rise and Progress of the African Race in America and its final Accomplishment, and Celebration on May 19ᵗʰ A.D. 1870.

This 1870 lithograph commemorates a parade held in Baltimore to celebrate the ratification of the Fifteenth Amendment. Federal judge Hugh Lennox Bond is in the pantheon between Abraham Lincoln and John Brown at top, while Martin Delany, the father of the Pan-African movement, the first African-American commissioned Union officer, and later a supporter of South Carolina governor Wade Hampton, is shown in uniform next to his longtime colleague Frederick Douglass on the right.

Unlike the twentieth-century KKK with its white robes and pointy hats, those in the post–Civil War Ku Klux Klan were responsible for designing and making their own disguises, with calico a preferred fabric. While the disguises were intended to prevent identification of the Ku Klux, the bizarre costumes were one reason the KKK gained national attention and approbation.
NORTH CAROLINA MUSEUM OF HISTORY

Major Lewis Merrill was described by a New York report as having the face "of a German professor, and the frame of an athlete." His skills as a detective and his diligence in investigating Ku Klux atrocities are a key reason York County became the focus of the national campaign against the Ku Klux.
COURTESY OF THE LIBRARY OF CONGRESS

A member of York County's most prominent family, Dr. J. Rufus Bratton, photographed here in the regalia of a 32nd-degree Scottish Rite Mason, became one of the leaders of the York County Ku Klux Klan.
YORK COUNTY CULTURE AND HERITAGE MUSEUMS

Susie King Taylor held the title of "regimental laundress" with the US 33rd Colored Infantry, the regiment in which Jim Williams probably served—the records are not definitive. Taylor, the wife of a regimental soldier, did far more than laundry, nursing sick and wounded soldiers and teaching others to read. Black and white women would also be actively engaged during the Ku Klux terror.
COURTESY OF THE LIBRARY OF CONGRESS

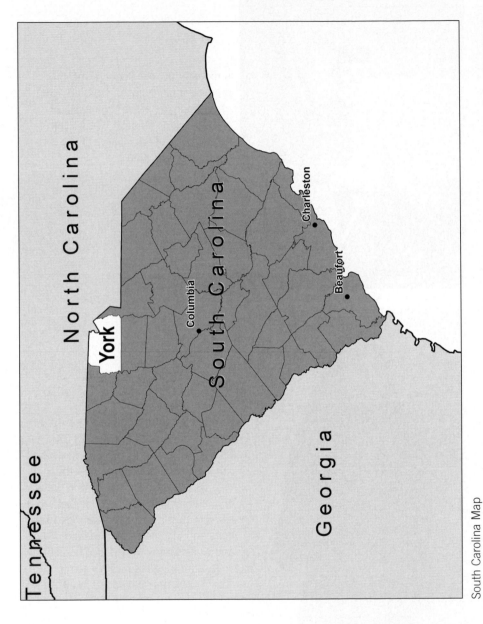

South Carolina Map

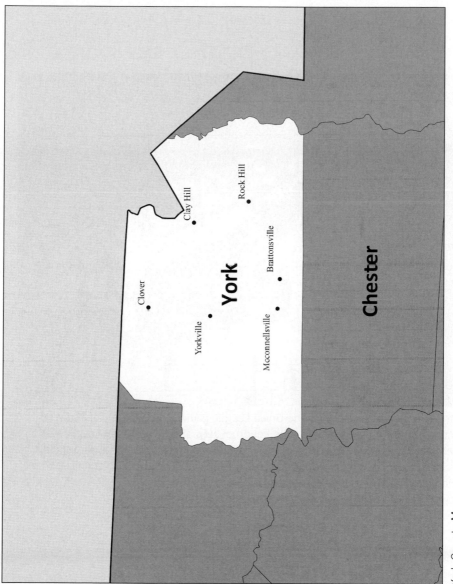

York County Map

African-American members of the Union League gather on the streets of Yorkville, South Carolina, to commemorate the Fourth of July, 1867. The Union League was a Republican political club and machine, raised funds for schools, resolved disputes that could not be heard in white courts, and served as a self-defense organization that later helped organize state-sponsored militias.

YORK COUNTY CULTURE AND HERITAGE MUSEUMS

or fifteen" guns in his possession.[29] When a Ku Klux suggested the group should not "tarry" because "we have to get back to hell before daybreak," they compelled Steel to ride mounted behind a Ku Klux so he could lead the way. But after a few hundred yards the Ku Klux claimed Steel was too heavy and holding back his horse, and so Steel was allowed to dismount and told to run home as a Ku Klux shouted, "We are going on to kill Williams, and are going to kill all these damned niggers that votes the Radical ticket; run, God damn you, run!"[30]

The next witness was Williams's unfortunate widow, Rosa, who recounted how the Ku Klux burst into her home, shoved her roughly aside, found her husband hiding under the floorboards, and dragged him away, ignoring her screams and pleas that they spare his life. Despite being asked to recount a horrific event that surely traumatized her and her children for life, an event that left her alone to care for several young children with only her ability as a cook to stave off homelessness and starvation, neither Corbin nor Stanbery offered her condolences. Stanbery spent the bulk of his cross-examination pestering Mrs. Williams to recall where her husband had purchased ammunition for his militia and what type of ammunition it was. Corbin intervened, "I don't see the relevancy in all this." To which Stanbery testily replied, "You don't see the relevancy of anything we ask."[31]

Following Rosa Williams, Hiram Littlejohn testified that the Ku Klux raided his house after the lynching and boasted, "We have hung Jim Williams tonight; we intend to rule this country or die." They then took the only gun in Littlejohn's possession, a double-barrel shotgun.[32]

Caldwell, the Ku Klux who participated in the raid but denied participating directly in the lynching, then took the stand for the prosecution and recalled how the raid unfolded. Under cross-examination, Johnson had Caldwell acknowledge that the purpose of the raid was to seize any and all firearms owned by those African Americans who were the targets of a raid. "Were you told that the object of the society was to prevent their voting?" Johnson asked. "I didn't hear anything of that said," replied Caldwell.[33]

Johnson then asked Caldwell about the alleged arsons being committed by African Americans, and Caldwell acknowledged he had heard about several suspicious fires. When questioned on redirect by Corbin, however, Caldwell admitted he had never heard Williams make any threats against the white community, nor did he know any man who claimed to have heard

Williams make such threats. "No, sir; I never saw a man who said he had heard them; nothing, only what Dr. Bratton told me," he said.[34]

It was not until the second day of the trial through the testimony of Elias Ramsay, another Ku Klux who agreed to testify for the prosecution, that someone finally identified the long-forgotten defendant, Robert Hayes Mitchell, as having participated in the raid on Williams. Despite the disguises worn, Ramsay said he easily recognized Mitchell's voice, as he had known him for ten years and the two had fought together in the same regiment during the war.[35]

It was here that Amzi Rainey, whose assailants had already pled guilty and been sentenced, provided testimony about the Ku Klux raid on his home in late March, two weeks after Williams was lynched, in which he was beaten and his clothes set on fire, his ten-year-old daughter was shot and wounded in the head, and his teenage daughter was raped.

Dick Wilson then took the stand to recount a raid on his home on April 11 when the Ku Klux was trying to find Wilson's grown son, Richard. The Ku Klux night riders asked the elderly Wilson if he was "a good old Radical?" Wilson replied, "I don't know whether I have been; I have tried to be." His fearlessness enraged the Ku Klux, who forced Wilson to drop his pants and then beat him with white oak ramrods as thick as a finger with such force that three of the rods broke in half. When Wilson begged the Ku Klux to stop, they told him they would shoot him if he said another word and beat him some more, and then demanded to know if he would now vote the Democratic ticket. "Yes, I will vote any way you want me to vote; I don't care how you want me to vote, master, I will vote," said Wilson, who was so badly beaten he could barely crawl when the Ku Klux ordered him to run. Wilson said the beating left him in such a state that he could not walk, sit, or lie on his back for two weeks.[36]

Johnson rose to object to the testimony of Rainey and Wilson as having little to do with Williams's murder except to provide "cumulative evidence" of the Ku Klux outrages, which was likely Corbin and Chamberlain's motivation.[37]

When it was time for Johnson and Stanbery to present Mitchell's defense, they focused on proving, as Stanbery said they would, that Williams was "an outlaw and a dangerous man" whose murder was warranted.[38] He did not explain why, if Williams was a criminal, he was not brought before civil authorities.

The first defense witness was Julia Rainey, who described Williams as "my former slave." Rainey said it was her impression that the militia company that Williams captained was "under his control entirely, and they were not very orderly managed. . . . Their conduct was disturbing indeed; they had begun to alarm the whole country." Rainey claimed that Williams's alleged threats "were very common to me," but acknowledged she had "never heard him myself" make any such threats.[39]

When court resumed the following day, the first witness called by the defense, indicating the weakness of their case, was John A. Moroso, editor of the *Charleston Courier*, who had toured York County six weeks prior to the 1870 election. Moroso said the election was marred by "excitement" instigated by Black militia members bearing arms who tried to disrupt a nearby Democratic Reform rally by constantly beating a kettle and bass drum, irritating local whites to the point that "a riot was imminent."[40]

Corbin objected to how testimony from "a newspaper reporter" recounting scenes from months before Williams's murder was relevant to the case at hand. Stanbery countered that he was showing that it was not those favoring the Democratic Reform ticket (which he was now equating with the Ku Klux Klan) who were trying to prevent people from voting, but rather the Union League, which was using not just loud drums but also "dangerous assaults [and] hurling stones" to disrupt Reform rallies and obstruct voting. Williams and his militia were "constantly drilling . . . as if he were preparing them for war" and doing so in an "inoffensive community . . . where nothing like the Ku Klux had ever been seen." This left local whites with no choice "but to disarm him, and put it out of his power to follow out his evil intentions," Stanbery said.[41]

Judge Bond was unpersuaded, stating that the disruption of a political rally the previous year had little to do with the alleged Ku Klux conspiracy. Stanbery replied that he was attempting to show there had been no interference at the polls with the right of African Americans to cast ballots in the 1870 election, and all the intimidation "came from the other side." Corbin said the charges against Mitchell and other Ku Klux were not about preventing their African-American victims from voting in 1870, but the raids were designed to prevent them from exercising the free right to vote in future elections. Bond added that the fact the Ku Klux were allegedly not active in August of 1870 did not prove they were not engaged in a conspiracy in the present day. "How does it go to negative a fact that a man committed an offense on Monday by showing that he was quiet on Tuesday?" Bond asked. On cross-examination, Chamberlain got Moroso to admit that he had not actually seen any African-American militia during his brief time in Yorkville, and so Stanbery moved on to other witnesses.[42]

The Democratic Reform candidate for governor in 1870, Judge Richard B. Carpenter, was called to the stand and said his impression was that the Black militias "held more terror" for "conservative colored people" who supported the Democratic Party than they did for whites. The issue, Carpenter said, was that politics in South Carolina was now practically war and one side, the Radicals, were being armed by the state and the other side was not.[43]

Bill Lindsay, an African American who said he had been acquainted with Williams for "four or five years," became the first witness to insist he had personally heard Williams threaten to kill local whites "from the cradle up."[44] Lindsay, who was known as "Gentleman Bill" and who said his support for the Democratic Party was the reason why he personally did not fear the Ku Klux, said Williams was angry that he had been ordered to disarm his militia. "He seemed to be in earnest when he said so," Lindsay said of Williams's threat, although he also acknowledged he had never known Williams "to do anything bad," and that Williams generally had a "good reputation."[45]

Another African American, David Thomasson, said he, too, had heard Williams make threats, though Thomasson had himself been arrested under suspicion of riding with the Ku Klux and spent three days in jail before being released by Merrill. Like Lindsay, Thomasson said he also voted the Democratic ticket and because of that was "under no obligation to feel afraid of [the Ku Klux]."[46]

A third African-American witness, William Bratton, also testified that he had heard Williams make threats against "the white ladies and children, gin houses and barns." But Bratton, who had worked alongside Williams when both were slaves on the Bratton plantation, was a member of Williams's militia company and had been reduced in rank from lieutenant to private by Williams. He said the reduction in rank "did not matter to me" and was not the reason he was now testifying on behalf of the Ku Klux. Stanbery charged that Williams had busted Bratton because Bratton became a supporter of the Democratic Party.[47]

Several white witnesses also said they heard Williams make threats of varying degrees. Scott Wilson, who lived near Williams, said the only threat he had heard Williams make was that he would never vote for a white man, "that was [the] only threat I heard."[48] W. H. Atkins said Williams had proposed that whites and Blacks settle their differences "in a manly way" by fighting it out with fists "out in the old field."[49] John B. Fudge, however, insisted he had personally heard Williams threaten to "kill from the cradle to the grave, and . . . lay waste to this country, generally." But when Corbin asked, "What did you do to prevent him from killing you and your family?" Fudge responded, "I did nothing."[50]

IV

One witness the defense never called to the stand was the accused, Mitchell, nor were any of the accused Ku Klux in any of the trials allowed to testify. It had been a long-standing practice under both English and American law to prevent those charged with a crime from testifying at their own trials. The legal *Commentaries* developed by eighteenth-century English jurist Sir William Blackstone, which systemized the entirety of English common law and which were therefore the lodestar for all legal practice in Great Britain and the United States, argued that no witness in a trial could be considered reliable and competent if they were "interested in the event of the cause" of the trial, i.e., a criminal defendant.

Only well into the nineteenth century did thinkers such as ultimate philosopher Jeremy Bentham in England and John Appleton, chief justice of the Supreme Court of Maine, begin to question the logic behind Blackstone's guidance. Appleton noted that in English and American law, the defendant is presumed innocent, and therefore the accuser is presumed a perjurer, but the "perjuror [*sic*] alone is heard." To allow neither the accuser nor the accused to testify, since both had a personal interest in the outcome of the case, was nonsensical, Appleton argued. In 1864, Maine became the first state to allow the accused to testify in court if they requested to do so with "the credit to be given to his testimony being left solely to the jury under instructions of the court," but no defendant could be compelled to testify. Other states began to follow Maine's lead, but the Southern and federal courts were among the last to make the change, and Georgia still refused to allow defendants to testify at their own trials until the early twentieth century.[51]

Mitchell's testimony would likely have been irrelevant. While he was the defendant, the trial and his defense had been all about Williams. In calling rebuttal witnesses, Corbin and Chamberlain sought only to refute the notion that Williams was a dangerous man. A white man named George Witherspoon said the only person he knew who claimed Williams had made threats was Dr. J. Rufus Bratton, and that was *after* Williams's murder.[52] Tims was recalled to the stand and emphasized that the only people who claimed they heard Williams vow to kill whites were "white people, and some few Democratic niggers." Williams, Tims said of his captain, was not "in any way a quarrelsome man. . . . He was not a profane man, and I had not heard him curse for over a year, not an oath."[53]

P. J. O'Connell, a white state legislator, said Williams was "a genial, jovial, and good-hearted fellow; he was a peaceable man," and added that "Jim Williams was opposed to anything like retaliation." O'Connell insisted that his white constituents only "pretended to be alarmed. . . . I did not believe that there was any white men in our County who were scared about the colored militia."[54]

Another Republican state legislator, J. H. White, said that while the defense had referenced the burning of white farmers' cotton gin houses and barns, the bigger problem was whites burning schools serving African-American children and adults; one such school, Green Pond, had been torched and rebuilt three times, he said.[55]

In his closing arguments, Chamberlain told the jury that "the entire country" was watching these Ku Klux trials "with unusual interest and anxiety, for . . . this trial and its results stretch far beyond this defendant, and far beyond this Court room, and touch the vital interests of every citizen, and go down to the very foundations of our American liberty and government."[56] He crisply defined what was meant by a criminal conspiracy:

> *A conspiracy is an agreement or combination between two or more persons, by their concerted action, to do an unlawful act. . . . The unlawful act may never be done. No step may ever be taken to accomplish that unlawful purpose; but the essence of the offense is present, the crime is completed, when the agreement and combination is formed to do the unlawful act. . . . If there are twelve men, twelve individuals, in the conspiracy, when that conspiracy begins, they are, in the eye of the law, one man; they*

breathe one breath; they speak one voice; they wield one arm . . . the declarations of one of these twelve individuals, while in the pursuit of their unlawful purpose, is the act, the word, the declaration of all.[57]

Chamberlain taunted the leaders of the Ku Klux who had organized the conspiracy but had since fled the country to avoid being held accountable. In planning the lynching of Williams, Dr. J. Rufus Bratton had deliberately organized an exceptionally large raiding party, far more than necessary to achieve the task. "You see here, gentlemen of the jury, as you will, perhaps, never see again, the terrible power of organization," Chamberlain said. "Probably no one, no two, no three of that party could have been induced to commit that murder; but, under the cloak and sanction of this vast organization, the responsibility of crime was divided until it was not felt. Murder, violent murder, excited no compunction, because behind Rufus Bratton was a column of seventy men, who were to divide the responsibility with him."[58]

At one level, Chamberlain said he felt "pity" for Mitchell, only a minor member of the Ku Klux, who had to stand trial while Bratton and other leaders like Avery remained free, but Mitchell was representative of a conspiracy that had "tens of thousands of members, stretching all over one entire section of this country."[59] And the stakes involved in dismantling this conspiracy could not be higher, Chamberlain said. The "appalling" purpose of the Ku Klux, he said, was nothing less than "the turning back of the entire tide of our history since the opening of the last great struggle on this continent between the spirit of slavery and the spirit of justice and liberty."[60]

And as for Williams, Chamberlain said, "There is not a drop of blood in my veins that does not stir today in grateful response to this heroism of an uneducated negro—five years, only, a freeman—who now determined to protect the lives and liberties of his fellow-citizens by the only means which the Government had given him. . . . And when the names of these conspirators, who murdered him, shall have rotted from the memory of men, some generation will seek for marble white enough to bear the name of that brave negro captain."[61]

In their closing remarks, Stanbery and Johnson made the remarkable choice to challenge the eleven African-American jurors to prove they and their race were worthy of the right to serve on juries by acquitting their client. Even when attempting to compliment the Black jurors, Stanbery insulted them. The men on the jury, "as intelligent men of that race," knew in their hearts that Williams was a dangerous man, Stanbery said, but the problem was that "you know what an influence over the race of colored people such a man will have, exciting their passions—accustomed to obedience as they are."[62]

The Black jurors, Stanbery said, now had to prove that "you are capable of divesting yourselves of the prejudices of race and color" in order to demonstrate that they were "entitled to sit in the jury box."[63] Mitchell was a "very young man, scarcely past his majority," Stanbery said. "Look at him. Does he look like a murderer?" Someone should pay for Williams's murder, but it was not Mitchell, who thought the raid was only intended to seize guns from Williams, not lynch him. "When you get Dr. Bratton, with such proof, deal with him; but, for God's sake, don't make this young man his scape-goat," Stanbery said. The problems in York County were all due to the militias, he said; the Ku Klux was already in decline until Governor Scott issued guns to predominantly Black militias. The African-American jurors needed to set aside their own prejudice against white people and vote to acquit, or else "I do not want to see one of your race on a jury again."[64]

Johnson was less aggressive in his remarks, but admitted that he was discomfited addressing "for the first time . . . a jury composed in part of your colored brethren." But Johnson insisted, "I have no prejudice," and expressed his belief that the "native intelligence" of the jurors "will not permit you to indulge in any prejudice against the race to which I belong. We are all of the same Father."[65]

Johnson strongly condemned the Ku Klux violence, acknowledging that the reports testified to were likely true. "I have listened with unmixed horror to some of the testimony which has been brought before you," Johnson said. "The outrages proved are shocking to humanity; they admit neither cause nor justification . . . the parties engaged were brutes, insensible to the obligations of humanity and religion. The day will come, however, if it has not already arrived, when they will deeply lament it. Even if justice shall not overtake them, there is one tribunal from which there is no escape."[66]

But that outrage did not change the fact that the Enforcement Acts approved by Congress were unconstitutional, Johnson said, and the government had not proved that the purpose of the Ku Klux was to prevent African Americans from voting. Besides, he added, if the Ku Klux had tried to obstruct suffrage by the Radicals, the Union League and the militias had done the same to Democrats.[67]

Corbin then rose to give his final remarks, noting that Johnson had hit on the key issue of what the Constitution now meant. Corbin said that when the Ku Klux stated in their bylaws that they were obedient only to the US Constitution as "bequeathed to us in its purity by our forefathers," they meant that they supported the Constitution only as it was ratified in 1789. They were explicitly stating that they would not abide by the terms of the subsequent Thirteenth, Fourteenth, or Fifteenth Amendments. In other words, Corbin said, "It means, we reject the results of the late war."[68]

The federal government had intervened because the "deaf, paralyzed" tribunals of the Southern states had done nothing to protect the rights or the lives of their African-American citizens or those of whites who supported the Republican Party.[69] African Americans had embraced their new freedom with no thoughts of revenge against the whites who had once enslaved them, Corbin said; the Ku Klux Klan had no genuine reason to exist. But it did exist, and the conspiracy had to be put down now or else the South would suffer anew: "The late war left you poor, in poverty and distress; if the arm of the American people has again to be raised to put down this organization, I fear it will make your homes desolate and your fields a wilderness," he concluded.[70]

In his charge to the jury, Bond reiterated Chamberlain's explanation of a conspiracy. Mitchell had been charged with being part of a conspiracy to prevent African Americans from voting; he had not been charged with the individual acts committed by that conspiracy. If the jury did not believe the prosecution had proved that a conspiracy like the Ku Klux Klan existed, or the defense had proved Mitchell was not part of the conspiracy, they should vote to acquit. But if they were convinced that Mitchell was aware of the Ku Klux's aims and was part of that conspiracy, then they should vote to convict. The jury deliberated thirty-eight minutes before returning a guilty verdict.[71]

At his sentencing, Mitchell noted that he had not been arrested but had turned himself in to Major Merrill "and told him all I knew." He admitted he had joined the raid, but had not participated in the lynching of Williams and had not known the purpose of the raid. "I didn't do anything," Mitchell said, to which Bond, who had heard the same in sentencing those who assaulted Amzi Rainey, archly replied, "You held the horses?" Bond said he did not doubt that Mitchell, who also admitted to participating in another Ku Klux raid, was now remorseful and had told the truth, but added, "Mr. Mitchell, it has been your unhappiness to have been connected with a great crime." For being part of a criminal conspiracy, Bond sentenced Mitchell to eighteen months imprisonment and a one hundred dollar fine.[72]

There had finally been a trial and a conviction in the Great South Carolina Ku Klux Klan Trials, but that victory for the prosecution in Columbia was tempered by a far greater setback that had occurred in Washington, DC, one that would dramatically impact future prosecution of the Ku Klux and the effect of the trials on posterity.

CHAPTER TEN

He tells a number of stories—one of a fellow being castrated—with terribly minute & tedious details of each case—it has got to be a bore, to listen twice a week to this same thing.
> —SECRETARY OF STATE HAMILTON FISH REGARDING HIS
> CABINET COLLEAGUE AMOS T. AKERMAN

I

Attorney General Amos T. Akerman never divulged why he mysteriously resigned in December 1871, or even whether he had resigned of his own volition or been forced from office. "The reasons for this step, I would not detail fully without saying what, perhaps, ought not to be said," Akerman wrote Corbin on December 15, the day the resignation became public and the day the defense rested its case in the trial of Robert Hayes Mitchell.[1] Corbin was no doubt distraught by the departure of a superior who had placed such trust in the young prosecutor.

Even three years after the fact, Akerman remained coy about the reasons for his departure. Looking back on his time as attorney general, he wrote in his diary, "My course in it was satisfactory to my conscience—I believe it was satisfactory to the President—but it was not satisfactory to certain powerful interests, and a public opinion, unfavorable to me, was created in the country."[2]

What those powerful interests were, Akerman did not say. There was speculation that the railroad interests, "the country's most powerful industry," were deeply discontented with Akerman's scrupulous honesty.[3] But there was also speculation that Akerman and President Grant no longer saw eye to eye on how to pursue the Ku Klux Klan, and, further, there were those in the administration who never believed Akerman was up to the task of being attorney general and who coveted his position.

Grant also never gave a specific reason why he replaced his attorney general. In his letter formally asking for Akerman's resignation, Grant vaguely stated that "circumstances convince me that a change in the office you now hold is desirable."[4] He added cryptically, "Nothing but a consideration of public sentiment could induce me to indite this."[5]

That Akerman and Grant parted on reasonably good terms is suggested by Grant softening the blow by offering to appoint Akerman to a federal judgeship or to "any foreign appointment that was vacant, or likely to be so," but Akerman concluded such positions "would not be to his taste."[6] He declined to consider any other post and planned a quiet return to Georgia. As he told his wife, his greatest concern was that he avoid "exposing the President to annoyance and perhaps the censure and dislike of powerful interests, on my part."[7]

Akerman's equanimity throughout this ordeal led Grant to send a follow-up letter, stating, "I can refer with pride to the uniform harmony which . . . has constantly existed, not only between us but between yourself and Colleagues in the Cabinet."[8] Here, Grant was laying it on a bit thick for, as Akerman well knew, he was not in harmony with several key members of Grant's Cabinet nor, toward the end, even with Grant himself.

Akerman had seen his dismissal coming. He was well aware he had made powerful enemies, and as a newcomer to national politics and the Republican Party, he did not have a network of defenders in Washington or the nation. As early as August 1871, he told his wife that he had become mindful of "a new effort which I am satisfied is going on to oust me from office because I will not subserve to certain selfish interests."[9]

New York Republican congressman Fernando Wood stated as fact that Akerman had been forced to resign because he had made decisions "adverse" to the railroad interests, making enemies of powerful railroad tycoons such as Collis P. Huntington and Jay Gould and their lawyers—one of whom was Akerman's predecessor as attorney general, Ebenezer Hoar. Weeks after Akerman's resignation, Wood called for an inquiry "into the case of the contest among certain railroad companies for public lands, to which none of them are entitled."[10]

It was one of Akerman's duties as attorney general to review railroad requests for lucrative federal land grants that had been offered as an incentive for railroad construction. It was up to Akerman to ensure that the railroads had complied with their agreements with the government, including whether the railroads had been built and that they had been built where they were supposed to be, before transferring title of what were previously public lands to private interests. Akerman had "an exceedingly sharp eye" and found several occasions where a denial or delay of the land grants was warranted.[11] In one note to a railroad, Akerman scolded, "Your road is not *completed* until it is finished . . . to a site legally fixed for a junction."[12]

Akerman's incorruptibility "in an age of ethical laxity" astonished and troubled those who wished to influence the workings of the Department of Justice.[13] Akerman rejected one railroad's attempt to offer him a fifteen-thousand-dollar bribe if he would reverse one of his opinions.[14] When another railroad lobbyist flexed his political connections and sought to pressure Akerman to change one of his rulings, Akerman tartly responded, "Should you have occasion to correspond further with this Department, it is proper that you should know that such considerations are wholly without influence here. When called on for an opinion as to the law, the only inquiry here is, What is the law?"[15]

Yet, it may *not* have been the railroad interests who drove Akerman from office. Despite the brazen offer of a bribe clearly presenting the opportunity to do so, Akerman did not mount a muckraking investigative crusade against the railroads, and, in fact, his "letter-of-the-law rulings won him the grudging respect of some opposing lawyers." For example, after his dismissal, when Akerman would travel back to Washington, DC, on business, he enjoyed several cordial visits with Hoar, neither man apparently bearing the other any ill will.[16]

But if Akerman had no problems with his predecessor, he had a less positive relationship with his peers and particularly one subordinate who very much wished to be his successor.

Thirty-eight-year-old Benjamin Bristow was the nation's first solicitor general, which was the second-highest post at the newly created Department of Justice and whose duties included arguing the federal government's cases before the US Supreme Court. But Bristow felt he was eminently qualified to hold the higher post of attorney general.

Bristow had been a "Kentucky blue jay," meaning he was an early supporter of the Union cause in that border state and later joined the Union army. He fought under Grant's command at Fort Henry, Fort Donelson, and Shiloh (being badly wounded in the latter battle), and rose to the rank of colonel. Considering himself a superior lawyer and a figure of greater national prominence who also had a personal relationship with the president, Bristow chafed at being Akerman's underling and undermined his superior's standing with Grant whenever he had the chance. Bristow told the president that Akerman "was altogether *too small* for the place in every particular, that he was ridiculed by the Court & profession generally and that he was a *dead weight* on the administration."[17]

Grant "expressed great surprise that [Akerman] had failed as disastrously" as Bristow alleged, and noted that he had not personally heard any Supreme Court justice criticize Akerman. While he conceded Akerman may have not met all his expectations, Grant considered him "an earnest man & thoroughly honest," and was troubled by the idea that he might need to replace Akerman for "want of capacity."[18]

As Akerman became entrenched in the prosecutions of the Ku Klux, Bristow became more aggressive in his intrigues to replace his boss. Bristow or his admirers were likely the source of a story in the *New York Herald* that adopted Bristow's line that the Supreme Court justices considered Akerman "hardly competent."[19] The *Herald* claimed that Akerman was "quite self-opinionated, tenacious in his own views and rather disagreeable in considering those of others." Further, leaving little doubt the source of these views, the *Herald* claimed it was widely known in Washington that Bristow "has been the real Attorney General," quietly compensating for the inadequacies of the obscure lawyer-farmer-politician from Georgia.[20]

Bristow, who preferred a more conciliatory policy toward the South, even did his best to undermine Akerman on his signature issue: dismantling the Ku Klux Klan. Bristow argued that further Ku Klux prosecutions were counterproductive and told Grant that Akerman was "doing no good" in South Carolina.[21] Because Akerman was out of Washington at the time, Bristow was tasked with issuing the proclamation suspending habeas corpus in the nine South Carolina counties that became the focus of Ku Klux prosecutions, which he did after "modestly entering my protest." As one historian of Grant's presidency noted of Bristow, "His attitude suggested that it was Akerman's vigor in pursuing the Klan as much as his supposed incompetence that drove Bristow's machinations against the attorney general."[22]

II

Bristow was hardly alone within the administration in criticizing Akerman for pushing Grant into more aggressive action against the Ku Klux than he might otherwise have taken. Just as he had no national following that might protect his standing, neither had Akerman cultivated close relationships with his peers in the Cabinet. He angered colleagues by refusing to grant them permission to hire outside legal counsel for their special projects. Akerman thought the hiring of outside counsel, which was expensive, had long been abused, and he had no funds in the Department of Justice budget to pay for them anyway. He also was proud of the team of US attorneys he had helped Grant put in place in all the states. In rejecting a request for outside counsel made by Secretary of War William Belknap, Akerman said, "The District Attorney for Massachusetts and his regular assistant are well qualified for any professional work which the Government needs to be done there."[23]

Akerman could come across as sanctimonious even when simply being sincere. In a letter of advice to his son, Benjamin, Akerman wrote, "Understand public questions. Ask what is right, not what is popular. When you have ascertained the right try to make it popular; but cleave to it, popular or not."[24]

But not everyone was ready to cleave to policies that had become unpopular, the president included. There is no doubt that Grant remained horrified by the Ku Klux and sympathetic to the plight of African Americans, but he also was being told by other advisors that the government was now going too far and it was time for African Americans to rely less on the government and take greater control of their fate by exercising their vote—which was, of course, what the Ku Klux was trying to prevent them from doing. Once resolute in taking on the Ku Klux, Grant had become, in the words of biographer William McFeely, "uneasy about Akerman's zeal" in securing civil rights for African Americans.[25]

One of those whispering in Grant's ear was Secretary of State Hamilton Fish, who disliked all federal interventions in the South and worried there would be far more unless Akerman was removed. Fish found Akerman's sometimes lengthy disquisitions on the Ku Klux annoying. In an entry in his diary in October 1871, Fish complained that "Akerman made a long, long statement about the Ku Klux" during that day's Cabinet meeting.[26]

Akerman freely acknowledged that he was "chronically garrulous on the Klan" but believed it was important to rouse the nation to further action on behalf of African Americans.[27] At a Cabinet meeting in late November, Akerman detailed a horrific assault on a forty-year-old African-American man in Georgia named Henry Lowther, who had been arrested on accusations that he had slept with a white woman and was plotting an insurrection of armed Black men. Nearly two hundred Ku Klux came to the jail and kidnapped Lowther, dragging him to a nearby swamp, where he was given the choice of being killed or castrated. He chose the latter, and this foul and bloody deed was performed by the town's doctor, a former Confederate army surgeon.[28]

Fish was unmoved by this gross indecency, and instead groused in his diary that Akerman had again brought up the topic of the "Ku Klux—he has it on the brain—he tells a number of stories—one of a fellow being castrated—with terribly minute & tedious details of each case—it has got to be a bore, to listen twice a week to this same thing."[29]

When rumors surfaced that Akerman might be replaced, there were also stories that Fish might be pushed out of the administration as well, following several foreign policy mishaps, such as the Santo Domingo annexation fiasco. Instead, Fish, whom Grant considered "the foremost statesman of the age" and his possible successor as president, stayed.[30] Not only that, Grant, knowing how much Fish would be pleased, gave his close confidant advance notice that he intended to remove Akerman.[31]

Fish's ennui with the fight for African-American rights reflected not only the opinion of much of Grant's Cabinet but also of the public at large where, barely a half dozen years into the effort to secure lasting rights for African Americans, "a certain moral fatigue began to afflict the North, where racism remained widespread."[32]

Native Southerner and railroad developer James W. Harrison had toured the North to find investors for his Blue Ridge Railroad and anxiously wrote back to some of his Southern Republican allies, including South Carolina governor Robert Scott, that they needed to end their crusade for African-American civil rights if they wished to attract Northern investment. Writing from New York City, Harrison said, "There is not only no sympathy for them here, but actual hostility and contempt. I don't allude to [just] this city, but all through the North and West. In other words, the

Negro is played out, and other more practical and exciting subjects will soon be brought on the political boards."[33]

The view that white Southerners were sympathetic victims of Reconstruction had been presaged in the *New York Times*, which editorialized in 1870, just when the Ku Klux was beginning to receive national attention, that "as a whole, the South is as free from lawlessness as any other part of the Country," adding of the South that the North "must not magnify its faults, or close our eyes to its merits."[34]

New York Tribune editor Horace Greeley made the decision in the fall of 1871 to challenge Grant for the presidency in 1872 in considerable part because he opposed Grant's Southern policies. Greeley favored a far more conciliatory policy toward former Confederates and moderation in the pursuit of civil rights for African Americans. He declared, for example, that he supported "equivalent" rather than equal education for Black children in the South, a foretaste of the "separate but equal" doctrine adopted by the US Supreme Court in its 1896 ruling in *Plessy v. Ferguson*.[35]

Akerman was taken aback that the North was losing interest in Reconstruction at the moment he had expected a redoubled effort on behalf of the rights of African Americans. He had been certain that the Ku Klux trials and the report of the congressional investigating committee would "horrify the north . . . [and] show them how active and cruel the Confederate temper still is in the south." Akerman had predicted the Ku Klux trials would dominate national news coverage and congressional debate "during the ensuing winter." But while the trials gained considerable national newspaper coverage, Akerman ruefully acknowledged that "the 'Tammany Frauds' in New York have occupied the public mind somewhat to the exclusion of affairs in the south."*[36]

Akerman tried to rally public opinion in the North when he had the opportunity. "In a speech at Brooklyn last Friday evening," Akerman wrote hopefully in early November 1871, "I tried to make some of the truth known, and the simple narration of some of the transactions in York county appeared to make a very deep impression upon the reflecting part of the audience."[37]

---

*The *New York Times* had recently run an exposé on how the Tammany Hall political machine had embezzled hundreds of thousands of dollars during construction of New York City's new courthouse, a revelation that led angry taxpayers to refuse to pay their taxes, which then caused a crisis in the city's credit rating.

But that audience, perhaps never as large or as reflective as Akerman hoped, was growing smaller and more reactionary by the day. Akerman acknowledged that Congress had no appetite for further civil rights legislation, and understood that while the Ku Klux crimes were morbidly fascinating to readers, the repetition of atrocities had become numbing. As Americans today often view the Middle East as full of intractable and insoluble conflicts, so then many in the North felt that the South would have to sort out its race relations on its own—and the North had no interest in addressing its own myriad means of oppressing African Americans within its own society.

In late November, Akerman acknowledged that "many Republicans of the North are anxious for an end of the Southern troubles." Northern Democrats, of course, were even more anxious to reestablish the prewar political status quo, as they stood to benefit from a return to power of their Southern fellow partisans. By the time he had submitted his resignation and was ready to depart Washington, Akerman forlornly acknowledged that in the North "even such atrocities as Ku-Kluxery do not hold their attention as long and as earnestly as we should expect. The Northern mind being active and full of what is called progress, runs away from the past."[38]

Despite flagging support within the administration and the public at-large, Akerman, following the advice he had given his son to always do what was right, not what was popular, reportedly was planning to increase the pace of prosecutions and implement a Ku Klux policy "more offensive than at present" that apparently included the possibility of suspending habeas corpus and sending additional federal troops to certain sections of Georgia. But the *New York Herald* reported that "the President does not seem to agree" with Akerman's plan to expand Ku Klux prosecutions, and it was the two men's "distinct difference of opinion on the Ku Klux policy" that was the "special impulse" that led to Akerman's removal from office.[39]

The real problem, historian McFeely noted, was that Akerman was "one of an exceedingly small group of white Republicans who were not embarrassed" to see African Americans assert the equality the party and the nation had promised.[40] The District of Columbia, being under federal control, had slowly pioneered a new relationship between the races, such as by integrating public transportation, and Northern Republicans were as discomfited being regularly in the presence of free Blacks as Reverdy Johnson had been in addressing Black jurors for the first time in the courtroom in Columbia. Akerman was targeted for removal from office, McFeely writes, "because men from the North as well as the South came to recognize, uneasily, that if he was not halted, his concept of equality before the law was likely to lead to total equality."[41]

Akerman had trouble believing that Grant's ardor in combatting the Ku Klux had cooled, and his loyalty to Grant never wavered. Even after he was pressured to resign, Akerman told a friend, "In his administration there is more to promise with less to blame, than in any that we have had for forty years. Its merits are in primary things, its faults in trivial things." His loyalty was undiminished nearly a decade later when he expressed hope that Grant would break precedent and come out of retirement to seek a third presidential term in 1880.[42]

The problem was that the resoluteness Grant had demonstrated time and again in war abandoned him in politics. His instincts were genuine and honorable, but he could be easily influenced by others and depart from a course to which he had once seemed resolutely committed.

An incident that involved Grant shortly after he appointed Akerman attorney general demonstrates both the hopeful promise of Reconstruction and the more typically infuriating and heartbreaking failures in the quest for racial justice. James Webster Smith, a former slave from Columbia, South Carolina, was the first African-American cadet appointed to the US Military Academy at West Point after having demonstrated considerable scholastic ability in high school and then at Howard University. Smith entered West Point as the lone African American after three other Black men were denied admission on spurious grounds. Smith was too well prepared to be kept out on a technicality, but his "welcome" at West Point in the summer of 1870 was atrocious. He was shunned and silenced—white cadets conspired to say not a single word to Smith all year unless it was to insult and degrade him—and he was mercilessly hazed far beyond anything a white plebe might encounter, including beatings and being doused while he slept with a slop bucket full of urine and feces.

One of his tormentors was Grant's own son, Frederick Dent Grant, who was a senior the year Smith was a plebe. Despite the relentless harassment and near-overwhelming loneliness, Smith persevered and maintained a strong academic record, which outraged his persecutors all the more.

When Northern philanthropist David Clark, who had championed Smith's West Point appointment, sought an audience with Grant at the White House to seek the president's intervention on Smith's behalf, Fred Grant sat in. After Clark had made his case, Fred Grant, who had his father's ear on the subject, spoke up: "Well, no damned nigger will ever graduate from West Point." His father offered no rebuke, and Grant, whose intervention would have made a decisive difference, made no effort to diminish Smith's torment. An outraged Clark later called Fred Grant, who would graduate forty-first in a class of forty-one in discipline, "a low miserable scamp," and actively worked against Grant's reelection the following year, calling him "unworthy of his position."[43]

Akerman had said of Grant, "The objections to his administration . . . are of the most frivolous sort. They do not go to essentials."[44] But ensuring that West Point was welcoming to African Americans, nearly two hundred thousand of whom had fought for the Union and played a decisive role in its victory, was hardly frivolous. By the second half of the twentieth century, the American military would become among the most integrated institutions in American society. But Grant's failure to intervene in Smith's case meant that was decidedly not the case in the nineteenth century.

When Smith could take no more and allegedly struck one of his cadet tormentors, he was brought up on charges and convicted, but the presiding judge was General O. O. Howard, first head of the Freedmen's Bureau, cofounder of the university Smith had attended, and an advocate for the integration of West Point. Aware of Smith's tribulations, Howard gave Smith a light punishment. The case was appealed to Secretary of War William Belknap, "who was well known for his own disinclination to assist black causes." Belknap pardoned Smith but also ruled that if Smith wished to stay at West Point, despite his outstanding academic record, he would have to start over as a plebe and redo his freshman year. Remarkably, Smith did return, but the torment continued and he, along with three other African Americans who had been admitted that fall, left West Point mid-year. A Black cadet, Henry O. Flipper, finally graduated from West Point in 1877, but after Jim Crow took hold there were no more African-American graduates until 1936.[45] Belknap summed up the Smith episode by saying he did for the cadet "what has never been done for a white boy in like circumstances"—which was absolutely true, but not the way Belknap meant it.[46]

III

"With Akerman's departure on January 10, 1872, went any hope that the Republican party would develop as a national party of true racial equality," historian William S. McFeely wrote, meaning that Southern Republicans, primarily African Americans, had lost their champion within the Grant Administration, and that white supremacist Democrats were destined to again dominate politics in the South for another century.[47] That Akerman and his efforts are now largely forgotten, McFeely added, is the result of a "conspiracy of historical silence that came down on Reconstructionist integrationists."[48] Certainly, Akerman's successor had no inclination to pick up the torch.

Even though Bristow had secured the support of nearly fifty, mostly Southern congressmen, his scheme to replace Akerman failed. The man Grant chose to replace Akerman as attorney general was former Oregon senator George Williams, who had gained a reputation as one of Grant's "chief flatterers and hangers-on" and who was the first presidential Cabinet member from the West Coast.[49] Williams was Akerman's opposite in almost every way, and was a "dim legal light" whose career would eventually be undone by his ambitious and extravagant wife.[50] While Williams's inadequacies seem to have been well known, he had been a member of the Senate club, and so his nomination drew no opposition. The *New York Tribune* reported that Williams "was confirmed within five minutes after the nomination was read, a compliment frequently paid to an ex-Senator appointed to office."[51]

Williams was born in 1833 in upstate New York and studied law there before moving west, first to Iowa, where he became a judge with fateful personal consequences, and later to Oregon where, at the age of thirty, he was appointed chief justice of the Oregon Territory by President Franklin Pierce. Originally a Democrat, Williams had argued for an anti-slavery provision at Oregon's constitutional convention, and when the Civil War began Williams switched allegiance to the Republican Party and was elected one of Oregon's US senators in 1864, though he was defeated for reelection in 1870.

His background led some to believe that, "on the all-important southern question, Williams was sound," and after his appointment Williams pledged to use "the whole power of the country in the most vigorous and effective manner to crush out every conspiracy against the peace of society and the safety of the unoffending citizens."[52] In truth, Williams was not "concerned with much of anything except his career and his exceedingly costly wife."[53]

Superficially, it did appear that Williams was continuing the campaign against the Ku Klux unabated. The number of convictions of Ku Klux under Williams's watch increased, with 456 convictions in 1872 and another 469 in 1873, but Williams never claimed "a deep concern" for the anti–Ku Klux crusade, and the "greater credit" for these successful prosecutions belongs to the dedicated US attorneys in the South, such as Corbin, who were still operating under a strategy and instructions developed by Akerman.[54]

Further, the handling of the case pending against J. Rufus Bratton and James W. Avery for the murder of Jim Williams underscored Attorney General Williams's lack of interest in using the Ku Klux cases to protect the rights of African Americans. In that case, one legal scholar said, his behavior appeared "downright obstructionist."[55]

As discussed earlier, Avery and Bratton were indicted for the March 1871 lynching of Jim Williams, but both men fled the country for Canada to avoid prosecution. The case involved two constitutional questions that Judges Bond and Bryan were loath to rule on without guidance from the US Supreme Court: Was the Second Amendment now a federally secured right because of the Fourteenth Amendment, and was using common law crimes as the measure of punishment in civil rights cases constitutional? Following an agreement between prosecutors and defense counsel, Bond and Bryan agreed they could not come to a single opinion and certified the case directly to the Supreme Court in hopes the high court would resolve both questions.

The Supreme Court received the certification in December but, wary of tackling any civil rights cases involving the new Fourteenth Amendment, had delayed taking up the case. Now, Williams gave the court a way of avoiding making a ruling at all by moving to invalidate the certification, arguing that the Supreme Court did not yet have jurisdiction in the case. He cited precedent from a Supreme Court ruling from two years before where the justices said they could not intervene in a case so long as a lower court still had broad discretion to address the disputed issues before it.

Williams said the trial of Avery and Bratton, even though both men were absent, could have gone forward in the Fourth Circuit, and Bond and Bryan could have first ruled on the constitutional questions at hand before forwarding the case for appeal to the Supreme Court, which could have then upheld, overturned, or modified those decisions.[56]

Reverdy Johnson, "who was certainly a finer constitutional lawyer than Williams," argued against dismissing the certification. The constitutional issues themselves involved whether the Fourth Circuit court had jurisdiction in the proceeding, Johnson said, and so the case against Avery and Bratton could not proceed in that venue "until the question is decided." Johnson had argued that the odd alternative penalty provision in the Enforcement Act meant that a federal court was, in the case of Avery and Bratton, essentially trying a murder case, which should therefore be under state, not federal, jurisdiction.[57]

Williams countered that the circuit court clearly had jurisdiction to try the defendants on conspiracy charges, and so the trials could have proceeded on those charges and the constitutional questions could have been addressed after there was a conviction and sentencing. The Supreme Court, this time acting with greater alacrity since it afforded the opportunity of *avoiding* a decision on civil rights, sided with Williams and ruled on March 21, 1872, that they could not provide direction on the constitutional questions at hand so long as the circuit court still had broad discretion to deal with the issues.[58]

The following month, in April 1872, Corbin decided to try once more to force a decision on the outstanding constitutional questions and indicted a Ku Klux on the charge of conspiring to deprive an African-American citizen of the right to bear arms under the Second Amendment, and he declared he would seek the common law penalty for murder in the case. This case involved a Ku Klux named Elijah Ross Sepaugh who was selected among several defendants to stand trial for the particularly grisly murder of Tom Roundtree, an African American who was targeted for death because he allegedly planned to buy a large number of guns with the three hundred dollars he had realized from the sale of his cotton crop. Nearly eighty nightriders descended on Roundtree's home in December 1870. When the Ku Klux broke into his house, Roundtree fired into the crowd, wounding Sepaugh, which led to a return barrage of fire from the Ku Klux that riddled Roundtree's body with thirty-five bullets. For good measure, one of the Ku Klux then slit Roundtree's throat from ear to ear.[59]

The law, Corbin told the jury, "says that when men commit murder, they shall die, and we have no right to complain of it."[60] The jury of six white and six Black men convicted Sepaugh of conspiracy to deny Roundtree his civil rights and a second count that he had helped commit murder as part of that conspiracy. Sepaugh's attorney, John Ficken (Johnson and Stanbery were no longer actively engaged defending the Ku Klux by this time), quickly moved for an arrest of judgment to defer sentencing by Judge Bond, and the case was certified to the Supreme Court. Ficken's argument was on the same grounds that Johnson had argued in the case of Avery and Bratton, which was that murder cases must be tried in state, not federal, court.

Once again, the Supreme Court procrastinated so that Sepaugh was still in jail awaiting sentencing in 1874 when Williams intervened and ordered Corbin to enter a *nolle prosequi* (a formal notice with the court that the government did not intend to proceed) on those counts related to murder, which removed it from the Supreme Court docket. Corbin protested, but Williams would only say he made the request "not for the sake of Sepaugh, but for the sake of the public good." Sepaugh, instead of facing execution, was convicted on a minor violation of the Enforcement Act and fined one hundred dollars and sentenced to one year in prison.[61]

Lacking clear guidance from the nation's high court, federal prosecutors no longer sought to include Second Amendment violations in their indictments against Ku Klux, nor did they seek penalties beyond the modest prison terms and fines that were one option for punishment under the Enforcement Acts. Ku Klux generally received short prison terms, rather than the possibility of execution, which in some cases worked in the federal government's favor. "They all plead guilty, if only you won't hang them," Judge Bond wrote his wife.[62]

It seems unlikely that Attorney General Williams, in his several interventions to avoid a Supreme Court ruling, was motivated by a desire to increase Ku Klux confessions, because everything he did suggested he wished to wind down the campaign against the Ku Klux.[63] Williams's focus was now on clearing the docket, for at the end of 1872, 1,188 Enforcement Act cases were still pending in South Carolina alone, a backload that without substantial new court resources would take years, if not decades, to resolve.

As one way to clear more cases, Corbin requested a special session of the circuit court for August 1872. Not only was Williams opposed to such a special session, so was Judge Bond, who felt he had done his part "to suppress this revolt . . . and I can do no more." Besides, the August weather in

South Carolina "is not particularly agreeable & trying Ku Klux less so," he said, adding as justification that the trials were expensive and the courts had been told to economize.[64]

As he began to wind down Ku Klux prosecutions, Williams first ordered federal prosecutors to focus only on the most heinous cases that involved murder; cases that involved brutal whippings and assaults were set aside. Then he ordered US attorneys in the Carolinas to suspend further prosecution of existing cases, and to instead focus only on new cases as they arose. Williams admitted he was less interested in convictions than in simply keeping public order. He also began a selective pardoning policy. Bizarrely, this was done at the initiative of an active prewar abolitionist named Gerrit Smith who had visited the federal prison in Albany, New York, where most convicted Ku Klux had been sent, and concluded that most of these inmates were not Ku Klux leaders, which was true, but were instead "ignorant men who had been duped into joining" the KKK. His report spurred Williams to begin pursuing pardons so that even most of those Ku Klux who were convicted never served the entirety of their already modest sentences.[65]

IV

Perhaps Williams preached leniency out of fear that he might also one day find himself in need of clemency, for Williams was the type of dishonest hack who gave the Grant Administration its long-standing reputation for incompetence and corruption. As biographer Jean Edward Smith wrote, "Grant's loyalty to his appointees went beyond prudence."[66] This was certainly true of Williams, who "whenever tested as attorney general had failed dismally," Smith wrote. During the Crédit Mobilier scandal, "the evidence was clear-cut" that Williams had badly managed lawsuits brought against the company, which meant the government was unable to retrieve any of the millions of dollars of which it had been "manifestly defrauded."[67]

More damning than Williams's incompetence was his second wife's avarice. Williams had first met the future Kate Williams when he was a judge in Iowa and had granted the beautiful young mother of a son a divorce from her husband, a miller eight years her senior. Over the next few years, Kate remarried and divorced again, while Williams's first wife, also named Kate, died, leaving him a widower. He and Kate renewed their acquaintance when Kate moved to Portland, Oregon, and they wed in 1867, midway through Williams's Senate term.[68]

Mrs. Williams, still in her late twenties and about seventeen years younger than her husband, was considered the most beautiful woman in official Washington. This made her popular with the men of Washington, but her social pretensions angered the wives of other administration officials and senators, most especially First Lady Julia Grant, who began excluding Kate Williams from official functions.[69] To appease his wife and remove Kate Williams from Washington, Grant at one point contemplated making Williams minister to the tsar's court in Russia.[70]

Akerman had been miserly spending public money even on public business. Mrs. Williams desired to have the most expensive carriage in Washington—grander even than the president's—and so one was purchased and equipped with a liveried coachman and footman at government expense. Williams also commingled his personal accounts with those of the Justice Department, "paying personal checks with government funds," although he ended up repaying the money.[71] Grant initially concluded the Williamses were only "indiscreet," but later concluded the use of government funds for personal use was "unjustifiable."[72]

Akerman had refused to be bribed. Mrs. Williams actively sought a bribe to cover her and her husband's opulent lifestyle. Kate Williams had solicited a thirty-thousand-dollar bribe—what in today's dollars would be in excess of a half-million dollars—from the New York mercantile firm of Pratt & Boyd in return for the promise that she would get her husband to stop proceedings against the firm for alleged fraudulent customhouse accounts.[73]

Where Akerman had engaged the US Secret Service to work undercover to expose the crimes of the Ku Klux Klan, Williams used the Secret Service to gather political intelligence for use in the 1872 elections.[74] He also enlisted Secret Service chief Hiram Whitley to help him and his wife dispose of an embarrassing personal problem: his wife's wastrel son by her first marriage.

The young man, clearly his mother's son, had moved to Washington to enjoy his own high living as the stepson of a member of the president's Cabinet. He reportedly brought known prostitutes as dates to official Washington functions, stole jewelry from some of his paramours, and robbed his stepfather of twenty-seven thousand dollars in cash that the attorney general had stashed in his personal safe. Whitley tracked the young man down in New York City and retrieved all the stolen money but for the twelve hundred dollars the young man had already spent.[75]

At the Williamses' request, Whitley developed an elaborate ruse to get the troubled young man out of Washington for good. Whitley, who described the young fellow as "a daisy to look at with hair wavy and nicely parted, a pair of keen, gray-blue eyes, rosy cheeks, and a mouth to kill," ensnared the boy in an elaborate scam whereby the young man was introduced to a bogus counterfeiter of government bonds. Whitley and his minions convinced the young man a murder had been committed and that he needed to flee to Mexico to avoid arrest for his part in the phony felony. Whitley proudly noted that Kate Williams's son "was never afterwards heard of by any of his relations in Washington."[76]

For other malfeasance, for which it appeared he might be indicted, Whitley resigned in 1874, claiming ill health, though Williams hung on.

When Chief Justice Salmon P. Chase died in May 1873, Grant passed over such luminaries as New York senator Roscoe Conkling and stellar future justice John Marshall Harlan (who would be appointed to the court by President Rutherford B. Hayes), and astonished official Washington by nominating Williams to the post. Made aware of Williams's many indiscretions, Grant withdrew the nomination, which drew the ire of a bitter Kate Williams, who had craved this even higher social position. She began to write a series of anonymous letters, with the help of a vengeful Whitley, who felt he had been unjustly ousted from his position, to Cabinet secretaries and their wives, including Mrs. Grant, alleging all manner of sexual and financial improprieties within the Grant Administration. This was all too much for Grant, who finally asked Williams for his resignation in April 1875.[77]

Williams, who became mayor of Portland, Oregon, twenty-five years later, was succeeded as attorney general by Edwards Pierrepont, who had been US attorney in New York. Pierrepont expressed strong support for the civil rights of African Americans, but he continued Williams's moratorium on Ku Klux prosecutions. But that was later. When Williams first became attorney general, there were still more Ku Klux cases to be tried in Columbia.

CHAPTER ELEVEN

After they got done with me, I had no sense for a long time. I laid there—I don't know how long.
      —HARRIETT SIMRIL FOLLOWING HER GANG RAPE BY KU KLUX

I

Following Robert Hayes Mitchell's conviction for his relatively minor role in the murder of Jim Williams, the next trial in Columbia involved two of the more prominent York County Ku Klux who had been arrested: John W. Mitchell, who was identified as a Ku Klux chieftain, and Dr. Robert W. Whitesides, a local physician. Both were the type of leaders that Akerman had hoped would be prosecuted aggressively as the most potent strategy to dismantle the Ku Klux.

Mitchell and Whitesides were charged with participating in an assault on an African American named Charles Leach, who was "severely" whipped "because he had been a Radical and voted the Radical ticket."[1] But the assault on Leach often seemed largely forgotten during long segments of the trial as Corbin and Chamberlain instead called witnesses to testify to the Ku Klux's often sexualized violence, noting that Ku Klux "not only whipped and beat colored men entitled to vote, but they whipped and ravished women in pursuance of their general conspiracy."[2]

With so many national newspaper reporters in the courtroom, Chamberlain and Corbin were deliberately calling witnesses to testify to Ku Klux atrocities irrelevant to the specific case at hand to further expose Ku Klux atrocities to a national audience, and give lie to the Ku Klux pretense that it was a chivalrous organization.

Southern white men had enjoyed "generations of nearly universal . . . sexual access to black women," and that had not really changed with emancipation.[3] The most graphic testimony during the trials came from a woman named Harriett Simril, whose wrenching witness (and the reaction to it) demonstrated both the several purposes for which rape was used by the Ku Klux and the especially vulnerable status of African-American women.

Simril was a neighbor of Elias Hill's in the Clay Hill district. She, along with her husband, Sam Simmons, who was known to support "Radical" politics, were the targets of three Ku Klux raids that eventually resulted in the Ku Klux burning down their home. During the first raid in the spring of 1871, Ku Klux dragged Simmons from his and Simril's home and beat him with a cowhide until he finally promised to "quit all politics, if that was the way they was going to do him."[4] Despite this recantation, and for reasons not explained at trial, the Ku Klux returned a few months later and demanded to see Simmons again, but Simril, who had young children in the house, said he was not home and that she did not know where he was. The Ku Klux then pushed their way into Simril's home.

"Well, they were spitting in my face, and throwing dirt in my eyes, and when they made me blind, they bursted open my cupboard," Simril testified. "I had five pies in my cupboard, and they eat all my pies up, and then took two pieces of meat; then they made me blow up the light again, cursing me."[5]

It is notable that Simril began her testimony by noting that the Ku Klux had broken into her cupboards to ransack her kitchen. The Ku Klux not only planned to defile her body, but as historian Kate Côté Gillin noted, "Their first act was to desecrate her home, the domestic haven most black women tried to reclaim once free."[6] Just as Elias Hill had felt a particular pang when the Ku Klux broke his treasured clock, Harriett Simril was receiving the same message from the Ku Klux that her aspirations of domestic middle-class respectability were futile.

Creating a safe, nurturing home was perhaps the greatest expression of what freedom meant to African-American women. During slavery, despite being the objects of white lust, Black women were deliberately defeminized. Females who were enslaved were made to wear ragged, desexualized clothing and were expected to work in the fields from before sunrise to after sundown alongside men as if there were no gender difference and as if they were no more than livestock.

The desire of African-American women after emancipation to fill the same domestic roles as white women infuriated Southern whites, especially the planter class, who, in part, blamed the postwar labor shortage on the refusal of Black women to continue to work in the fields. Lucretia Adams told the congressional committee that held hearings in Yorkville that she had been whipped because she had refused to work in the fields and the Ku Klux who beat her said their mission was "to make the damned niggers work," regardless of gender.[7]

Another African-American woman named Jane Surratt also testified before the congressional subcommittee that both she and her daughter had been whipped by the Ku Klux for failing to work in the fields. Surratt said the Ku Klux forced her to lie on the ground and struck her forty times with a switch "bigger than my thumb . . . from my ankles clear up to about here, above my waist." Surratt was hurt so badly she could not hold her youngest child on her lap, and could only nurse the child by laying it on the bed and then bending over it. Surratt added that her landlord, a man named Dennis Scruggs, came to their cabin after the Ku Klux raid not to see if she was healing, but to complain that no one in the family was out in the fields working.[8]

After recounting how the Ku Klux destroyed her pantry, Simril said the Ku Klux kept demanding to know where her husband was. They searched the house again and again, Simril said, decided to wait until her husband returned, and forced Simril to make a fire for warmth as they pestered her for assurances that her husband had learned his lesson and would vote Democratic in future elections. After an hour had passed, by Simril's estimation, they grabbed her and dragged her outside.

"They dragged me into the big road, and they ravished me out there," Simril testified.

"How many of them?" Corbin asked.

"There was three," Simril replied, adding that she was able to recognize her attackers and identified them by name: Tom McCollum, Ches McCollum, and "Big Jim" Harper. The three took turns raping Simril as her children waited inside the house.

"One right after the other?" Corbin asked.

"Yes, sir," Simril replied, and she then detailed "all [the] nasty talk [that] came out of their mouths" as they raped her, but we do not know exactly what they said because the court reporter declared the words "of too obscene a nature to permit publication," and so he refused to put it in the court transcript.[9]

When Reverdy Johnson later demanded to know how the rape of Simril or any woman was related to the violation of voting rights and the case at hand, Chamberlain replied that it was clear that rape was used regularly by the Ku Klux to force African-American women to reveal the whereabouts of their husbands and to punish them when they would not do so.[10]

It is also notable that while the Ku Klux might have simply raped Simril in her home, they instead deliberately brought her outside the house and raped her in the middle of the "big road." It was common for the Ku Klux to outrage Black mothers, wives, and daughters out-of-doors in what they hoped was in plain view of an anguished husband or father hiding nearby. The Ku Klux hoped these husbands and fathers would become so enraged that they would emerge from hiding and expose themselves to Ku Klux violence, including death, but even if they remained in hiding the Ku Klux had the satisfaction of knowing that such an open display of depravity sent the message that Black men were as hobbled in protecting their families in freedom as they had been in slavery.

Rape, then, as it often is in times of war and strife, was used to brutalize women and humiliate the men in their communities. In a time and culture where women were considered primarily extensions of their husbands or fathers, to assault a woman was by extension to assault the man to whom she "belonged." To rape an African-American woman was to reassert white "power and sexual dominance over the black community."[11]

The more prosperous, the more assertive, the more independent African-American men were, the more the Ku Klux sought to "demasculinize" them by violating "their" women. In this regard, Rosa Williams, widow of Black militia captain Jim Williams, was fortunate in avoiding being assaulted herself, for the Ku Klux particularly targeted the wives and daughters of African-American Union army veterans for rape in retaliation for their men having demonstrated the initiative to fight for their freedom.[12]

After completing their crime, the three Ku Klux rejoined the larger raiding party and left Simril lying in the road. "After they got done with me, I had no sense for a long time," she said. "I laid there—I don't know how long."[13] Hours passed, but before the sun rose, she made her way back to her house. When her husband returned, they and their children gathered their belongings and slept outside for the next several nights for fear of another raid. This proved to be prudent. When she and her husband returned to her house, Simril discovered the Ku Klux had returned once more and burned it to the ground. "The next morning when I went to my house it was in ashes," she said.[14]

Following this appalling testimony, Johnson and Stanbery declined to cross-examine Simril, but several Democratic newspapers did their best to impugn and ridicule her testimony. Allowances had to be made "for the exaggerations of the witnesses who are mostly ignorant negroes," said the *Charleston Daily Courier*, adding that if the rape occurred, it could only have been perpetrated by "lower-class whites." The *New York World* was outraged that such a story would be brought up during the trial of community leaders such as Whitesides and Mitchell, "gentlemen of wealth and refinement, having charming families," who would never have had anything to do with such a "filthy-looking fright of a negress."[15]

In questioning whether the rape occurred, the *Courier* was not simply questioning whether a crime had occurred but whether such a crime was even possible, for up until three years previous, it was not a crime in South Carolina (or most of the South) to rape a Black woman. During slavery, white men who assaulted Black women justified their debauchery with the calumny that African-American women were innately licentious. As one scholar has noted, the portrayal of Black women as sexual aggressors "served both to exonerate White men of their inhuman rapes and to mask their human attractions to the supposed beast-like women."[16]

This idea that there was literally no such thing as the rape of an African-American woman because they were always sexually willing continued even following emancipation, when the Black Codes instituted by the holdover Confederate state governments in South Carolina and elsewhere defined a rapist as someone who did "unlawfully and carnally know any *white* woman [emphasis added], against her will or consent."[17] After Radical state legislatures made rape laws race neutral, Black women were so strongly discouraged from pursuing rape charges against white assailants that "the number of white-on-black cases officially filed and heard was quite small," one scholar concluded.[18] Even when they filed rape charges against Black assailants, the status of African-American women in Southern law and tradition was so degraded that these cases were not treated seriously by the white judicial system. In one instance when a Black man was convicted of raping a Black woman in Virginia, a white magistrate's sentence was only a directive to the man's father to give the rapist a "good whipping."[19]

The lack of legal protection for African-American women was one reason Corbin and Chamberlain were keen to expose the savage violence regularly inflicted by the Ku Klux upon them. Corbin and Chamberlain were still hopeful that they could find a way to extend some form of federal protection to both African-American women and children. The federal prosecutors had passionately argued that the Fourteenth Amendment provided all American citizens with the personal protection of the Bill of Rights, but Judges Bond and Bryan had been unwilling to go beyond acknowledging that the Reconstruction amendments protected only the right of African-American men to vote in federal elections. Therefore, despite the horrific stories shared on the witness stand, no federal indictments against Ku Klux included counts of violence against women or children, since they were not provided the right to vote.

II

If the Ku Klux thought this literal domestic terrorism would break the spirit of the African-American community by breaking the spirit of its women, they were wrong. The brutal abuse of African-American women only made them more militant in asserting their new rights and in supporting African-American men, including their men's use of violence, if necessary, in the quest for civil and political equality. They encouraged their men to join the Union League and militia and used often extraordinary measures to get them to vote.

A man named Mack Taylor recalled that Black ministers, perhaps drawing on the lesson of the ancient Aristophanes play *Lysistrata*, urged Black women to withhold sexual favors from their husbands if they refused to vote. Taylor, interviewed decades later by the Federal Writers Project, said when he failed to vote in 1872 for the Republican candidate for governor, Franklin Moses, "my wife wouldn't sleep wid me for six months."[20]

A white man named Alexander Wylie was stunned when he heard three young Black women, whom he claimed had been treated "just as a white person," express violent rhetoric both in defense of their rights and in bitterness about their treatment at the hands of whites. One of the young Black women said she would like to be in hell and "have a churn-paddle, and churn the whites to all eternity."[21]

Other African-American women still had hopes there would be judgment in this life. Some went to authorities to press charges against those who tormented them and their families. The widow of Tom Roundtree, whose murder had been ordered by William C. Black, a well-to-do Ku Klux and former state legislator, went to the sheriff and identified several of her husband's attackers, who were arrested. Black, however, helped the accused establish false alibis and they were never tried, while Mrs. Roundtree and her children were instead forced from their home and thereafter subsisted on charity from the local Army garrison under Merrill's command.[22]

Many African-American women tried to intervene to prevent the beating of a husband or father. Twenty-two-year-old Margaret Blackwell grabbed a pistol from the hand of a Ku Klux to prevent him from shooting her brother. For her resistance, she was kicked and beaten, but her brother was not killed.[23]

Other women sometimes volunteered to accept a beating in the place of their husbands or sons as an act of both love and resistance. An African-American man named Isham McCrary told congressional investigators that when the Ku Klux came to his home and announced they planned to whip him to death, his wife ran out of the house to plead that the Ku Klux should beat her instead. In her haste, she tripped and fell, injuring her leg so badly that she could not walk for nearly two weeks. The Ku Klux mocked her as she lay writhing in pain, but McCrary, while beaten, was not killed thanks to his wife's devotion.[24]

Black women were also occasionally able to resist their attackers. During the Mitchell and Whitesides trial, an African-American woman named Mary Robertson testified that she had been able to fend off an attempted rape by Ku Klux even while held at knife and pistol point. The Ku Klux had forced Robertson's young son to lead them to her home. When they could not find her husband, they first whipped Robertson's son and "gave my little baby boy two cuts."[25] A neighbor, James Crosby, a local African-American preacher who would also be raided by the Ku Klux that night, said he also heard "the lash of a whip—whipping a little boy."[26]

A Ku Klux named Jim Leach then dragged Robertson to a field more than one hundred yards from her house, possibly hoping to use her rape to flush her husband out of hiding. According to Robertson, Leach "snapped a pistol in my face three times" and screamed, "There is no help for you. Damn you, lie down." Robertson refused, and Leach then put a knife to her throat, but still could not force Robertson to the ground. In retaliation, he struck Robertson so hard with a hickory stick that, "I thought I was cut in two," she said. Three other Ku Klux arrived and took turns striking Robertson until, after another fifteen blows, the Ku Klux finally left. One of the other men who struck her, Robertson said, was John Mitchell, and as she surveyed the rest of the raiding party she saw, watching the scene unfold from nearby, Whitesides whose "face was not covered a bit."[27]

Just as Black women supported their men in resisting the Ku Klux, so, too, did the trials demonstrate that white women actively and often enthusiastically supported their men participating in the Ku Klux. Most white women in York County believed the Ku Klux to be "necessary . . . for the protection of white womanhood."[28] Some Ku Klux suggested they had been pushed into joining the conspiracy at the insistence of their mothers, wives, and fiancées. A white man named James Long claimed during his testimony that white women were "worse than the men" in their agitation at the sight of armed African Americans in the militias and by the recent spate of fires. They were, he said, more determined than their men to put African Americans back in their pre-emancipation place.[29]

At least two York County women, Lucy Zipporah Smith Howell and Willie Williams, insisted they had actually been initiated into the Ku Klux "oath and all," allegedly to ensure their secrecy as they knew so much about a variety of Ku Klux raids. Howell is the woman who said the Ku Klux killed the blacksmith Charles Good because they believed he was marking the shoes of the Ku Klux's horses so authorities could identify who had been on what raids. It is also possible, however, that Howell and Williams's "initiation" was simply a lark involving male admirers.[30]

While they could not go on raids, white women sometimes became physically involved, including in an incident involving my great-grandfather's younger brother, Moses P. Farris, and another man, William Carter, who spent most of 1872 in hiding to avoid arrest for their own crimes as Ku Klux. The two men were spending the night at the home of Moses's fiancée, Rachel Robbins, when his fiancée's sister, Laura, noted an African-American man named Bill Palmer observing the house. Believing Palmer was watching the property in order to report the "whereabouts" of Carter and Farris to federal authorities, the young woman snuck up on Palmer and began striking him with a stick until he fled.[31]

More typically, white women provided support services for the Ku Klux, most notably by sewing the outlandish disguises intended to frighten

African Americans while concealing the identity of the wearers. A Ku Klux pamphlet would later claim that Southern women had sewn more than four hundred thousand robes for Ku Klux men and their horses during the Reconstruction period, and while they were fully aware of what their men were doing in those robes "not a word was said by these women . . . and not one single secret . . . was ever revealed."[32]

During the Mitchell and Whitesides trial, fellow Ku Klux Charles Foster said he was summoned to the home of Milton Watson and told to bring his disguise, described as "a gown . . . solid red [with a] sack came over your head, and a string to draw around your neck," so that Watson's sister, Mary, and two other young women, Rose Leach and Jerusha Moss, could make matching outfits for other Ku Klux using Foster's as a pattern.[33] As York County minister and historian Jerry West said, "The old southern attitudes of rights, honor and womanhood were intricately woven into the robes of the Klansmen."[34]

But white women could also be the victims of Ku Klux, for while the Ku Klux constitution claimed that women were to "ever be special objects of our regard and protection," this in no way applied to African-American women or to white women who were the wives of white Republicans, nor to any white woman who had any type of relationship with African-American men.

On February 3, 1871, the Ku Klux raided the home of a white Republican named William Wilson. Wilson's wife, Faithy, said she could recall the date vividly because she had given birth to her son at 4:00 p.m. that afternoon.[35] When the Ku Klux raided that night, they killed the family's dog, fired shots into the house, and beat Wilson. Even though she had given birth hours before, several Ku Klux prepared to rape Mrs. Wilson. Her ten-year-old stepson, Harvey Hambright, begged the Ku Klux to leave his mother alone. Young Harvey was plump—"he was a damned big fine Radical . . . mighty nigh fat enough to make soap grease," one Ku Klux said—and so amused the Ku Klux with his defiance that they ended the rape attempt and left.[36]

The next witness to take the stand after Harriett Simril was a "puking" Klansman named Shaffer Bowens, who first testified to his role in the murder of Tom Roundtree, and then how he participated in raids on the homes of two white women, one named in court records as Jane Boheliers and another identified only as "Skates." Bowens said the Ku Klux were out looking specifically for three African-American men. Two were brothers,

John and Jake Wright, and the third was named John Moss. When the Ku Klux could not find the men at their homes, they traveled to Skates's house and broke down the door of her cabin, but found no one at home.

The Ku Klux then broke into Boheliers's home, about two miles from Skates's residence, where they found Moss and the Wrights hiding under the floorboards. The Ku Klux pulled the men outside, where the leader of the raid, a Ku Klux named Joe Harden, had twenty-five hickory switches cut and they began to whip the three men. Two of the men escaped and ran away, but the Ku Klux grabbed John Wright and tied his hands around a tree. Harden then began to whip Wright in a frenzy. "We all tried to get him to quit whipping him, but couldn't do it," Bowens said. Finally, Harden knocked Wright to the ground with the butt of his stick, but his violent urges were still not satiated.[37]

Bowens said he thought the raid was now over, but Harden then demanded that Boheliers be brought outside as well. "They had a pot of tar and lime, and was going to pour her full of it," Bowens said. Bowens claimed that he protested, but Harden "said he was going to have it done. [He] went back and ordered her out; made her lie down and held up her clothes." One of the Ku Klux attorneys asked the court to halt Bowens's testimony before it became too graphic, but Judge Bond replied that Corbin had promised to explain how this related to the Mitchell and Whitesides case. "We might as well let the people hear, and let the jury know what things exist about us," he said.[38]

Harden ordered Boheliers to now hold up her dress on her own, Bowens said, and directed a Ku Klux named Elijah Ross Sepaugh, who had been involved in Roundtree's murder, to fetch the pot of hot, steaming mixture "and told him to pour it in."

"Did he obey them?" Corbin asked.

"[Sepaugh] then poured it into her, as much as he could, and took a paddle and rubbed it in," Bowens replied.

"Pour it in her where?" Corbin asked.

"I don't like to tell," Bowens replied.

Judge Bond persisted: "In her privates?"

"He poured it in her privates," Bowens acknowledged. "They then told me to give her orders to leave there in three days."[39]

A disgusted Bond asked Corbin whether Harden was in jail awaiting trial. "No, sir," Corbin replied. "He has not been caught yet. There is some difficulty in finding him."[40]

It is doubtful Bond was particularly shocked by this assault on Boheliers; he had heard similar stories while presiding earlier at the trials of Ku Klux in North Carolina. There, he heard testimony in two cases, one involving a twenty-year-old Black mother of two and another involving an eighteen-year-old white woman, where in both cases the Ku Klux stripped the women naked, beat them, and cut them with knives before burning off their pubic hair with lit matches. The court records never listed the motivation for such horrendous acts, but in the case of the white woman, who was named Frances Gilmore, it was alleged she was a "strumpet" who slept with Black men.[41]

Bowens also insisted he did not know of any "special reasons" why the Ku Klux assaulted Boheliers and, presumably, intended to do the same to Skates. The nature of the relationship between Boheliers and the three African-American men was never specified. Corbin asked Bowens if Moss and the Wright brothers were "grown men," and Bowens replied that they appeared to be. It is possible the relationship was platonic, and if Corbin thought the men were young, perhaps Boheliers was in some way mentoring or teaching them. But the nature of the Ku Klux assaults suggests Boheliers's perceived sin was sexual in nature, though apparently consensual, and perhaps Boheliers, as Gilmore may have been, was a prostitute who catered to Black clients.[42]

According to historian Diane Miller Sommerville, interracial relationships were more tolerated during the times of slavery and Reconstruction than is generally understood. Southern fixation on what is called the "rape myth," the idea that Black men actively sought to rape white women and that this was the primary motivation for the lynching of African-American men, was the fanciful product of Jim Crow times, not Reconstruction, Sommerville argues.

The perverse work of the so-called "Dunning School" historians, whose histories of Reconstruction were written at the beginning of the twentieth century, used fear of Black-on-white rape to defend the Ku Klux as a necessary self-defense organization for the white community. One of these historians, Claude Bowers, wrote that Black men as slaves posed no threat to white Southern womanhood, but Yankee carpetbaggers instilled in African-American men the desire for social equality that resulted in Black lust for white women. "Rape is the foul daughter of Reconstruction," Bowers wrote.[43]

There is no evidence for this at all and a great deal to counter it. Bowers and his cohorts in the Dunning School were unable to find documentation of these alleged outrages, and instead were influenced by a new genre of fiction that emerged from Jim Crow, including the particularly infamous book by Thomas Dixon, *The Clansman* (1905), which became the basis for the film *Birth of a Nation* (1915) that was filled with "inflammatory black-on-white rape scenes."[44]

Nowhere in the records of the Great South Carolina Ku Klux Klan Trials is there a single instance where a Ku Klux raid was justified by Ku Klux defenders on the grounds that the intended target of the raid had raped a white woman. South Carolina–born journalist and historian Wilbur Cash concluded that the chance a white woman would be raped by a Black man "was much less, for instance, than the chance she would be struck by lightning."[45]

There was violence aimed at those, white and Black, who engaged in consensual interracial relations, as seen in the case of Boheliers and the three young Black men. The Ku Klux in York County also raided the homes of "white men living in adultery with Negro women and to Negroes living in adultery with white women." In neighboring Union County, a white family killed an African-American man and whipped his stepdaughter because the latter had given birth to a child fathered by one of the white family's members.[46] There is no record whether the white man of the family who fathered the child suffered any consequences whatsoever.

The Ku Klux even indulged in sexualized violence against white men in attacks that had strong homoerotic overtones. Commodore Perry Price testified before the congressional inquiry that the Ku Klux raided him because he was a local constable with Radical sympathies. He was taken from his home, blindfolded, and, when he refused to strip himself, his clothes were torn from his body so he lay naked on the ground while the Ku Klux focused their blows with whips, a hickory stick, and a brush on his buttocks until he lost all feeling. Asked to describe what the Ku Klux disguises looked like, Price replied that it appeared that each Ku Klux was wearing "something like a lady's dress."[47]

William Champion, who was white, and Clem Bowden, who was an African-American neighbor near what is now Gaffney, South Carolina, told congressional investigators an even more sordid tale. Champion, a farmer active in Republican politics, had taught Sunday school at a church Bowden also attended, and Champion, who was poor and looking for extra income, had offered to expand the school to two days a week and offer regular literacy lessons for any interested Black students.

In October 1870, the Ku Klux raided Champion's home, blindfolded him, and led him to a field where other Ku Klux had also brought Bowden and Bowden's wife. The Ku Klux pulled down Champion's and Bowden's pants and forced Mrs. Bowden to pull up her dress. They then beat them with sticks and branches before forcing Bowden to whip Champion, and then forced Champion to whip Bowden. They then demanded that Champion first kiss Bowden's "posterior" and then Mrs. Bowden's "private parts," before demanding that he have intercourse with Mrs. Bowden. "I told them they knew, of course, that I could not do that," Champion said, and the Ku Klux, who included a local trial judge, beat Champion some more and "asked how I liked that for nigger equality."[48]

Historian Francis B. Simkins, onetime president of the Southern Historical Association and considered a racial progressive in the 1920s when he wrote one of the first remotely critical histories of the post–Civil War Ku Klux Klan, recounted several of these stories in a 1927 article for the *Journal of Negro History* that was actually quite brave for its time. Yet Simkins insisted that such "disgusting" stories were proof that the Ku Klux was composed of "a much lower type than is popularly believed," noting that the Ku Klux's strength in the South Carolina Piedmont "where the uncultured white were predominant is indication of the type of membership. One must lose complete faith in Southern chivalry to believe that South Carolinians of standing could have committed the horrible crimes of which the Klan was actually guilty."[49]

That, of course, was not true. There was no South Carolinian of greater standing than Wade Hampton, and while he was not accused of committing these crimes personally and claimed to find them abhorrent, he paid for the legal counsel to defend them and sat at the defense table during the trial. The reason was that the purpose of the Ku Klux, as these sex crimes against women and others prove, was not about regulating sexual mores or cultural values. Its purpose was power. That had been the message that Corbin, Chamberlain, and Akerman had hammered home again and again. The *New York Herald* was convinced. As the Mitchell and Whitesides trial wound down, it noted, "The political purpose of the Klan has been indubitably shown."[50] Politics is all about power, and wherever power is at stake there will always be men of "standing," including Mitchell and Whitesides, who were still standing trial.

III

It was not until the second day of the trial that Charles Leach, whose assault was the basis for the indictment against Mitchell and Whitesides, took the stand to describe the assault that left him unable to work for a week. When the Ku Klux arrived on the raid, they demanded Leach hand over any guns in his possession, warning that if he did not turn them over voluntarily and they found one while searching his house, "we will kill you." Leach demonstrated remarkable courage and poise during the raid. When a Klansman accused Leach of being "a God damned Radical," Leach steadily replied, "Yes, I voted the Radical ticket." When they asked if he belonged to the Union League, he responded, 'Yes, I went to the League meeting twice," but he added, "I didn't see much sense in it [and] I didn't go back any more, gentlemen."[51]

If Leach had hopes this might satisfy the Ku Klux and they would leave him unharmed, he was mistaken. Charles W. Foster, a Ku Klux who testified for the prosecution, expressed admiration for Leach's cool demeanor. Instead of letting Leach be, Foster said the Ku Klux gave Leach a choice: He could be killed quickly, or they could give him one hundred lashes. "He said he would rather [receive] five hundred lashes," Foster testified. But the raid on Leach was one of a half dozen raids made by this klan on a night that had started at 9:00 p.m. They had the energy to give Leach only "about fifty lashes, I think," Foster testified, "with hickories and cowhides, probably a whip attached to it."[52] It was still enough to leave Leach "cut . . . all to pieces" from his hips up to his neck.[53] Exhausted, the Ku Klux let Leach go, and Foster said it was 4:00 a.m. when he arrived back at his home.[54]

Leach's testimony ended the prosecution's case, and attorneys for Whitesides and Mitchell then took very different tacks in offering their defense. Johnson and Stanbery were now acting solely in advisory capacities, so attorney W. B. Wilson argued the case that Whitesides "utterly denies" he was ever a member of the Ku Klux, despite Mary Robertson's testimony that she saw him observe the attempt to rape her. Wilson said the crimes enumerated during the trial "shock and disgrace humanity," but noted several prosecution witnesses supported the claim that Whitesides was not Ku Klux. One government witness said he had heard Whitesides publicly condemn the Ku Klux in March, long before he had reason to fear arrest, while another said he had once given Whitesides a Ku Klux secret signal but Whitesides did not respond.[55]

Foster, the one Ku Klux "puker" who claimed to have seen Whitesides on Ku Klux raids, was either mistaken or had a mysterious vendetta against Whitesides, Wilson said. He was only seeking to "rescue himself from prosecution," Wilson said, suggesting Foster may have been offered other inducements to testify. Wilson put several witnesses on the stand who testified that on the night Leach was assaulted, Whitesides was at Mitchell's home and was one of two physicians attending to Mitchell's mother, an epileptic who had had a seizure that night. Corbin expressed amazement that these witnesses could, nearly a year later, recall the exact date of Mrs. Mitchell's seizure and that it happened to be on the same night that Leach was assaulted.[56]

Mitchell's fourteen-year-old son, Samuel, took the stand to testify that he had heard his father refuse to join the Ku Klux when approached by a group of men at Christmastime 1870. But in his closing arguments, Mitchell's attorney, C. D. Melton, acknowledged Mitchell was a Ku Klux but said just because the Ku Klux was a secret organization did not make it "necessarily obnoxious to the law." Melton, as Johnson and Stanbery had done, equated the Ku Klux with the Union League. "Was it political?" Melton said of the Ku Klux. "Perhaps it was. But was not the League political?"[57]

Maybe some Ku Klux wished to prevent African Americans from voting, Melton said, but Mitchell was not one of them. He was "kindly disposed towards the colored people," Melton said. Mitchell, despite allegations he was a klan chieftain, did not instigate "mischief," but joined the Ku Klux to prevent it. "Cannot such a thing be?" he asked.[58] In accordance with standard trial practice throughout the United States, Melton was denied permission by the court to have Mitchell take the stand in his own defense, and he expressed frustration that neither Mitchell nor any accused klansman was allowed to "explain their conduct, their motives, or their purposes."[59]

Melton was particularly indignant that Corbin had called so many witnesses, including the women themselves, to testify to the rapes committed by the Ku Klux, with the implication that sexual violence was an essential purpose of the Ku Klux. "Now, I ask you, do you believe it," Melton asked the jury, "and that there did exist upon the face of God's earth an organization which would have among its purposes that of committing these gross outrages upon helpless women?"[60] He was perhaps fortunate that African Americans on the jury, like his client, were forbidden from speaking during the trial, for their answer, from both their own experience and the testimony provided, would likely have been "yes."

Chamberlain closed for the prosecution, pointing out that Whitesides and Mitchell were "nobody's dupes." Unlike some of the young men previously on trial, they did not occupy humble positions within their community but were "men of standing, men of substance, and men of education, men who have been accustomed to lead and influence [their] community," he said. Chamberlain reminded the jury that the government did not need to prove that Whitesides and Mitchell had participated or even approved of every act of the Ku Klux. The charge was being part of a conspiracy that seemed to have acted like a "terrible tornado" that had swept up virtually all the white men in York County.[61]

Addressing the jury of mostly freedmen, Chamberlain reminded them that when the Ku Klux called for a return to "Constitutional liberty, as bequeathed to us by our forefathers," this seemingly "innocent phrase" meant returning to the society that existed before the approval of the Thirteenth, Fourteenth, and Fifteenth Amendments, when "national law sanctioned slavery." A return to this form of constitutional liberty, Chamberlain said, "would have seized you, and brought you back and planted you again upon the plantation, and within the reach of your former masters."[62]

Chamberlain ridiculed Melton's assertion that the Ku Klux was a "political club." An organization devoted to distributing pamphlets and encouraging people to vote would not require members to take an oath that promised death if they revealed any of the group's secrets.[63] No, he said, the purpose of the Ku Klux was quite simple to understand; it was to "so terrorize that community that no colored man who had been set free by the Thirteenth Amendment, and made a citizen and a voter by the Fourteenth and Fifteenth Amendments, should be any better, or gentlemen, as well off, as when he was a slave." For if African Americans had no rights, Chamberlain said, "you had better be property."[64]

Chamberlain noted that while Mitchell and Whitesides's attorneys had impugned the testimony of Foster, the Ku Klux turned prosecution witness, they had presented no witnesses to rebut his testimony. One man whom the defense insisted could support Whitesides's contention that he was not a Ku Klux member had disappeared, Chamberlain noted, "gone, we know not where, a terrified and self-convicted Ku Klux." As for Foster, Chamberlain insisted he had been offered no inducements to testify and had every reason not to. Instead, Foster had shown extraordinary courage. "Two thousand loaded pistols—pointed at him, and every man sworn to kill him; and, yet, he comes and tells his story," Chamberlain said.[65] Chamberlain might have noted that women like Simril and Robertson had displayed equal if not greater courage in telling their stories, but he did not.

The jury received the case on Friday afternoon and deliberated all that day into the evening and night, and resumed deliberations the next morning before announcing their verdict at 9:00 a.m. on December 23, two days before Christmas. Demonstrating the sobriety with which the juries approached their duties, the jury deliberated over two days before finding Mitchell and Whitesides guilty of two counts. One was being part of the general Ku Klux conspiracy and the other of seeking to prevent Charles Leach from voting in the 1872 elections. But, for reasons not listed in the court transcript, they acquitted the men of two other counts that alleged Mitchell and Whitesides beat Leach to punish him for voting the Radical Republican ticket in the 1870 election.[66]

In preparation for sentencing, Mitchell was finally allowed to address the court. He began with, "I don't know hardly what to say," stating that his "poor" education left him inarticulate in "how to express my desires." Mitchell did not deny being a member of the Ku Klux, but insisted he had only joined to "save myself" because he had been threatened when he was not a member. He acknowledged he had been chosen as a klan chieftain because "they wanted a man that was sober and discreet." He had participated in two Ku Klux raids, Mitchell admitted, but in neither raid had a crime been committed—and he flatly denied he had been part of the raid when Leach was beaten. He added that at his wife's insistence, he had burned his Ku Klux disguise back in February and had left the order, which left him worried he would be the target of a raid.

Mitchell appealed for mercy, noting that he had seven children at home and was his family's sole means of support.[67]

Bond said it was appropriate that Mitchell appealed for mercy "on account of your family . . . but you never thought of the families of these other people. Men were taken out and murdered within sight of their wives, and men were scourged, and their wives were scourged, by this infamous organization, of which you were a chief." Whatever his lack of formal education, Bond said Mitchell was a "prominent man" in his neighborhood and the community deserved better leadership and judgment from him. Bond sentenced Mitchell to five years in prison and levied a one-thousand-dollar fine.[68]

Whitesides also addressed the court, but his remarks were comparatively brief. He maintained that he never belonged to the Ku Klux "and was always opposed to it." Quietly prompted by his attorney, Whitesides specifically denied having been part of the raid on Leach. Bond acknowledged that it appeared Whitesides had played a minor role in the Ku Klux, but lectured Whitesides that a man of his "position" might have helped stop the outrages. The Enforcement Acts, the suspension of habeas corpus, the presence of federal troops, and these trials would all have been unnecessary, Bond told Whitesides, "if gentlemen in your position in York County, having found out what was going on, had united to put it down. It seems that the people preferred to live in amongst this outrageous Klan rather than under the government of law." Bond fined Whitesides one hundred dollars and sentenced him to one year in prison. The court then adjourned for four days to observe the Christmas holiday.[69]

The two men's trials had ranged far beyond the primary crime of Leach's beating, but, as Chamberlain noted in his summation, that had largely been the point. The depraved nature of so many Ku Klux crimes was now part of an official record and would now "go forth to the world in the public prints."[70]

Chapter Twelve

I never considered, sir, that I had any right to preach against raids of that kind; I have no colored people belonging to my congregation at all.
—The Reverend Robert E. Cooper
TESTIFYING TO HIS ROLE IN WITNESS INTIMIDATION

I

Harriett Postle knew that Edward T. Avery was not only a respected local physician but also the father of a young family. So, even though Postle was aware of just how cruel the Ku Klux could be, she was nonetheless stunned when Avery, whom she recognized despite his disguise, placed his boot on the body of her infant as the child lay on the floor, put his weight upon it, and threatened to crush the life out of the baby unless she told the Ku Klux where her husband, a preacher named Isaac Postle, was hiding.*

A dozen Ku Klux had come to the Postle home between the hours of 3:00 and 4:00 a.m. on a Tuesday in March; Mrs. Postle could not remember the exact date. "I was asleep when they came," she said. "They made a great noise and waked me up, and called out for Postle. My husband heard them and jumped up, and I thought he was putting on his clothes, but when I got up I found he was gone." Mrs. Postle, who said she was "about thirty years old," was the mother of six children, the oldest being a fourteen-year-old boy, and she was pregnant with her seventh child.[1]

---

*Before Dr. Avery's trial began, a man named John S. Millar was tried and convicted of a single count of conspiring to prevent African Americans from voting. It was a strange case for prosecutors to bring to trial, as Millar was not accused of participating in any Ku Klux outrages, only of attending two Ku Klux meetings, which he said he did in order to protect his African-American laborers. Millar owned a large plantation, which was likely why Corbin, under orders to target community leaders, was "overzealous" in filing the charge. Several African Americans testified on Millar's behalf, stating he was adamantly against the Ku Klux. Bond agreed Millar was the "least guilty" of anyone brought to trial, and sentenced him to only three months in jail and a twenty-dollar fine. (Lou F. Williams, 91)

When the Ku Klux burst into her home with guns drawn, Mrs. Postle was so terrified she had trouble dressing. Her oldest son jumped under a bed to hide and the Ku Klux, thinking he was the father, aimed their pistols and prepared to shoot. "I then cried out, 'It is my child!'" Mrs. Postle said, and she pulled the young teen out from under the bed. As he was "hallooing and crying, I begged them not to hurt my child," she said. The Ku Klux shoved the boy hard against the wall, and a petrified Mrs. Postle slumped down in a chair, holding her infant in her arms. Thinking she was using the chair to disguise the fact her husband might be hiding under the floorboards, the Ku Klux knocked Mrs. Postle from the chair and she and her baby fell to the floor, which is when Avery pressed his foot down upon the child.[2]

Mrs. Postle continued to deny that she knew where her husband had fled. "You are a damned, lying bitch, and you are telling a lie," one of the Ku Klux said. The man who had put his boot on her baby now placed a noose around her neck, and she instinctively grabbed his hand. It was his left hand and it was "lame," which is how Mrs. Postle recognized Avery, for his left hand had been badly injured in the war and the injury was known and recognizable to all who knew him. Even though Avery was outfitted in a garish outfit of a red gown, a blue mask, and a cap with two, foot-long horns sewn onto it, "I said to myself right then," Mrs. Postle said. "I knows you." And the discovery made her melancholy. "Dr. Avery, I know, has a little family of his own, of little children."[3]

"We are men of peace," Avery told Mrs. Postle, as he now pressed his boot into the abdomen of the prostrate woman, "but you are telling me a damned lie, and you are not to tell me any lies to-night." He pressed harder and "mashed me badly," Mrs. Postle said, adding, "but not so badly as he might have done," for Avery apparently suddenly realized that Mrs. Postle was seven or eight months pregnant and raised his foot off the woman. With her children in tears, Mrs. Postle called them to her side and led them outside as the Ku Klux fired their guns wildly throughout the house on the chance Isaac Postle was hiding in an unseen nook or cranny. As she sat outside the house, leaning against a wall, a Ku Klux grabbed her by the throat and "beat my head against the side of the house till I had no sense hardly left; but I still had hold of my babe," Mrs. Postle testified.[4]

At that moment, the Ku Klux, shining their torches, discovered Postle hiding under the house. "Come out," ordered Avery; "if you don't I'll kill you."[5] The Ku Klux pulled Postle up through the floorboards by his hair, threw a rope around his neck as they had his wife's, and led him into the woods 250 yards from the house. They accused Postle, who was known as "Isaac the Apostle," of preaching "burning and corruption and telling the people to set fire to the gin houses and barns." Postle replied, "I have never preached anything but peace and harmony."[6]

The Ku Klux then threw the rope that was lassoed around Postle's neck over the branch of a tree. As they questioned Postle about who had been setting fires and whether he knew where African Americans were hiding their guns, they pulled on the rope to raise him off the ground so that "only my toes touched the ground.... I was choked and could not tell them anything," Postle said. "Then they slackened the line a bit and put all those questions to me over again." As they raised and lowered Postle with the rope, the Ku Klux repeatedly struck him with a leather strap an inch and a half wide, "two licks apiece as hard as they could," and tried to get Postle to say something that would justify even more abuse.[7]

They asked if he supported President Grant and had voted for the Radicals in the last election. Postle replied that he had not voted because he was on his circuit preaching during the time of the election. Then a Ku Klux asked if it were true that Postle had said "you would raise your children as good and as nice as anybody's children?" Aware the Ku Klux hoped to trick him into a statement suggesting he believed in social equality, Postle replied, "No, sir. I cannot raise my children so well, because I am not able." With that, the Ku Klux let him down and removed the rope from his neck. He was told that for every gin house set on fire, the Ku Klux would hang ten African Americans, beginning with Postle. As Postle looked at his assailants, he recognized several, including Avery and a man he identified as Howard White, "a colored man," Postle said, "and I believe a Democrat. He has left our part of the country, and I don't know where he is now." Postle said he and some neighbors who had also been raided by the Ku Klux that night compared notes and thought about leaving York County, but decided to stay when the federal troops arrived a few weeks later to provide protection.[8]

Avery's trial then took a strange turn when his attorney, W. B. Wilson, rose to cross-examine Postle and produced an affidavit drawn up by a local Presbyterian minister, Reverend Robert E. Cooper, signed by Postle, and witnessed by trial judge A. C. Cook, which said Postle confessed that he had been "incorrect and false" in accusing Avery of being one of his assailants.[9]

Postle explained that after the notice of Avery's arrest appeared in the *Yorkville Enquirer*, Cooper came to his home to discuss a matter that Cooper said "is in your behalf as well as in mine." Cooper asked Postle if he would withdraw his charges if presented with evidence that proved he had been mistaken in identifying Avery as one of his assailants. Postle said he doubted such evidence existed but said he would listen, as "it is not the mind of any Christian man, much less a preacher, to punish a man if he is innocent." Cooper insisted Postle come with him to visit Avery's wife, Mary. Postle noted to Cooper that he had neither put Avery in jail nor did he have the power to release him. "Never mind, you just come and see her," Cooper said, adding, "he won't be in prison always." Postle said he understood this remark to be a threat. "I began to think when they got out it might be that they would oppress, or arrest, or whip and disturb us, as they had done," he said.[10]

Mrs. Avery was "a high-spirited woman," Postle said, and after she invited Postle to sit with her by a fire she began to harangue him and demand he withdraw his complaint, insisting her husband had never left their house the night of the raid. "I felt very small, being with a lady like her—of her ability and position—and I felt it was almost wrong not to submit to her," Postle said, but he still refused to recant his testimony. "Our talk is all in vain!" Mrs. Avery exclaimed, and tired of being a supplicant to an African American, now switched to threats, telling Postle, "I would bring you to the same condition [as my husband], and, as such, to be cropped and branded and penitentiaried [*sic*] for ten years, and perhaps for your lifetime." She then summoned two of her African-American servants, her cook, Kizzy Avery, sixty-six, and the family nursemaid, Louisa Chambers, twenty-one, who both told Postle they would swear he was lying if he claimed Avery had been part of the Ku Klux raid.[11]

Postle said he had never been in trouble with the law and he was frightened by Mrs. Avery's and Reverend Cooper's threats. "I will withdraw on *your* oath, but not on *my* oath," Postle told them. Admitting he knew nothing of the law, Postle said when he signed the affidavit produced by Cooper, he thought he was simply allowing them to swear that they believed Avery to be innocent. On the witness stand, Postle said, "I still believe he (Avery) was one of the men with that party."[12]

II

Reverend Cooper took the stand and told a different story. He said Postle had come to him for "counsel and advice," and claimed that Postle admitted "he didn't know a single person" among the men who raided his home. Cooper said he asked Postle why he had been the target of a Ku Klux raid, and alleged that Postle acknowledged he had given a sermon in which he urged his fellow African Americans to set fires "and inflict great suffering and punishment upon the white people." Cooper added that he had told Postle that he would "counsel them against such a course as that."[13] Cooper did not explain why he did not advise the authorities of such a threat.

Cooper denied that he insisted Postle go visit Mary Avery, and said when he told Postle that he might face legal consequences if it was proved he was lying, he denied he had been making a threat. "I simply stated what I conceived to be the law," Cooper said. Cooper also denied Mrs. Avery had been either condescending or threatening toward Postle, but rather humble and sincere. He quoted Mrs. Avery, "rising to the importance of the occasion," as offering Postle the melodramatic pledge that "if my hopes of salvation depended upon the statement which I am now about to make to you, I would still say that Dr. Avery, my husband, was in my chamber the entire night." Cooper acknowledged that he and Mrs. Avery might have "referred to the penalty of perjury," but they had not threatened Postle with imprisonment or having his ears cut off. Asked why he had authored the affidavit, Cooper said it was because he used better grammar than the magistrate, R. C. Crook, and he did not want to submit a document filled with improper "syntax and prosody" to "the authorities of the United States."[14]

Corbin was infuriated that a Christian minister would play the role of enforcer for the Ku Klux Klan. He demanded to know why Cooper had even brought up the issue of perjury with Postle? "I wanted to get the old negro to tell what I believed to be the truth," Cooper replied. How did Cooper know the charges against Avery were false? Cooper said it was solely "upon the testimony of Mrs. Avery, a lady of uncompromising veracity." As to his own truthfulness, Cooper offered the favored genealogical defense of the Southern white aristocracy: "If I was speaking to those who knew my antecedents, you wouldn't question it." This was too much for Judge Bond, who demanded Cooper answer directly whether Postle had been threatened with perjury and, if so, who made the threat: Cooper or Mrs. Avery? Cooper admitted the possibility of perjury had been raised, but he could not remember by whom.[15]

Corbin then asked whether Cooper, as a Christian minister, had ever preached against the violence committed by the Ku Klux? "I am not a Ku Klux," Cooper said. "I didn't ask you that question," Corbin responded. "Did you ever preach against this Ku Klux business?" Cooper said he "wasn't commissioned to preach against those things; I don't preach political sermons at all." Corbin was incredulous. Did he think Ku Kluxing, with its whippings and murders, was only "a political matter to you?" An increasingly uncomfortable Cooper replied, "I never considered, sir, that I had any right to preach against raids of that kind; I have no colored people belonging to my congregation at all." Did he not worry, Corbin asked, that the commission of these crimes endangered the "bodies and souls" of his congregation? Cooper said he had assumed none of his congregation had participated in such crimes and so had no need to preach on the topic. "If I had had any reason to believe that they did, I suppose I would have done it, because I am pretty fearless," the disingenuous Cooper said.[16]

The two Avery servants, Louisa Chambers and Kizzy Avery, appeared as witnesses, but neither was particularly helpful to Avery's case. Avery was observed by a juror coaching Chambers in her testimony before she took the stand, and this was reported to the court, and while Kizzy Avery insisted her employer had not left the house the night Postle and others were raided, she confirmed that Mrs. Avery and Reverend Cooper had *both* threatened to ensure Postle was sent to the penitentiary if he did not change his story.

Major Merrill then took the stand for the first time during the trials to testify that Reverend Cooper had lied to him about his witness tampering. Merrill said Cooper came to his home just a few weeks before the trial and, despite being warned that anything he said might be used against him in court, insisted to Merrill that neither he nor Mrs. Avery had mentioned perjury to Postle. "He distinctly and repeatedly said that no allusion was made to it at all," Merrill said, which Cooper himself had just testified under oath was not true.[17]

Mrs. Avery, Cooper, Chambers, and Kizzy Avery were all indicted for seeking to intimidate a witness in a federal court proceeding. The four never went to trial and were never convicted, but the shenanigans surrounding Avery's trial were only just beginning.[18]

III

While the focus of the trial had been on the testimony of Isaac and Harriet Postle, only one of the four counts of the indictment issued against Avery, that of being involved in the general Ku Klux conspiracy, involved the attack on the couple. The other three counts involved the whipping and torture of sixty-one-year-old Samuel Sturgis, who was a neighbor of the Postles near Rock Hill and who had been raided the same night as the Postles while staying at the home of Abram and Emeline Brumfield.

Sturgis said a dozen Ku Klux arrived, including Avery, whom he said he had known for more than twenty years. Not only did he recognize Avery's injured hand, he saw Avery's face in profile when the Ku Klux bent over and his mask briefly slipped down. The Ku Klux beat Sturgis, threatened him with a pistol, and then threw a rope around his neck, dragged him roughly along the ground, and then, as they had with Postle, threw the rope over a beam in the house and raised and lowered Sturgis until he swore that "I would never vote a Radical ticket any more."[19] Sturgis was disturbed that at least five of the Ku Klux on the raid were fellow African Americans, including Howard White, plus Samuel Stewart, Frank Cowans, Hampton Avery, and Henry Toole. Neither the prosecution nor the defense seemed interested in questioning why these African-American men would join the Ku Klux on the raid, and so their motives were never discussed.[20]

It was New Year's Day 1872, the fourth day of the Avery trial, when his attorney, Fitz William McMaster, rose to give his closing argument and began by assailing the racial makeup of the jury that consisted of nine Black and three white men. McMaster was in the middle of drawing a parallel with how the Irish Catholic patriot Daniel O'Connell had been wrongfully convicted in 1844 by an all-Anglican jury when Corbin interrupted him and addressed the Court. "I don't notice the defendant in Court," he said. "I have just asked the counsel where the defendant was, and the reply I received was, that was for me to find out."[21]

Judge Bond was not amused, particularly when McMaster declined to answer whether he knew where Avery was and whether the defendant intended to reappear. Avery's three-thousand-dollar bond was ordered forfeited, and Bond threatened McMaster with both contempt of court and disbarment. McMaster begged to be allowed to consult counsel before Bond ordered his disbarment. There was uncertainty about how to proceed in a trial where the accused had participated through most of the trial and then simply disappeared. The court adjourned to the following day. Meanwhile, rumors abounded that Avery was certain he would be convicted and had fled, like my great-grandfather, to Arkansas.[22]

When court reconvened the next day, the decision was made to proceed as if Avery were still present. Chamberlain noted Avery had been present to enter his plea and had had the opportunity to confront all the witnesses called against him. If he was now absent by his choice, there was no reason the case could not be sent to the jury. Bond agreed and said if Avery wished, he could appeal later.

McMaster was aggressive and defiant in his closing argument. He resumed his argument from the previous day that Black jurors could not reach a fair verdict since Avery was charged with assaulting African Americans. "Can you be other than naturally indignant at these outrages?" McMaster asked. "Will not your hostility be naturally greater than a white man would feel? Therefore, it is that I say the world has never seen a greater outrage than in the jury that is now trying this question."[23]

When Avery realized the deck was stacked against him and that he could not count on the jury to act impartially, it was natural that he should flee, his attorney said. "I hope he is [now] in country that is freer than this by this time," McMaster said, insisting that Avery's flight should not be taken as an admission of guilt. Avery had once been a member of the Ku Klux, McMaster acknowledged, when it was an organization devoted solely to "home protection," but the "horrid and unnatural" crimes elucidated by the witnesses were the work of the lowest class of men, "the coal-field men of York County," and could not be ascribed to Avery, who was, according to McMaster, "a gentleman."[24] If prosecutors were simply using a man of Avery's high standing to set an example, McMaster said, "How delightful it would be to have Wade Hampton as a vicarious substitute for all the gentlemen of the South, and put him in the Penitentiary for ten years!"[25]

All this talk of gentility infuriated Corbin. Never in the practice of law, he said, had he seen a case where a defendant entered a plea, helped select the jury, heard all the testimony, "and then, in the darkness of night flees." There was only one conclusion to be made, Corbin said: "This gentleman—may God spare the name," had confessed his guilt when he ran away. Witnesses had him playing an integral role in the raids on the Postles, Sturgis, and even the one on the home of my great-grandfather's cousin, John R. Faris, where Avery had been "knocked down" with a fire shovel to prevent him from entering Faris's house.[26]

In addition to lambasting the concept that anyone in the Ku Klux was a gentleman, Corbin questioned the definition of "minister." He said, "I wish I could find the ministers of York County in better company." Not only had the Reverend Cooper refused to condemn Ku Klux violence from the pulpit, he engaged in witness intimidation and perjury to assist the Ku Klux. Nor was Cooper the lone pastoral apologist for the Ku Klux. Corbin noted that just the previous week, one of Charleston's most prominent ministers, the Reverend Dr. E. T. Winkler, pastor of the Citadel Square Baptist Church, had published a lengthy letter in New York and South Carolina newspapers, bitterly denouncing the Ku Klux trials. Winkler claimed it was men of low class, like my great-grandfather, "Crackers" and "Clay-Eaters . . . many of them are the offspring of illicit connections," who had committed these heinous crimes and then turned informers to falsely soil the reputations of the innocent, "the most respectable, wealthy and influential citizens of the State." As if Carolina's most prominent citizens were not already persecuted enough, Winkler said in a jarring and tasteless non sequitur, when "their property is assessed above its market value" for tax purposes.[27]

"What do you think of a minister of this kind?" Corbin asked the jury, referencing both Winkler and Cooper, who admitted he had never preached against Ku Klux violence. "What have you to say for a man who preached Christ and Him crucified—had a commission for that—but who says, 'I never said a word against Ku Kluxism. Whipping, killing and murdering could be done, and I say nothing about it because I don't preach politics.' Is there any surprise that Ku Klux could exist in York County?" The case was then sent to the jury, "and after a lapse of fifteen minutes," the court record says, they returned a verdict of guilty.[28]

Avery was not sentenced, however, because he was not there, and he remained in hiding while his wife attempted to clear his conviction.

Mrs. Avery wrote US attorney general George Williams in 1873, urging that the case against her husband and the father of their six children be dismissed and that he be allowed to return home. She submitted affidavits from two other Ku Klux who claimed they had been on the raids of Postle and Sturgis and swore that Avery had not been with them. Williams wrote

Corbin, who strongly objected, directing that he allow Avery to return to York County without further prosecution. Judge Bond also needed to agree to discontinue the case against Avery, but Bond not only clearly considered Avery to be guilty of the crimes with which he was charged, he was also personally offended that Avery had "jumped bail and disappeared after the government had spent so much time and effort on his trial." When Bond received the closing orders on Avery's case in April 1873, he signed only after striking through the section that excepted Avery from arrest. Aware he might yet be sentenced and jailed, Avery continued to remain in hiding until the middle of 1874, when the Ku Klux trials finally were discontinued.[29]

McMaster was not disbarred. Given his "known reputation as an able lawyer and an accomplished gentleman," in the words of the *Charleston Daily News*, the hearing on his possible disbarment drew attorneys from throughout South Carolina. Chamberlain admitted that he made the case for disbarment with limited enthusiasm, professing to hold McMaster in high esteem as an attorney, but said attorneys are officers of the court and that he had abused attorney-client privilege in being aware his client intended to run without notifying the court. Bond was clearly angry with McMaster, but declined to rule after the two-day hearing, and then left for home in Baltimore to begin a term of the circuit court there. There is no record that Bond ever formally issued a decision, and McMaster simply continued to practice law and eventually served in the state legislature and as mayor of Columbia, although he lost a race for Congress.[30]

The *Daily News* noted that before he departed, Bond pronounced sentencing on dozens of men who had pled guilty to a variety of charges for having been engaged in the Ku Klux conspiracy. The trial juries had been dismissed, which led the *Daily News* to state, "the trials are at end for the time, and perhaps forever."[31] That was wishful thinking on the newspaper's part. The grand jury was not discharged, and it was during this session in early 1872 that it issued the two indictments against my great-grandfather, John Clayton Farris. When the criminal trials resumed in April, several of the defendants were represented by McMaster.

IV

John Clayton had been away in Arkansas for months when he was finally indicted by the grand jury, and he never returned to South Carolina and so never had to stand up in court to explain his actions or motivations. As the circuit court session for the winter of 1871–72 wound down, Bond sentenced dozens of Ku Klux who had confessed and pled guilty to a variety of crimes associated with the conspiracy. Before he passed sentence, Bond questioned each "at considerable length . . . as to their reasons for joining the Ku-Klux, their complicity in the deeds of the Klan and their knowledge as to whether or not their more respectable neighbors knew, or were members, of the organization." The *Charleston Daily News*, so sympathetic to "gentlemen," ridiculed them, stating that it was obvious "from their appearance, [they belonged] to the lowest classes of society."[32]

Since John Clayton never publicly explained his behavior, the remarks of the men who stayed to face the consequences of their actions offer the only insight into his own possible motivations. Whether they truly do can never be answered.

Most of these convicted men acknowledged they could not read or write, although the 1860 Census states John Clayton could, though at what level is unknown. Most also insisted they had been coerced into joining the Ku Klux. William Shearer, one of four brothers who were Ku Klux and who participated in the raid that led to the lynching of Jim Williams, said, "Well, everybody else was in, and I didn't exactly feel safe without I belonged to it."[33] William Jolly, who estimated that he was "about eighteen years old," said, "I joined the Klan because I was afraid they would whip me if I didn't." He added that he was so terrified of the Ku Klux that he slept outside and away from his home for three weeks before he decided it was simpler to just join the conspiracy.[34]

Martin Hammett said the Ku Klux made him lie down and receive a hard lick from a hickory switch so he would know what to expect if he failed to join.[35] W. P. Burnett said the Ku Klux gave him a choice: Pay five dollars and receive fifty lashes or join.[36] That was a bargain compared to the offer Andrew Cudd received. He said the Ku Klux threatened to kill his common-law wife and give him five hundred lashes if he did not join. Asked why he did not go to his church for protection, Cudd said "pretty much" all the men in his congregation were Ku Klux.[37] Asked why he didn't go to the authorities, Alexander Bridges, a father of seven, said he was afraid of being killed if he divulged anything about the Ku Klux. Asked why he didn't just go away someplace to escape the Ku Klux, he said, "I could not take my family with me; I had to stay"—an impediment that did not burden my divorced and childless great-grandfather.[38]

Some, like Sylvanus Shearer, William's younger brother, still insisted that they "only held horses" when on a Ku Klux raid, and begged Bond "to be as light as possible" in meting out his sentence. Turning back to William Shearer, Bond asked if he recalled that when he was paroled from the Confederate army, he had taken an oath to never "take up arms or resist the laws of the United States?" Shearer replied, "A man can be scared to forget a good many things sometimes." Bond sentenced each of the Shearer brothers to eighteen months in prison and fined them each one hundred dollars.[39]

A few defendants were candid in admitting the depravity of their crimes. Junius B. Tyndall, who was only nineteen, said he had been on several raids. In one, the Ku Klux forced an African-American woman to whip her husband, and then forced the husband to whip his wife. On another raid, Tyndall said his klan noticed a group of African Americans holding a picnic, "a frolic [with] dancing and they didn't want them to have it so they were whipped." Tyndall was sentenced to a year in prison.[40]

Far more Ku Klux tried to minimize the severity of what they had done. Shearer said one raid was a spur-of-the-moment "spree" where they dropped by a freedman's home "and made Charley Russell dance some," though he declined to say how they compelled Russell to perform his jig.[41] Thomas J. Price, of Spartanburg, acknowledged that he had been on two raids in which the wives and daughters of several Black women had received a "light whipping." Asked what he meant by that, Price said they received "twenty-five or thirty lashes with hickories," adding what he believed was the further exculpatory explanation that they were "grown girls."[42]

Price insisted he had done only what he was told to do by Ku Klux leaders and that failure to obey meant he would have been "whipped or used roughly in some way or other." This led Bond to retort, "I think there ought to be another proclamation of emancipation." When Price said he had been too afraid to go to the authorities, Bond asked why he didn't seek guidance from the ministers he knew. Echoing Corbin's disgust with the local clergy, Price replied, "I did not know but they might belong to the order." He received a prison sentence of six months, less than the Shearers, likely because no one died in the raids in which Price participated.[43]

D. Lewis Jolly also admitted to having participated in two raids. In one, the Ku Klux broke a white man out of jail before he could be "hung for killing a negro." The other raid Jolly participated in was done at the request of the wife of a Ku Klux leader who was angry her husband had slept with a Black woman named Mary Bean in what was possibly a consensual relationship. Jolly said the Ku Klux took Bean from her bed "and whipped her a little . . . for breaking the peace between a white man and wife." The white husband, who was Ku Klux "and one of these big wealthy men," was not whipped or punished, Jolly said.[44]

Some of the defendants were genuinely pathetic figures. Jesse Tait, a self-acknowledged "unlearned man," admitted he had joined the Ku Klux but had never been able to go on a raid because he was a farm laborer, like my great-grandfather, but without enough money to own a horse. Tait noted he had turned himself into Major Merrill "without being put under arrest"; Bond released Tait on five hundred dollars bond, and Tait was never sentenced.[45] The court record states that Lewis Henderson was "so ignorant that he seemed incapable of understanding the simplest English, or of expressing himself with any coherence." He somehow communicated he had been on one raid but never whipped anyone; he still received a three-month jail sentence.[46] Twenty-four-year-old M. T. Phillips had a speech impediment so severe that another Ku Klux, William Robbins, had to serve as his interpreter in court and conveyed that Phillips had only joined the Ku Klux after being beaten himself.[47]

A handful of defendants seemed genuinely remorseful. M. T. Philips, not to be confused with the similarly named person in the previous paragraph, admitted he had helped whip several Black men and one fifteen-year-old African-American girl. Philips said the two men who brought him into the Ku Klux and administered the oath were both magistrates, and when he asked if being in the Ku Klux would be against the law, they assured him it would not. "If punishment will put down this thing, I am willing to be punished [for] my part," Philips said. Apparently impressed with Philips's contrition, Bond suspended judgment.[48]

William F. Ramsey expressed remorse for being on a raid in which he helped whip an elderly Black man named Reuben Phillips and Phillips's wife. The elderly woman received three blows apiece from each of the seven Ku Klux on the raid, though Ramsey acknowledged that he had no idea "what we whipped them for." He said he had joined the Ku Klux because his uncle advised him he would have to "leave the country" if he did not. "I felt ashamed after I had been on this raid, and said if God would forgive me, I would never go on another, and I never did," Ramsey said, "though I was warned to go on some three or four more. I know most of those who joined the Klan did it for self-protection. I supposed we did not unite and resist them because we did not have sense enough, but I know a good many didn't join voluntarily." Because of his seeming sincerity, Bond sentenced Ramsey to just three months in jail.[49]

Other Ku Klux simply lied about their crimes. Milus Carroll had also been on the raid in which Jim Williams was lynched. Years later, in a memoir he prepared for his family, he wrote about the incident in detail, suggesting he had directly participated in the murder, and he spoke freely about it fifty years later in an interview with the *Yorkville Enquirer*. But on the day he was sentenced, Carroll insisted he had stayed "with the horses" during the raid and said, "I did not see Jim Williams hung." Bond still sentenced him to eighteen months in prison and fined him one hundred dollars.[50]

Stephen B. Splawn feigned regret that he had helped form a klan with himself elected its leader, but when he learned a key mission of the Ku Klux was to whip men who "didn't comply with their notions" of how to vote, he ordered his klan to disband and tried to file a report with the justice of the peace, Bank Lyles, only to learn that Lyles was also Ku Klux. Corbin interrupted Splawn and presented as a witness a member of Splawn's klan, Robert Cash, who testified that Splawn was not being honest and that he had participated in a raid. Bond sentenced Splawn to two years in prison and fined him fifty dollars.[51]

Bond was particularly irritated by Samuel G. "Squire" Brown, in whose office Major Merrill had discovered the Ku Klux Klan constitution and bylaws. Brown insisted he had never read those documents, and also insisted he had once prevented a raid. But Bond countered that testimony during the several trials suggested Brown "took a prominent part" in Ku Klux activities. Noting that Brown was a man "advanced in years" who had served as a magistrate, Bond said that "those who were young and ignorant had a right to look to you for direction and advice." Bond sentenced Brown to five years in prison and levied a one-thousand-dollar fine. When Brown tried to "make some further explanation," Bond silenced him, saying, "You evidently don't propose to tell all you know, and I don't, therefore, propose to hear further."[52]

The failure of the so-called respectable members of the community to provide moral and ethical guidance to those beneath them in the social order had been a key point of wonderment throughout the trial. This is odd given that Corbin and Chamberlain emphasized repeatedly that the Ku Klux's aims were essentially political. Why, then, would it be shocking that those in power would be part of a conspiracy designed to either keep them in power or return lost power? But the elite, with exceptions such as Dr. J. Rufus Bratton's direct participation in the murder of Jim Williams, did their best to stay arm's length from many atrocities. As W. P. Burnett complained, the wealthy and prominent tended to skip the raids and instead "pushed the poor people into it, and made them go."[53]

Several defendants, including Christenberry Tait, stated they joined the Ku Klux at the urging of "respectable men, and [those] well off."[54] William Robbins, too, said, "The best men and the highest men belonged to the order, and they advised me to join for my protection." Asked if he feared retribution for appearing in court, Robbins acknowledged that the "leading men" in his community had advised him and others called to testify to leave the state, and warned that those who did not heed that advice and testified at the trials, named names, and divulged secrets, "it would be their day next."[55]

Some Ku Klux insisted they had lost the ability to distinguish between right and wrong. Frederick Harris admitted to helping whip at least five African-American men during raids, including a man named James Gaffney. "Did you not know that this was all wrong?" Bond asked incredulously. "No, sir, I didn't know nothing about it," Harris replied. "Would you not have thought it wrong if James Gaffney had dragged you out of bed and whipped you?" Bond asked. "Well, I suppose I would have thought hard of it," Harris said. "Don't you suppose he thought the same?" Bond asked. "I didn't know whether it was wrong or not," Harris said, again declining to reflect on the morality of his actions. He simply said, "I was ordered to do it by the committee."[56]

Convinced this Socratic inquiry would yield nothing of value, Bond ended his inquisition and sentenced Harris to six months in prison. He was roused to remonstrate the assembled defendants:

The Court seeks to find palliation for the enormities, the unmanly enormities, that have been committed. Striking men where men could not strike back to protect themselves, and where they had no redress or hope of redress; striking with masks on, and, therefore, striking without any responsibility. Whether these enormities have been committed on men, still more on women, they were wholly unmanly, and let me say utterly un–South Carolinian.[57]

As the court prepared to adjourn for this term, Corbin expressed dismay that so many leaders of the Ku Klux had been able to flee South Carolina, so justice could only be meted out to those unable to take flight. Bond, in a particularly reflective mood after having heard six weeks of often nauseating testimony, made a lengthy closing statement:

But what is quite as appalling to the Court as the horrible nature of these offenses is the utter absence, on your part, and on the part of others who have made confession here, of any sense of feeling, that you have done anything very wrong in your confessed participation in outrages which are unexampled outside of the Indian territory. Some of your comrades recite the circumstances of a brutal, unprovoked murder, done by themselves, with as little apparent abhorrence as they would relate the incidents of a picnic, and you yourselves speak of the number of blows with a hickory, which you inflicted at midnight upon the lacerated, bleeding back of a defenseless woman, without so much as a blush or sigh of regret. None of you seem to have the slightest idea of, or respect for, the sacredness of the human person.[58]

Bond suggested that something was wrong with the South itself because of slavery and its class system. Men were used to taking orders and being subservient to those higher in social caste. The "flagellation" of Black men and women during slavery "was no unusual occurrence," and so had lost the ability to shock. Not being able to see the humanity of African Americans, Bond said, too many Southerners had lost "the sacred character in yourselves":

It will appear strange to your fellow-countrymen, who read your story and that of your confederates, however willing they may be to believe you, that so large a portion of the young white men of your County can be in such a state of abject slavery to the men of property above them, as to be willing to commit murder at their command. In no case has there been any resistance to these midnight raiders, except on the part of the colored people.[59]

Fear of a whipping or other retribution was not justification to whip, rape, or murder others, Bond said. Each man was free to choose whether to resist the vile Ku Klux conspiracy or obey the laws of the nation. "They cannot both exist together; and it only needs a little manliness and courage, on the part of you ignorant dupes of designing men, to give supremacy to the law," Bond said, perhaps thinking of one designing man, in particular, who should have been one of the first Ku Klux in the dock and who some still hoped would face his day in court.[60]

CHAPTER THIRTEEN

The shortest cut by which criminals can be extradited from Canada is known as the "shanghaiing process."
—HIRAM WHITLEY, CHIEF OF THE US SECRET SERVICE

I

Despair that so many Ku Klux leaders were escaping justice led authorities to concoct a convoluted kidnapping scheme involving Dr. J. Rufus Bratton that initiated the first significant international incident between the United States and a newly independent Canada. Bratton was chloroformed, kidnapped, and spirited across the border into the United States to the chagrin of Canadian authorities, who demanded not only Bratton's return but also the waiving of his bail. "The Bratton case was very important in Canadian legal—and political history," wrote Canadian author and journalist Henry Orlo Miller, who came to know and admire Bratton's son, Andral. "At the time our nation was only five years old and this was the first challenge to our national sovereignty."[1]

The United States and British Canada had a rocky relationship long before the Bratton incident. American troops invaded Canada during the Revolutionary War, and tens of thousands of Americans who wished to remain loyal to the Crown emigrated to Canada after that war. During the War of 1812, the British sacked Washington, DC, in retaliation for American soldiers burning down the legislative assembly and other government buildings in the Canadian capital of York (now the site of Toronto). Over the next twenty-five years, skirmishes involving American filibusters who hoped to incorporate bits of Canadian territory large and small into the United States left dozens dead, as did raids in 1866 by Irish-American Fenians anxious to strike a blow for their homeland's independence against

British-held territory. War also seemed possible during heated diplomatic disputes involving the boundaries of the Oregon Territory and Alaska, the latter which the United States acquired the same year, 1867, that Canada became an independent federal dominion, a status that left Canada's foreign policy under the control of Great Britain.

As part of the British Empire, Canada was officially neutral during the American Civil War, although Canadians generally held anti-slavery views. Roughly fifty thousand Canadians volunteered to fight in the Civil War, primarily for the Union side, with seven thousand killed. But there were significant numbers of Confederate sympathizers in Canada, and Canada served as a base for Confederate spies operating in the North. In sum, there was considerable distrust between the two peoples well before several leading Ku Klux decided to flee to Canada and seek refuge there in a perverse inversion of the prewar Underground Railroad that had brought an estimated thirty thousand to forty thousand escaped slaves to freedom in Canada.

One of those Ku Klux refugees was Bratton who, like my great-grandfather, fled York County in October 1871 to avoid arrest and, also like John Clayton, first found refuge with a sister. In Bratton's case this was Sophia O'Bannon, who lived in Barnwell, South Carolina, near the Georgia border. Worried about arrest, Bratton quickly moved on to Selma, Alabama, where he stayed with an old colleague, Dr. William Barron. While living in Selma, Bratton allegedly contemplated purchasing an interest in some local coal and iron mines which, had he not been on the lam, relatives asserted, "would have made him a rich man."[2] Where Bratton would have found funds for such an investment is unknown, for he was nearly broke; at the time, his mother had to borrow money to pay the taxes due on her farm, and Bratton would later have to ask friends to put up money for his bail.[3]

With the federal government stepping up efforts to capture runaway Ku Klux leaders, Bratton left Selma for Memphis, where he was reunited with his older brother, John, who had also fled York County to avoid arrest. Upon meeting, they learned that, by chance, they had both adopted the same alias, Simpson, which was a family name and John's middle name. Bratton stayed in Memphis only a short while before separating from his brother and heading north to London, Ontario, where he knew that a South Carolina expatriate named Gabriel Manigault now lived, and where his former York County Ku Klux colleague, Major James W. Avery, was also in hiding.

Unlike Wade Hampton, Manigault was a former Confederate who believed emigration was preferable to remaining a citizen under a government he despised. Manigault later testified that he left South Carolina after the war because he refused to take an oath of allegiance to the United States and assumed Bratton had similarly refused to do the same.[4]

On the lam for months, Bratton arrived in London on May 21, 1872, and immediately sought out Manigault, who found Bratton lodgings in a home owned by a neighbor named Sarah Hill. Bratton had suspicions he had been followed into Canada, but still walked freely about the city, though usually armed with a Colt revolver. Not only had he been warmly welcomed by his fellow Southern refugees, but as a 32nd-degree Mason, the second-highest achievable level within the Scottish Rite, Bratton also tapped the goodwill of local Masonic brethren. He felt so comfortable in his new home that he had no qualms about going out in public to attend a cricket match that was played in honor of Queen Victoria's birthday.[5]

Bratton had reason to feel safe and out of reach of American authorities. Despite its neutrality during the war and the previous general anti-slavery sentiments of its citizens, the Canadian government under its first prime minister, Sir John Macdonald, took a benign view of former Confederates seeking asylum. The United States had made several attempts to extradite Ku Klux who had fled to Canada, but the Canadian government refused to cooperate; they considered the Ku Klux "political refugees worthy of protection."[6]

The official reason given for the noncooperation was that, unlike murder, for example, the peculiar federal charge against the Ku Klux of "interfering with the voting rights of a Negro citizen" was a "non-extraditable" crime. Manigault had even managed to secure written guidelines from the Canadian government for Ku Klux exiles as to what their rights were under Canadian law should American authorities seek to arrest them. That the government provided such assistance to suspected Ku Klux seemed "proof of the extent to which Canada was at this time acting as an asylum" for these "political refugees."[7]

This posture of the Canadian government frustrated and infuriated American officials. Major Merrill was among those agitating for the American government to act boldly. If the federal government truly wished to eradicate not only "Ku-Kluxism" but also the root causes that led to the establishment of the Ku Klux, Merrill wrote to General Terry, it was necessary to ensure that the "higher grade leaders" who held such sway over the "lower orders" received "firm and impartial administration of justice."[8]

The urgings of Merrill and others had an effect, for at some point in the spring of 1872 a warrant was issued for the arrest of Ku Klux fugitives living in Canada. According to witnesses who testified later at trial, the warrant bore the signature of President Grant, though the government remained coy about who had told whom to do what.[9] Hiram Whitley, chief of the US Secret Service, enjoyed hinting at Secret Service involvement in the plot without confirming or denying it. In his memoirs he wrote:

> Government detectives do not always pay attention to State lines. They take a criminal where they find him, and land him where he is most wanted. The shortest cut by which criminals can be extradited from Canada is known as the "shanghaing process," which means that a refugee from justice might be smuggled across the line for a consideration. This was a measure occasionally resorted to in my time. Of course, I only suspected this, as I never assisted in an affair of this kind. No locality should be made an Arcadia for the retreat of rogues. Why allow them to rest upon a bed of roses? Let such men ever bear the toughest kind of a thorn in their sides, an essential ingredient of their every-day life.[10]

The shadiness of the enterprise involving Bratton was deepened by the man chosen to carry out the "shanghaiing."

A few days after Bratton arrived in London, a man who was mischievously using the alias of "Hunter" arrived from Detroit by train and checked into London's Tecumseh Hotel, the largest in Canada at the time. "Hunter" was Deputy US Marshal Joseph G. Hester, a man with a sketchy past who had been active in the arrest of Ku Klux in the Carolinas and who was now tasked, perhaps by the Secret Service, with whom he had worked before, with kidnapping Ku Klux fugitives living in Canada. Hester's personality prevented him from blending in anywhere, and he attracted immediate attention as he "began to move about in a quiet and mysterious manner," according to a Canadian newspaper. "He had a professional air, and appeared now as a clergyman and then as an ordinary gentleman of leisure."[11]

A North Carolina native who had served in the Confederate navy, Hester shot his commanding officer as the man slept on the CSS *Sumter* after the officer had accused Hester of stealing supplies. Hester was charged with murder but was released on a technicality and returned to service. While later commanding his own Confederate ship, the *Pocahontas*, Hester was captured outside Charleston Harbor while trying to run through the federal blockade. It appears he then made a deal to switch sides and work as a Union operative.[12]

After the war, Hester was hired as a US marshal and became a determined pursuer of the Ku Klux in North Carolina. While habeas corpus had not been suspended anywhere in North Carolina, the number of arrests of suspected Ku Klux in that state rivaled what was occurring in South Carolina. A total of 763 indictments against suspected Ku Klux had been issued in North Carolina by the end of 1871, with Hester gaining renown for his detective work in tracking down fugitives.[13] His work was so well known that in 1876 Grant wrote a personal letter of recommendation, urging that Hester remain on the Department of Justice payroll because "it was through his exertions and fearlessness that so many were brought to justice."[14]

In addition to this alleged fearlessness, Hester was a clever and apparently persuasive man. Somehow, he convinced London officials to allow him access to the local post office, where he spent "hours there daily," going through mail that had arrived from the South to find clues to the whereabouts of refugee Ku Klux.[15] Hester opened letters from South Carolina addressed to a man named "Simpson" that urged him to "keep out of the public eye" and to not reply lest his return letters lead authorities to his hideaway.[16] Noting the delivery address of the letter, Hester began staking out the Hill boarding house and observing Bratton's daily routine as he hatched his abduction plan.

Hester realized he would need local assistance to find and arrest Bratton and recruited Isaac B. Cornwall, a deputy clerk in the office of Middlesex justice of the peace Charles Hutchinson. It is unknown what induced Cornwall to assist Hester. Hester may have offered Cornwall a significant financial incentive, as there was reward money available for bringing Ku Klux to justice, or perhaps Cornwall had learned of the Ku Klux atrocities and was happy to help bring a leading perpetrator to justice. Or, as Cornwall later testified, he may have simply believed Hester held a valid warrant that needed to be honored—though the method used to arrest Bratton suggests Cornwall was aware that he and Hester were operating well outside Canadian law.

II

At about 4:30 p.m. on June 4, 1872, a Tuesday and two weeks after his arrival in Canada, Bratton left Hill's boardinghouse to take a stroll northward on Cheapside Street toward a gravel pit that is now the site of Doidge Park in modern London. Bratton's increasing level of comfort in his new home can be ascertained by the fact that he did not bother to bring the Colt revolver that he usually carried on his constitutionals. This area of town was sparsely populated, with only a few scattered houses. At the time Bratton took his stroll, neighboring streets were deserted except for an eight-year-old girl named Mary Alice Overholt, who was walking with a milk pail in her hand.[17]

As Bratton hiked along the gravel pit, a horse-drawn cab driven by a cabbie named Robert T. Bates pulled up to the edge. Cornwall and Hester emerged from the cab, with Hester walking away from the gravel pit to observe from afar while Cornwall walked slowly toward Bratton as Bates stayed with the cab. Bratton stopped and stared apprehensively, hoping to ascertain the approaching man's business. When he was about six feet away, Cornwall suddenly lunged toward Bratton and "seized him in a rude and violent manner by the arm and shoulder, telling him he arrested him under a warrant." Bratton demanded to see the warrant, and Cornwall answered that Bratton would be able to do so soon enough. Cornwall tried to place handcuffs on Bratton, who resisted. A struggle ensued, with both men falling to the ground. Bratton, at six feet, was taller than Cornwall, but the clerk was younger and stronger and lay on top of Bratton, pinning his arms and body to the ground. Both Bratton and Cornwall appealed to Bates for assistance, Bratton shouting that Cornwall did not know who he was arresting, but the cabbie stayed in his box.[18]

As Cornwall sat on Bratton, Mary Alice Overholt saw Cornwall "take something out of his pocket" and hold it near Bratton's face as the two men continued to struggle. Mary Alice said Bratton was "moving his head from side to side, as if he were trying to keep away from the object being held to his face." Bratton slowly stopped fighting and succumbed to the manacles placed on his wrists; Cornwall had used a bottle of chloroform to drug and subdue Bratton. An alarmed Mary Alice ran to the home of a neighbor, Euphemia Dixon, who emerged from her house just in time to see Bratton shoved into the cab. Dixon oddly did not notify the police but instead, recognizing Bratton as Sarah Hill's new boarder, went to alert the landlady of the strange incident.[19] Hill also did not notify the police but sent word to Manigault, who did rush to file a report, but by that time Bratton and his abductors were long gone.[20]

Placing Bratton in the cab, Cornwall read aloud the arrest warrant. Bratton, sedated and wearing a "stupid, vacant look" from the chloroform, insisted he was not the man Cornwall was looking for, nor did he consider the warrant valid.[21] Bratton demanded to be taken before a local magistrate, as he thought "that in a place of some 20,000 inhabitants there should be some authority competent to deal with him."[22] Cornwall ignored that demand as well as Bratton's request that they stop by Hill's boardinghouse so he might gather some clothing and personal effects.

Instead, the cab went to the Grand Trunk Railroad station, but the westbound Pacific Express was running forty-five minutes late. Cornwall instructed Bates to drive up and down one of the back streets near the station until the train arrived. When it did, the cab pulled up to the side of the train opposite the depot to avoid public view. Cornwall paid Bates his four-dollar fare, grabbed Bratton from the cab, and took him to a Pullman car where he "thrust him in the anterior part of it, into a small apartment with one or two seats." Bratton later testified that neither he nor Cornwall appeared to have tickets, and the only persons he saw during the trip except for Cornwall were the train's porter and conductor.[23]

Bratton thought the train would stop in Windsor and told Cornwall that he knew the names of several good attorneys there (perhaps fellow Ku Klux exiles or sympathizers) and that he wished to be allowed to contact one upon their arrival. Cornwall ignored him, and the two had no further conversation until the train, surprising Bratton, pulled into Detroit without having stopped in Windsor. Cornwall opened the train compartment door and in stepped Hester, who had also boarded the train at London but rode in a separate compartment.[24]

Bratton recognized Hester from several sightings around town when Hester was tailing him, including at the cricket match. "You go with me now," Hester told Bratton, and he took his prisoner to the Detroit police station, where he was searched by a police sergeant and discovered to be carrying "$108.85 in money, a watch, pocketbook, and surgeon's lancet," but no identification with a name. Bratton continued to insist he was an Alabama farmer named James Simpson.[25]

Bratton was briefly placed in a cell until Hester came to get him about midnight, and the two men plus Cornwall went to a Detroit hotel, the Russell House, to wait for the train that would take Hester and Bratton farther south while Cornwall returned to Canada.[26] Awaiting the train, Bratton again demanded to see Hester's authorization for his arrest. Hester produced the warrant and Bratton noted that it had been signed by President Grant, but he also noted the murder victim listed in the warrant was not Jim Williams, but another York County African American named Anderson Brown. Brown was known to be an effective political speaker, and he had been dragged from his home and shot in the head two weeks before Williams was murdered.[27] But the name listed in the warrant as the suspect in Brown's murder was not Bratton's, but that of Bratton's co-leader of the Ku Klux in York County, Major James W. Avery.[28]

III

How Hester managed to confuse Bratton with Avery is not known, but a man impulsive enough to shoot his slumbering commanding officer was perhaps not as scrupulous with details as he should have been.

Avery had been a key target for federal prosecutors. A wealthy Yorkville merchant, Avery reportedly held the title of grand giant, meaning he was the top Ku Klux leader in York County, the only man to outrank Bratton within the local KKK organization. While, like Bratton, he occasionally personally participated in raids, apparently including the one in which Brown was murdered, his primary duty was to direct the Ku Klux's overall strategy in York and, at least as far as Major Merrill was concerned, "there is no question that he controlled many Klan operations" there.[29]

Unlike Bratton, who seemed to enjoy the limelight and the notoriety associated with being a Ku Klux leader, Avery kept a lower profile. For example, he declined an invitation to testify before the congressional subcommittee investigating Ku Klux atrocities, while Bratton seemed to relish the opportunity to play cat and mouse, with the congressional inquisitors.

Avery in the dock would have afforded federal prosecutors the opportunity to further undercut the claim that the Ku Klux was an organization
dedicated to self-defense. Avery's well-known primary goal for the Ku Klux
had been "largely political—to disarm and destroy the black militia, drive
Republican officials from power, and bludgeon Republican voters into qui-
escence." He was irritated when Ku Klux rank and file used raids to settle
personal scores or regulate moral behavior. Avery worried this type of violence was too random to serve the purpose of the Ku Klux and too much
uncontrolled violence would do what it did—invite federal intervention.
Before he ran away to Canada, Avery allegedly spent the summer of 1871
"trying to stop or slow down the terror which he had helped to begin."[30]

Hester was zealous in his hunt for Ku Klux and unfazed by his mistake. His job was to bring wanted Ku Klux to justice, particularly leaders.
Cornwall said when the two men discovered the mistake, Hester expressed
no reservations about keeping Bratton in custody because he was also an
"important" Ku Klux leader.[31] As things turned out, having the correct Ku
Klux in custody would likely have not changed the eventual outcome.

The journey from Detroit to South Carolina was lengthy and circuitous,
requiring several changes of trains and coaches with stops at inns and hotels
along the way. If Bratton was uncooperative along the way, Hester would
again chloroform the prisoner, changing Bratton's usually shrewd expression
into a vacant stare.[32]

While waiting at a small stop in Virginia, Bratton, with renewed confidence now that he was again south of the Mason-Dixon Line, leapt from
the train and ran into the woods, where he spent the night. The next day,
confident that Hester would not think he would be so audacious, Bratton
returned to the train station in hopes of purchasing a ticket back to Canada.
Instead, he was startled to see Hester waiting for him on the platform. "Glad
to see you," Hester said. "Well, let's go home," a subdued Bratton replied.[33]

When Hester and Bratton arrived in Yorkville on June 10, six days after
the abduction in Ontario, "the best people in the community rushed to greet
[Bratton] and offer their support," reflecting the continued status of Bratton, his family, and the Ku Klux cause in York County.[34] Bratton was placed
in Merrill's custody, where the major tried to engage Bratton in a hoped-for
confession, but Bratton was as elusive as ever and refused to "puke," instead
continuing to deny, as he had from his first meeting with Merrill more than

a year before, that he was unaware such a group as the Ku Klux even existed, let alone that he was a member and leader. Still, Bratton was the type of KKK leader that Merrill (and Akerman) had long hoped would be brought to justice, and so there is a subdued note of triumph in Merrill's short telegram to Attorney General Williams: "Dr. James Rufus Bratton arrested and now in jail here."[35]

The triumph was short-lived, for Bratton was not in jail long. Two days later, on June 12, Bratton appeared before Judge Bryan, who set Bratton's bond at twelve thousand dollars, the equivalent of more than a quarter-million in today's dollars. Thirteen men, neighbors and fellow Ku Klux, most of them prominent residents of the community, came forward with the money to collectively guarantee Bratton's bond, and he was released, likely going to his stately plantation-style home on North Congress Street to be reunited with his wife and children. A month later he appeared at trial—not his, but that of the unfortunate Cornwall back in London, Ontario.

IV

After his release on bond, Bratton laid low for a few weeks, perhaps hoping Merrill and the other authorities would assume he had become resigned to his fate and so let down their guard. Or perhaps Merrill had received word from Washington to let Bratton quietly depart as the simplest solution to an escalating dispute with Canada. His departure from South Carolina meant that the thirteen friends and admirers who guaranteed his twelve-thousand-dollar bond would forfeit their money.

Meanwhile, the story of Bratton's abduction had put London, Ontario, "in a state of wild excitement" and had deeply vexed the Canadian government.[36] On June 10, the day Bratton arrived back in Yorkville, Cornwall was fired from his job as a clerk in the Middlesex justice of the peace office and was arrested and charged with kidnapping, even though he insisted to his superiors that Hester had presented a proper warrant for Bratton's arrest.

Cornwall was arraigned on June 13. Among those who testified at the arraignment were Bratton's friend Manigault, who insisted that Bratton had committed no crime and was being harassed by the US government as "a political offender." Canadian newspaper accounts of Bratton's abduction made no mention of the Ku Klux crimes committed in South Carolina, and instead expressed outrage that the writ of habeas corpus had been suspended in parts of South Carolina, and that Hester had violated the privacy and secrecy of the Canadian mail.[37]

The *Toronto Globe* stated that whatever crimes might have been committed by Bratton were irrelevant compared to this insult to Canadian sovereignty:

> *It is the duty of the Government to act promptly and decidedly in this matter, and demand that the stranger taken with violence from under the protection of the British flag, be returned unharmed, and rendered secure from further molestation. If he has been guilty of any extraditable offense there is a proper and lawful way of obtaining his arrest and removal. Official outrages of the above nature must not be tolerated if we desire to maintain the national honour unsullied.*[38]

Also portraying Bratton as a persecuted asylum seeker, the *Ottawa Daily Citizen* placed the story of Bratton's abduction on the front page under the headline "An International Outrage!" and said the incident would "lead to a grave international question between the Canadian and United States governments." The *Daily Citizen* opined that "in taking this high-handed proceeding, the man Hester has violated our laws in a manner which demands speedy reparation and apology from his Government. We feel sure the act will arouse the utmost indignation throughout the country."[39]

Prime Minister Macdonald appeared before the Canadian House of Commons to announce that he had telegraphed the British ambassador in Washington (since Great Britain still handled Canadian foreign affairs) with instructions to inquire what the abduction was about and to protest that the arrest had not been handled through proper channels.[40] The British government sent a sharp note to Secretary of State Hamilton Fish. Despite his opposition to the Ku Klux trials, Fish, who had recently referred to Britain as "perfidious Albion," sent back a tart response.[41] The Canadian writer Orlo Miller insists that anger had escalated to the point that Great Britain had "threatened war unless Dr. Bratton was returned at once," but this is false hyperbole.[42] There was never a genuine threat of war over such a small incident, especially so soon after the United States and Great Britain had resolved a variety of grievances between the two nations.

Just the year before, Grant had won an international arbitration with Great Britain regarding claims associated with the significant American shipping losses to the Confederate warship, the CSS *Alabama*, which had used British shipyards as a base for its predations during the Civil War. The settlement was accompanied by a new treaty affirming friendly relations between the United States and Great Britain, though Macdonald was personally irritated by concessions granted the Americans at Canadian expense, particularly around North Atlantic fisheries. Grant was in no mood to sour these improved relations with Britain. Besides, Hester had arrested the wrong man.

While bringing Bratton to justice was a worthy goal, the incident had been an embarrassment. Grant ordered that Bratton be released, though by the time Grant issued his order it was moot; Bratton had slipped out of Yorkville around July 11. "Naturally," the *Yorkville Enquirer* noted, "under the circumstances, various rumors are afloat on the street as to where he has gone." All that was known at the time, the *Enquirer* added, is that "up to the present time no requisition has been received for the return of Dr. Bratton to Canada."[43]

V

Monday, July 15, shortly after noon, Cornwall's trial began in the Middlesex County Criminal Court with Judge William Elliott presiding. The first witness called to testify was Bates, the cab driver, who denied providing any assistance to Cornwall in subduing Bratton "beyond performing the duties as a driver." After Bates stepped down, in a scene that should only occur in fiction, the rear doors of the courtroom swung open and a commotion ensued as Bratton entered and strode to the witness box to testify "to the great surprise of the defendants [*sic*]" and the courtroom gallery. Bratton had arrived in London on Saturday, but "kept concealed until after the opening of the court, when he made his appearance."[44]

On the stand Bratton recounted how Cornwall had grabbed him in a "rude and violent manner," while Bates refused his pleas even as he shouted that "Cornwall did not know who he was arresting." Bratton said he told Cornwall that he was willing to appear before any magistrate, but "objected to the humiliation of the irons." When Cornwall handed him over to Hester, Bratton, playing to the courtroom crowd, stated that when Hester advised him that he would be returning to the United States, he replied with the following disquisition: "No, I'm under Canadian law, now; that warrant does not allow you to detain me here, and I, under protest, refuse to obey you; neither your government, or you sir have a right to detain me here, and if you do you will pay for it." The *London Free Press* reported that "at the conclusion of this oration the crowd in the Court made demonstrations of approval, which the Court immediately suppressed."[45]

Cornwall's attorney, William Bartram, was taken aback by Bratton's surprise appearance and asked the court to adjourn so he might adjust his defense in light of this unexpected testimony. The Crown prosecutor, William Barker, disingenuously noted that Bartram had never asked "if Bratton was not coming," and Elliott ordered the trial to continue. In his cross-examination, Bartram asked Bratton why he was living in Canada under an assumed name. Bratton replied he did so for "prudential reasons" that he did not want to divulge unless ordered to do so by the court, which Judge Elliott did not do. Bratton then recounted that he had advised Cornwall that he was not James W. Avery and could prove it if given the chance, but that Cornwall insisted that he knew Bratton was Avery because he had seen Bratton walking along the street with a young girl known to be Avery's daughter.[46]

Cornwall's superior, Charles Hutchinson, clerk of the Middlesex County justice of the peace, then testified that Cornwall was only a deputy clerk and not a constable, and therefore had no authority to arrest anyone, even under a valid warrant. When it was Bartram's turn to present the case for the defense, he recalled Bratton to the stand to ask the question the court had not pressed before, which was whether Bratton had been charged with any "grave offenses" in the United States. "The witness said there was a charge of murder against him, but so far as he knew there was no truth in it whatever," the *Free Press* reported.[47]

The trial now wrapped up quickly. Bartram delivered a lengthy closing argument in which he now asserted that Bratton had gone to Detroit "of his own accord," even while acknowledging that Bratton was in manacles during the journey. Barker recounted that the testimony of Bates, as well as that of young Mary Alice Overholt, supported Bratton's assertion that he had been forcibly kidnapped. Judge Elliott asked Cornwall if he had anything to say before sentencing, to which Cornwall replied, "I have nothing to say, sir." Elliott commended Cornwall for being known as "a man of undoubted ability and well versed in criminal law," but Elliott said that it seemed to him that Cornwall had agreed to participate in an extrajudicial kidnapping "for gain," and he sentenced Cornwall to three year's imprisonment in the Provincial Penitentiary.[48]

Cornwall appealed his conviction and sentence, but in the appeal of *Cornwall v. The Queen*, he lost and served his sentence. Bratton sent for his family and remained in Canada for another six years, establishing a medical practice in London where he "acquired the reputation of a good and compassionate physician, well-loved by local Canadians."[49]

Bratton received yet another consideration. Hoping to return to South Carolina someday, Bratton knew he had left thirteen supporters in the lurch when he forfeited the twelve-thousand-dollar bond they had posted before he absconded back to Canada. Hoping to avoid an awkward reunion when the time came, with these men still hoping to recoup their money, Bratton appealed to the British government for "protection." The British ambassador in Washington advised Secretary of State Fish "that Her Majesty's Government does not tolerate interference with her laws, and that the proceedings against Bratton, having followed his abduction from British territory, they must be cancelled," and that the case against Bratton should be returned "as far as practicable, in the same position as before his forcible abduction from Canada."[50]

Attorney General Williams ordered Corbin to agree to a motion filed by Bratton's attorney to annul and cancel the surety bonds, which Judge Bryan granted. A copy of Bryan's order was then forwarded to the British ambassador in Washington.[51]

And so, while mercenary in purpose or not, Cornwall, the man who tried to bring a murderer to justice, spent three years in prison. The murderer himself went free, and his friends were refunded the twelve thousand dollars they thought had been forever lost so that the murderer could return to Yorkville without any embarrassing obligations.

In 1985, more than 110 years after Bratton's abduction, the Canadian author Orlo Miller, by then the seventy-four-year-old chairman of the London Library Board's historical sites committee, sought to erect a plaque on the grounds of St. Joseph's Hospital near where Bratton was abducted to commemorate "the first time Canada flexed its muscles internationally." When it was learned that Bratton had been a suspected Ku Klux involved in murder, Miller, a Bratton family friend, defended Bratton by noting he had never been prosecuted—though that was, of course, what his abduction had tried to achieve. One of the unions representing the hospital workers organized local opposition, arguing that erecting the plaque would be "tantamount to honoring someone connected with the notorious Klan." The union rejected a library board proposal to have the marker omit any reference to the KKK, and with the union pledged to picket the plaque were it ever installed anywhere, the board ultimately rejected Miller's proposal and the memorial was never erected.[52]

CHAPTER FOURTEEN

It seems . . . that now, as long ago, freedom is not and cannot be made safe in the United States as long as we have a Supreme Court.
— HARRISBURG *(PA)* TELEGRAPH

I

That Bratton (and my great-grandfather and hundreds of other Ku Klux) were able to evade justice was shameful, but their desire to avoid prison was understandable. The facility that housed the sixty-five Ku Klux who were eventually sent to prison was an unpleasant place and a long way from home. Though even if they had received the prison terms they deserved, they, like most of the Ku Klux who were imprisoned, would likely have not served their full sentences.

With the national government having had a minimal role in criminal justice prior to the Civil War, there were no federal prisons until the first was opened in Leavenworth, Kansas, in 1903. Before then, the federal government contracted with state and local penal facilities to house federal prisoners, and the Ku Klux sentenced in federal court in Columbia and elsewhere in the South in 1871–72 were sent to New York to the penitentiary owned and operated by Albany County, which leased space for state convicts as well.

Prisoners sentenced in Columbia were first marched to Charleston, where they boarded a steamship that would transport them to New York City, and from there they were escorted by federal infantry up the Hudson River to Albany—more than eight hundred miles north of South Carolina. In Albany, the average low temperature in February is 17 degrees Fahrenheit and the average high barely above freezing; in Columbia, the average high temperature in February is 60 degrees. The cold was the first shock of many.

Built by inmate labor in the 1840s, the Albany Penitentiary was located "on a green hill overlooking New York's capital city, with fourteen-foot whitewashed brick walls and crenelated guard towers" and resembled "nothing so much as a medieval fortress."[1] The prison building covered three acres and was surrounded by another twelve acres of "well laid out grounds, ornamented with trees, shrubs and flowers with a meandering brooklet." For a fee of twenty-five cents, locals could picnic on the grounds, heedless of the misery behind the walls. When the prison was razed in 1933, demolition crews uncovered "dungeons" that were likely used to keep rule-breaking inmates in deep isolation.[2]

Isolation, however, was the norm even when the prisoners were together. The Albany Penitentiary subscribed to what was known as the Auburn penal system, a "silent system altogether." Each inmate was kept in a solitary cell that measured three feet by six and a half feet, and they took their meals alone. Inmates were forbidden from conversing with one another at any time without permission, even while working together.[3] When not working, they were expected to keep their arms folded. "The ringing of a gong" preceded any movement of the inmates, who then lined up and marched in step with the right hand placed on the shoulder of the inmate in front as they shuffled in silence.[4]

A *New York World* reporter who was allowed to tour the penitentiary concluded that the Ku Klux prisoners "appear to be treated as well as is to be expected," and, looking on the bright side, emphasized that a modern prison like Albany at least no longer used flogging or pillorying as punishments.[5] It's true that the Auburn system was less extreme than the competing Pennsylvania system of penal reform, where conversation was also prohibited but inmates were always kept in solitary cells and were never brought together as a group.[6]

There were extraordinarily bitter debates among prison reformers over which system was best suited to introspection, penance, and rehabilitation. Advocates of the Auburn system argued that the total inmate isolation advocated under the Pennsylvania system would drive prisoners insane (which it sometimes did), but the real and particular benefit of the Auburn system for authorities was that it allowed inmates to be engaged in group industrial labor that could make the prison self-sufficient and even profitable.

With the arrival of the sixty-five Ku Klux prisoners (forty of whom were from York County), the Albany Penitentiary held 625 prisoners, of whom ninety were women, and all were made to work. Able-bodied male inmates worked six days per week at "hard labor" in one of the prison's four large shoemaking shops, while women and older men were employed making cane-bottomed chairs.[7] Not only did the products produced by inmates cover all prison operating costs, it was said that in its first twenty-two years of existence the Albany prison turned a $170,000 profit, described in the *Yorkville Enquirer* as "unexampled prosperity in the history of prisons."[8]

Reverend C. E. Chichester, a minister from Charleston who traveled to Albany to investigate conditions, proclaimed the food there "ample and of good quality," the cells "comfortable," and the shoe manufacturing work "easy and pleasant."[9] The *World* also provided a similarly upbeat assessment and commended the penitentiary for offering classes two nights per week for those inmates who wished to learn to read and write, and adding that each prisoner was issued a Bible and was allowed to check out one book per week from the prison library. The few white-collar criminals housed in Albany worked in the prison library (and the prison hospital), so they were spared the further humiliation of performing the manual labor assigned to inmates of a lower social order.

Inmates were allowed to send mail or receive visitors once every four weeks, but incoming mail was distributed each Sunday and often included care packages with canned fruit or other supplements for the prison's bland and meager diet. The *World* article made it sound as if inmates enjoyed a healthy and balanced diet, stating that dinners included such fare as pork and beans or salt beef and vegetables, while on Saturday nights inmates could "luxuriate on fish chowder." The newspaper also insisted that the health of the prisoners from South Carolina was "uniformly good," but this was no more accurate than its review of prison food. A Ku Klux inmate named Hezekiah Porter had died in July of spinal meningitis, and another was hospitalized with pneumonia when the reporter took his tour.[10]

The Ku Klux inmates offered far less rosy accounts of their stay in Albany, not that their travails were unwarranted. Hugh Shearer, who had been on the raid in which Jim Williams was lynched, complained that prison food was "very poor" and consisted of a modest daily serving of meat that was usually gristly, while evening suppers often consisted of a single piece of bread. Linen for sleeping was a straw mattress and a straw pillow along with three blankets that were never laundered, he said.[11]

Nor were the prisoners themselves regularly washed. Randolph Shotwell, a North Carolina newspaper editor who was sentenced to six years in Albany for masterminding a Ku Klux assault on a Republican legislator, said that inmates were allowed to wash only once per week for what he estimated was a sixteen-second bath in cold water in a common "wash tank." But what particularly outraged Shotwell was that when inmates received their weekly shave, the prison trustee charged with lathering the faces of all inmates was "a filthy negro," while the barber was a "mulatto" who used a dull razor with so little care that "blood was left oozing from various portions" of Shotwell's face "for half an hour after the operation."[12]

What is absent from the prisoners' accounts, then or later, is introspection or regret for the crimes that placed them behind bars. Yet their complaints found sympathetic ears, including those of a man running for president of the United States.

II

Horace Greeley, the eccentric and erratic editor of America's most widely read newspaper, the *New York Tribune*, had been a founding member of the Republican Party, had cheered the North into war, and was initially extremely critical of Lincoln for dawdling on emancipation. But midway in the Civil War, Greeley changed course. He urged Lincoln to seek a negotiated peace with the South (even personally trying to recruit a foreign mediator), and after the war he helped jailed Confederate president Jefferson Davis post bail because of what Greeley said was a combination of "Christian compassion and anger that the government was holding Davis, in violation of his constitutional rights, without any specific charges."[13]

Greeley had supported Grant's candidacy in 1868, but he believed presidents should serve only one term and he had become disillusioned with corruption within the Grant Administration and its alliance with big business. Greeley had originally planned to challenge Grant for the Republican nomination but then joined Missouri senator Carl Schurz and other like-minded souls "alarmed at growing federal power" to form a third party that they named the Liberal Republican party, which advocated for civil service reform, tariff reductions, lower taxes, and an end to subsidies for railroads.[14]

Greeley became the Liberal Republican presidential nominee, and when the Democrats concluded they could nominate no better candidate and did not want to split the anti-Grant vote, they conferred their nomination upon Greeley as well.

As a presidential candidate, Greeley retreated from his former advocacy for civil rights for African Americans. He condemned the Ku Klux Klan as an "execrable" organization but was disillusioned with Reconstruction and wished to accelerate reconciliation with the white South.[15] In a bid for Southern votes, he said the federal government should pay off the Confederate government's war debts, and he favored widespread amnesty for all former Confederates. And despite his critiques of the Ku Klux, he began to push for the pardons of those in prison as another step toward a conciliation that might pacify the South. His position might not only earn him Southern votes, but might also help him carry New York, where there was keen opposition to Radical Republicanism and sympathy for the Ku Klux.

Greeley reached out to a friend, the wealthy former abolitionist Gerrit Smith, and requested that Smith travel to Albany to investigate the condition of the Ku Klux held there, with a particular eye toward identifying prisoners worthy of clemency. Smith had given a speech at the Republican convention just the week before in which he strongly endorsed Grant's campaign to eradicate the Ku Klux, saying, "Let President Grant withdraw his repressing hand for even a week, and the flames of hell would again burst."[16] But Smith acquiesced to his old friend's appeal, which he sold as Christian charity, and visited the Albany Penitentiary on July 8, 1872. The day after his tour, Smith wrote President Grant a lengthy letter, urging that several Ku Klux be pardoned due to illness or old age.

Grant, who at that stage of the campaign was concerned about the threat posed by Greeley's candidacy, hesitated for several weeks before responding to Smith. In a letter dated July 22, 1872, when most of the Ku Klux prisoners had been in the Albany Penitentiary for only a few months and some only a few weeks, Grant said issuing pardons before the upcoming election might be "misinterpreted."[17] But he pledged to send someone from his administration to review conditions at Albany and delegated the task to Attorney General Williams, who asked Secret Service chief Hiram Whitley to conduct the investigation.

Whitley arrived at the penitentiary on August 7. As Ku Klux inmates were brought to him for interviews, Whitley realized that, despite the enforced silence at Albany, "the prison grapevine" had alerted the Ku Klux to who he was and why he was there. When Reverend Chichester had visited Albany the month before, he said the Ku Klux prisoners had confidently predicted to him that they would be pardoned in 1873 after the election. Their theory was that if Grant won reelection he could "afford to release them, as they will have fully accomplished the work for which the Enforcement Act was passed, i.e., the reelection of Grant, and if Greeley is elected he will see that innocent men shall no longer be incarcerated in prisons for crimes which they have never committed."[18]

But now that a possible arbiter of their freedom was present, the Ku Klux adopted a less sincere but far more contrite tone. Whitley met with forty Ku Klux prisoners and claimed that most said "they had been justly sentenced" but pled extenuating circumstances. As they had before Judges Bond and Bryan, these men, "some of them very poor and unlearned," told Whitley that they had not known what the aims of the Ku Klux were when they joined and that they "had been incited to violence by their leaders, who had managed to escape from the country, leaving them to bear the responsibility and the punishment of their misdeeds."[19]

Whitley sympathized with this point of view. He praised their "general expression of regret," and agreed "they were betrayed by unscrupulous and designing men of more enlightened minds." Those who were caught, convicted, and sentenced to prison, Whitley said, were "not only truly repentant, but absolutely ashamed." Such men could be pardoned "not only with great safety, but fully in the interest of the public good," Whitley said. In his report to President Grant, Whitley recommended clemency for twenty-two individuals, although he specifically recommended against a pardon for one of the few Ku Klux leaders sent to Albany, sixty-three-year-old Samuel G. "Squire" Brown, who had also irritated Judge Bond by his lack of remorse and his lack of candor in telling all he knew.[20]

Despite his earlier expressed concern that pardons before the election would seem politically motivated, Grant immediately agreed to grant clemency to four Ku Klux, all low-ranking Klansmen who were either elderly or seriously ill.[21] Grant's leniency inspired former Confederate vice president

Alexander Stephens to travel to Washington in September to meet with Attorney General Williams and urge clemency for everyone convicted under the Enforcement Acts.

Major Merrill learned of the meeting and wrote Williams to vehemently protest consideration of any further paroles, given that the government had already indulged in "an amazing degree of clemency." He noted that just in York County, more than five hundred low-level Ku Klux who had confessed to participating in the conspiracy had not been prosecuted, but had simply been told to go home with an assurance that if they committed no further offense they never would be prosecuted. Because of the "inadequacy of the machinery of the United States courts and the utter worthlessness of the state courts in this section [of the country] hundreds of participants in murder even will never be brought to justice," Merrill said.[22]

The assurances provided by Stephens and others that clemency would help pacify the South were ludicrous, Merrill argued. "The blind, unreasoning bigoted hostility to the results of the war is only smothered not appeased or destroyed," Merrill said. "The only safety or assurance for safety for citizens is the protection of the general government." Clemency was not an act of mercy, Merrill said, but "a confession that wrong has been done," which was hardly the case with the Ku Klux. Merrill reminded Williams of the men and women, particularly African Americans, who risked their lives by coming forward with information on the Ku Klux, by testifying before the congressional committee or at the trials, and by serving on the juries or as witnesses at the trials that had decimated the Ku Klux. Clemency was a betrayal of all those people, as well as himself and the men in his command, Merrill said.[23]

Williams ignored Merrill. While he rejected Stephens's appeal for immediate pardons, he held out the promise of future clemency by stating that Grant would consider such action after the election, "when the President is satisfied that the danger from Ku Klux violence has ceased and that such unlawful associations have been abandoned." When that happens, Williams said, Grant "will be ready to exercise executive clemency in all cases in the most liberal manner."[24]

Conservative Democrats in the South took the hint and suppressed what remained of the Ku Klux for the rest of the fall, with the result that 1872 was "the most violence-free election during the entire period of

Reconstruction."[25] In that election, Grant crushed Greeley, winning nearly 56 percent of the popular vote. Greeley carried only three Southern and three border states. He was also beset by personal tragedy. His wife, Mary, died a week before the election, and Greeley himself died on November 29, just twenty-four days after the election.

Grant might have used his renewed mandate to complete the job of uprooting the Ku Klux and pursue more aggressive policies that might have guaranteed that the rights of African Americans would be respected from then on. But he did not.

Grant perceived that the North, whose mind was, as Amos Akerman had lamented, "full of what is called progress [and] runs away from the past," had lost interest in the plight of African Americans. The president was also preoccupied with charges of corruption and wasteful spending within his administration, and he was tired of being accused of being a military despot. Most concerning, the nation was slipping into what would be a deep economic recession now known as the "Panic of 1873," though at the time it was called the "Great Depression" until it was supplanted in that distinction by the misery of the 1930s.

Using the comparative lack of violence around the November election as justification, Williams openly invited convicted Ku Klux to submit individual applications for pardons, which the president began issuing in January 1873. While preference was allegedly given to those who insisted they had been coerced into joining the Ku Klux, among the first to receive pardons were Robert Hayes Mitchell, Milus Carroll, and Hugh Shearer and his brothers, all of whom had been involved in one way or another in the murder of Jim Williams. More than half of the York County Ku Klux who had been sent to Albany were pardoned in 1873, as were several who had been serving their time in the York County jail.[26]

Now free, the Ku Klux who had been held in Albany still had to make their way home. Retrieving their vermin-infested clothing, which had been stored since their incarceration in a damp vault at the prison, each man was given ten dollars upon release. The money was not nearly enough to purchase a ticket home by stage, rail, or ship, so most walked or hitchhiked the eight hundred miles, hungry for most of the way, while their shaved heads and ragged clothes identified them as former convicts subject to heckling, especially from children. But, as Randolph Shotwell said, "we managed to get home at last"—something Jim Williams, Thomas Roundtree, and the Ku Klux's other murdered victims never got to do.[27]

III

If the Grant Administration was now letting Ku Klux *out* of prison, it is not surprising that it soon determined that no more Ku Klux should be put *into* prison. After taking over from Akerman, Williams had continued the Justice Department's aggressive prosecution of the Ku Klux throughout most of 1872. In South Carolina, US Attorney Corbin reported an astounding 90 percent conviction rate in Ku Klux cases, though he had only been able to try ninety-six cases. This meant that another twelve hundred cases just in South Carolina were held over to 1873.[28]

Judge Bond had fretted over the "fearful" cost of the Ku Klux trials, which he estimated at two hundred dollars per hour when the court was in session.[29] Before he turned the reins at Justice over to Williams, Akerman was already raising the alarm that neither the administration nor Congress seemed willing to devote the resources necessary to deal with the backlog of cases. "If it takes a court over one month to try five offenders," Akerman said, "how long will it take to try four hundred, already indicted, and many hundreds more who deserve to be indicted?"[30]

Resources for Ku Klux prosecutions were further depleted when Grant diverted a large amount of the Justice Department's enforcement budget to New York to preclude election fraud by Democrats and the Tammany machine. Williams had expected Congress would provide a supplemental appropriation to cover the deficit, but Congress did not. Williams had higher political ambitions and did not want a reputation as a profligate spender of public funds (despite or perhaps because of his own personal use of government funds). With increasing urgency, he demanded US attorneys prosecuting Ku Klux trim their expenses. Despite the backlog of hundreds and hundreds of cases involving murder, rape, and assault, Williams accused Corbin and others of engaging in "frivolous and vexatious prosecutions" and engaging in "the most unwarrantable extravagance."[31]

A month after Grant's landslide victory, at the same time that he was inviting convicted Ku Klux to appeal for clemency, Williams stepped back from vigorous enforcement of the Enforcement Acts. In a letter to Corbin dated December 7, 1872, Williams said, "My desire is that pending prosecutions be pushed only as far as may appear to be necessary to preserve the public peace and prevent further violations."[32] By the spring of 1873, all prosecutions under the Enforcement Acts had been postponed or discontinued. Williams directed Corbin and other federal prosecutors in the Carolinas to *nolle prosequi* (file a formal notice with the court that a prosecution has been abandoned) in all cases but those involving the very worst crimes.

Rather than continue the fight, Williams, with the full concurrence of President Grant, decided to declare victory and call it good, an approach that was, remarkably, endorsed by Republican officials in the South. To the dismay of Corbin, Merrill, and state attorney general Chamberlain, South Carolina governor Robert K. Scott and his successor, Franklin J. Moses, also a Republican, both urged an end to prosecutions and a general pardon for all Ku Klux already convicted in South Carolina.[33]

It was a novel legal concept: Laws would be observed and the peace kept if lawbreakers were *not* prosecuted. Yet that was the hope on which the Grant Administration and its Southern Republican allies hung their hats. The idea that the victims of Ku Klux crimes deserved justice was ignored, and the ever-present possibility that the Ku Klux might rise again was discounted. Instead, "the Government," Williams proclaimed, "has reason to believe that its general intentions in prosecuting these offenses . . . have been accomplished, that the particular disorder has ceased, and that there are good grounds for hoping that it will not return. At all events it affords the Government pleasure to make an experiment based upon these views."[34] A US marshal in Texas could only shake his head at such naivete, saying of the Ku Klux and their many supporters in the South: "In their hearts the rebellion has never been 'crushed out.'"[35]

Even though Williams had now retreated to a position where the Justice Department only *threatened* to prosecute Ku Klux, Southern Democrats sought complete capitulation. In July 1873, a delegation bearing a letter of introduction from Judge Bryan visited President Grant at his summer retreat in Long Branch, New Jersey. They gave the president assurances the Ku Klux had been destroyed, the South was at peace, and the rights of all people, Black as well as white, would be respected. Perhaps out of wishful thinking as much as anything, Grant accepted these assurances and directed Williams to send a follow-up letter that pledged the administration to a new course of leniency that stemmed from "the belief that the Ku Klux Klan have, through said convictions, been almost if not altogether broken up, and that those, who were concerned in, or sympathized with, them have come to see the folly, wickedness and danger of such organizations."[36]

Now, when federal officers arrested suspected Ku Klux, no matter the seriousness of the alleged crime, they received an angry rebuke from the attorney general. Several US attorneys and marshals resigned rather than tolerate censure and criticism from superiors for doing their duty.[37] Corbin, however, stayed on as US attorney for South Carolina until the change of presidential administrations in 1877. By then, President Grant had pardoned every convicted Ku Klux from South Carolina and every other state and all prosecutions under the Enforcement Acts had ceased.[38]

IV

There was some validity to the belief that the short-lived implementation of the Ku Klux Klan Acts, even as limited and as focused as prosecution efforts were, had served its intended purpose just as Akerman and General Alfred Terry had hoped. Senator Adelbert Ames, a Mississippi Republican, said that the crackdown on the Ku Klux in South Carolina "had a very subduing effect all over the South. It is perceptible here."[39] Frederick Douglass said the arrests, the trials, the convictions, and the flight of so many Ku Klux meant that "peace has come to many places as never before. The scourging and slaughter of our people have so far ceased."[40]

The creative combination of military force and aggressive prosecution in the courts "was successful in breaking the back of the Klan," not only in South Carolina but in much of the South. The change in the treatment of African Americans in the South might have been even more dramatic had the federal government expanded such focused efforts to other areas of the South, "but the resources and the will were simply not there."[41]

Still, the Ku Klux Klan as a viable organization was no more. Night riding, with exotic costumes worn while committing horrific crimes, had stoked national outrage and forced federal military intervention. Ku-Kluxing was no longer a viable strategy for Southern conservative Democrats who wished to keep African Americans and white Republicans in line. Other, more subtle strategies for reestablishing and enforcing white racial dominance would need to be developed and would, in fact, soon emerge.

Most leaders of the Ku Klux Klan had avoided accountability and punishment for their crimes. Convictions of lower-ranking Ku Klux had been made under a very narrow reading of the scope of the Enforcement Acts. The sentences received had been comparatively light, and most of those had been commuted. Now, the Grant Administration had stopped enforcing civil rights laws completely.

Yet, in this interlude of comparative tranquility, there still remained a window of opportunity and one more forum where the Fourteenth Amendment's expanded vision of individual rights and personal freedoms, as articulated by the amendment's authors, might still be protected and thereby alter the trajectory of American history. This was the US Supreme Court. But there, too, justice was left undone.

The first civil rights case decided by the Supreme Court actually predated the Enforcement Acts of 1870 and 1871 and the Ku Klux trials. It instead arose from a particularly horrific crime committed in Lewis County, Kentucky, which was prosecuted in federal court under the Civil Rights Act of 1866. In the summer of 1868, two white men, John Blyew and George Kennard, took a pair of axes and massacred and mutilated the African-American family of Jack and Sallie Foster. Not only were the Fosters hacked to death, but so was Foster's blind grandmother and the couple's sixteen-year-old son, Richard, who made a dying declaration that identified Blyew and Kennard as the murderers.*

At that time, Kentucky law forbade African Americans from testifying in any trial in which there was a white defendant. Richard Foster's dying declaration was therefore inadmissible as evidence in state court, and African-American neighbors who had witnessed elements of the crime would not be allowed to testify either. Citing the Civil Rights Act of 1866 as the basis for doing so, the US attorney for Kentucky, Benjamin Bristow, who would soon become solicitor general of the United States, charged and tried Blyew and Kennard in federal court, where they were convicted and sentenced to death by Judge Bland Ballard.

Kentucky governor J. W. Stevenson called a special session of the legislature to appropriate funds to finance Blyew and Kennard's appeal. Jeremiah Black, who had been US attorney general under President Buchanan, was hired as special counsel to argue Kentucky's case that murder should always be tried in state not federal court. Bristow countered that the Civil Rights

---

*An eight-year-old daughter of the Fosters successfully hid and avoided the attack, but Blyew and Kennard did axe their six-year-old daughter, Amelia Foster, who survived but was hideously scarred. She never married and worked as a housekeeper until her death in 1934. (Source: Notable Kentuckian African Americans Database: https://nkaa.uky.edu/nkaa/items/show/2045)

Act gave federal courts jurisdiction in criminal cases when it was clear citizens would not be able to have their rights enforced by a state court, and Kentucky's ban on African-American witnesses in the trial guaranteed there would be no justice for the Fosters.

Oral arguments were heard in February 1871, but the court deliberated for more than a year before announcing on April 1, 1872, that Blyew and Kennard's convictions were overturned, but on narrow technical grounds.* The high court declined to offer any guidance on the constitutional issues at play and left "no record explaining why the Court refused to resolve the questions surrounding the scope of the federal government's authority to enforce civil rights."[42] Judge Ballard was disgusted by the justices' timidity and provided his paraphrase of the Beatitudes as they applied to the Court: "Blessed are they who expect little for they shall not be disappointed. But if Congress meant what the Court says they meant is not all of their legislation which relates to the negro a mockery?"[43] Further events would prove so.

The first case to arrive at the Supreme Court arising from the Ku Klux trials and the Enforcement Acts was *United States v. Avery*, the case against several Ku Klux, including York County KKK leaders James W. Avery and J. Rufus Bratton, who were involved in the raid in which Jim Williams was murdered. Divided in opinion on how large the scope of the indictments against the men should be, Judges Bond and Bryan had agreed to certify the case directly to the Supreme Court to resolve two questions. First, was the right to bear arms under the Second Amendment a common law right that fell under state authority or a constitutionally guaranteed right that could be protected by the federal government under the authority of the Enforcement Acts? Second, could persons convicted under the Enforcement Acts be punished using the sentences established under state law for the type of crime committed? Of most particular interest was the question of whether federal courts could impose the death penalty for a civil rights violation if that violation involved committing a murder.

*Blyew and Kennard were retried in state court in Kentucky, which had by then changed its law to allow Black witnesses in the trials of whites, but the first trial ended in a hung jury. Blyew then escaped, but Kennard was tried again, convicted, and sentenced to life in prison at hard labor. He was pardoned in 1885 because of alleged poor health—though he lived another thirty-eight years. Blyew was recaptured in 1890, tried, convicted, and sentenced to life in prison, but was pardoned in 1896, having served less than a half dozen years for the murders of four people, including two children.

Whereas Corbin and Chamberlain had been keen to get the case certified to the Court in hopes that resolution of the constitutional questions involved would speed up the indictment and prosecution process, there was now a twist. Attorney General Williams had determined that the federal government now did not want a Supreme Court ruling on the constitutionality of the Enforcement Acts. Williams personally argued the case before the justices and asserted the Court had no jurisdiction in the case, while Ku Klux legal counsel Reverdy Johnson and Henry Stanbery pleaded with the justices to take up the case and resolve the constitutionality of the Enforcement Acts.

The Supreme Court deliberated for all of a day before agreeing "that it had no jurisdiction, and therefore could not hear arguments on the merits of the enforcement act or ku-klux law [*sic*]." In an 8–1 decision, the Supreme Court noted that the difference of opinion between Bond and Bryan involved a motion to quash counts of an indictment. Such a disagreement did not fall "within the proper scope of a writ of error," the Court said, and the issue should and could be properly resolved at the lower federal district court level without guidance from the Supreme Court.[44] In one of the many ironies that would keep appearing in civil rights cases before the Court, the lone dissenter in the case was Chief Justice Salmon P. Chase, who had written the opinion in *United States v. Rosenberg* on which the Court now based its majority opinion.[45]

Given that Williams would, within the year, lead the Grant Administration's retreat on civil rights enforcement, his urging the Supreme Court not to involve itself in the civil rights cases demonstrates to some scholars Williams's "astounding indifference" to the plight of African Americans and the need to buttress their civil rights with constitutional law. Williams had told the Court that the questions presented in the civil rights cases were not "of such pressing public importance as to require immediate decision." Four million African Americans who remained under the constant threat of violence would have certainly disagreed, and legal scholar Robert J. Kaczorowski said the urgency of the Enforcement Acts cases was "too obvious for Williams to have believed this statement."[46]

But a plausible alternative explanation, given that Williams at this time was still committed to prosecuting the Ku Klux Klan, is that Williams did not expect a favorable ruling from the Supreme Court in the *Avery* case.

Better some of the issues remain in limbo and unresolved than have them answered in a way that would undermine successful prosecutions going forward. This theory was the view of several newspapers at the time, who claimed there was "general rejoicing among the supporters of the administration at the failure to have the act tested in the Supreme Court."[47] One news account said it was common knowledge that the Grant Administration had "a great dread of the result of an inquiry, before the Supreme Court, into the constitutionality of the Enforcement or Ku-Klux law, and every opportunity will be seized of evading that issue."[48]

V

In truth, the Supreme Court needed little encouragement to avoid ruling on the scope of federal enforcement of civil rights, and it seems clear that at least the majority of the Court had developed "a masterful political stratagem . . . to decide politically explosive legal questions in a seemingly nonpolitical way."[49] This became evident when the Court decided to finally address the issues raised by the Fourteenth Amendment not, ironically (that word again), by taking a case involving the protection of civil rights for beleaguered African Americans, but rather a case that involved white butchers in New Orleans who objected to the State of Louisiana creating a corporate monopoly for animal slaughtering.

As America became increasingly urbanized and policymakers more knowledgeable about health and sanitation, several states began to actively regulate the meat-packing industry. Being close to the Texas cattle market, New Orleans had become a major slaughter and meat-packing center where an estimated one thousand butchers, most plying their trade upstream of the city, slaughtered more than three hundred thousand animals per year. Offal and effluence from the slaughter seeped into the water supply and was blamed for an outbreak of cholera in the city.

A variety of other states and major cities had similarly chartered monopoly corporations to regulate the slaughter industry, but Louisiana's efforts were distinctive by the level of corruption and graft involved. In 1869, the Louisiana Legislature created the Crescent City Live-Stock Landing and Slaughter-House Company, which was authorized to create, at a site two miles *downstream* from the city, the sole location where meat could be landed, inspected, slaughtered, and butchered. Independent butchers who wished to continue their trade were required to pay a regulated fee to rent space at the facility.

More than four hundred members of the local Butchers' Benevolent Association (all white men) sued and hired as their legal counsel former US Supreme Court justice John A. Campbell, who had resigned from his seat to become the Confederacy's secretary of war when his native Alabama seceded from the Union. Campbell set aside his previously fervent belief in states' rights and based his appeal on the argument that the "privileges and immunities" now guaranteed to all citizens under the Fourteenth Amendment included the right to freely pursue a legal occupation, which he argued the Louisiana monopoly made impossible for local butchers.

But in a 5–4 decision issued on April 14, 1873, shortly after the Grant Administration had determined it would end prosecution of Ku Klux cases, the Supreme Court ruled against the white butchers and upheld the state law creating the slaughterhouse monopoly. The Court agreed with the corporation attorneys that the butchers were not being prevented from plying their trade, but rather the state was simply exercising its traditional police power to protect public health and safety.

The Court might have left it there with a decision of limited applicability to the broader issue of civil rights. Instead, in a case that did not involve the issue of racial justice, the majority opinion, written by Justice Stephen J. Miller, offered a sweeping interpretation of the Fourteenth Amendment anyway—and undermined the amendment's intentions of promoting racial equality.

That Miller would be the justice to articulate this position is odd given that he was a Lincoln appointee born in Kentucky who was so opposed to slavery that he freed his family's few slaves and moved to free Iowa. Miller explained that the Court decided to use the *Slaughter-House Cases* to examine whether the Civil War and the Fourteenth Amendment had changed the constitutional structure of the Union because there were "no questions so far reaching and pervading in their consequences."[50] Miller and the Court majority then answered those questions so narrowly as to make the Fourteenth Amendment and the privileges and immunities associated with national citizenship "all but meaningless."[51] Nor did the majority explain why they used the *Slaughter-House Cases* to reach these conclusions, rather than a genuine civil rights case of more relevance to the Fourteenth Amendment's intended purpose.

The sole cause of the Civil War, Miller wrote, was slavery, which is a defensible statement but one that also allowed Miller to avoid addressing the argument that the war had changed the federal system and the relationship between the national and state governments. He ignored how Lincoln had also framed the conflict as a struggle between the South's commitment to states' rights and the North's concept of a national sovereignty necessary to preserve the Union. Miller argued that the Thirteenth Amendment was solely about abolishing the institution of slavery, and the purpose of the Fourteenth Amendment was solely to reverse the *Dred Scott* decision by explicitly stating that African Americans were citizens of the United States and entitled to all rights associated with that status. By declaring that the purpose of the Reconstruction Amendments was *only* to rectify the wrong of slavery, the Court had no reason to delve into the possibility that the war and the amendments had changed the structure of the Union and the nature of national citizenship for all people, Black or white.*

Miller's opinion ignored the record of the debate around the Fourteenth Amendment, such as statements by its principal author, Ohio congressman John Bingham, and others who stated that the purpose of the Fourteenth Amendment was to assure that every citizen, regardless of who they were or where they lived, could count on the federal government to protect their rights as listed in the first eight of the ten amendments that constitute the Bill of Rights.

Without citing a source, Miller stated as fact that proponents of the amendment could not possibly have been contemplating a revolutionary change in the federal system that "radically changes the whole theory of the relations of the State and Federal governments to each other and of both these governments to the people." Had that been the intent, Miller argued, the Fourteenth Amendment would have included "language which expresses such a purpose too clearly to admit of doubt."[52]

---

*Some scholars have suggested the Court had a very practical reason for wishing to limit federal authority. The federal courts were already tremendously backlogged with Enforcement Act cases prosecuted under the aegis of the Fourteenth Amendment and dreaded how many cases would inundate the federal courts if the Court became, in Miller's phrasing, a "perpetual censor" of state laws. There is also some thought that Miller thought he was helping the freedmen and women in the South by strengthening the Reconstruction state governments there, and some Southern newspapers did condemn the *Slaughter-House* ruling for strengthening what they believed were illegitimate state governments. But biracial political system of the Reconstruction South soon ended, and so *Slaughter-House* was a major setback in the enforcement of civil rights for the next seventy-five years. (Foner, *Second Founding*, 136)

Reflecting the arguments made by Reverdy Johnson and Henry Stanbery during the Ku Klux trials, Miller differentiated between the rights associated with national citizenship from those associated with state citizenship. Those rights considered "natural rights" under common law, such as freedom of speech and the right to bear arms, were under the protection of the states—even though there was ample evidence that states were not protecting these rights and had conspired, certainly in the case of African Americans, to prevent the exercise of these rights. The only rights specifically associated with national citizenship, the Court majority ruled, were those explicitly listed in the body of the Constitution, which included the right to use navigable waters, to be protected from pirates on the high seas, to peacefully assemble, and to petition Congress.

One of the things that makes the Court's majority position remarkable is that it was composed of all Northern men. Except Miller, who was born in Kentucky but spent his adult career in Iowa, not a single justice on the Court was from a former slave-holding state, and eight of the nine were Republican appointees.* Yet the majority opinion approximated the view held by Democratic Conservatives in the South and those articulated by attorneys defending the Ku Klux Klan in South Carolina. No wonder that it is often said that while the North won the war, the South won the peace.

There were several strong dissents issued by three of the four justices, who declined to join the majority opinion. Justice Noah Swayne of Ohio, who had represented runaway slaves in court and been Lincoln's first appointee to the Court, said that while the prewar interpretation of the

*A justice from a former slave-holding state would not join the Court until 1877, when John Marshall Harlan of Kentucky was appointed by Rutherford B. Hayes after having been passed over by Grant when there was a Court opening in 1873. Had Grant appointed Harlan, perhaps the *Slaughter-House Cases* would have been decided differently for, ironically—the word that we return to again and again when discussing civil rights litigation during this period—Harlan would become the Court's foremost advocate for civil rights for African Americans, a distinction he would hold for three-quarters of a century, mostly by default, given the lack of concern most subsequent justices held for civil rights. Several white supremacists would serve on the Court, such as Justice Lucius Quinus Lamar of Mississippi, who believed Blacks were unfit to vote, and Chief Justice Edward D. White of Louisiana, who was likely a member of the Reconstruction-era Ku Klux as a young man, or at least a similar group such as the Knights of the White Camelia, though he seems to have regretted it. He once told a law clerk, "Young man, you'll be lucky when you're my age if you've only been a damned fool once." To make a statement against integration, the Louisiana Legislature voted to have Justice White's statue placed in Statuary Hall in the US Capitol in 1955, which was the year after the Supreme Court overturned *Plessy v. Ferguson*, which White had supported, by ruling in *Brown v. Board of Education* that segregated public schools are unconstitutional.

Constitution protected citizens from oppression by the national government, there was little protection from "oppression by the states." He argued that the Reconstruction Amendments marked a "new departure . . . in the constitutional history of the country." In a second dissent, Justice Joseph P. Bradley, a former railroad attorney from New Jersey, also argued for an expansive interpretation of the Fourteenth Amendment, saying it had fundamentally altered the federal system and made national citizenship primary and state citizenship secondary.[53]

But the main dissent, which Swayne and Bradley joined, was authored by Justice Stephen J. Field, who had become chief justice of the California Supreme Court when his predecessor killed one of the state's US senators in a duel and had to leave the state. Field said that if the Fourteenth Amendment had not created a robust definition of national citizenship then it had been a "vain and idle enactment, which accomplished nothing, and most unnecessarily excited Congress and the people on its passage." The twist was that Field made this argument not in defense of the civil rights of African Americans or any citizen, but in the interest of corporations. Field was concerned less by violence against Blacks than by the populist sentiment that emerged after the war, especially in state capitals, that was forcing large businesses, especially railroads, to conform to what they considered an intolerable patchwork of regulations that varied from state to state.[54]

Perversely, Field's argument would eventually sway the Court into supporting a strong national government, but for the benefit of corporations, not individuals. A dozen years after writing the majority opinion in the *Slaughter-House Cases*, Miller wrote the Court's majority opinion in *Wabash v. Illinois*, which severely limited the right of states to regulate interstate commerce and which led to the formation of the Interstate Commerce Commission. As Justice Robert J. Jackson would note more than a half-century later, "Never in its entire history can the Supreme Court be said to have for a single hour been representative of anything except the relatively conservative forces of the day."[55]

VI

The *Slaughter-House Cases* had been decided by a single vote, but it is the majority opinion, not the minority opinion (no matter how well reasoned), that sets precedent, and subsequent Court rulings reinforced the limitations the *Slaughter-House* decision had placed on the Fourteenth Amendment's impact on American life. This included any change in the status of American women, Black or white.

The day after the *Slaughter-House* ruling, which had stated that the right to pursue the livelihood of your choice is not a right of national citizenship, the Court voted 8–1 to reject an appeal from a woman named Myra Bradwell who sued to overturn an Illinois Supreme Court ruling that barred women from the practice of law. Justice Bradley wrote the majority opinion, arguing that "nature" and "divine ordinance" did not give women the same rights as men, adding superciliously that women should "properly" devote their energies to "the domestic sphere."[56]

Meanwhile, Congress forged ahead with additional civil rights legislation. In February 1875, Congress gave final approval to what was known as Sumner's Supplemental Civil Rights Bill, so named because it supplemented the original Civil Rights Act of 1866 and was primarily authored by the late Massachusetts senator Charles Sumner. This legislation authorized a new set of entitlements that included equal access to public transportation and public accommodations, which included lodging, theaters, "and other places of amusement." Ohio senator John Sherman, brother of General William Tecumseh Sherman, said that if the right to travel, attend school, or go to a public inn were not protected by the Constitution, "then what in the name of human rights are the privileges of citizens?"[57]

But what Congress gave, the Supreme Court took away. In 1876 the Court ruled in a case involving one of the worst incidents of racial violence in postwar America that had occurred on April 13, 1873, which had been Easter Sunday and the day before the Supreme Court issued its decision in the *Slaughter-House Cases*.

While nationally the 1872 election had been comparatively peaceful as Southern Democrats tried to convince the Grant Administration that the Ku Klux Klan had been suppressed and tranquility had returned to the South, there were still pockets of horrific violence. In Grant Parish, Louisiana, the election had been marred by widespread fraud and intimidation of Black voters so that, even though the parish had a majority Black population, local whites claimed victory. To prevent whites from fraudulently seizing power, Black militia members occupied the parish courthouse in the central Louisiana town of Colfax, even digging a trench around the building in anticipation of a white siege.

The anticipated attack came on Easter Sunday 1873, when more than three hundred armed whites surrounded the courthouse and began firing into the building as the Black militia responded in kind. When the whites brought up a cannon, however, the badly outgunned African Americans waved a white flag in surrender, but whites instead set the building on fire. African-American militiamen were shot as they fled the burning building, and many of those who managed to break through the white cordon were later hunted down and murdered. An estimated 150 African-American and three white men were killed in what became known as "The Colfax Massacre."[58]

Louisiana officials refused to press charges, so federal attorneys drew up indictments against nearly one hundred white men believed to have participated in the massacre, including a local planter named Bill Cruikshank. As in the Ku Klux cases in South Carolina and elsewhere, large numbers of defendants fled to avoid prosecution and the initial trial of a remaining handful of defendants ended with a hung jury, but three men, including Cruikshank, were ultimately convicted of civil rights violations and appealed those convictions to the Supreme Court.

In a unanimous decision issued on March 27, 1876, and authored by new chief justice Morrison Waite of Ohio, a Grant appointee, the Court overturned the convictions and ruled that individual rights were still under the protection of the states, not the federal government, and that the Bill of Rights, including the Second Amendment right to bear arms, only protected citizens from infringement of those rights by Congress, not individuals.

The Fourteenth Amendment had added "nothing to the rights of one citizen against another," Waite wrote, meaning that he had adopted the reasoning argued by Johnson and Stanbery in the Ku Klux trials that "ordinary" crimes, such as murder, should be tried in state, not federal court. The Court placed some of the blame for its decision on federal prosecutors, charging that they had drawn up faulty indictments. Federal prosecution might have been justified, the Court said, had prosecutors explicitly stated that the assault in Colfax was intended to prevent African Americans from voting on account of their race. "We may suspect that race was the cause of the hostility, but it is not averred," was the Court's remarkable assessment.[59]

On the same day it issued the ruling in *Cruikshank*, the Supreme Court issued a second ruling known as *United States v. Reese* that overturned the convictions of Kentucky officials who had conspired to prevent African Americans from voting in a local election. In doing so, the Court declared significant sections of the Enforcement Acts unconstitutional because they prohibited interference in voting when the Fifteenth Amendment only prohibited interference based on race. Historian Leonard Levy said the decisions in *Cruikshank* and *Reese* had "paralyzed the federal government's attempt to protect black citizens . . . and, in effect, shaped the Constitution to the advantage of the [now defunct] Ku Klux Klan."[60]

Remarkably, despite these judicial setbacks, in 1880 a majority of African-American males in the Southern states still were able to vote, and they still voted overwhelmingly Republican. African Americans also continued to enjoy access to most public accommodations enjoyed by whites, including restaurants, theaters, and public transportation.[61] But the decade would produce even more egregious Supreme Court decisions that encouraged states, particularly but not exclusively in the South, to devise new and superficially legal means to deny African Americans the right to vote, taking their cue as to how from the strong hints coming from the Court.

In 1878 Congress barred the use of the Army to police elections, while Republican proposals for federal supervision of federal elections were defeated in Congress in 1888 and 1890. In 1878 the Supreme Court overturned a one-thousand-dollar judgment awarded to an affluent free-born Black woman named Josephine DeCuir who had been denied accommodations on a Mississippi River steamboat on the grounds that a Louisiana law that guaranteed color-blind access to public transportation was a burden on interstate commerce because different states might have different laws on integration. Justice Nathan Clifford, the lone holdover on the Court from the Buchanan Administration, wrote a concurring opinion that helped lay the groundwork for the 1896 *Plessy v. Ferguson* opinion that would legalize segregation by arguing that integration would drive away white customers and ruin businesses. Segregation, therefore, actually promoted the public interest, in Clifford's view.[62]

In 1883 the Supreme Court took another large step in launching Jim Crow* when it ruled segregation was permissible in a consolidation of cases arising from the Sumner Supplemental Civil Rights Act that had integrated public accommodations. The cases included where African Americans had been denied hotel accommodations in Kansas and Missouri, were excluded from first-class train travel in Tennessee, and were barred from sitting in the dress circle at a theater in New York City that was showing the Victor Hugo play *Ruy Blas*, ironically the story of a slave disguised as a nobleman that starred Edwin Booth, the brother of Lincoln's assassin.

The majority opinion in the *Civil Rights Cases* was written by Justice Bradley and stated that while the Fourteenth Amendment empowered Congress to prevent states from taking action that impaired a citizen's civil rights, the federal government could do nothing about "the wrongful acts of individuals." Bradley, who had argued in *Slaughter-House* that national citizenship should only benefit corporations and who had notoriously argued that it was "repugnant" for women to have a career independent of their husband, now took a gratuitous slap at African Americans for seeking government protection of their rights. Even though African Americans had been out of bondage for less than twenty years, were still often confined to a situation akin to indentured servitude, and had been whipped, raped, and murdered by the thousands, Bradley told them that it was time they stopped seeking "to be the special favorite of the law." A variety of newspapers, North and South, praised the ruling, including the *Chicago Tribune*, which lauded the Court for refusing to place Blacks "above the white man" and for ending the status of African Americans as "wards of the government."[63]

The *Harrisburg* (PA) *Telegraph* was much closer to the mark when it placed the *Civil Rights Cases* in the tradition of the nefarious *Dred Scott* decision. Referencing Chief Justice Roger Taney, the author of *Dred Scott*, the *Telegraph* said "[t]he Taneys are not all dead, or else they are a race who succeed each other; and when blind, brutal prejudice wishes to indulge itself in imposing disabilities and humiliations upon the weak and defenseless, a decision of the Supreme Court can be found or procured to help them." The

---

*Jim Crow was the collective name for the various state and local laws approved in the late nineteenth and early twentieth centuries that legalized and enforced racial segregation. The name comes from a blackface minstrel show character played by New York–born actor Thomas D. Rice and by the late 1830s had become a widely used epithet that conformed to the white caricature of African Americans as lazy, dumb, and untrustworthy.

Telegraph said the Court was unchanging. "It seems . . . that now, as long ago, freedom is not and cannot be made safe in the United States as long as we have a Supreme Court."[64]

There was one justice on the Court whose feelings mirrored the *Telegraph*'s and he, John Marshall Harlan, provided the lone dissent in the *Civil Rights Cases*.

Like Amos Akerman, Harlan had been a slave owner, and he agonized over his dissent until his wife, Malvina, placed on his desk the same inkstand that Taney had used to write his *Dred Scott* opinion. Inspired to urge the Court never to issue so dastardly an opinion again, Harlan traced the Court's sorry history of defending slavery, including it upholding laws that required private citizens to assist in the recapture of runaway slaves. Harlan argued that the Thirteenth Amendment did more than abolish slavery, it created a national entitlement to "universal civil and political freedom" and empowered Congress to prohibit all actions that were "inconsistent with the fundamental rights of American citizenship." He added that all forms of racial discrimination were a "badge of servitude" (though it should be noted that Harlan incongruously harbored deep prejudices against the Chinese and sought to restrict their right to immigrate to the United States and become citizens).

Harlan also added prophetically that the United States was entering "an era of constitutional law when the rights of freedom and American citizenship cannot receive from the nation that efficient protection which heretofore was unhesitatingly accorded to slavery." Thirteen years later, in 1896, Harlan was again the lone dissenter in *Plessy v. Ferguson*. The author of that execrable decision was Justice Henry Brown, who hailed from the "social elite" of Massachusetts and had attended Yale. Brown's decision ruled that segregation was permissible provided separate facilities for African Americans were "equal" with those provided for white Americans.[65]

The facilities would not be equal, of course, and the Court would not seriously revisit the issue of racial equality for another fifty-eight years. In the meantime, when Court opinions did touch on Reconstruction measures, the Court would remarkably cite as justification for its inaction on racial equality the discredited accounts of Reconstruction authored by the Dunning School of historians. This meant the Court was not taking its cue from historical fact, but from the fanciful fiction of men like Thomas Dixon and his romanticized account of the Ku Klux Klan in his book *The Clansman*. Court opinions still quoted the malicious and misguided Dunning School historians as late as 1965.[66]

That fact did not bother most white Americans. Even though the Reconstruction Amendments and the accompanying Enforcement Acts were intended to protect the civil rights of all Americans, not just African Americans, they were viewed by most white Americans as the *Chicago Tribune* saw them, providing preferential treatment for Blacks over whites. Far from being infamous, these Court decisions, virtually all written by men from Northern states, were so in tune with white American public opinion, North and South, that, historian Eric Foner observed, they "helped rehabilitate the Court's public reputation, at low ebb, at least in the North, ever since the *Dred Scott* decision."[67]

The South then—though, again, not exclusively the South—began completing the primary task of the Ku Klux, which was to deny African Americans the right to vote. Having received the very strong hint from the Supreme Court that the only time the federal government could intervene was when states passed laws that *explicitly* used race to disqualify African Americans from voting in federal elections, the South sought new means to exclude Blacks from participating in elections without explicitly mentioning race. Property ownership became a requisite, poll taxes were levied, residency and registration requirements were tightened, literacy and civics tests were administered, and if that still did not block Black participation then registrars could, as a stop-gap measure, randomly administer "good character tests" that African Americans, no matter their character, would not be allowed to pass.[68]

When poor, illiterate whites became concerned these requirements would also exclude them from participating as voters too, Southern states implemented what was known as the "Grandfather Clause," which stated that no voter need meet any of the literacy, property ownership, or poll tax requirements if they or an ancestor had voted prior to 1867 or had fought in the Civil War. "Virtually no blacks would pass through the Grandfather Clause. Most whites, on the other hand, were able to meet one of the requirements."[69]

The impact on African-American participation in elections was immediate and extraordinary. In Louisiana, one hundred thirty thousand Blacks had voted in the 1896 election; in 1900, only 5,320 were able to register to vote, and in 1904 that number decreased to 1,342.[70] Ninety-nine percent of Black voters had been disqualified in the space of eight years.

The Ku Klux Klan Trials had been the highpoint of Reconstruction and represented our nation's greatest and most sincere attempt to achieve racial justice during the one-hundred-year period between the end of the Civil War and the civil rights movement of the 1960s. The trials destroyed the Ku Klux Klan and created a moment pregnant with hope and possibility. The year 1872 might have been an extraordinary inflection point that changed American history for the better in a dramatic and glorious way.

Instead, less than twenty-five years after its demise, due to Southern obstinacy, Northern indifference, and a Supreme Court that forgot justice is the most important component of the law, the Ku Klux's mission was accomplished and was done so all *within* rather than *outside* the law.

Chapter Fifteen

Old Jim Williams's body lies a-mouldering in the grave . . . his truth is marching on.

—*Emancipation Day celebrants altering the lyrics to "John Brown's Body"*

I

On New Year's Day 1872, hundreds of local African Americans, accompanied by the "booming of cannons and tooting of brass horns," braved high winds and heavy rains to gather at noon in the yard before the colonnaded courthouse in Chester, South Carolina, to celebrate Emancipation Day. It was the ninth anniversary of what the white editor of the local newspaper, the *Chester Reporter*, called the "natal day of their freedom," as the Emancipation Proclamation that President Lincoln had issued in September 1862 had officially taken effect on January 1, 1863.[1]

The crowd listened to speeches that celebrated "the virtues of their patron saint, Abe Lincoln," the newspaper said, and then to other speeches that revealed squabbling within the South Carolina Republican Party. Judge William M. Thomas, for example, railed that Governor Robert Scott should have requested federal troops much sooner the previous year to quell the Ku Klux violence in York and Union Counties.[2]

Left unstated in this charge of dawdling incompetence by Scott, but certainly understood by the crowd, was that had federal troops arrived two months sooner than they did, then perhaps Jim Williams, who had been lynched in March, and many other murder victims would still be alive to join in this celebration of freedom, while many, many more would have been spared painful and humiliating whippings, rapes, and other outrages.

Williams was well known to the Chester crowd. He had lived in Chester County as a boy when he was the property of Quay Donivan, and his murder had occurred just ten miles north of Chester near Williams's home on the Bratton plantation just inside the York County line. They were also well aware of how he had been murdered, which was key to why the Ku Klux did what they did.

Had the Ku Klux led by Dr. J. Rufus Bratton simply wanted Williams dead, they could easily have shot him outside his home and it would have been over in an instant. But lynching was for white supremacists what crucifixion had been for the ancient Romans, the most mortifying and sordid of deaths, usually reserved for "troublesome slaves," a public spectacle of prolonged suffering that provided a vivid warning to the lowly to remember their place in society.[3] But a crucifixion, whether the victim is nailed to or hung from a tree, has been known to create martyrs.

For frightened whites, Williams was a criminal, deserving of death; for local African Americans he was a symbol of pride and hope, a man who held firm that the American creed would not apply to him and his progeny at some vague future someday, but that it applied to them then and there, what Martin Luther King Jr. would describe ninety years later as "the fierce urgency of now." Despite being five-foot-six in height, he had stood tall and defiant in expressing his personal dignity. When he captained his militia and drilled them into a formidable force, he did so in broad daylight, in full view of all. He did not hide or apologize for his aspirations. He had also, along with Elias Hill, sought to make peace with his white neighbors, but would accept only an equitable peace fair to Blacks as well as whites.

This sought-for peace did not occur—it did not even last that day—and when confronted with the possibility that Black militias might be disarmed, an act of capitulation, Williams resolutely traveled to Columbia as a full citizen of South Carolina to make an appeal directly to the leader of the state. Whether Governor Scott ever granted him an audience is unknown. What we do know is that not long after he returned from the Capitol and in what was his last public act, he stood on the steps of the courthouse in Yorkville and before the whole town asserted that he possessed the same inalienable rights as any American citizen. There is no record that Williams ever committed a violent act, but he was ready to do what was necessary to defend his rights and those of his family and his community.

Because he was committed to his ideals, he was killed, specifically, lynched, and the Black citizens of Chester equated his death with the hanging of another man, a white man, John Brown, who became a martyr because he had taken up arms in the pursuit of freedom for the enslaved. And so, according to the *Chester Reporter*, the crowd at Chester took the lyrics of the song that Union soldiers had dedicated to Brown and substituted the name of Jim Williams. Then, in the tune of the old folk song that Julia Ward Howe would also adapt as "The Battle Hymn of the Republic," they loudly sang these new improvised lyrics:

> Old Jim Williams's body lies a-mouldering in the grave,
> While weeps the sons of bondage whom he ventured all to save;
> But though he lost his life in struggling for the slave,
> His truth is marching on.
> Glory, Glory, Hallelujah!
> His truth is marching on!

The hymn acted as a benediction, the *Chester Reporter* said, and "the crowd dispersed, feeling no doubt, that the emancipation proclamation had been duly celebrated."[4]

While being a (now forgotten) martyr ennobled Williams's death (though certainly not in the eyes of most local whites), he was still dead, and Rosa Williams was still a widow with five children to raise. These included Gil, the child Williams fathered with his second wife, Ollie, who had been sold away during slavery and was never heard from again; Rosa's two children, Henry and Lula, that she had with her first husband, Green Bratton; and the children Rosa had with Jim, James Williams Jr., and the daughter named Patience who was an infant when her father was murdered.

Rosa never remarried and struggled on what she could make as a cook and laundress for various white households. Rosa had briefly received a small pension provided by the State of South Carolina to the survivors of men killed by the Ku Klux. Though it had been limited to ten dollars per month for a widow and six dollars per month for each orphan under the age of majority, it was a substantial benefit to a family that had lost its primary breadwinner. But in what was one of the very first acts taken after assuming office, Governor Wade Hampton and the newly Democratically controlled legislature abolished the pension program in 1877.

In 1893 Rosa, as the widow of a Union army veteran, applied for a survivor's benefit shortly after Congress, in 1890, broadened the original Union army pension program. As with the Carolina pension, the amount available was small, ranging from six dollars to twelve dollars per month in total, but such pensions were an immense boon to African Americans in the South, where nearly one in six African-American men of age had served in the Union army and whose wages after the war were a fraction of what white laborers earned for the same work.[5]

When Rosa applied for the pension, she was required to submit as many affidavits as possible attesting to her husband's service. Unfortunately, Rosa's run of misfortune never seemed to cease. In 1892 her house had burned down, and whatever formal discharge or other papers that would have verified her husband's service were lost. Nor could Rosa recall exactly in which regiment her husband had served. It had been too long ago, and the number and names of military units likely meant little to an unschooled woman who was simply happy to have her husband at home once more—and free for the first time. "I did hear him tell about it," Rosa said of Williams's war service, "but have forgot it." Given that he was eleven years old when his father returned from the war, Rosa hoped Gil might recall his father's war stories, including his regiment, but Gil had moved to North Carolina and could not be immediately located.[6]

There was a further snafu when the War Department confused Rosa's application with that of another widow, named Delia, who had been the wife of another deceased Jim Williams who had served with an African-American regiment in Tennessee. The War Department initially became convinced that these women were "contesting widows" seeking a pension claim for the same man, but the two cases were eventually separated—and neither woman was approved for a pension. The Tennessee widow, the former Delia Williams, had remarried, which made her ineligible for a pension. In Rosa's case, because she could not produce any records, such as a discharge paper, and because the affidavits submitted on her behalf were all from family members or

African-American friends, the War Department concluded that she had not provided sufficient proof that Williams had served during the war.

Affidavits from white people were given more weight by the War Department, and Rosa was so desperate that she sought the help of her former owner, Harriet Rainey Bratton, who was not only the sister of Samuel Rainey, who had been Jim Williams's owner, but also the widow of John S. Bratton Jr. and sister-in-law of J. Rufus Bratton, her husband's killer. Rainey declined to submit an affidavit on Rosa's behalf but appeared before a special examiner reviewing Rosa's request and stated dismissively, "I do not remember whether James Williams went to the army when Sherman came through here. . . . There were so many of them (slaves) went away about that time that I did not keep track of them."[7]

Rosa never received a pension, and according to census records, she kept working to provide for herself and her children until they became of age, but she now toiled as a farm laborer rather than a cook while she lived next door to her son, Henry. Henry worked as a farmer, but in testament to the ambitions instilled in him by his parents, all his children attended school and his eldest daughter became a schoolteacher. When she was no longer able to continue working to support herself, Rosa alternated living with Henry and Patience until she died of kidney disease in 1920, having lived a hard life that might have been modestly easier had she successfully obtained the veteran's pension that was her due.

The failure of Rosa Williams to obtain a pension was not unique. Even though nearly two hundred thousand African-American men had fought in the war, had a mortality rate 50 percent higher than their white comrades, and even though their late entry into the war provided the boost that likely tipped the war in favor of the North, they were not treated any more equitably in the pension program than they were in any other aspect of American life.* While 81 percent of white applicants obtained pensions under the 1890 program, only 44 percent of African-American applicants did so. Economist Dora L. Costa, who did a detailed analysis of the Union army pension program, said "the conditions for which white pensions were

---

*Economist Dora L. Costa's study comparing white and Black veterans' pensions notes that the mortality rate for white Union troops was 14 percent compared to 22 percent for Blacks, who were housed in less sanitary conditions and not given equal access to adequate medical care. Over 90 percent of the deaths of Black soldiers in the war were from disease compared to two-thirds of the deaths of white soldiers. (Costa, "Pensions and Retirement among Black Union Army Veterans," 567–92)

granted often had a tenuous link to service in the war. But black veterans were not granted the same leniency." Further, when pensions were granted African-American veterans or their survivors, they received far smaller amounts. By 1900 the average pension for Black recipients was $7.59 per month, while it was $12.94 per month for white recipients.[8]

Confederate veterans, having fought against the Union, were not eligible for federal pensions, so the Southern states established their own pension program for those who fought for the Confederacy. Given the South's destitution after the war and the region's traditional antipathy toward taxes and government spending, the initial Southern state pension systems were usually limited to paying for artificial limbs for those soldiers who needed them as a result of a war injury, though some states also provided housing for indigent veterans. But over time, as Confederate veterans grew older and more disabled, there was a strong push to broaden the pension systems.

Confederate veterans applied for pensions not in the state where they mustered, but in the states where they now lived. My great-grandfather, John Clayton Farris, had enlisted in his native South Carolina but had been a resident of Baxter County, Arkansas, since 1871. In fact, while he may have done so, there is no record he ever returned to South Carolina, even to visit family. In 1891 Arkansas began granting pensions to Confederate veterans who could prove they were indigent, which was defined as having an income of less than $150 per year and no personal or real property that was cumulatively valued at more than four hundred dollars.*

Nearly ten years after he relocated to Arkansas, on February 14, Valentine's Day 1881, John Clayton married his second wife, Edith Cranfil, my great-grandmother, who was eighteen years John Clayton's junior. Together they had seven children who lived to adulthood, including their third child, William Francis Farris, who is my grandfather. For reasons unknown and incomprehensible, not only did John Clayton not allow my grandfather to attend school, he failed to teach him the rudimentary reading and writing skills that he allegedly possessed and could seemingly have passed on.

John Clayton made his living in Arkansas as a sharecropper, a hard life made harder by the lingering effects of his several war wounds. In 1909, at age seventy-two, tired and poor, he applied for a veteran's pension from

---

*An income of less than $150 was abject poverty. Costa's study says a typical white laborer of the time made an average of $432 per year and a Black laborer an average of $194 per year.

the State of Arkansas but was denied by the Baxter County pension board, who claimed the destitute sharecropper had provided "insufficient proof of indigency."[9]

John Clayton tried again in 1910. This time, he provided affidavits attesting to his lack of worldly possessions, as well as testimony from a doctor who proclaimed John Clayton "at least ¾ disabled." The doctor noted that due to war wounds John Clayton sported scars on the top of his head, on his right thigh, and also over the right shoulder blade, while suffering from a "large hernia" brought on by a lifetime of heavy lifting and pushing from manual labor. Several friends and relatives from South Carolina provided testimonials, including his younger brother, Moses, who vouched for John Clayton's service in the 5th South Carolina Infantry and assured the pension board that his injuries were war-related and not the result of "vicious habits." This time, his application was approved, though he had few years to enjoy the modest extra income, for he died July 25, 1916.[10]

This was a year after my own father, Neil Farris, was born near Gassville, Arkansas, the third of eight children who lived to adulthood. In 1927 my grandfather, William Francis, moved his family to Oklahoma, yet despite the handicaps of being an illiterate sharecropper, he was not a strong advocate for letting his children attend school past the sixth grade. My grandmother, the former Effie Davis, insisted my father continue school, although because he was still periodically held out to help farm, my father did not graduate from Excelsior High School near Okemah, Oklahoma, until he was twenty years old.

His Future Farmers of America teacher had particularly encouraged my father to attend college. Certain that anything was preferable to the backbreaking work of picking cotton for a penny a pound, my father hitchhiked to Stillwater, Oklahoma, with fifty cents in his pocket and enrolled at what was then known as Oklahoma A&M University. With the help of a fifteen-dollar loan from his faculty advisor, Charles Pierce, to cover his first semester tuition, my father worked his way through school, arising every day at 3:00 a.m. to milk two dozen cows and sweep out the stalls at the college dairy, and supplemented that with work as a hasher at a fraternity and as a janitor in the dormitories. He graduated in four years and then earned a master's degree after his service in World War II, spending the bulk of his career as a soil scientist for the federal Bureau of Indian Affairs.

Meanwhile, my great-grandmother, known as "Eda" and now a widow, applied for a Confederate veteran's survivor benefit in 1917. Unable to read or write, she made her mark on her application that asserted she owned no property valued at more than five hundred dollars and earned no income in excess of $250 per year, which was the new threshold. Her application was granted, and my great-grandmother continued to receive a pension for the remainder of her life. The income was vital, as it allowed her, by 1932, to own three cows and a mare, as well as a small interest in a tract of land, where she lived with her eldest son. She died in 1954, three days after her one hundredth birthday, when Southern states were still paying out millions of dollars per annum to the widows of Confederate veterans.*

And so my great-grandmother, by all accounts a good woman who had a hard life, received a pension for thirty-seven years as the widow of a Confederate veteran who had been in the Ku Klux Klan, while Rosa Williams, also a good woman and who, if anything, had a far more difficult life, whose husband had served honorably in the Union army and who was murdered by the Ku Klux Klan for the "crime" of defending his rights and those of his fellow citizens, never received a cent.[11]

II

By the end of Grant's presidency, virtually all convicted Ku Klux had either completed their prison terms or been pardoned by the president. Active cases against Ku Klux were dismissed, including eleven hundred cases just in South Carolina in 1874.[12] No new arrests were made, and the search for those still wanted had ended, though not all Ku Klux felt free to return to the homes they had abandoned. Dr. J. Rufus Bratton and his York County co-conspirator Major James W. Avery remained in exile in Canada, aware that the seriousness and notoriety of their lynching of Jim Williams, and Bratton's success in making the federal government look foolish in its attempt to abduct him from his hiding place in Canada, had made each man persona non grata as far as the US government was concerned.

But the 1876 presidential election changed things. Exhaustion with Reconstruction, rampant corruption within the Grant Administration, and,

---

*In 1958, when there was believed to be only one surviving Confederate veteran and an estimated fifteen hundred widows of Confederate veterans still alive, the federal government assumed the obligation of paying out their pension benefits. A daughter of a Civil War veteran who had fought for both North and South during the war was still receiving a pension benefit of $73.13 per month until she died in 2020.

particularly, the lingering economic effects of the Panic of 1873 had taken their toll on the Republican Party. In an election in which an astonishing 82 percent of registered voters participated, it initially appeared that the Democratic governor of New York, Samuel Tilden, had prevailed over the GOP nominee, Ohio governor Rutherford B. Hayes, and ended sixteen years of Republican occupancy of the White House. But shenanigans in Florida, Louisiana, and South Carolina had left the vote count in those three states in dispute, and so neither candidate could claim an Electoral College majority.*

This unprecedented situation led Congress to form a special bipartisan commission composed of members of Congress and the Supreme Court to resolve the dispute. It soon became clear that there would be no thoughtful process to resolve this constitutional impasse, but instead a secret bargain was reached among party leaders that gave the election to Hayes in return for a Republican guarantee that the few remaining federal troops still stationed in the South would be removed. Radical Reconstruction, already petered out, would officially end, and conservative Democrats would be allowed to regain political control of the South.†

Throughout the South, Democrats regained control of state houses, including in South Carolina, where General Wade Hampton unseated Republican governor Daniel Chamberlain in a tumultuous and contested election. Chamberlain had been elected governor in 1874 after completing his term as state attorney general. In his campaign for governor, Chamberlain had pledged to cut state taxes and spending and to root out the corruption associated with the previous Republican administrations.

Once in office, Chamberlain did his best "to please the Democrats" by following through on his pledges of fiscal austerity and also by appointing Democrats to key positions in his administration. This, in turn, antagonized Republicans, who grew frustrated when Chamberlain proved impotent in tamping down renewed white violence against African Americans. Chamberlain came to the same conclusion that Governor Scott had reached:

*There is evidence Republicans altered vote totals in the three states to give Hayes majorities in all three, but the Republicans likely committed the fraud with a clear conscience, as in 1876 armed whites once again used violence and intimidation on a large scale to prevent Blacks from voting the Republican ticket.
†As noted earlier in the book, I use the adjective "conservative" because that is how most Southern Democrats described themselves and, for a decade after the war, preferred to say they belonged to the "Conservative" rather than "Democratic" Party. (See Woodward, *Origins of the New South, 1877–1913*.)

He could not call out the state militia without antagonizing Democrats and inviting more violence. But unlike Scott he did not have the option of requesting federal troops given the Grant Administration's pullback from Southern affairs.[13]

Increasingly a politician without a party, Chamberlain even lost the support of his friend US Attorney Daniel T. Corbin. Corbin was just as politically ambitious as his former Ku Klux co-prosecutor and, at a time when there was still no direct election of senators, was angling for election by the state legislature to the US Senate. Aware that Chamberlain had made enemies in both parties, Corbin charged that Chamberlain was culpable in the corruption that he was now pledging to root out.

Corbin's own moral authority in making such an accusation was dubious. He, too, was hounded by allegations of corruption. Winning a twenty-eight-thousand-dollar judgment while representing the State of South Carolina in a civil suit against the South Carolina Phosphate Company, Corbin kept virtually the entire amount for himself as his fee and turned over "a mere $206 to the state."[14] This scandal would be a great impediment to Corbin's senatorial ambitions.

Like Chamberlain, Corbin was also increasingly powerless to combat escalating white violence. Under pressure from Attorney General Williams to stop prosecutions under the Enforcement Acts, and perhaps also engaging in some political calculation related to his Senate bid, Corbin declined to prosecute those responsible for one of South Carolina's worst incidents of racial violence since the Ku Klux trials.

On July 4, 1876, in the town of Hamburg, a Black militia celebrating Independence Day and the nation's centennial started what appeared to be a minor kerfuffle by refusing to allow two white men to cross Main Street and cut through the militia parade. The men filed charges against the militia captain, a man named Doc Adams, but rather than wait for the issue to be resolved in court, hundreds of local whites surrounded the militia, who were now holed up in an old brick warehouse. Shooting broke out between the two groups and then, as had occurred in Colfax, Louisiana, the whites brought up a cannon and fired into the warehouse. When the militia surrendered, the whites, furious that one of their own had been killed in the skirmish (as had two Black militiamen), selected six Black captives "and shot them dead" in retribution.[15]

Chamberlain personally traveled to Washington to appeal to Grant for assistance. The president, as he had after the Colfax Massacre, again issued high-minded and stern declarations about ensuring "an untrammeled ballot" but, worried about the political impact so close to the presidential election, declined to send federal troops to restore order.[16]

Corbin, perhaps also concerned about the lack of military support, declined to arraign any of the offenders in federal court, offering the rationale that prosecutions might simply lead to more atrocities. One of the consequences, certainly unintended by Corbin, was that one of the leaders of the white mob, former Confederate general Matthew C. Butler, whom Northern newspapers labeled "The Murderer of Hamburg" and Southern newspapers hailed as "The Hero of Hamburg," would win the Senate seat coveted by Corbin.[17]

Unlike the comparatively peaceful 1872 election, violence around the 1876 election killed scores of people, almost all of them African Americans, but with no resulting federal intervention or federal (or state) prosecutions. Even a sympathetic biographer has acknowledged that Hampton, whose supporters implemented a plan of intimidation that had already proven effective in Mississippi, won the 1876 South Carolina gubernatorial election "largely through violence and electoral fraud."[18]

While the Ku Klux had disappeared in form, its spirit survived, but now those seeking to intimidate African Americans did so openly and brazenly. So-called "rifle clubs," whose members drilled and marched openly and without disguises, were the new preferred method of menacing Blacks. Hampton had considered the Ku Klux with its bizarre costumes and grotesque violence against women and children an embarrassment to the South and a provocation to the North. By contrast, an open display of power and unity seemed to him a far manlier expression of the supposed natural order of Southern white male dominance far less likely to invite federal interference. Just as the public drilling of Black militias had frightened whites, so now the brazen display of will displayed by the rifle clubs intimidated Blacks.

In South Carolina, club members wore shirts of dyed red flannel, and the march of these heavily armed paramilitary "Red Shirts" down the main streets of every town and hamlet was a fixture of Hampton's rallies throughout the state. Over the two-month campaign, Hampton stumped in fifty-seven communities, drawing crowds of three thousand to ten thousand at each stop.[19] His rally at Yorkville, where Hampton claimed both to have been "the first man in America who advocated Negro suffrage" and that African Americans had more rights in South Carolina than in Chamberlain's native Massachusetts, was described as the second-largest held in the state.[20]

A racial moderate compared to most conservative Southern Democrats (with an emphasis on the comparative), Hampton continued to superficially condemn violence, preferring not to know what his more zealous supporters were up to. On the stump, however, he endorsed "force without violence" and "peaceful coercion," Orwellian descriptions of the hoped-for effect of the Red Shirts.[21] Corbin clearly saw the Red Shirts as an extension of the Ku Klux, saying they had "reorganized under the names of rifle clubs [but] have entered upon and intend to pursue the purposes and general plans of 1871 and 1872 of the old organizations."[22]

To a large degree Corbin was correct, but the destruction of the Ku Klux had had some lasting meritorious impact on Carolina politics, as demonstrated by Hampton who, even as he sought to "redeem" South Carolina from Radical Republican rule, actively courted Black voters and pledged to be "Governor of the whole people."[23]

In pledging, for example, to provide more money for the education of African-American children, Hampton, of course, was not addressing African Americans as equals. Rather, his promises to Black voters were, a biographer noted, "paternalistic ones . . . like those a powerful patron might make to his clients."[24] And when he boasted of the good relationships he enjoyed with African Americans, he was primarily referring to kind words uttered by certain of his former slaves.

Yet Hampton won the backing of a startlingly large number of African Americans who likely just wanted peace and believed Hampton had the status to maintain law and order. Hampton even won the backing of African Americans such as Martin Delany, Frederick Douglass's journalistic partner and the first African American to be a commissioned officer in the Union army. In 1874 Delany ran for lieutenant governor on what was labeled the Independent Republican party ticket that lost to Chamberlain. Passed over by Grant for appointment to various federal positions, including consul general to Liberia, Hampton appointed Delany as a trial justice in Charleston in 1877 and resisted repeated calls by Democrats to have Delany removed.

Ultimately, Hampton received an estimated ten thousand votes from African Americans, which accounted for his margin of victory, for Hampton defeated Chamberlain by a mere 1,134 votes in a contested election that was not finally resolved until the spring of 1877—just like the presidential race.[25]

Hampton did keep several of his promises to African Americans. He ensured funding was provided for schools for African-American children and appointed not just Delany but more than one hundred African Americans to various minor government posts. Hampton was in no way promoting racial equality, a concept completely foreign to him, but was reassuming the role of aristocratic protector. His meager effort on behalf of African Americans "was not about the character and virtues of black people at all," biographer Rod Andrew Jr. wrote, "but rather about his own."[26]

Still, it was more than had been expected, and Hampton increased his share of the Black vote in his reelection in 1878. Dismayed conservatives finally sent the too-accommodating Hampton to the US Senate in 1879 to get him out of Columbia, but while Hampton served as governor, South Carolina spent an equal amount per student on white and Black education, and he appointed more than one hundred African Americans to positions within his administration, though most were lower-level positions at the county or municipal level.[27]

Yet, and why we must always call Hampton a "comparative" racial moderate, among the first acts of his administration was the institution of the notorious convict lease system that became a new means of enslaving thousands of African Americans who were arrested on minor or trumped-up charges to secure their forced labor. Also among his first acts as governor, he took the remarkably petty and cruel step of repealing the modest state pensions that had been awarded to the widows and orphans of those killed by the Ku Klux.[28]

He also closed the newly integrated University of South Carolina in order that it might be reopened three years later as an all-white college, and he began working diligently for the return of Bratton and other Ku Klux exiles to South Carolina.*

III

When Hampton assumed office in April 1877, the State of South Carolina was $5.6 million in debt. There were cries from newly empowered conservative Democrats to repudiate that debt and prosecute former Republican officeholders for alleged fraud and malfeasance as well as general political retribution. Hampton desired a good relationship with President Hayes and a definitive end to federal intervention in the South, while Hayes, aware of the unusual circumstances surrounding his selection as president, was anxious to promote national harmony. He even convinced Hampton to join him and other governors for a multistate national unity and reconciliation tour that included cordial meetings with former Union officers, who amicably shook hands with their former foe. A touched Hampton repeatedly asserted, "We are all on the same side now."[29]

But two sets of potential prosecutions stood as a barrier to this new national amity. Hayes wished Hampton to refrain from prosecuting former Republican officeholders in South Carolina, while Hampton wanted assurances that, despite the recent horrific violence in Hamburg and elsewhere, there would be no renewed wave of Enforcement Acts prosecutions in federal courts. In correspondence and private meetings, in which apparently each man "liked what they saw in the other," Hayes and Hampton colluded to ensure prosecutions on both sides were dropped.[30]

---

*In 1869 the University of South Carolina began the process of becoming the only university in the South during Reconstruction to admit and grant degrees to African-American students. The first African-American student to obtain a degree was Henry Hayne, who was also South Carolina's secretary of state, who had enrolled to study medicine. Its first African-American faculty member was Richard Theodore Greener, who had been the first African American to graduate from Harvard and who taught philosophy while also attending the USC college of law. USC had never been a large school, with enrollment seldom topping two hundred before the war, and after the war had only about fifty students. When the school was integrated, most white students and faculty left, leaving just eight students. South Carolina then offered more than 120 full-ride scholarships to boost enrollment. Most of those who applied were African-American, and by 1875, 90 percent of the student body was Black. Hampton closed the university in 1877, citing lack of state funds. When he reopened the school three years later, it was an all-white school. The legislature ignored Hampton's tepid call for a state-funded Black college, and so the only higher education option for Carolina Blacks was the private Claflin University in Orangeburg. (See: Current, *Those Terrible Carpetbaggers*, 328; Andrew, *Wade Hampton*, 430l; and Reynolds, *Reconstruction in South Carolina*, 231–38.)

SCOTT FARRIS

In South Carolina, three (one white and two Black) former Republican officeholders were made scapegoats and convicted for the alleged sins of the previous Republican state administrations, but they were also quickly pardoned by Hampton, who pledged to Hayes that there would be no more "political" prosecutions.[31] In return, Hampton advised Hayes that it would "strengthen my hands" and help keep extremists at bay, maintain peace, and allow him to maintain his comparatively moderate racial course if Hayes would grant clemency to the few Ku Klux still in prison and issue a proclamation that it was safe for all exiled Ku Klux to return to their homes without risk of prosecution or harassment.[32]

On June 14, 1878, Hampton wrote J. Rufus Bratton's brother, John, who was a close Hampton advisor, to alert him that he had just met with Hayes in Washington and the president had specifically guaranteed that J. Rufus "and all others connected with the Ku Klux troubles can return to the state with perfect safety." For political reasons, the president did not want to issue a public statement, Hampton said, but the president privately promised that "no activity shall be taken" against Bratton or any Ku Klux fugitive. The Ku Klux who fled to avoid prosecution "are no longer exiles," Hampton said, expressing his hope to Bratton "that your brother will soon be at home."[33]

The day he received Hampton's letter, John Bratton wrote J. Rufus, advising him that the efforts by Hampton to bring him home, which had been ongoing "for some time now," had finally borne fruit. He enclosed Hampton's letter and advised J. Rufus that by the time he received the letter in Ontario, he expected that a sympathetic federal judge would have formally entered a *nolle prosequi* in his case, formally blocking any possible federal prosecution.[34]

It took several months for Bratton to close out his medical practice and settle his affairs in London, Ontario.* He did not arrive back in Yorkville until November 1878, when he was greeted not with a coldness usually due

*The record is unclear whether Major James W. Avery, the reputed head of the Ku Klux in York County, ever joined Bratton and returned to Yorkville. There is no announcement of his return in the archives of the *Yorkville Enquirer* and instead evidence that Avery remained in Canada. In August 1878, after he would have received word that it was safe for him to return to the United States, Avery had a notice published in the *Enquirer* that his son, Ralph, had been admitted as a cadet to the Royal Military College, Canada's equivalent of West Point, and so it appears at least some of the Averys had heartily embraced Canadian citizenship. ("A Yorkville Boy Abroad," *Yorkville Enquirer*, August 29, 1878, 2)

a wanted criminal, but warmly as a martyr for the cause.[35] Still considered "a fine looking, black-eyed, dark haired man" of aristocratic bearing, Bratton quickly and easily resumed his role as civic leader as if he had not spent six years in an enforced exile in a foreign country.[36]

Several years after his return, in 1887, one of his tasks was to chair a group charged with setting up a public school system in Yorkville for children ages six to sixteen. Under the proposal advanced by Bratton, who still fancied himself a self-appointed guardian of African-American interests, the budget for the school that would educate the area's estimated 225 white children would be nineteen hundred dollars per year, while the budget for the school expected to educate 185 Black children would be $550. The principal of the white school would be paid one hundred dollars per month and have three assistants, while the principal of the Black school would be paid twenty-five dollars per month and have two assistants.[37] Less than ten years later, in its 1896 *Plessy v. Ferguson* decision, the US Supreme Court would essentially ratify such an arrangement as "separate but equal."

In his 1871 testimony before the investigating congressional committee, Bratton had denied any knowledge of the Ku Klux, let alone confessing to being a member and leader. Even after his return from Canada, unsure if the political winds had changed direction for good, Bratton and his family continued to insist that he had been wrongly accused. But as Jim Crow arrived and the South embraced the Ku Klux as a heroic rather than shameful part of its history, past pretense was dropped.

Bratton died in 1897 and his obituary in the *Yorkville Enquirer*, presumably authored or approved by his family, now proudly noted that Bratton had been one of the key community leaders outraged that "the ignorant Negroes, under the lead of the scoundrelly carpetbaggers, began to overrun the state after the war." The obituary stated that "Dr. Bratton was one of those who became convinced, and who acted upon that conviction, that the only defense which would be secured for home and fireside, was through the Ku-Klux organization, and with this he became directly or indirectly connected."[38]

In this eulogy, Bratton's "apparent gruffness" was praised as "of the kind that is always indicative of sincere honesty and nobility of soul, and beneath it all there was a consistent tenderness and sympathy, which would but reveal to those who knew the doctor well, that he was a practical Christian."[39]

Far from being a mark of shame, the lynching of Jim Williams and Bratton's role in it had become the stuff of legend, recounted with gusto around the firesides of white homes and gatherings and the subject of periodic fond recollections recorded by the *Yorkville Enquirer* in which the participants spoke of their involvement with the pride soldiers convey when recounting their role in a war's great battle. One of those who heard the stories was the son of a Baptist preacher who would also enter the ministry but who fancied himself to be—and who achieved grate fame and fortune as—a pseudo-historian and novelist. His name was Thomas Dixon.

Dixon was born in 1864 in Shelby, North Carolina, located just thirty miles northwest of Yorkville. His family inculcated a sympathy for the Lost Cause in the boy early on with tours of famous battlefields and an excursion to Columbia so he might see how South Carolina's capital had been devastated by the war and be repulsed by the sight of a state legislature that included African-American members.

As a boy, Dixon reported that he once caught a glimpse from a bedroom window of the "strange, terrifying spectacle" of a robed and disguised klan, getting ready for an evening raid.[40] Dixon drew on this scene when, more than thirty years later, he described the Ku Klux in flowing robes, bathed in moonlight, and making "a picture such as the world had not seen since the Knights of the Middle Ages rode on their Holy Crusades."[41]

Family members, particularly his York County relatives, told young Dixon other fables of Reconstruction that clearly included the lynching of Jim Williams under the leadership of an admired local physician and planter. These stories left no doubt in Dixon's mind but that the Ku Klux had been a righteous cause. When, as an adult, he viewed a New York theatrical production of *Uncle Tom's Cabin*, which he considered a slander on the South, he vowed to produce a rebuttal. His first book, *The Leopard's Spots*, even co-opted the character of Simon Legree, transforming the brutal slaveholder of Harriet Beecher Stowe's novel into a "champion" of the freed slaves.[42]

Dixon would write eighteen novels, most of them wretched melodramas panned by literary critics, but which collectively sold hundreds of thousands of copies. His most influential book was his second, *The Clansman*, published in 1905. The novel's hero, named Ben Cameron, is credited in the story with establishing the Ku Klux after the war. The Cameron character is a physician who was a colonel in the Confederate army and is an aristocrat who lives in a magnificent home looking out over the central square of his hometown. He is kind to African Americans who know their place and follow his guidance, but the climax of this bizarre amalgam of histrionics and propaganda is the lynching of a freedman named Gus, who is identified as the "Captain of the African Guards" and whose crime is the rape of a white girl who later commits suicide out of shame.

As was the case in the lynching of Jim Williams, once the character of Gus is murdered, Dr. Cameron pins a note to the dead man's breast pocket, which in the book's telling are the letter's "K.K.K." written in blood-red ink. Further in parallel to Williams's murder, Cameron then orders all African Americans to immediately surrender their firearms. White people are filled with "exultant joy" as African Americans again "yield to white men and women the right of way on the streets."[43]

These parallels make it clear, as most scholars agree, that the Cameron character was largely based on Dr. J. Rufus Bratton.[44] Reviews of the book ranged from labeling it "repellant" to (and this from a reviewer in the *New York Times*) "a thrilling romance." For his part, Dixon claimed to not care whether the book was considered "literature or trash."[45] What was important was that he, in his mind, had set straight the historical record of the South and the Ku Klux. He had conveyed to an otherwise ignorant North "the awful suffering of the white man during the dreadful Reconstruction period."[46]

Believing this vital message needed to reach a far wider audience, Dixon sold the film rights to *The Clansman* to a fellow Southerner, Kentucky-born director D. W. Griffith, who turned the book into Hollywood's first blockbuster, *Birth of a Nation* (1915). Griffith took considerable liberties with Dixon's book, to Dixon's disgust. Dr. Cameron is no longer a tall, vital man still in his prime, but because Griffith cast a shorter, older actor named Henry B. Walthall in the part, the character based on Bratton in the movie is called "the Little Colonel."

Like Dixon, Griffith was obsessed about assuring his audience that the film was based on historical fact. He and Dixon both had the inspiration of getting an imprimatur for the film from fellow Southerner and historian Woodrow Wilson, the Virginia-born president of Princeton University before he became president of the United States. Griffith flattered Wilson that the president's own work, *A History of the American People* (1902), had provided source material for the script. Wilson, whose views on race were akin to Dixon's and who had completely resegregated the federal government, wiping out all the modest civil service integration gains made since Grant, agreed to screen the film at the White House. Wilson then offered the memorable review that *Birth of a Nation* was "like writing history in lightning," and added without irony, "My only regret is that it is all so terribly true."[47]

The film also caught the active imagination of a Georgia man named William J. Simmons, a born "joiner" who had failed in careers in teaching and medicine and whose dream was to form and lead a fraternal organization of his own. Following the screening of the film in Atlanta on Thanksgiving night 1915, Simmons and fifteen other men rode to the top of a granite formation outside Atlanta known as Stone Mountain,* lit a wooden cross aflame (a Simmons invention), and announced the rebirth of the Ku Klux Klan.[48]

This new iteration of the KKK initially had few members until Simmons hired two crack publicity agents of limited scruples, Mary Elizabeth Tyler and Edward Young Clarke, who sent one thousand solicitors working on commission across the country to sign up members at ten dollars a pop—not to mention income from sales of official hats, robes, and other Klan accoutrements. With its focus on enmity toward Jews, Catholics, immigrants, and any citizens not part of the white Anglo-Saxon Protestant tradition, the Klan grew to perhaps five million members by 1925. The KKK gained political control in many cities and states, including states outside the South such as Indiana and Oregon. But internal squabbles, scandal, and the growing realization among members that the organization was primar-

---

*Stone Mountain became the site of the largest monument to the Confederacy in America, a 75-foot-high bas-relief of the figures of Robert E. Lee, Jefferson Davis, and Thomas "Stonewall" Jackson. Idaho-born Gutzon Borglum, creator of Mount Rushmore and a high-ranking member of the new Ku Klux Klan, was the first sculptor hired for the work, and among the designs initially suggested by the head of the Georgia chapter of the United Daughters of the Confederacy was a sculpture commemorating the Reconstruction Ku Klux. That idea was eventually discarded and Borglum began carving, starting with Lee's face, in 1923 but soon quit in a dispute with his patrons. Despite substantial funding from the KKK and both the federal and Georgia government, the project continually stalled until the 1954 *Brown v. Board of Education* Supreme Court decision integrating public schools created a new sense of urgency to finish the monument as an act of defiance to the Court ruling. The official opening of Stone Mountain Park occurred on April 14, 1965, the one-hundredth anniversary of the assassination of Abraham Lincoln.

ily a money-making scam led interest in the group to wane, and the onset of the Great Depression in 1929 sounded the death knell of the organization.[49]

A third iteration of the Klan arose in the 1950s and 1960s in response to the growing civil rights movement, and the KKK remains with us today, albeit with comparatively few members, a lingering legacy of the Ku Klux troubles in York County after the Civil War and of a local physician who committed murder.

IV

The perversion of Reconstruction history portrayed in *Birth of a Nation* was mirrored in the life of Daniel H. Chamberlain. The former prosecutor of the Ku Klux Klan was embittered by his loss in the 1876 governor's race to Wade Hampton and what he considered the betrayal of African Americans in the South by Rutherford B. Hayes and the Northern Republican Party. Rather than stay and continue the fight, however, he left South Carolina in 1877 and moved to New York, where he became a successful Wall Street attorney and annually taught a course in American constitutional law at Cornell University.

Initially, Chamberlain remained a champion of the ideals of Reconstruction. In an 1879 article in the *North American Review*, he asserted that African Americans had proved their worthiness of the vote by approving "wise, liberal, and just constitutions," and in those states where African Americans were in the majority there had been "steady progress toward good government." He continued:

> It is said that the inability of a people to cope, in physical and material resources, with its enemies, is proof that such a people is not entitled to retain its political power. Such conclusions are as illogical as they are immoral. Under the principles of our Government and of all just government, rights are not dependent on numbers or physical strength or material resources. The right to vote, and to have that vote honestly counted—the right to hold and exercise the political power conferred by a majority of the votes when honestly counted—these are rights, under our Government, totally independent of the power or wealth or education of the voters.[50]

In the following issue, the *North American Review* hosted a symposium in which public figures from the North and South addressed the questions: "Ought the Negro to be Disfranchised? Ought He to have been Enfranchised?" One contributor was Wade Hampton who, despite his active pursuit of the Black vote and pledge to be governor of "the whole people," said that "the policy of conferring the right to vote upon the negro, ignorant and incompetent as he was," had been a "dangerous experiment."[51]

Chamberlain, in a sad about-face described by one historian as "a carpetbagger's conversion to white supremacy," came to agree with Hampton out of a combination of vanity, self-interest, and an embrace of social Darwinism.[52] In correspondence with a sympathetic President-Elect James Garfield, Chamberlain blamed his loss in 1876 not on any fault with his own administration, but on the state legislature and the African Americans within it, stating that white South Carolinians "could never have been persuaded to oppose my re-election but for the acts of a Republican Legislature, in denying to them decent government and officers."[53]

After Garfield was assassinated just six months into his presidency, the increasingly wealthy Chamberlain resigned from the Republican Party to protest the alleged liberal fiscal policies of Garfield's successor, Chester Arthur. Chamberlain particularly condemned Republican proposals to provide federal funding for public education, saying it would be especially wasted upon African Americans. By then, Chamberlain had become a devotee of the writings of Charles Darwin and Sir Henry Maine, whom he credited with articulating a "law of all natural existence" that equally applied to human relations.[54]

This embrace of social Darwinism led Chamberlain to conclude that the rapid reforms of Reconstruction were a mistake, and meaningful change was an evolutionary process that would take eons to occur. Chamberlain said that it was now clear to him that people of African descent were inferior to Anglo-Saxons, who, he argued, would not have tolerated 250 years of enslavement. Chamberlain, who had commanded brave African-American troops during the war and witnessed the struggle for suffrage firsthand, now grotesquely argued that the African American "was set free by others, not by his own efforts . . . and enfranchised by no efforts of his own."[55]

Because of his past service in South Carolina, Chamberlain's new opinions held weight. This was especially true since he was articulating them during a time when Americans, normally champions of self-government, sought to justify American rule of Hawaii, Puerto Rico, and, especially, the Philippines.* That nonwhites were not suited to self-government had already been demonstrated in Reconstruction America, Chamberlain said. In a 1901 article he wrote for the *Atlantic Monthly* he marveled at how it had not been obvious from the start "that good government, or even tolerable administration, could not be had from such an aggregation of ignorance and inexperience and incapacity?" Chamberlain included a swipe at Theodore Roosevelt for being "ignorant and feckless" in inviting an African American, Booker T. Washington, to dine at the White House.[56]

Chamberlain said that he now understood how including African Americans in state government had provoked South Carolina whites "beyond endurance." In his most repulsive statement, Chamberlain blamed African Americans for inviting violence upon themselves because of the "nameless crime" of Black men raping white women, ignoring—as he would have well known—that Black-on-white rape was never alleged during the Ku Klux trials as a trigger for white violence, nor is there any record of whites expressing serious concern about interracial rape during Reconstruction. Yet Chamberlain now argued that if only Black men would stop raping white women, then lynchings would cease and African Americans would find whites ready to "yield and defend all the ordinary civil rights."[57]

While these revised (and perverse) views cost Chamberlain a good many Northern friends from his days as an abolitionist, they made him new friends in South Carolina. On trips to the state he discovered his brief tenure as governor was now being positively reevaluated, and he became friends with Hampton, whom he praised as a "true 'natural leader.'" Chamberlain died in 1907 at the age of seventy-two, and a South Carolina newsman who had covered the 1876 campaign said it had been a blessing that Chamberlain lived long enough "to allow his natural character and clarity of judgment to prevail."[58] Perhaps that was true.

---

*The Spanish-American War of 1898 had ended Spanish rule of the Philippines, but the United States declined to grant the archipelago its independence. A Filipino insurrection lasted three years, killing four thousand American troops, twenty thousand Filipino fighters, and an estimated two hundred thousand Filipino civilians. This largely forgotten war spurred a fierce national debate over American imperialism. When a Republican senator argued American rule was necessary because Filipinos, being nonwhite, "are not of a self-governing race," South Carolina senator Ben Tillman rose to ask if this meant Republicans were now acknowledging Reconstruction had been a mistake and asked, "Do you acknowledge that you were wrong in 1868?" (Lepore, 368–69)

Unlike Chamberlain, US Attorney David T. Corbin never repudiated the policies of Reconstruction for which he had fought, nor did he immediately leave South Carolina following the 1876 election—in part because he spent the next two years trying to secure the US Senate seat that he believed was his. But he, too, felt betrayed by Hayes and was haunted by his own past poor judgment.

In South Carolina, the contested votes in the 1876 election resulted not only in a disputed governor's race but also two separate and competing state legislatures, one controlled by Republicans and the other by Democrats, with each claiming legitimacy. The Democratic-led House chose Matthew Butler to be South Carolina's junior senator, while the Republican-controlled House, which occupied the Capitol, selected Corbin. The Republican-led legislature eventually ceded the Capitol to the Democrats, and the Senate dispute was resolved by Congress.

In 1877 the US Senate was evenly divided between Republican and Democratic members, but when the full Senate voted to resolve the contested Senate seat, it was South Carolina's senior Republican senator, who held the deliberately sarcastic nickname of "Honest" John Patterson, whose vote gave the seat to the Democrat Butler. Patterson explained that Hayes, still anxious to maintain good relations with Hampton, told Patterson that he would have no influence over patronage appointments in South Carolina unless he supported Butler.[59]

Corbin, not reappointed US attorney, remained in South Carolina and did not abandon his appeal of the Senate's decision until February 1879. The South Carolina Legislature, now firmly in Democratic hands, pressured Corbin to give back his fee from the South Carolina Phosphate Company case. The state finally dropped its claims against Corbin in 1884, by which time Corbin had moved to Chicago, where he practiced law until his death in 1905.

Major Lewis Merrill was another key Ku Klux trial participant hounded by controversy for the rest of his career. The crackdown on the Ku Klux and the attendant local hostility toward him and his men had taken a serious emotional and physical toll on Merrill. In July 1872 Merrill seems to have suffered a minor stroke that left him partially paralyzed. As these symptoms subsided, Merrill, still only thirty-seven years old, was plagued with blinding headaches, insomnia, short-term memory loss, and impaired vision.[60]

Still, Merrill's request for a one-year leave of absence was not granted for another full year, until an Army surgeon provided the diagnosis that Merrill was suffering from "exhaustion of brain power."[61] Most of his troops had left South Carolina by December 1872, reassigned to duty back on the western frontier, while Merrill stayed behind to assist with the few remaining trials as prosecution of the Ku Klux wound down.

For all his many virtues, in early 1873 Merrill again displayed, as he had when gambling with a defendant while serving as a judge advocate, a shocking lack of judgment, perhaps even greed, when it came to money. In February 1873 the South Carolina Legislature finally honored Governor Scott's earlier pledge of reward money for those who provided information leading to the arrest and conviction of Ku Klux. But in appropriating thirty-five thousand dollars for this purpose, a claims commission set up to disburse the funds first gave themselves five hundred dollars apiece and then divvied the rest up among a handful of federal officials who had made the arrests while simply performing their duties. Merrill was granted more than half of the available appropriation, $20,700—and he gave five thousand dollars of that amount to the man who had successfully lobbied the rewards bill through the legislature.[62]

The scandal gave Ku Klux apologists fodder to support their contention that the prosecutions had been a sham. Hostile South Carolina newspapers began referring to Merrill as "Dog Merrill," and the issue did dog Merrill for the rest of his career.[63] A Senate inquiry into the matter came to nothing, though Merrill was also the focus of a second congressional inquiry, this in 1876, to rehash the allegations made as a result of the gambling debt he had sought to collect a half dozen years earlier.[64] That inquiry, too, came to nothing, but in 1886, shortly before his scheduled retirement, when Merrill was recommended for promotion to lieutenant colonel in recognition of his past service, Southern senators used the two controversies to block Merrill's promotion for four years, finally gaining a measure of retribution for Merrill's work in destroying the Ku Klux conspiracy.[65]

But before he retired and in the wake of the infamous Colfax Massacre, Merrill was sent to Louisiana to once again stem violence committed by white supremacists. A group known as the White League had violently taken control of a large section of the central part of the state and proved more difficult to dismantle than the Ku Klux Klan. Part of the theory behind the prosecutions of the Ku Klux, who operated in secret, at night, and in disguise, was that exposure would bring shame and an end to violence. But the White League, like most "rifle clubs" that emerged in the wake of the Ku Klux's destruction, operated openly and boldly. In one incident, a "posse" of two hundred White League members had the temerity to "arrest" a squad of Merrill's soldiers on trumped-up charges they had cut telegraph lines. No longer benefiting from Amos T. Akerman's bolder leadership, Merrill was denied permission to launch a military operation to free his men and was directed to simply work with local authorities to resolve the impasse. The spurious charges against Merrill's men were dropped, but the White League had demonstrated both the Grant Administration's self-imposed impotency and who had the real authority in Louisiana's Red River District.[66]

Before he returned to the frontier, Merrill received a choice assignment to serve as a liaison for foreign military officials attending the Centennial International Exhibition of 1876 in Philadelphia, the first world's fair held on American soil, which was scheduled in conjunction with the nation's Centennial. The exhibition was notable for unveiling a host of items that demonstrated American ingenuity, including the telephone, the typewriter, Heinz Ketchup, and Hires Root Beer. Most significant to Merrill, his presence in Philadelphia meant that he was not with his comrades of the 7th Cavalry when, under the command of Merrill's nemesis, Colonel George Armstrong Custer, they were annihilated by a large combined force of Lakota Sioux and Cheyenne warriors in a battle near the Little Bighorn River in the Montana Territory. Merrill did return to the West in 1877, and his assignments on the Great Plains continued into the 1880s. But poor health and never-ending money problems made his last years difficult. He died in Philadelphia in 1896 at the age of sixty-one and was buried at Arlington National Cemetery.[67]

V

Other Ku Klux participants spent their last years less eventfully. Despite Corbin's suspicions, Reverdy Johnson did not use the Ku Klux trials as a springboard for a run at the presidency. He continued to practice law and argued his last case before the US Supreme Court in 1875. On February 10, 1876, Johnson was in Annapolis preparing to argue a case before the state court of appeals. He was a guest at the governor's mansion, and after dinner, feeling unwell, the nearly blind Johnson decided to take a walk to get some fresh air. Johnson stumbled over a lump of coal lying in the path next to the house, and fell headfirst against the wall of the mansion, fracturing his skull. Tributes abounded for the man considered by "common consent . . . the leader of the bar of the Supreme Court of the United States."[68]

Poor eyesight was also a factor in Henry Stanbery's death. After the Ku Klux trials, he had returned to Cincinnati to practice law, which he did until 1880. Troubled by cataracts, he traveled to New York City, but the surgery to restore his eyesight failed. Now blind, he spent the last six months of his life in New York until he died there in 1881. His last words were, "I have been neither saint nor savage, but have tried to do my best."[69]

Judge Hugh Lennox Bond may have considered his fellow jurist, George Seabrook Bryan, an old man during the Ku Klux trials, but Bryan outlived Bond by a dozen years. Bryan served as a federal judge in South Carolina until he retired in 1886 at the age of seventy-seven, but he lived another nineteen years, dying in 1905 at the age of ninety-six.

Bond died in 1893 in his native Baltimore at the age of sixty-four, two years after having been elevated to the Fourth Circuit Court of Appeals. But if his life was short, Bond's legacy is continuing to grow in the public consciousness.

In 2017, in a move that would have deeply offended Reverdy Johnson, statues of his friend Roger Taney, author of the *Dred Scott* decision, were removed from Baltimore and Annapolis on the orders of the Republican governor of Maryland and the Democratic mayor of Baltimore. They did so in response to violence that had occurred in August that year in Charlottesville, Virginia, following competing demonstrations between those in favor of and those against the planned removal of several Confederate monuments in that city. A twenty-year-old avowed white supremacist attending a "Unite the Right" rally rammed his car into a crowd of those demonstrating in favor of the monuments' removal, killing one woman and injuring nineteen other people.* The man was later sentenced to life in prison.

---

*Attorneys for those injured in Charlottesville filed suit against the "Unite the Right" rally organizers, invoking that remaining provision of the Enforcement Act of 1871, the so-called Ku Klux Klan Act (1871), that allows citizens to bring civil suit for damages against individuals whom they believe have infringed on their civil rights.

The bronze Taney statue in Annapolis had been erected at the front entrance to the Maryland State House in 1872, intended by the conservative Democratic-controlled legislature of the time as a message of defiance against Reconstruction and notions of racial equality. Interestingly, the descendants of Taney and Dred Scott had met at the foot of the statue in the summer of 2017, the 160th anniversary of the *Dred Scott* decision, as a gesture of forgiveness and reconciliation. *Both* families made a plea for the statue to remain, with the suggestion that statues of Dred Scott and Maryland native Frederick Douglass be placed nearby in a "position of dialogue" with the Taney statue. The Taney statue was removed anyway and as of 2020 remained in storage.[70]

Absent the arrangement suggested by the Scott and Taney families, *Washington Post* columnist Charles Lane suggested that the Taney statue that had stood in Baltimore be replaced with a statue of Bond, who "deserves far better treatment from history than the obscurity that set in almost from the moment of his death in 1893. No public installation in Maryland—not a park, school or courthouse—bears his name."[71]

Bond was certainly more enlightened on racial issues than Taney, but his views were also complicated. Bond said his Christian faith taught him that all people, regardless of race, were part of God's "single family of man." But though he fearlessly advocated for the civil rights of African Americans, he never believed that Blacks were equal to whites. He supported their education not because he believed in their potential for upward mobility—he did not—but because education would make them more productive workers and "the security of each class in society depends upon the measure and security of the freedom of the lowest and weakest class."[72]

More deserving of a memorial somewhere is the first head of the US Department of Justice, Amos T. Akerman, who after his dismissal as US attorney general fearlessly returned to his home in Cartersville, Georgia, where he focused on his law practice, his church, and his family. Despite the enemies he had made, his law practice thrived, and he was in demand nationally both as a public speaker and as an attorney, taking cases as far north as New York and as far west as Louisiana, though he also took much smaller cases close to home if they allowed him to continue to advocate for racial justice.[73]

In 1875 Akerman defended an African-American man named Cordy Harris who had been accused, as Jim Williams had been in York County, of plotting an "insurrection" in Washington County, Georgia. In the panic that followed the rumors of this supposed plot, Akerman said, "innocent acts were supposed to have criminal significance, and the mass of white people really believed themselves in danger. In this belief they were encouraged by a few demagogues who fanned the flame." Making inquiries, Akerman concluded the charges against Harris were a "fabrication," and he secured Harris's acquittal in his trial in Sandersville, Georgia. "Considering the excitement in the community, I think the result rather remarkable," Akerman said, praising the judge and jury in the case for being able to rise "above prejudice."[74]

Akerman remained despondent that his adopted South had birthed and nurtured something as awful as the Ku Klux Klan. On a train trip from Charlotte to Atlanta in 1874, he overheard one of his fellow passengers tell another as they passed through York County, "That is . . . where Tom Rountree [sic] was killed by the Ku Klux," and, Akerman noted in his diary, "they talked about the affair without an expression of horror." As Akerman ruminated on how Roundtree and others had been "butchered," he again marveled that "to persons who had not the strongest evidence of the facts, a history of the Ku Klux would be incredible. That any large portion of our people should be so ensavaged as to perpetuate or excuse such actions is the darkest blot on Southern character in this age."[75]

Akerman never abandoned his Radical Republican principles. In fact, he thought they had in some ways triumphed in the South in small ways. He observed that Democrats campaigning in the 1876 election, with their appeals to Black voters and expressions of patriotism on the nation's Centennial, seemed to have "taken up the cardinal doctrines of the Republican Party. If it were sincere, we might have less bitter politics now. But it is not sincere. Strike out the anti-North and anti-negro feeling, and the Democratic party would fall to the ground."[76]

Akerman, however, also worried that the Republican Party had gone too far in passing the Sumner Supplemental Civil Rights Act in 1875, with its integration of public transportation and accommodations. "The measure is not required to secure justice to the negroes and will have a contrary effect by inflaming whites against them," he wrote. "What they need is something to protect them in independent suffrage. With this, they can get every other public right that they ought to have."[77]

Akerman's unrelenting advocacy for the rights of African Americans and his dismay at how they continued to be "dreadfully wronged" won the grudging admiration of his often-hostile neighbors and colleagues. Following a lengthy public speaking tour in Connecticut and Ohio in the fall of 1880, Akerman fell ill. Days before his death, members of the bar and leading citizens of Bartow County, Georgia, signed and sent a resolution to President Hayes, urging that Akerman be appointed a federal judge for the Fifth District as a testimony to his distinguished career. "Although every member of this meeting is a democrat [*sic*], and differing entirely from Mr. Akerman politically," the resolution said, "yet such is our confidence in him, as a citizen and lawyer, that we feel his appointment would prove eminently satisfactory to the people of the state wherein he will be called to preside, and will do much to conciliate them and strengthen their faith in the administration appointing him."[78]

Following Akerman's death on December 21, 1880, at the age of fifty-nine, the *Atlanta Constitution*, a fierce critic of Akerman, editorialized, "Even his bitterest political opponents gave him credit for honesty in his convictions and courage in their support. Few men have passed through such trials and come out so spotless in the public gaze."[79]

And yet Akerman, the US attorney general who took the greatest risks pursuing equal rights, is largely forgotten and ignored, a sign of how we have erased so much of the true history of Reconstruction, perhaps to assuage our guilt and to justify the behavior of ancestors who behaved less nobly than Akerman.*

VI

Perhaps the "strange national amnesia" regarding Reconstruction noted by historian Ron Chernow is due to Reconstruction's great unsettling message, which is that progress is neither inevitable nor irreversible. And so an era that began with great promise in righting the great wrong of slavery is still ongoing. Great progress has been made, but even the election of a Black president has not meant that the goals of Reconstruction have been achieved.

---

*In 2019 the Georgia Historical Society erected a marker outside Akerman's former home in Cartersville, Georgia, recognizing his fight against the Ku Klux Klan. Prominent Georgians present for the marker's dedication, including Georgia's attorney general, acknowledged they did not know who Akerman was prior to being asked to participate in the marker's unveiling. (*Atlanta Journal-Constitution*, https://www.ajc.com/blog/politics/discovering-amos-akerman-lost-gop-hero-the-19th-century-south /9VqXrSZsoRXYT8SvGXOIUP)

Voter suppression, the key goal of the Reconstruction-era Ku Klux Klan as the means to political power, has remained a major issue. A 2019 study by the Leadership Conference on Civil Rights found that following a 2013 Supreme Court ruling that weakened the Voting Rights Act of 1965, states with "a history of racial discrimination" had closed twelve hundred polling places in the five years following that ruling. The study found Arizona had closed one in five of its polling places and Texas one in ten. Closures in Georgia left seven counties in that state with only a single polling place.

Reporting on the study, the Reuters news service noted that the polling place closures occurred while "Republican-led states impose[d] a range of other restrictions, from shorter voting hours to photo-ID requirements."[80] These poll closures, purges of voter rolls, and other measures, such as an Oklahoma requirement that absentee ballots be notarized, were not overtly racial, per the Fifteenth Amendment, but the implication was that the intent was to depress the votes of Blacks and other minorities, who were most likely to be inconvenienced (or disenfranchised) by these measures and who, unlike during Reconstruction, have overwhelmingly supported the Democratic Party since the 1960s.*

In 2020 there was a nationwide and global surge of protests demanding greater progress toward racial justice that were triggered by the death of a Black man named George Floyd at the hands of Minneapolis, Minnesota, police officers. Included among the demands of protestors were calls to take down a host of monuments and other symbols that honored those whom protestors charged had promoted injustice, violence, and racial division in American history.

South Carolina had previously removed the Confederate battle flag from its Capitol grounds in 2015 in response to the murder of nine African-

---

*The Republican and Democratic parties have realigned since Reconstruction so their constituencies are nearly exactly the inverse of what they were 150 years ago. African Americans, once nearly unanimously supportive of the Republican Party, are now the most loyal of Democratic constituencies, as the Democrats, beginning in the mid-twentieth century, began to aggressively embrace the cause of civil rights. Republicans, meanwhile, began actively courting conservative white Southerners, particularly during the 1964 presidential campaign of Arizona Republican senator Barry Goldwater, who was one of the few Republican senators to oppose the Civil Rights Act of 1964. Whereas Republican presidential candidate Richard Nixon won just under a third of the African-American vote in 1960, Goldwater won just 6 percent of the African-American vote, and no Republican candidate for president has been able to win even 15 percent of the Black vote since. (See the author's previous book, *Almost President*, chapters eight and nine, for a more detailed explanation of how and why this realignment occurred.)

American worshippers at Charleston's Emanuel AME Church by a self-described white supremacist who had been invited to join the group's Bible study. In 2020 Mississippi voted to change its state flag, which included the Confederate emblem, following threats the state would no longer be allowed to host college sports championships. That same year, the Tennessee Legislature voted to no longer honor the June 13 birthday of the first grand wizard of the Ku Klux Klan, Nathan Bedford Forrest, which from 1921, at the instigation of the reborn KKK, until 1969 had also been an official state holiday. The Tennessee Capitol Commission also voted to remove a bust of Forrest from the Capitol, but for unarticulated reasons simultaneously removed the bust of another Tennessean, Admiral David Farragut, hero of the Union navy.[81]

Whether these symbolic gestures will lead to more substantive change remains to be seen, but other less noticed but not necessarily less notable gestures may also be part of a trend that significantly improves race relations in the United States. While an oft-suggested "national conversation on race" is unlikely (such a cacophony is logistically impossible and likely futile, as demonstrated by any daily check of our interactions on social media), there are many dialogues happening at the more human scale of families and communities, including in York County.*

South Carolina did not have a state historical marker that mentioned the Ku Klux Klan until 2017, when a campaign led by the Allison Creek Presbyterian Church and its pastor, Sam McGregor Jr., convinced the South Carolina Department of Archives and History to erect a marker

---

*One act of grace that received national attention in 2009 was when a Ku Klux Klansman named Elwin Wilson traveled to Washington, DC, to apologize to civil rights icon Congressman John Lewis for a beating he gave Lewis in York County in the spring of 1961. That year, Lewis was one of a group of civil rights activists known as the Freedom Riders who were testing a Supreme Court ruling that desegregated interstate transportation. When the Freedom Riders arrived at the Rock Hill Greyhound bus station, Wilson, then a physically imposing twenty-four-year-old pipe welder, was one of several Klansmen who assaulted Lewis and other riders. Wilson said he had an epiphany in 2009 when the local newspaper, in the wake of Barack Obama's election as president, did a retrospective on the county's history during the 1960s civil rights movement. Troubled by his role in defending segregation, Wilson accepted the invitation of a friend to attend a church with a large number of Black parishioners. Wilson said he was stunned to find he was accepted by people he had once persecuted. Lewis said Wilson's trip to Washington was the first apology he had received for the acts of violence committed against him during the civil rights era. Wilson and Lewis made several appearances together on national television to talk about the power of remorse and forgiveness to facilitate change, including a change of heart. (See: "I Need To Tell Some People I Am Sorry," *Rock Hill* (SC) *Herald*, January 24, 2009, https://www.heraldonline.com/news/local/article12248426.html.)

to commemorate the 1871 Ku Klux attack on Elias Hill. The marker, like the church, is located at the corner of South Carolina State Highway 274 and Allison Creek Road, or about one-quarter mile west of where Hill is believed to have lived. One side of the marker reads:

> *During Reconstruction (1865–1877), the Ku Klux Klan persecuted Rev. Hill and other freedmen in York County. In October 1871, 166 free blacks from Clay Hill emigrated to Liberia, West Africa, led by Elias Hill, Solomon Hill, June Moore, and Madison, Harriet, and George Simril. Arriving in Liberia in December, they began new lives at Arthington as planters and political leaders.*

The church, which dates to 1854, became interested in Hill while doing research on an adjacent cemetery that had from 1859 to 1896 served as a burial ground for enslaved and free Blacks from the local Clay Hill community. The church, with the help of local Eagle Scouts, identified three hundred gravesites in the cemetery, among them one belonging to Hill's mother, Dorcas. Church and other volunteers transformed the cemetery from an overgrown weed patch into a tranquil area of prayer and meditation with well-tended walking paths through its woods.

At the dedication ceremony for the marker, held on the 146th anniversary of the assault on Hill in a ceremony the church called "Let the Land Say . . . Amen," parishioner Patrice Gaines, a former reporter for the *Washington Post*, said that while the history of the Ku Klux is "ugly, shameful and . . . the type of history we don't like to talk about . . . I think it strengthens all of us to acknowledge the truth. To learn from it, and move on from it."[82]

As of 2020, the Culture and Heritage Museums of York County was in the process of developing a second marker in South Carolina to mention the Ku Klux, a marker at Historic Brattonsville that will tell the story of the murder of Jim Williams. These markers are, hopefully, a trend to retrieve in the American memory those currently forgotten pioneers of civil rights who served as community leaders, informants, witnesses, and jurors during the Great South Carolina Ku Klux Klan Trials.

The year after the Elias Hill marker was put in place, several members of the Allison Creek Church traveled to Liberia to meet with the descendants of Hill's family and those of other African Americans from York County who had migrated to Africa in 1871. As they toured the Arthington area where the Hill party settled, congregant Spenser Simril sought to explain his connection to a descendant of Hill's nephew, Solomon Hill, who became a wealthy coffee planter in Liberia. "I feel uncomfortable saying this—he was enslaved by my family," Simril said. To which the Liberian man replied that he hoped this connection would bind them "closer," adding that Simril should not feel badly about his ancestors. "You are not responsible," he said. "It is [the] time that is responsible for what happened." Simril then invited the Liberians to come to South Carolina, where the Simril family, as have the Brattons and many other families throughout the South and the nation, now holds regular biracial reunions for anyone descended from those who use the same surname.[83]

The purpose of this book, as ought to be the purpose of any work of history, whether of family, community, or nation, is not to shame but to enlighten and to understand why things are the way they are. But the descendant of Solomon Hill is only partly correct. While we are only responsible for our own actions, enlightenment does occasionally require, if not penance, at least initiative. If for no other reason than to ensure my great-grandfather's soul is at rest, the author royalties from this edition will be donated to reputable organizations devoted to the causes he sadly worked against: racial justice, voter participation, and a fuller and more honest interpretation of the Reconstruction era.

Our understanding, as well as the work, of Reconstruction continues. As Akerman discovered, many support equality in the abstract and when it is a task assigned to others, but are uncomfortable when it becomes too personal. The process of Reconstruction is not over, and how it finally turns out depends on whether we move beyond the abstract and symbolic and can remain committed to the pursuit of justice, or whether, like too many in this story, we become distracted and lose our sense of urgency in fulfilling our founding national creed of human equality.

Acknowledgments

As with all my books, the first person I need to acknowledge is my wife, Patricia, who is a talented and dogged researcher and editor. I literally could not do these books without her and wish she would accept the coauthorship that she justly deserves. I also thank our two children, William and Grace, who display great patience when I embark on these writing adventures.

This book has greatly benefited from the extraordinary generosity of many people, some scholars or archivists, some just folks, who have shared their knowledge, their skills, and their own family histories. The latter include writer and filmmaker Dr. Spenser Simril Jr., who will soon publish a book on his own family's quest to reconcile its history entwined with both the fight for freedom and slavery, and Dr. Lisa Bratton, associate professor of history at Tuskegee University and a descendant of those enslaved at Brattonsville, who has conducted many valuable oral histories and who is working on her own book about her ancestors Malinda and Green Bratton, the latter who appears in this book.

Pastor Sam McGregor of the Allison Creek Presbyterian Church not only gave me many hours of his time and provided copies of prodigious research done by him and his parishioners on Elias Hill, he also introduced me to many of the people receiving thanks here, and he provided a blessing for this work that touched me deeply. I thank Wali Cathcart, whose ancestors migrated to Liberia with Elias Hill but later returned, for telling me his family's story as we toured the Clay Hill cemetery at Allison Creek Church.

Several members of the University of South Carolina faculty were very generous with their time and advice, including my dear friend Dr. David J. Snyder, as well as his colleagues Dr. David Dangerfield, who directed me to many helpful archives, and Dr. Thomas Brown, an expert on the history of

Columbia, South Carolina. I also thank McKenzie Lemhouse, a very helpful specialist at the South Caroliniana Library at USC.

The more I do research, the more I remain in genuine awe at the helpfulness and good cheer of so many archivists. Those whom I wish to thank for their help, dedication, and knowledge are Gina White, director of archives and special collections, and V. Emily Deinert, archivist, reference librarian, and assistant professor, at the Louise Pettus Archives at Winthrop University; Robert W. Pease Jr., at the National Archives in Atlanta (who helped track down the indictments listed against my great-grandfather); Nancy Sambets, director of archives, and Wanda Fowler, researcher, at the Historical Center of York County; John Skardon, who has earned the title "genealogy master" at the York County Library; and Catherine Allen at the Columbia Historical Society.

I am very grateful to my friend and colleague Britney Schopf for developing the map of South Carolina and York County that appears in the book, and I also thank those who helped locate photographs used in this book, including Erin Beasley at the National Portrait Gallery, Eric Blevins at the North Carolina Museum of History, and Paul Carnahan at the Vermont Historical Society.

I offer a special thanks to Bernice Bennett, professional genealogist and also a true master of research at the National Archives in Washington, DC, who dug up invaluable information on Jim and Rosa Williams, and also to several of the staff at Historic Brattonsville, including site manager Kevin Lynch, historian Zach Lemhouse (who also offered helpful corrections to the manuscript), site interpreter Jonah Stephens, and visitor services coordinator Dabney Roberts, who turned out to be a distant cousin. Other relatives who provided very helpful information include Jamie Jones and Daniel Troublefield, and friends who offered helpful editing suggestions include Dave Kingham, Hank Stern, Ken Morrison, and Rick Thamer.

In addition to providing extremely useful information from their own works cited extensively in my book, several authors were also kind enough to offer advice and guidance. This most especially includes J. Michael Martinez and also Lou Falkner Williams. I also want to acknowledge the work of two York County, South Carolina, authors, now deceased, whom I am very sorry not to have had the chance to meet: the Reverend Jerry West and Michael C. Scoggins, who was a dynamic and beloved research historian with the Culture & Heritage Museums of York County. I hope this book exposes their work to an even larger audience.

Last, but hardly least, I again thank my loyal, talented, and hardworking agent, Laura Dail, who is also an excellent editor in her own right, and I thank Rick Rinehart, my editor at Lyons Press, and the excellent team at Lyons, including project editors Meredith Dias and Alexander Bordelon, copy editor Joshua Rosenberg, and cover designer Sally Rinehart.

NOTES

Note: Citations of "Congressional report" refer to one of the three volumes listed in the bibliography as *Report of the Joint Select Committee to Enquire Into the Condition of Affairs in the Late Insurrectionary States.*

INTRODUCTION

1. Foner, *Reconstruction*, 431.
2. McFeely, *Grant*, 372.
3. Hamilton, "Amos T. Akerman and His Role In American Politics," 74.
4. Williams, *Great South Carolina Ku Klux Klan Trials*, 16.
5. Foner, *Reconstruction*, 458, and Trelease, *White Terror*, 404.
6. Egerton, *Wars of Reconstruction*, 287.
7. Foner, *Reconstruction*, 443.
8. Chernow, *Grant*, xxii.
9. Chernow, *Grant*, 857.
10. *Proceedings*, 62.

CHAPTER ONE

1. McPherson, *Battle Cry of Freedom*, 849–50.
2. Leyburn, *Scotch-Irish*, 219, 252.
3. "Notices," *Yorkville Enquirer*, July 16, 1868, 2.
4. Mendenhall, *Tales of York County*, 48.
5. Scoggins, *Brief History of Historic Brattonsville*, 11.
6. Witt, *Patriots and Cosmopolitans*, 115.
7. West, *Reconstruction Ku Klux Klan in York County*, 2.
8. Peter Judge, "'Charleston of the Upcountry,' Yorkville Offered Genteel Living," *Rock Hill* (SC) *Evening Herald*, March 4, 1985, C4.
9. Hall, "Dr. James Rufus Bratton," 6.
10. Bratton, "For My Children in Future Life," 9.
11. Long and Long, *Civil War Day by Day*, 711–12.
12. Bratton, "For My Children in Future Life," 7.
13. Bratton, "For My Children in Future Life," 9.
14. Bratton, "Dr. J. R. Bratton," 3.
15. Pearl, "K Troop."
16. Bratton, "Dr. J. R. Bratton," 15.
17. West, *Reconstruction Ku Klux Klan in York County*, 127.
18. Witt, *Patriots and Cosmopolitans*, 97.

19. Scoggins, "Inventory of Slaves Belonging to the Estate of Dr. John Bratton, August 1843."
20. Winik, *April 1865*, 330.
21. Don Worthington, "150 Years ago, Jefferson Davis Stopped in York County," *Rock Hill* (SC) *Herald*, April 27, 2015, https://www.heraldonline.com/news/local/article19778199.html.
22. Mendenhall, *Tales of York County*, 48.
23. West, *Reconstruction Ku Klux Klan in York County*, 2.
24. Winik, *April 1865*, 334.
25. Andrew, *Wade Hampton*, 300.
26. Andrew, *Wade Hampton*, 300.
27. Congressional report, 4:1237.
28. McPherson, *Battle Cry of Freedom*, 318.
29. Andrew, *Wade Hampton*, 301.
30. West, *Bloody South Carolina Election of 1876*, 21.
31. Andrew, *Wade Hampton*, 566, n33.
32. Willoughby, *The "Good Town" Does Well*, 35.
33. Swinney, "Suppressing the Ku Klux Klan," 215.
34. "The Ku Klux," *New York Tribune*, November 14, 1871, 1.
35. Winik, *April 1865*, 352.
36. "The Mass Meeting," *Yorkville Enquirer*, September 3, 1868, 2.
37. "Letter from Gen. Hampton," *Yorkville Enquirer*, August 17, 1865, 1.
38. Williams, *Great South Carolina Ku Klux Klan Trials*, 3.
39. Wilkerson, *Warmth of Other Suns*, 37.
40. Bratton, "For My Children in Future Life," 16.
41. Bratton, "For My Children in Future Life," 18.
42. "The Crops," *Yorkville Enquirer*, August 17, 1865, 2.
43. Parsons, *Ku-Klux*, 37.
44. Trelease, *White Terror*, 4.
45. Parsons, *Ku-Klux*, 41.
46. Trelease, *White Terror*, 4.
47. Parsons, *Ku-Klux*, 43.
48. Parsons, *Ku-Klux*, 43.
49. Parsons, *Ku-Klux*, 63.
50. Trelease, *White Terror*, 26–27.
51. Zuczek, *State of Rebellion*, 56–57.
52. Parsons, *Ku-Klux*, 50.
53. Trelease, *White Terror*, 19–20.
54. Trelease, *White Terror*, 62.
55. Trelease, *White Terror*, 26–27.
56. "K.K.K.," *Yorkville Enquirer*, April 2, 1868, 3.
57. "K.K.K.-Mysterious," *Yorkville Enquirer*, April 2, 1868, 2.
58. "The KuKlux—What Is It?", *Yorkville Enquirer*, April 9, 1868, 2.
59. West, *Reconstruction Ku Klux Klan in York County*, 35–38.
60. Trelease, *White Terror*, 363.
61. Trelease, *White Terror*, 45.
62. Trelease, *White Terror*, 362.
63. West, *Reconstruction Ku Klux Klan in York County*, 5.
64. Willoughby, *The "Good Town" Does Well*, 45.
65. Proctor, "Whip, Pistol, and Hood," 73.
66. Hadden, *Slave Patrols*, 209.
67. Epps, *Democracy Reborn*, 196.

68. Epps, *Democracy Reborn*, 83.
69. Du Bois, *Black Reconstruction*, 54.
70. Proctor, "Whip, Pistol, and Hood," 96–98.
71. *Proceedings*, 764.
72. *Proceedings*, 771.

CHAPTER TWO

1. *Proceedings*, 325.
2. "Views and Interviews: Remembers the Jim Williams Raid," *Yorkville Enquirer*, February 18, 1921, 1.
3. Post, "Carpetbagger in South Carolina," 60.
4. West, *Reconstruction Ku Klux Klan in York County*, 123.
5. Congressional report, 4:1223.
6. Emberton, "The Limits of Incorporation," 616.
7. Foner, *Reconstruction*, 199.
8. Foner, *Reconstruction*, 201.
9. Zuczek, *State of Rebellion*, 73.
10. Current, *Those Terrible Carpetbaggers*, 224.
11. Faris, *Faris Family of Washington County, Indiana*, 29.
12. Hall, *Shell in the Radical Camp*, 35–36.
13. Zuczek, *State of Rebellion*, 74.
14. Williams, *Great South Carolina Ku Klux Klan Trials*, 24.
15. Williams, *Great South Carolina Ku Klux Klan Trials*, 26.
16. Merrill report to Terry, June 9, 1871, 9, Letters Received by the Adjutant General, 1871–1880, File 2586—Terry, A. J., National Archives, Washington, DC.
17. Zuczek, *State of Rebellion*, 74.
18. Rosa Williams Union army widows pension application No. 524175, National Archives, Washington, DC.
19. Higginson, *Army Life in a Black Regiment*, 247.
20. Boritt, ed., *Why the Confederacy Lost*, 158.
21. Taylor, *Reminiscences of My Life in Camp with the 33rd United States Colored Troops*, 19.
22. Taylor, *Reminiscences of My Life in Camp with the 33rd United States Colored Troops*, 27.
23. Higginson, *Army Life in a Black Regiment*, 14.
24. Higginson, *Army Life in a Black Regiment*, 41.
25. Higginson, *Army Life in a Black Regiment*, 23.
26. Higginson, *Army Life in a Black Regiment*, 34.
27. Boritt, ed., *Why the Confederacy Lost*, 162.
28. *Proceedings*, 296.
29. *Proceedings*, 227.
30. *Proceedings*, 224.
31. Post, "Carpetbagger in South Carolina," 60.
32. "Views and Interviews: Remembers the Jim Williams Raid," *Yorkville Enquirer*, February 18, 1921, 1.
33. "The Anderson Militia," *Yorkville Enquirer*, February 16, 1871, 2; Trial transcript, 240.
34. "The Union Outrage," *Yorkville Enquirer*, February 23, 1871, 2.
35. *Proceedings*, 311.
36. *Proceedings*, 332.
37. *Proceedings*, 333, 348.
38. "Views and Interviews: Remembers the Jim Williams Raid," *Yorkville Enquirer*, February 18, 1921, 1.
39. *Proceedings*, 259.
40. "Views and Interviews: Remembers the Jim Williams Raid," *Yorkville Enquirer*, February 18, 1921, 1.

41. *Proceedings*, 247.
42. Rosa Williams Union army widows pension application No. 524175, National Archives, Washington, DC.
43. *Proceedings*, 248.
44. Rosa Williams Union army widows pension application No. 524175, National Archives, Washington, DC.
45. "Views and Interviews: Remembers the Jim Williams Raid," *Yorkville Enquirer*, February 18, 1921, 1.
46. *Proceedings*, 237.
47. "Views and Interviews: Remembers the Jim Williams Raid," *Yorkville Enquirer*, February 18, 1921, 1.
48. West, *Reconstruction Ku Klux Klan in York County*, 124.
49. *Proceedings*, 237.
50. *Proceedings*, 237.
51. "Views and Interviews: Remembers the Jim Williams Raid," *Yorkville Enquirer*, February 18, 1921, 1.
52. West, *Reconstruction Ku Klux Klan in York County*, 124.
53. *Proceedings*, 223.
54. Merrill to Terry, June 9, 1871, 22, Letters Received by the Adjutant General, 1871–1880, File 2586—Terry, A. J., National Archives, Washington, DC.
55. *Proceedings*, 266.
56. *Proceedings*, 248.
57. *Proceedings*, 248.
58. *Proceedings*, 266.
59. "Views and Interviews: Remembers the Jim Williams Raid," *Yorkville Enquirer*, February 18, 1921, 1.
60. *Proceedings*, 269.
61. Trelease, *White Terror*, 367.
62. Scoggins, "The Jim Williams Incident," 7.
63. Trelease, *White Terror*, 367.
64. West, *Reconstruction Ku Klux Klan in York County*, 71.
65. Congressional report, 4:709.
66. Trelease, *White Terror*, 368.
67. Congressional report, 4:709–10.
68. Rosa Williams Union army widows pension application No. 524175, National Archives, Washington, DC.
69. Rosa Williams Union army widows pension application No. 524175, National Archives, Washington, DC.
70. Rosa Williams Union army widows pension application No. 524175, National Archives, Washington, DC.
71. *Proceedings*, 289.
72. Higginson, *Army Life in a Black Regiment*, 269.
73. *Proceedings*, 289.
74. Higginson, *Army Life in a Black Regiment*, 25.
75. Epps, *Democracy Reborn*, 129.
76. Foner, *Reconstruction*, 153.
77. Reid, *After the War*, 221.
78. Foner, *Reconstruction*, 97–98.
79. Williams, *Great South Carolina Ku Klux Klan Trials*, 5.
80. Foner, *Reconstruction*, 70–71.
81. Foner, *Reconstruction*, 159–60.
82. Brattonsville Oral History Project, Interview with former US congressman John Spratt, October 10, 2009, Historical Center of York County.
83. *Proceedings*, 671–72.
84. *Proceedings*, 339.

CHAPTER THREE

1. "Remarkable Man for Liberia," *African Repository*, Vol. XLVII, 280.
2. "Remarkable Man for Liberia," *African Repository*, Vol. XLVII, 281.
3. "Departure of Our Fall Expedition," *African Repository*, Vol. XLVII, 354.
4. Congressional report, 5:1412.
5. Congressional report, 5:1415.
6. "Remarkable Man for Liberia," *African Repository*, Vol. XLVII, 281.
7. Congressional report, 5:1477.
8. Congressional report, 5:1406.
9. Congressional report, 5:1406.
10. Congressional report, 5:1407.
11. Congressional report, 5:1407.
12. Congressional report, 5:1407.
13. Congressional report, 5:1407.
14. Congressional report, 5:1408.
15. "Views and Interviews," *Yorkville Enquirer*, May 23, 1933, 1.
16. Congressional report, 5:1408.
17. Congressional report, 5:1408.
18. Congressional report, 5:1413.
19. Congressional report, 5:1412.
20. Congressional report, 5:1411.
21. Congressional report, 5:1477.
22. Faust, *James Henry Hammond*, 157.
23. Congressional report, 5: 1406.
24. Congressional report, 5:1406.
25. "Remarkable Man for Liberia," *African Repository*, Vol. XLVII, 281.
26. "Remarkable Man for Liberia," *African Repository*, Vol. XLVII, 281.
27. Witt, *Patriots and Cosmopolitans*, 94.
28. Witt, *Patriots and Cosmopolitans*, 93.
29. Witt, *Patriots and Cosmopolitans*, 95–96.
30. Witt, *Patriots and Cosmopolitans*, 85.
31. "Remarkable Man for Liberia," *African Repository*, Vol. XLVII, 281.
32. "Departure of Our Fall Expedition," *African Repository*, Vol. XLVII, 354.
33. Witt, *Patriots and Cosmopolitans*, 113.
34. "Remarkable Man for Liberia," *African Repository*, Vol. XLVII, 281.
35. "Remarkable Man for Liberia," *African Repository*, Vol. XLVII, 281.
36. Foner, *Reconstruction*, 283–85.
37. Hall, *Shell in the Radical Camp*, 5.
38. Williams, *Great South Carolina Ku Klux Klan Trials*, 16.
39. Williamson, *After Slavery*, 354.
40. Williams, *Great South Carolina Ku Klux Klan Trials*, 15–16.
41. Zuczek, *State of Rebellion*, 78.
42. Zuczek, *State of Rebellion*, 74.
43. Williams, *Great South Carolina Ku Klux Klan Trials*, 15–16.
44. West, *Reconstruction Ku Klux Klan in York County*, 61.
45. West, *Reconstruction Ku Klux Klan in York County*, 61.
46. Congressional report, 5:1411.
47. "Former Slave, 100, Recalls Civil War," *Rock Hill* (SC) *Evening Herald*, August 3, 1959, York County Public Library.
48. West, *Reconstruction Ku Klux Klan in York County*, 62.
49. Congressional report, 5:1410.

50. Witt, *Patriots and Cosmopolitans*, 128.
51. "Public Meeting at Clay Hill," *Yorkville Enquirer*, February 16, 1871, 2.
52. "Public Meeting at Clay Hill," *Yorkville Enquirer*, February 16, 1871, 2.
53. Congressional report, 5:1410.
54. Congressional report, 5:1410.
55. Congressional report, 5:1415.
56. "More Ku-Kluxing," *Yorkville Enquirer*, February 16, 1871, 2.
57. Congressional report, 5:1411.
58. Witt, *Patriots and Cosmopolitans*, 87.
59. "Remarkable Man for Liberia," *African Repository*, Vol. XLVII, 281.
60. "When Portland Banned Blacks: Oregon's Shameful History as an 'All-White' State," *Washington Post*, June 7, 2017, https://www.washingtonpost.com/news/retropolis/wp/2017/06/07/when-portland-banned-blacks-oregons-shameful-history-as-an-all-white-state/?utm_term=.4f0cc31d2228.
61. Congressional report, 5:1412.
62. Witt, *Patriots and Cosmopolitans*, 133–34.
63. Witt, *Patriots and Cosmopolitans*, 103.
64. "The Colored Convention," *Yorkville Enquirer*, October 26, 1871, 2.
65. Witt, *Patriots and Cosmopolitans*, 137.
66. "Gone to Liberia," *Yorkville Enquirer*, November 2, 1871, 2.
67. Witt, *Patriots and Cosmopolitans*, 137.
68. Congressional report, 5:1410.
69. Witt, *Patriots and Cosmopolitans*, 138.
70. "Former Slave, 100, Recalls Civil War," *Rock Hill* (SC) *Evening Herald*, August 3, 1959, York County Public Library.
71. "Former Slave, 100, Recalls Civil War," *Rock Hill* (SC) *Evening Herald*, August 3, 1959, York County Public Library.
72. "Letter from Rev. Elias Hill," *Yorkville Enquirer*, February 22, 1871, 2.
73. "Letter from Rev. Elias Hill," *Yorkville Enquirer*, February 22, 1871, 2.
74. "Letter from Liberia," *Yorkville Enquirer*, August 6, 1874, 2.
75. Witt, *Patriots and Cosmopolitans*, 149–50.
76. "Letter from Rev. Elias Hill," *Yorkville Enquirer*, February 22, 1871, 2.
77. Witt, *Patriots and Cosmopolitans*, 147.
78. "Former Slave, 100, Recalls Civil War," *Rock Hill* (SC) *Evening Herald*, August 3, 1959, York County Public Library.
79. Witt, *Patriots and Cosmopolitans*, 147.

Chapter Four

1. Epps, *Democracy Reborn*, 234–35.
2. Wills, *Lincoln at Gettysburg*, 145.
3. Wills, *Lincoln at Gettysburg*, 146–47.
4. Wills, *Lincoln at Gettysburg*, 130–31.
5. Wills, *Lincoln at Gettysburg*, 38–39.
6. "South Carolina Re-establishing Slavery," *New York Tribune*, November 14, 1865, 4.
7. Curtis, "Curious History of Attempts to Suppress Antislavery Speech, Press, and Petition in 1835–37," 796.
8. Curtis, "Curious History of Attempts to Suppress Antislavery Speech, Press, and Petition in 1835–37," 805–7.
9. Schurz, *Report on the Condition of the South*, 61.
10. Epps, *Democracy Reborn*, 96.

11. Epps, *Democracy Reborn*, 226–27.
12. Epps, *Democracy Reborn*, 227.
13. Foner, *Reconstruction*, 258.
14. Epps, *Democracy Reborn*, 239.
15. McPherson, *Ordeal by Fire*, 517.
16. Bond, "Original Understanding of the Fourteenth Amendment in Illinois, Ohio, and Pennsylvania," 435.
17. Epps, *Democracy Reborn*, 234.
18. Blight, *Frederick Douglass*, 490–91.
19. Chernow, *Grant*, 623.
20. Swinney, "Suppressing the Ku Klux Klan," 21.
21. White, *American Ulysses*, 130.
22. Chernow, *Grant*, 283.
23. Chernow, *Grant*, 450.
24. Chernow, *Grant*, 282.
25. Smith, *Grant*, 425.
26. Calhoun, *Presidency of Ulysses S. Grant*, 102–103.
27. White, *American Ulysses*, 525.
28. Trelease, *White Terror*, 385.
29. Kousser and McPherson, eds., *Region, Race and Reconstruction*, 395.
30. Hamilton, "Amos T. Akerman and His Role in American Politics," 47.
31. "Washington: Talk at the Capital About the Resignation of Mr. Hoar," *New York Times*, June 17, 1870, 1.
32. Kousser and McPherson, eds., *Region, Race and Reconstruction*, 397.
33. Chernow, *Grant*, 700.
34. Kousser and McPherson, eds., *Region, Race and Reconstruction*, 397–98.
35. Hamilton, "Amos T. Akerman and His Role in American Politics," 2.
36. Kousser and McPherson, eds., *Region, Race and Reconstruction*, 398.
37. Hamilton, "Amos T. Akerman and His Role in American Politics," 12.
38. Hamilton, "Amos T. Akerman and His Role in American Politics," 15.
39. Hamilton, "Amos T. Akerman and His Role in American Politics," 20–22.
40. Hamilton, "Amos T. Akerman and His Role in American Politics," 24.
41. Hamilton, "Amos T. Akerman and His Role in American Politics," 42.
42. Kousser and McPherson, eds., *Region, Race and Reconstruction*, 400.
43. Kousser and McPherson, eds., *Region, Race and Reconstruction*, 402.
44. Hamilton, "Amos T. Akerman and His Role in American Politics," 47.
45. Kaczorowski, *Politics of Judicial Interpretation*, 62.
46. "How Mr. Akerman's Appointment Is Perceived by the Press of Georgia," *New York Times*, June 22, 1870, 1.
47. Trelease, *White Terror*, 385–86.
48. Chernow, *Grant*, 704.
49. Chernow, *Grant*, 705–6.
50. Hamilton, "Amos T. Akerman and His Role in American Politics," 81.
51. Williams, *Great South Carolina Ku Klux Klan Trials*, 44–45.

CHAPTER FIVE

1. Williams, *Great South Carolina Ku Klux Klan Trials*, 45.
2. Martinez, *Carpetbaggers, Cavalry, and the Ku Klux Klan*, 83–84.
3. Martinez, *Carpetbaggers, Cavalry, and the Ku Klux Klan*, 86.

4. Budiansky, *Bloody Shirt*, 110.
5. Budiansky, *Bloody Shirt*, 110.
6. McNeil, "Retaliation in Missouri," 476.
7. Congressional report, 5:1482.
8. Congressional report 5:1487.
9. Williams, *Great South Carolina Ku Klux Klan Trials*, 41.
10. Chernow, *Grant*, 704.
11. Trelease, *White Terror*, 387.
12. Swinney, "Suppressing the Ku Klux Klan," 190.
13. Kaczorowski, *Politics of Judicial Interpretation*, 112.
14. Swinney, "Suppressing the Ku Klux Klan," 193.
15. Zuczek, *State of Rebellion*, 97.
16. Swinney, "Suppressing the Ku Klux Klan," 223.
17. McFeely, *Grant*, 372.
18. "Ku-Klux: Crushing Them Out in South Carolina," *New York Tribune*, November 13, 1871, 1.
19. Budiansky, *Bloody Shirt*, 109.
20. Martinez, *Carpetbaggers, Cavalry, and the Ku Klux Klan*, 83.
21. Congressional report, 5:1472.
22. Martinez, *Carpetbaggers, Cavalry, and the Ku Klux Klan*, 96–98.
23. Martinez, *Carpetbaggers, Cavalry, and the Ku Klux Klan*, 99–101.
24. Martinez, *Carpetbaggers, Cavalry, and the Ku Klux Klan*, 99–101.
25. West, *Reconstruction Ku Klux Klan in York County*, 72.
26. Pearl, "K Troop."
27. Budiansky, *Bloody Shirt*, 120.
28. West, *Reconstruction Ku Klux Klan in York County*, 81.
29. Merrill report to Terry, June 9, 1871, 3, Letters Received by the Adjutant General, 1871–1880, File 2586—Terry, A. J., National Archives, Washington, DC.
30. Massy, "Dr. Bratton's Adventures as Ku-Klux Leader."
31. Budiansky, *Bloody Shirt*, 121–22.
32. Congressional report, 5:1482.
33. Congressional report, 5:1477.
34. Congressional report, 5:1482.
35. Merrill report to Terry, June 10, 1871, 5–6, Letters Received by the Adjutant General, 1871–1880, File 2586—Terry, A. J., National Archives, Washington, DC.
36. Merrill report to Terry, June 10, 1871, 6, Letters Received by the Adjutant General, 1871–1880, File 2586—Terry, A. J., National Archives, Washington, DC.
37. Post, "Carpetbagger in South Carolina," 49.
38. Congressional report, 5:1486.
39. Congressional report, 5:1486–87.
40. Congressional report, 5:1485–86.
41. "The Mass Meeting," *Yorkville Enquirer*, September 3, 1868, 2.
42. "Negro Suffrage," *Yorkville Enquirer*, December 3, 1868, 2.
43. Williams, *Great South Carolina Ku Klux Klan Trials*, 21.
44. *Proceedings*, 680–81.
45. Merrill report to Terry, June 10, 1871, 1–2, Letters Received by the Adjutant General, 1871–1880, File 2586—Terry, A. J., National Archives, Washington, DC.
46. *Proceedings*, 657.
47. *Proceedings*, 638.
48. West, *Reconstruction Ku Klux Klan in York County*, 63.
49. "Just A-Rolling Along the Way," *Yorkville Enquirer*, July 14, 1933, 7.

50. Budiansky, *Bloody Shirt*, 123.
51. Martinez, *Carpetbaggers, Cavalry, and the Ku Klux Klan*, 138.
52. Congressional report, 5:1481–82.
53. Merrill report to Terry, June 9, 1871, 11, Letters Received by the Adjutant General, 1871–1880, File 2586—Terry, A. J., National Archives, Washington, DC.
54. Merrill report to Terry, June 9, 1871, 4, Letters Received by the Adjutant General, 1871–1880, File 2586—Terry, A. J., National Archives, Washington, DC.
55. Martinez, *Carpetbaggers, Cavalry, and the Ku Klux Klan*, 139.
56. Congressional report, 3:36.
57. Merrill report to Terry, June 9, 1871, 1–6, Letters Received by the Adjutant General, 1871–1880, File 2586—Terry, A. J., National Archives, Washington, DC.
58. "Washington: Astounding Disclosures Concerns the Objects of the Order of the Invisible Empire," *New York Herald*, November 3, 1871, 3.
59. Merrill report to Terry, June 9, 1871, 7, Letters Received by the Adjutant General, 1871–1880, File 2586—Terry, A. J., National Archives, Washington, DC.
60. Williams, *Great South Carolina Ku Klux Klan Trials*, 45.
61. Swinney, "Suppressing the Ku Klux Klan," 186.
62. Whitley, *In It*, 76.
63. Lane, *Freedom's Detective*, 58–59.
64. Swinney, "Suppressing the Ku Klux Klan," 186.
65. Lane, *Freedom's Detective*, 160.
66. Williams, *Great South Carolina Ku Klux Klan Trials*, 45.

CHAPTER SIX

1. Trelease, *White Terror*, 391.
2. Trelease, *White Terror*, 392.
3. Trelease, *White Terror*, 393.
4. Trelease, *White Terror*, 49–50.
5. Trelease, *White Terror*, 513 n39.
6. Congressional report, 5:1354.
7. Congressional report, 5:1342.
8. Congressional report, 5:1352.
9. Congressional report, 5:1344.
10. Congressional report, 5:1346.
11. Congressional report, 5:1344–45.
12. Congressional report, 5:1351.
13. Congressional report, 5:1348.
14. Congressional report, 5:1344–45.
15. Congressional report, 5:1348.
16. Congressional report, 5:1344.
17. Congressional report, 4:1221.
18. Congressional report, 4:1224.
19. Congressional report, 4:1226.
20. Foner, *Reconstruction*, 326.
21. Foner, *Reconstruction*, 375.
22. Congressional report, 4:1219.
23. Congressional report, 4:1222.
24. Congressional report, 4:1230.
25. Congressional report, 4:1237.

26. Zuczek, *State of Rebellion*, 208.
27. Congressional report, 5:1565–66.
28. Congressional report, 5:1569.
29. Congressional report, 5:1572.
30. Congressional report, 5:1575.
31. "South Carolina," *Yorkville Enquirer*, August 3, 1871, 3.
32. Congressional report, 5:1591–92.
33. Congressional report, 5:1475.
34. Congressional report, 5:1470.
35. "The Sub-Outrage Committee" and "How Testimony Was Obtained for the Sub-Committee in York," *Yorkville Enquirer*, August 3, 1871, 2.
36. "South Carolina," *Yorkville Enquirer*, August 3, 1871, 3.
37. "The Barry-Wallace Difficulty," *Yorkville Enquirer*, August 3, 1871, 2.
38. "Street Affray," *Yorkville Enquirer*, July 27, 1871, 2.
39. West, *Reconstruction Ku Klux Klan in York County*, 86.
40. "U.S. vs. Walker Smith et al," Record Group 21.43, Roll 97, Records of the District Courts of the United States, Fourth Circuit, National Archives, Atlanta, GA.
41. "U.S. vs. Charles Jamison et al.," Record Group 21.43, Roll 95, Records of the District Courts of the United States, Fourth Circuit, National Archives, Atlanta, GA.
42. "Noted Lynching Case Recalled," *Yorkville Enquirer*, October 10, 1919, 1.
43. "The Gallows," *Yorkville Enquirer*, April 16, 1885, 2.
44. Williams, *Great South Carolina Ku Klux Klan Trials*, 105.
45. Foner, *Reconstruction*, 440.
46. "U.S. vs. Walker Smith et al.," Record Group 21.43, Roll 97, Records of the District Courts of the United States, Fourth Circuit, National Archives, Atlanta, GA.
47. McFeely, *Grant*, 370.
48. Hamilton, "Amos T. Akerman and His Role in American Politics," 72.
49. Hamilton, "Amos T. Akerman and His Role in American Politics," 79.
50. Hamilton, "Amos T. Akerman and His Role in American Politics," 82.
51. Hamilton, "Amos T. Akerman and His Role in American Politics," 72.
52. McFeely, *Grant*, 370.
53. McFeely, *Grant*, 371.
54. Congressional report, 5:1413.
55. Congressional report, 5:1411.
56. Zuczek, "Federal Government's Attack on the Ku Klux Klan," 54.
57. Hamilton, "Amos T. Akerman and His Role in American Politics," 79–80.
58. Kousser and McPherson, eds., *Region, Race and Reconstruction*, 408.
59. Calhoun, *Presidency of Ulysses S. Grant*, 323.
60. Merrill report to Terry, January 4, 1872, 11, Letters Received by the Adjutant General, 1871–1880, File 2586—Terry, A. J., National Archives, Washington, DC.
61. Williams, *Great South Carolina Ku Klux Klan Trials*, 47.
62. Merrill report to Terry, January 4, 1872, 11, Letters Received by the Adjutant General, 1871–1880, File 2586—Terry, A. J., National Archives, Washington, DC.
63. Foner, *Reconstruction*, 458.
64. West, *Reconstruction Ku Klux Klan in York County*, 93.
65. Williams, *Great South Carolina Ku Klux Klan Trials*, 47.
66. Brown, *Oil in Our Lamps*, 190.
67. Brown, *Oil in Our Lamps*, 190–91.
68. Reynolds, *Reconstruction in South Carolina*, 198–99.
69. "The Ku-Klux in Jail," *New York Tribune*, November 23, 1871, 2.

70. Merrill report to War Department, April 17, 1872, 21–25, Record Group 94, Records of the Adjutant General's Office, Letters Received by the Adjutant General, 1871–1880, File 1432, National Archives, Washington, DC.
71. "The Ku Klux: Crushing Them Out in South Carolina," *New York Tribune*, November 13, 1871, 1.
72. West, *Reconstruction Ku Klux Klan in York County*, 95.
73. "The Ku-Klux in Jail," *New York Tribune*, November 23, 1871, 2.
74. West, *Reconstruction Ku Klux Klan in York County*, 90.
75. Post, "Carpetbagger in South Carolina," 44.
76. Williams, *Great South Carolina Ku Klux Klan Trials*, 47.
77. Post, "Carpetbagger in South Carolina," 44.
78. Merrill report to Terry, January 4, 1872, 12, Letters Received by the Adjutant General, 1871–1880, File 2586—Terry, A. J., National Archives, Washington, DC.
79. Merrill report to Terry, January 4, 1872, 12, Letters Received by the Adjutant General, 1871–1880, File 2586—Terry, A. J., National Archives, Washington, DC.
80. "The Ku-Klux in Jail," *New York Tribune*, November 23, 1871, 2.
81. "The Ku-Klux in Jail," *New York Tribune*, November 23, 1871, 2.
82. Post, "Carpetbagger in South Carolina," 48.
83. Post, "Carpetbagger in South Carolina,"46.
84. Post, "Carpetbagger in South Carolina," 48.

Chapter Seven

1. *Proceedings*, 6.
2. "The Ku-Klux Trials, Notes and Comments by Mail," *Charleston Daily News*, November 29, 1871, 1.
3. Alschuler and Deiss, "Brief History of the Criminal Jury in the United States," 884 and 884 n93.
4. Alschuler and Deiss, "Brief History of the Criminal Jury in the United States," 885 n96.
5. Forman, "Juries and Race in the Nineteenth Century," 912.
6. Alschuler and Deiss, "Brief History of the Criminal Jury in the United States," 885.
7. Steiner, *Life of Reverdy Johnson*, iii.
8. Forman, "Juries and Race in the Nineteenth Century," 913.
9. Andrew, *Wade Hampton*, 317.
10. Zuczek, *State of Rebellion*, 100.
11. Andrew, *Wade Hampton*, 363.
12. Andrew, *Wade Hampton*, 361.
13. Zuczek, *State of Rebellion*, 100.
14. Steiner, *Life of Reverdy Johnson*, 4.
15. Steiner, *Life of Reverdy Johnson*, 18.
16. Steiner, *Life of Reverdy Johnson*, 4.
17. Steiner, *Life of Reverdy Johnson*, 15–16.
18. Steiner, *Life of Reverdy Johnson*, 22.
19. Steiner, *Life of Reverdy Johnson*, 32.
20. McPherson, *Battle Cry of Freedom*, 174.
21. Steiner, *Life of Reverdy Johnson*, 38.
22. McPherson, *Battle Cry of Freedom*, 172–74.
23. Steiner, *Life of Reverdy Johnson*, 38 n38.
24. Steiner, *Life of Reverdy Johnson*, 51–54.
25. Steiner, *Life of Reverdy Johnson*, 119.
26. "Hon. Henry Stanbery Dead," *Cincinnati Enquirer*, June 27, 1881, 4.
27. Reed, ed., *Bench and Bar of Ohio*, 84.
28. "Hon. Henry Stanbery Dead," *Cincinnati Enquirer*, June 27, 1881, 4.

29. Wineapple, *The Impeachers*, 200.
30. Reed, ed., *Bench and Bar of Ohio*, 85.
31. Williams, *Great South Carolina Ku Klux Klan Trials*, 56.
32. Williams, *Great South Carolina Ku Klux Klan Trials*, 56.
33. Safire, *Safire's Political Dictionary*, 103.
34. Current, *Those Terrible Carpetbaggers*, xi.
35. Foner, *Reconstruction*, 295.
36. Reynolds, *Reconstruction in South Carolina*, 511.
37. www.vermontcivilwar.org/get.php?input=1430 (Retrieved 4/20/19).
38. Williams, *Great South Carolina Ku Klux Klan Trials*, 56.
39. Crosswell, "In the Shade of the Palmetto," 9, 12, 27, 30.
40. "The Ku-Klux Trials, Notes and Comments by Mail," *Charleston Daily News*, November 29, 1871, 1.
41. Current, *Those Terrible Carpetbaggers*, 92–93.
42. Current, *Those Terrible Carpetbaggers*, 92–93.
43. Current, *Those Terrible Carpetbaggers*, 94.
44. Current, *Those Terrible Carpetbaggers*, 94.
45. Williams, *Great South Carolina Ku Klux Klan Trials*, 49–50.
46. Vile, ed., *Great American Judges*, 104.
47. Brooks, *South Carolina Bench and Bar*, 338.
48. Williams, *Great South Carolina Ku Klux Klan Trials*, 52.
49. Brooks, *South Carolina Bench and Bar*, 340.
50. Williams, *Great South Carolina Ku Klux Klan Trials*, 53.
51. Williams, *Great South Carolina Ku Klux Klan Trials*, 53.
52. "The Ku-Klux: Progress of the South Carolina Trials," *New York Tribune*, December 18, 1871, 2.
53. Fuke, "Hugh Lennox Bond and the Radical Republican Ideology," 575.
54. Fuke, "Hugh Lennox Bond and the Radical Republican Ideology," 574.
55. Vile, ed., *Great American Judges*, 103.
56. Fuke, "Hugh Lennox Bond and the Radical Republican Ideology," 576.
57. Fuke, "Hugh Lennox Bond and the Radical Republican Ideology," 578.
58. Fuke, "Hugh Lennox Bond and the Radical Republican Ideology," 582.
59. Williams, *Great South Carolina Ku Klux Klan Trials*, 58–59.

CHAPTER EIGHT

1. Williams, *Great South Carolina Ku Klux Klan Trials*, 57.
2. "The Ku-Klux Trials, Notes and Comments by Mail," *Charleston Daily News*, November 29, 1871, 1.
3. Williams, *Great South Carolina Ku Klux Klan Trials*, 57.
4. "The Ku-Klux Trials, Notes and Comments by Mail," *Charleston Daily News*, November 29, 1871, 1.
5. *Proceedings*, 6.
6. *Proceedings*, 7.
7. *Proceedings*, 10.
8. *Proceedings*, 9.
9. *Proceedings*, 12.
10. Williams, *Great South Carolina Ku Klux Klan Trials*, 58–59.
11. *Proceedings*, 155.
12. *Proceedings*, 162.
13. Forman, "Juries and Race in the Nineteenth Century," 910 n84.
14. *Proceedings*, 279–80.
15. *Proceedings*, 281.
16. Hamilton, "Amos T. Akerman and His Role in American Politics," 79.

17. Williams, *Great South Carolina Ku Klux Klan Trials*, 62.
18. *Proceedings*, 825–32.
19. Williams, *Great South Carolina Ku Klux Klan Trials*, 62.
20. Congressional report, 3:70.
21. *Proceedings*, 30.
22. *Proceedings*, 21.
23. *Proceedings*, 19.
24. *Proceedings*, 24.
25. *Proceedings*, 25.
26. *Proceedings*, 28.
27. *Proceedings*, 31.
28. *Proceedings*, 62.
29. *Proceedings*, 64.
30. *Proceedings*, 63.
31. *Proceedings*, 65.
32. *Proceedings*, 67–68.
33. *Proceedings*, 46.
34. *Proceedings*, 65.
35. *Proceedings*, 72.
36. *Proceedings*, 74.
37. *Proceedings*, 74–75.
38. *Proceedings*, 131.
39. *Proceedings*, 79–80.
40. *Proceedings*, 81.
41. *Proceedings*, 86–87.
42. *Proceedings*, 89.
43. *Proceedings*, 90.
44. *Proceedings*, 92.
45. Williams, *Great South Carolina Ku Klux Klan Trials*, 72.
46. *Proceedings*, 66.
47. Williams, *Great South Carolina Ku Klux Klan Trials*, 73.
48. *Proceedings*, 137.

CHAPTER NINE

1. Halbrook, *Securing Civil Rights*, 104.
2. *Proceedings*, 147.
3. Williams, *Great South Carolina Ku Klux Klan Trials*, 74.
4. *Proceedings*, 147.
5. *Proceedings*, 146–47.
6. *Proceedings*, 146–47.
7. *Proceedings*, 148.
8. *Proceedings*, 149.
9. *Proceedings*, 150.
10. *Proceedings*, 150–51.
11. Fuke, "Hugh Lennox Bond and the Radical Republican Ideology," 579.
12. *Proceedings*, 151.
13. *Proceedings*, 153.
14. *Proceedings*, 163.
15. *Proceedings*, 175–78.

16. *Proceedings*, 175–78.
17. *Proceedings*, 178.
18. *Proceedings*, 187.
19. *Proceedings*, 201–2.
20. *Proceedings*, 203.
21. *Proceedings*, 205.
22. *Proceedings*, 216.
23. *Proceedings*, 219.
24. *Proceedings*, 222.
25. *Proceedings*, 223.
26. *Proceedings*, 228.
27. *Proceedings*, 231.
28. *Proceedings*, 233–34.
29. *Proceedings*, 248.
30. *Proceedings*, 234.
31. *Proceedings*, 239.
32. *Proceedings*, 242.
33. *Proceedings*, 250.
34. *Proceedings*, 252.
35. *Proceedings*, 263.
36. *Proceedings*, 284–85.
37. *Proceedings*, 281.
38. *Proceedings*, 296.
39. *Proceedings*, 289.
40. *Proceedings*, 294.
41. *Proceedings*, 296.
42. *Proceedings*, 297–99.
43. *Proceedings*, 300–301.
44. *Proceedings*, 301–302.
45. *Proceedings*, 307–10.
46. *Proceedings*, 340–41.
47. *Proceedings*, 346–47.
48. *Proceedings*, 348–49.
49. *Proceedings*, 353.
50. *Proceedings*, 320.
51. Popper, "History and Development of the Accused's Right to Testify," 454–64.
52. *Proceedings*, 369.
53. *Proceedings*, 358–59.
54. *Proceedings*, 360–62.
55. *Proceedings*, 366.
56. *Proceedings*, 375.
57. *Proceedings*, 376.
58. *Proceedings*, 391.
59. *Proceedings*, 398.
60. *Proceedings*, 381.
61. *Proceedings*, 394.
62. *Proceedings*, 412.
63. *Proceedings*, 400.
64. *Proceedings*, 413–15.
65. *Proceedings*, 416.

66. *Proceedings*, 419.
67. *Proceedings*, 428.
68. *Proceedings*, 432.
69. *Proceedings*, 446.
70. *Proceedings*, 449.
71. *Proceedings*, 449–51.
72. *Proceedings*, 457–59.

CHAPTER TEN

1. Williams, *Great South Carolina Ku Klux Klan Trials*, 101.
2. Hamilton, "Amos T. Akerman and His Role in American Politics," 109.
3. Chernow, *Grant*, 710.
4. Hamilton, "Amos T. Akerman and His Role in American Politics," 107.
5. Calhoun, *Presidency of Ulysses S. Grant*, 325–26.
6. "Washington: The Expected Cabinet Changes," *New York Tribune*, December 12, 1871, 1.
7. Hamilton, "Amos T. Akerman and His Role in American Politics," 107.
8. "Washington: Another Change in the Cabinet," *New York Tribune*, December 15, 1871, 1.
9. Hamilton, "Amos T. Akerman and His Role in American Politics," 107.
10. "Congress Yesterday—Propositions in the House—Anti-Administration Senators Defending Their Positions," *New York Herald*, January 9, 1872, 3.
11. Kousser and McPherson, eds., *Region, Race and Reconstruction*, 405.
12. McFeely, *Grant*, 373.
13. Hamilton, "Amos T. Akerman and His Role in American Politics," 90.
14. Hamilton, "Amos T. Akerman and His Role in American Politics," 107.
15. Hamilton, "Amos T. Akerman and His Role in American Politics," 90.
16. Kousser and McPherson, eds., *Region, Race and Reconstruction*, 409.
17. Calhoun, *Presidency of Ulysses S. Grant*, 322–23.
18. Calhoun, *Presidency of Ulysses S. Grant*, 323.
19. Calhoun, *Presidency of Ulysses S. Grant*, 325.
20. "The Rumored Cabinet Changes—Attorney General Akerman to Retire," *New York Herald*, December 5, 1871, 1.
21. Calhoun, *Presidency of Ulysses S. Grant*, 322.
22. Calhoun, *Presidency of Ulysses S. Grant*, 323.
23. Hamilton, "Amos T. Akerman and His Role in American Politics," 90.
24. Hamilton, "Amos T. Akerman and His Role in American Politics," 92.
25. McFeely, *Grant*, 373.
26. Chernow, *Grant*, 709.
27. Hamilton, "Amos T. Akerman and His Role in American Politics," 78.
28. Lane, *Freedom's Detective*, 185.
29. Chernow, *Grant*, 709.
30. Chernow, *Grant*, 826.
31. Kousser and McPherson, eds., *Region, Race and Reconstruction*, 410.
32. Chernow, *Grant*, 710.
33. Current, *Those Terrible Carpetbaggers*, 229.
34. "Lawlessness in the South," *New York Times*, July 26, 1870, 4.
35. Williams, *Horace Greeley*, 295, 300.
36. Hamilton, "Amos T. Akerman and His Role in American Politics," 84.
37. Hamilton, "Amos T. Akerman and His Role in American Politics," 84.
38. Hamilton, "Amos T. Akerman and His Role in American Politics," 85.

39. "The Rumored Cabinet Changes—Attorney General Akerman to Retire," *New York Herald*, December 5, 1871, 1.
40. McFeely, *Grant*, 374.
41. Kousser and McPherson, eds., *Region, Race and Reconstruction*, 409.
42. Hamilton, "Amos T. Akerman and His Role in American Politics," 94.
43. McFeely, *Grant*, 375–77.
44. Chernow, *Grant*, 710.
45. Hansen, "Racial History of the U.S. Military Academies," 111–16.
46. McFeely, *Grant*, 377–79.
47. McFeely, *Grant*, 374.
48. McFeely, *Grant*, 367.
49. Williams, *Great South Carolina Ku Klux Klan Trials*, 101.
50. Smith, *Grant*, 554.
51. "Washington: Another Change in the Cabinet," *New York Tribune*, December 15, 1871, 1.
52. Calhoun, *Presidency of Ulysses S. Grant*, 327.
53. McFeely, *Grant*, 383.
54. Kousser and McPherson, eds., *Region, Race and Reconstruction*, 410–11.
55. Williams, *Great South Carolina Ku Klux Klan Trials*, 102.
56. Williams, *Great South Carolina Ku Klux Klan Trials*, 102.
57. Williams, *Great South Carolina Ku Klux Klan Trials*, 102.
58. Williams, *Great South Carolina Ku Klux Klan Trials*, 102.
59. West, *Reconstruction Ku Klux Klan in York County*, 135.
60. Williams, *Great South Carolina Ku Klux Klan Trials*, 109.
61. West, *Reconstruction Ku Klux Klan in York County*, 134–35.
62. Williams, *Great South Carolina Ku Klux Klan Trials*, 107.
63. Williams, *Great South Carolina Ku Klux Klan Trials*, 102.
64. Williams, *Great South Carolina Ku Klux Klan Trials*, 110.
65. Trelease, *White Terror*, 415–17.
66. Smith, *Grant*, 554.
67. Smith, *Grant*, 560.
68. Lane, *Freedom's Detective*, 218–19.
69. Calhoun, *Presidency of Ulysses S. Grant*, 489.
70. Calhoun, *Presidency of Ulysses S. Grant*, 489.
71. Smith, *Grant*, 560–61.
72. Calhoun, *Presidency of Ulysses S. Grant*, 435.
73. White, *American Ulysses*, 557.
74. Lane, *Freedom's Detective*, 217.
75. Lane, *Freedom's Detective*, 219.
76. Whitley, *In It*, 260–67.
77. Calhoun, *Presidency of Ulysses S. Grant*, 489–90.

CHAPTER ELEVEN
1. *Proceedings*, 460.
2. *Proceedings*, 460–61.
3. Sommerville, *Rape and Race in the Nineteenth-Century South*, 155.
4. *Proceedings*, 501.
5. *Proceedings*, 502.
6. Gillin, *Shrill Hurrahs*, 67.
7. Congressional report, 5:1578.

8. Congressional report, 3:524.
9. *Proceedings*, 502.
10. *Proceedings*, 594.
11. Gillin, *Shrill Hurrahs*, 67.
12. Sommerville, *Rape and Race in the Nineteenth-Century South*, 149.
13. *Proceedings*, 502.
14. *Proceedings*, 503.
15. Williams, *Great South Carolina Ku Klux Klan Trials*, 89.
16. Kendi, *Stamped from the Beginning*, 42.
17. Sommerville, *Rape and Race in the Nineteenth-Century South*, 148.
18. Sommerville, *Rape and Race in the Nineteenth-Century South*, 150.
19. Sommerville, *Rape and Race in the Nineteenth-Century South*, 155.
20. Proctor, "Whip, Pistol, and Hood," 148.
21. Gillin, *Shrill Hurrahs*, 66.
22. Trelease, *White Terror*, 364.
23. Congressional report, 3:373–79.
24. Congressional report, 3:539–40.
25. *Proceedings*, 511.
26. *Proceedings*, 514.
27. *Proceedings*, 511–13.
28. West, *Reconstruction Ku Klux Klan in York County*, 5–6.
29. *Proceedings*, 312.
30. West, *Reconstruction Ku Klux Klan in York County*, 4.
31. Proctor, "Whip, Pistol, and Hood," 296.
32. Proctor, "Whip, Pistol, and Hood," 286.
33. *Proceedings*, 479, 572.
34. West, *Reconstruction Ku Klux Klan in York County*, 6.
35. *Proceedings*, 576.
36. *Proceedings*, 491–92.
37. *Proceedings*, 508.
38. *Proceedings*, 508.
39. *Proceedings*, 508.
40. *Proceedings*, 509.
41. Proctor, "Whip, Pistol, and Hood," 268–70.
42. *Proceedings*, 508.
43. Sommerville, *Rape and Race in the Nineteenth-Century South*, 178.
44. Sommerville, *Rape and Race in the Nineteenth-Century South*, 177.
45. Wilkerson, *Warmth of Other Suns*, 40.
46. Simkins, "The Ku Klux Klan in South Carolina," 633.
47. Congressional report, 3: 297.
48. Congressional report, p 3: 365–73 (Champion's testimony) and also 3:379–86 (Bowden's testimony).
49. Simkins, "The Ku Klux Klan in South Carolina," 618.
50. "The Ku Klux Trials," *New York Herald*, December 25, 1871, 3.
51. *Proceedings*, 519.
52. *Proceedings*, 483–84.
53. *Proceedings*, 519.
54. *Proceedings*, 483–84.
55. *Proceedings*, 576–77.
56. *Proceedings*, 539.
57. *Proceedings*, 581.

58. *Proceedings*, 584.
59. *Proceedings*, 583.
60. *Proceedings*, 582.
61. *Proceedings*, 586.
62. *Proceedings*, 589.
63. *Proceedings*, 590.
64. *Proceedings*, 592.
65. *Proceedings*, 595.
66. *Proceedings*, 603.
67. *Proceedings*, 603–604.
68. *Proceedings*, 605.
69. *Proceedings*, 606.
70. *Proceedings*, 593.

Chapter Twelve

1. *Proceedings*, 689.
2. *Proceedings*, 690.
3. *Proceedings*, 691–92.
4. *Proceedings*, 690.
5. *Proceedings*, 692.
6. *Proceedings*, 694.
7. *Proceedings*, 693.
8. *Proceedings*, 693–94.
9. *Proceedings*, 695.
10. *Proceedings*, 696.
11. *Proceedings*, 696–98.
12. *Proceedings*, 699.
13. *Proceedings*, 707.
14. *Proceedings*, 709–10.
15. *Proceedings*, 711–12.
16. *Proceedings*, 713–14.
17. *Proceedings*, 744.
18. West, *Reconstruction Ku Klux Klan in York County*, 100.
19. *Proceedings*, 686.
20. *Proceedings*, 688.
21. *Proceedings*, 749.
22. Willoughby, *The "Good Town" Does Well*, 51.
23. *Proceedings*, 752–53.
24. *Proceedings*, 753–54.
25. *Proceedings*, 756.
26. *Proceedings*, 760–63.
27. "A Powerful Letter: Charleston Clergyman on the Ku-Klux Cases," *Charleston* (SC) *Daily News*, December 20, 1871, 5.
28. *Proceedings*, 763.
29. Williams, *Great South Carolina Ku Klux Klan Trials*, 99.
30. "Notes and Details by Mail," *Charleston* (SC) *Daily News*, January 6, 1872, 1.
31. "The State Capital: An End for the Present to the Ku-Klux Trials," *Charleston* (SC) *Daily News*, January 6, 1872, 1.
32. "The Ku Klux Trials," *Charleston* (SC) *Daily News*, January 5, 1872, 1.
33. *Proceedings*, 764.

34. *Proceedings*, 770.
35. *Proceedings*, 782.
36. *Proceedings*, 779.
37. *Proceedings*, 781–82.
38. *Proceedings*, 779.
39. *Proceedings*, 766–67.
40. *Proceedings*, 784.
41. *Proceedings*, 765.
42. Proceedings, 771–72.
43. *Proceedings*, 772.
44. *Proceedings*, 777.
45. *Proceedings*, 774.
46. *Proceedings*, 782.
47. *Proceedings*, 775.
48. *Proceedings*, 776.
49. *Proceedings*, 771.
50. *Proceedings*, 769.
51. *Proceedings*, 779–80.
52. *Proceedings*, 767–68.
53. *Proceedings*, 779.
54. *Proceedings*, 773.
55. *Proceedings*, 775–76.
56. *Proceedings*, 774–75.
57. *Proceedings*, 777–78.
58. *Proceedings*, 789.
59. *Proceedings*, 790.
60. *Proceedings*, 791.

CHAPTER THIRTEEN

1. Miller to Mallaney, May 13, 1985, "Dr. James Rufus Bratton," Bratton Papers, York County Library, Rock Hill, SC.
2. Massy, "Dr. Bratton's Adventures as Ku-Klux Leader."
3. West, *Reconstruction Ku Klux Klan in York County*, 190 n4.
4. Landon, "Kidnapping of Dr. Rufus Bratton," 330.
5. Miller, *Century of Western Ontario*, 181.
6. Williams, *Great South Carolina Ku Klux Klan Trials*, 105–6.
7. Miller, *Century of Western Ontario*, 181–82.
8. Merrill report to Terry, January 4, 1872, 19–20, Letters Received by the Adjutant General, 1871–1880, File 2586—Terry, A. J., National Archives, Washington, DC.
9. "The Case of Dr. J. R. Bratton," *Yorkville Enquirer*, June 27, 1872, 2.
10. Whitley, *In It*, 120–21.
11. "An International Outrage!" *Ottawa Daily Citizen*, June 11, 1872, 1.
12. Pearl, "K Troop," Slate online.
13. Trelease, *White Terror*, 408.
14. Simon, ed., *Papers of Ulysses S. Grant*, Vol. 27, 328.
15. "Post Office Espionage," *Ottawa Daily Citizen*, October 12, 1872, 3.
16. Pearl, "K Troop."
17. Fred Landon, "Kidnapping on London Street in 1872 Developed Into International Incident," *London* (Ont.) *Free Press*, April 23, 1964, 28.
18. "The Abduction of Dr. Bratton: Full Report of the Trial," *Yorkville Enquirer*, August 1, 1872, 4.

19. Fred Landon, "London Kidnapping Led to Jail Term for Court Official," *London* (Ont.) *Free Press*, May 9, 1964, 26.
20. Miller, *Century of Western Ontario*, 180.
21. West, *Reconstruction Ku Klux Klan in York County*, 128.
22. "The Abduction of Dr. Bratton: Full Report of the Trial," *Yorkville Enquirer*, August 1, 1872, 4.
23. "The Abduction of Dr. Bratton: Full Report of the Trial," *Yorkville Enquirer*, August 1, 1872, 4.
24. Pearl, "K Troop."
25. Pearl, "K Troop."
26. "The Abduction of Dr. Bratton: Full Report of the Trial," *Yorkville Enquirer*, August 1, 1872, 4.
27. West, *Reconstruction Ku Klux Klan in York County*, 71.
28. "The Abduction of Dr. Bratton: Full Report of the Trial," *Yorkville Enquirer*, August 1, 1872, 4.
29. Trelease, *White Terror*, 363.
30. Trelease, *White Terror*, 353–54.
31. Fred Landon, "London Kidnapping Led to Jail Term for Court Official," *London* (Ont.) *Free Press*, May 9, 1964, 26.
32. Pearl, "K Troop."
33. Massy, "Dr. Bratton's Adventures as Ku-Klux Leader." (In his article for *Slate* magazine, Matthew Pearl states that Hester recaptured Bratton near Norfolk, Virginia, where he was hoping to find a boat headed north to Canada.).
34. Trelease, *White Terror*, 416.
35. Pearl, "K Troop."
36. Miller, *Century of Western Ontario*, 182.
37. Landon, "Kidnapping of Dr. Rufus Bratton," 332–33.
38. Miller, *Century of Western Ontario*, 182–83.
39. "An International Outrage!" *Ottawa Daily Citizen*, June 11, 1872, 1.
40. Fred Landon, "London Kidnapping Led to Jail Term for Court Official," *London* (Ont.) *Free Press*, May 9, 1964, 26.
41. Calhoun, *Presidency of Ulysses S. Grant*, 329.
42. Miller, *Century of Western Ontario*, 183.
43. "Personal," *Yorkville Enquirer*, July 18, 1872, 2.
44. "Editorial Inklings: The Kidnapping Case," *Yorkville Enquirer*, July 25, 1872, 2.
45. "The Abduction of Dr. Bratton: Full Report of the Trial," *Yorkville Enquirer*, August 1, 1871, 4.
46. "The Abduction of Dr. Bratton: Full Report of the Trial," *Yorkville Enquirer*, August 1, 1871, 4.
47. "The Abduction of Dr. Bratton: Full Report of the Trial," *Yorkville Enquirer*, August 1, 1871, 4.
48. "The Abduction of Dr. Bratton: Full Report of the Trial," *Yorkville Enquirer*, August 1, 1871, 4.
49. West, *Reconstruction Ku Klux Klan in York County*, 129.
50. "The Bratton Abduction Case Again," *Ottawa Daily Citizen*, November 15, 1872, 3.
51. "The U.S. Circuit Court," *Yorkville Enquirer*, December 5, 1872, 2.
52. "Plan to Honor Alleged Klansman Sparks Furor," *Toronto Star*, June 1985, Bratton Papers, York County Library, Rock Hill, SC.

Chapter Fourteen

1. Lane, *Freedom's Detective*, 199.
2. https://friendsofalbanyhistory.wordpress.com/2018/01/23/the-albany-penitentiary/.
3. "The Albany Penitentiary," *Yorkville Enquirer*, August 22, 1872, 3.
4. West, *Reconstruction Ku Klux Klan in York County* , 140–41.
5. "The Albany Penitentiary," *Yorkville Enquirer*, August 22, 1872, 3.
6. Morris and Rothman, eds., *Oxford History of the Prison*, 118.
7. "The Albany Penitentiary," *Yorkville Enquirer*, August 22, 1872, 3.

8. "Scraps and Facts," *Yorkville Enquirer*, September 26, 1872, 2.
9. "South Carolina Prisoners in Albany," *Yorkville Enquirer*, August 1, 1872, 2.
10. "The Albany Penitentiary," *Yorkville Enquirer*, August 22, 1872, 3.
11. West, *Reconstruction Ku Klux Klan in York County*, 140–41.
12. West, *Reconstruction Ku Klux Klan in York County*, 139–41.
13. Farris, *Almost President*, 295.
14. White, *Republic for Which It Stands*, 191.
15. Williams, *Horace Greeley*, 295, 300.
16. Lane, *Freedom's Detective*, 198.
17. Lane, *Freedom's Detective*, 199.
18. "South Carolina Prisoners in Albany," *Yorkville Enquirer*, August 1, 1872, 2.
19. "Col. Whitely's Ku-Klux Report," *Yorkville Enquirer*, August 22, 1872, 3.
20. "Col. Whitely's Ku-Klux Report," *Yorkville Enquirer*, August 22, 1872, 3.
21. Lane, *Freedom's Detective*, 203.
22. Williams, *Great South Carolina Ku Klux Klan Trials*, 123.
23. Williams, *Great South Carolina Ku Klux Klan Trials*, 123.
24. Kaczorowski, *Politics of Judicial Interpretation*, 87–88.
25. Kaczorowski, *Politics of Judicial Interpretation*, 88.
26. West, *Reconstruction Ku Klux Klan in York County*, 143–44.
27. West, *Reconstruction Ku Klux Klan in York County*, 142.
28. Kaczorowski, *Politics of Judicial Interpretation*, 84.
29. Kaczorowski, *Politics of Judicial Interpretation*, 70.
30. Kaczorowski, *Politics of Judicial Interpretation*, 73.
31. Kaczorowski, *Politics of Judicial Interpretation*, 81.
32. Williams, *Great South Carolina Ku Klux Klan Trials*, 123.
33. Trelease, *White Terror*, 416.
34. Williams, *Great South Carolina Ku Klux Klan Trials*, 124.
35. Kaczorowski, *Politics of Judicial Interpretation*, 80.
36. Kaczorowski, *Politics of Judicial Interpretation*, 90.
37. Kaczorowski, *Politics of Judicial Interpretation*, 91.
38. West, *Reconstruction Ku Klux Klan in York County*, 116.
39. Chernow, *Grant*, 710.
40. Egerton, *Wars of Reconstruction*, 301.
41. Coakley, *Role of Federal Military Forces in Domestic Disorders*, 312.
42. Kaczorowski, *Politics of Judicial Interpretation*, 116.
43. Kaczorowski, *Politics of Judicial Interpretation*, 115.
44. "The Supreme Court and the Ku-Klux Act," *Yorkville Enquirer*, March 28, 1872, 2.
45. "The Ku-Klux Cases," *Charleston* (SC) *Daily News*, March 22, 1872, 1.
46. Kaczorowski, *Politics of Judicial Interpretation*, 106.
47. "The Supreme Court and the Ku-Klux Act," *Yorkville Enquirer*, March 28, 1872, 2.
48. "Decision on the Ku-Klux Cases," *Yorkville Enquirer*, April 4, 1872, 2.
49. Kaczorowski, *Politics of Judicial Interpretation*, 116.
50. Kaczorowski, *Politics of Judicial Interpretation*, 122.
51. Foner, *Second Founding*, 134.
52. Kaczorowski, *Politics of Judicial Interpretation*, 126.
53. Foner, *Second Founding*, 135.
54. Foner, *Second Founding*, 135.
55. Baum, *Supreme Court*, 179.
56. Foner, *Second Founding*, 138.
57. Foner, *Second Founding*, 142.

58. Winkler, *Gun Fight*, 144.
59. Foner, *Second Founding*, 146.
60. Winkler, *Gun Fight*, 145.
61. Schmidt, "Principle and Prejudice," 835.
62. Foner, *Second Founding*, 150–51.
63. Foner, *Second Founding*, 154.
64. "The Freaks of Courts," *Harrisburg* (PA) *Telegraph*, October 16, 1883, 2.
65. Foner, *Second Founding*, 161.
66. Foner, "Supreme Court and the History of Reconstruction—and Vice-Versa," 1596.
67. Foner, "Supreme Court and the History of Reconstruction—and Vice-Versa," 1589.
68. Schmidt, "Principle and Prejudice," 836.
69. Schmidt, "Principle and Prejudice," 836.
70. Schmidt, "Principle and Prejudice," 847.

CHAPTER FIFTEEN

1. "Emancipation Day," *Chester* (SC) *Reporter*, January 4, 1872, 2.
2. "Emancipation Day," *Chester* (SC) *Reporter*, January 4, 1872, 2.
3. Holland, *Dominion*, 2.
4. "Emancipation Day," *Chester* (SC) *Reporter*, January 4, 1872, 2.
5. Costa, "Pensions and Retirement Among Black Union Army Veterans," 571.
6. Rosa Williams Union army widows pension application No. 524175, National Archives, Washington, DC.
7. Rosa Williams Union army widows pension application No. 524175, National Archives, Washington, DC.
8. Costa, "Pensions and Retirement Among Black Union Army Veterans,"572–74.
9. Arkansas Confederate Pension Records, 1901–1929, Arkansas State Archives, "John C. Farris," accessed via familysearch.org.
10. Arkansas Confederate Pension Records, 1901–1929, Arkansas State Archives, "John C. Farris," accessed via familysearch.org.
11. Arkansas Confederate Pension Records, 1901–1929, Arkansas State Archives, "John C. Farris," accessed via familysearch.org.
12. Trelease, *White Terror*, 417.
13. Current, *Those Terrible Carpetbaggers*, 342–44.
14. Croswell, "In the Shade of the Palmetto,"56, 67.
15. Zuczek, *State of Rebellion*, 164.
16. Calhoun, *Presidency of Ulysses S. Grant*, 550–51.
17. Croswell, "In the Shade of the Palmetto,"61–62.
18. Andrew, *Wade Hampton*, 370–71.
19. Andrew, *Wade Hampton*, 380.
20. "Hampton: Grand Demonstration by the York Democracy," *Yorkville Enquirer*, October 19, 1876, 2.
21. Andrew, *Wade Hampton*, 379.
22. Zuczek, *State of Rebellion*, 170.
23. Andrew, *Wade Hampton*, 422.
24. Andrew, *Wade Hampton*, 381.
25. Andrew, *Wade Hampton*, 384, 395–96.
26. Andrew, *Wade Hampton*, 422.
27. Andrew, *Wade Hampton*, 423.
28. Andrew, *Wade Hampton*, 431.
29. Andrew, *Wade Hampton*, 427.

30. Jarrell, *Wade Hampton and the Negro*, 134–35.
31. Andrew, *Wade Hampton*, 428.
32. Jarrell, *Wade Hampton and the Negro*, 137.
33. Wade Hampton to John S. Bratton, June 14, 1878, Folder 154, Bratton Family Papers, University of South Carolina Caroliniana Library.
34. John S. Bratton to J. Rufus Bratton, June 15, 1878, Bratton Family Papers, University of South Carolina Caroliniana Library.
35. "Return of Dr. Bratton," *Yorkville Enquirer*, November 21, 1878, 2.
36. "Reminiscences of Western York," *Yorkville Enquirer*, December 5, 1888, 1.
37. "Public Meeting," *Yorkville Enquirer*, November 30, 1887, 2.
38. "Death of Dr. Bratton," *Yorkville Enquirer*, September 4, 1897, 2.
39. "Death of Dr. Bratton," *Yorkville Enquirer*, September 4, 1897, 2.
40. Cook, *Fire from the Flint*, 13–14.
41. Dixon, *The Clansman*, 138.
42. Cook, *Fire from the Flint*, 121.
43. Dixon, *The Clansman*, 143.
44. Slide, *American Racist*, 41.
45. Slide, *American Racist*, 44–45.
46. Carnes, ed., *Past Imperfect*, 138.
47. Carnes, ed., *Past Imperfect*, 136–38.
48. Rothman, "When Bigotry Paraded Through the Streets."
49. Rothman, "When Bigotry Paraded Through the Streets."
50. Current, *Those Terrible Carpetbaggers*, 397.
51. Current, *Those Terrible Carpetbaggers*, 456 n19.
52. Fowler, "Carpetbagger's Conversion to White Supremacy," 286.
53. Fowler, "Carpetbagger's Conversion to White Supremacy," 294.
54. Fowler, "Carpetbagger's Conversion to White Supremacy," 296.
55. Fowler, "Carpetbagger's Conversion to White Supremacy," 296.
56. Current, *Those Terrible Carpetbaggers*, 397–98.
57. Fowler, "Carpetbagger's Conversion to White Supremacy," 299–301.
58. Current, *Those Terrible Carpetbaggers*, 399–400.
59. Croswell, "In the Shade of the Palmetto," 72–73.
60. Budiansky, *Bloody Shirt*, 142.
61. Martinez, *Carpetbaggers, Cavalry, and the Ku Klux Klan*, 221.
62. Trelease, *White Terror*, 417.
63. Budiansky, *Bloody Shirt*, 143.
64. Martinez, *Carpetbaggers, Cavalry, and the Ku Klux Klan*, 223.
65. Trelease, *White Terror*, 417.
66. Martinez, *Carpetbaggers, Cavalry, and the Ku Klux Klan*, 223.
67. Martinez, *Carpetbaggers, Cavalry, and the Ku Klux Klan*, 235.
68. Steiner, *Life of Reverdy Johnson*, 270.
69. Reed, ed. *Bench and Bar of Ohio*, Vol. 1, 85.
70. Brooks Dubose, "Two Years After Its Removal from Annapolis, Taney Statue Sits in Storage," *Annapolis* (MD) *Capital Gazette*, September 30, 2019, https://www.capitalgazette.com/maryland/annapolis/ac-cn-taney-statue-20190926-20190930-hirgfzbu3zaylp7mbfkectquz4-story.html.
71. "Replace Roger Taney's Statue in Maryland with One of This Man," *Washington Post*, August 16, 2017, https://www.washingtonpost.com/opinions/five-confederate-statues-in-maryland-will-be-removed-here-are-some-candidates-to-replace-them/2017/08/16/1681478a-8299-11e7-902a-2a9f2d808496_story.html.
72. Fuke, "Hugh Lennox Bond and the Radical Republican Ideology," 578–80.

73. Hamilton, "Amos T. Akerman and His Role in American Politics," 110.
74. Kousser and McPherson, eds., *Region, Race and Reconstruction*, 412.
75. Kousser and McPherson, eds., *Region, Race and Reconstruction*, 411.
76. Hamilton, "Amos T. Akerman and His Role in American Politics," 112.
77. Hamilton, "Amos T. Akerman and His Role in American Politics," 111.
78. Hamilton, "Amos T. Akerman and His Role in American Politics," 117.
79. Hamilton, "Amos T. Akerman and His Role in American Politics," 118.
80. https://www.reuters.com/article/us-usa-election-locations/southern-us-states-have-closed-1200 -polling-places-in-recent-years-rights-group-idUSKCN1VV09J.
81. https://www.tennessean.com/story/news/politics/2020/07/09/tennessee-capitol-commission -votes-remove-nathan-bedford-forrest-bust/5380243002.
82. Catherine Muccigrosso, "York Church Brings 'Ugly' History to Forefront with Festival Event, Marker Unveiling," *Rock Hill* (SC) *Herald*, May 5, 2017, https://www.heraldonline.com/news/ local/article148883959.html.
83. Quotes taken from video produced by Allison Creek Presbyterian Church: https://youtu.be/ LGUqofAQgMM.

BIBLIOGRAPHY

Anderson, Eric, and Alfred A. MossJr., eds. *The Facts of Reconstruction: Essays in Honor of John Hope Franklin.* Baton Rouge and London: Louisiana State University Press, 1991.

Andrew, Rod, Jr. *Wade Hampton: Confederate Warrior to Southern Redeemer.* Chapel Hill and London: University of North Carolina Press, 2008.

Andrews, Sidney. *The South Since the War.* Baton Rouge: Louisiana State University Press, 2004.

Ball, Edward. *Slaves in the Family.* New York: Farrar, Straus and Giroux, 2014.

Baum, Lawrence. *The Supreme Court.* Washington, DC: CQ Press, 2016.

Blair, William. *Cities of the Dead: Contesting the Memory of the Civil War in the South, 1865–1914.* Chapel Hill and London: University of North Carolina Press, 2004.

Blight, David W. *Frederick Douglass: Prophet of Freedom.* New York and London: Simon and Schuster, 2018.

———. *Race and Reunion: The Civil War in American Memory.* Cambridge, MA, and London: The Belknap Press of Harvard University Press, 2001.

Boritt, Gabor S., ed. *Why the Confederacy Lost.* New York and Oxford: Oxford University Press, 1992.

Brooks, U. R. *South Carolina Bench and Bar.* Columbia, SC: The State Company, 1908.

Brown, Douglas Summers. *A City without Cobwebs: A History of Rock Hill, South Carolina.* Columbia: University of South Carolina Press, 1955.

Brown, Mary Davis. *Oil in Our Lamps: The Journals of Mary Davis Brown from the Beersheba Presbyterian Church Community, York, SC, 1854–1901.* Columbia, SC: Self-published by The Descendants of Mary Davis Brown, 2010.

Budiansky, Stephen. *The Bloody Shirt: Terror after the Civil War.* New York: Plume, 2009.

Calhoun, Charles W. *The Presidency of Ulysses S. Grant.* Lawrence: University Press of Kansas, 2017.

Carnes, Mark C., ed. *Past Imperfect: History According to the Movies.* New York: Henry Holt and Company, 1995.

Chernow, Ron. *Grant.* New York: Penguin Press, 2017.

Coakley, Robert W. *The Role of Federal Military Forces in Domestic Disorders, 1789–1878.* Washington, DC: Center of Military History, United States Army, 1988.

Cook, Raymond Allen. *Fire from the Flint: The Amazing Careers of Thomas Dixon.* Winston-Salem, NC: John F. Blair, 1968.

Current, Richard Nelson. *Those Terrible Carpetbaggers: A Reinterpretation.* New York and Oxford: Oxford University Press, 1988.

Dawsey, Cyrus B., and James M. Dawsey, eds. *The Confederados: Old South Immigrants in Brazil.* Tuscaloosa: University of Alabama Press, 1998.

Dennett, John Richard. *The South as It Is, 1865-1866.* Tuscaloosa: University of Alabama Press, 2010.

Dixon, Thomas. *The Clansman: A New Edition.* Monee, IL: CreateSpace Independent Publishing Platform, 2015.

Du Bois, W. E. B. *Black Reconstruction in America: 1860–1880.* New York and London: The Free Press, 1992.

Edsall, Thomas Byrne, and Mary D. Edsall. *Chain Reaction: The Impact of Race, Rights, and Taxes on American Politics*. New York and London: W.W. Norton & Company, 1991.

Egerton, Douglas R. *The Wars of Reconstruction: The Brief, Violent History of America's Most Progressive Era*. New York: Bloomsbury Press, 2015.

Epps, Garrett. *Democracy Reborn: The Fourteenth Amendment and the Fight for Equal Rights in Post–Civil War America*. New York: Henry Holt and Company, 2006.

Faris, David. *The Faris Family of Washington County, Indiana*. Baltimore: Gateway Press, 1984.

Farris, Scott. *Almost President: The Men Who Lost the Race but Changed the Nation*. Guilford, CT: Lyons Press, 2012.

Faust, Drew Gilpin. *James Henry Hammond and the Old South: A Design for Mastery*. Baton Rouge: Louisiana State University Press, 1985.

Fleming, Walter L. *The Freedmen's Savings Bank: A Chapter in the Economic History of the Negro Race*. Chapel Hill: University of North Carolina Press, 1927.

Foner, Eric. *Forever Free: The Story of Emancipation and Reconstruction*. New York: Vintage Books, 2005.
———. *Reconstruction: America's Unfinished Revolution, 1863–1877*. New York: Harper & Row, 1988.
———. *The Second Founding: How the Civil War and Reconstruction Remade the Constitution*. New York: W.W. Norton & Company, 2019.

Franklin, John Hope. *Reconstruction after the Civil War*. Chicago and London: University of Chicago Press, 1994.

Franklin, John Hope, and Alfred A. Moss Jr. *From Slavery to Freedom: A History of Negro Americans*. New York: McGraw-Hill, 1988.

Frazier, Charles. *Cold Mountain: A Novel*. New York: Atlantic Monthly Press, 1997.

Freeman, Joanne B. *The Field of Blood: Violence in Congress and the Road to Civil War*. New York: Farrar, Straus and Giroux, 2018.

Gallagher, Gary W., and Alan T. Nolan, eds. *The Myth of the Lost Cause and Civil War History*. Bloomington and Indianapolis: Indiana University Press, 2000.

Gates, Henry Louis, Jr. *Stony the Road: Reconstruction, White Supremacy, and the Rise of Jim Crow*. New York: Penguin Press, 2019.

Gillette, William. *Retreat from Reconstruction, 1869–1879*. Baton Rouge: Louisiana State University Press, 1979.

Gillin, Kate Côté. *Shrill Hurrahs: Women, Gender, and Racial Violence in South Carolina, 1865–1900*. Columbia: University of South Carolina Press, 2013.

Hadden, Sally E. *Slave Patrols: Law and Violence in Virginia and the Carolinas*. Cambridge, MA, and London: Harvard University Press, 2001.

Halbrook, Stephen *Securing Civil Rights: Freedmen, the Fourteenth Amendment, and the Right to Bear Arms*. Oakland, CA: The Independent Institute, 2010.

Hall, S. B. *A Shell in the Radical Camp, or an Exposition of the Frauds of the Republican Party of South Carolina*. Charleston, SC: John C. Hundley & Brother, 1873.

Harris, Trudier. *Exorcising Blackness: Historical and Literary Lynching and Burning Rituals*. Bloomington: Indiana University Press, 1984.

Higginson, Thomas Wentworth. *Army Life in a Black Regiment*. Cambridge, MA: Riverside Press, 1900.

Holland, Tom. *Dominion: How the Christian Revolution Remade the World*. New York: Basic Books, 2019.

Horwitz, Tony. *Confederates in the Attic: Dispatches from the Unfinished Civil War*. New York: Vintage Departures, 1998.

Jarrell, Hampton M. *Wade Hampton and the Negro: The Road Not Taken*. Columbia: University of South Carolina Press, 1949.

Kaczorowski, Robert J. *The Politics of Judicial Interpretation: The Federal Courts, Department of Justice, and Civil Rights, 1866–1876*. New York: Fordham University Press, 2005.

Kendi, Ibram X. *Stamped from the Beginning: The Definitive History of Racist Ideas in America*. New York: Nation Books, 2016.

Kousser, J. Morgan, and James M. McPherson, eds. *Region, Race and Reconstruction: Essays in Honor of C. Vann Woodward*. New York and Oxford: Oxford University Press, 1982.

Lane, Charles. *Freedom's Detective: The Secret Service, the Ku Klux Klan and the Man Who Masterminded America's First War on Terror*. Toronto: Hanover Square Press, 2019.

Langguth, A. J. *After Lincoln: How the North Won the Civil War and Lost the Peace*. New York and London: Simon & Schuster Paperbacks, 2014.

Leland, John A. *A Voice from South Carolina: Twelve Chapters before Hampton, Two Chapters after Hampton with a Journal of a Reputed Ku-Klux*. Charleston, SC: Walker, Evans & Cogswell, 1879.

Lepore, Jill. *These Truths: A History of the United States*. New York and London: W.W. Norton & Company, 2018.

Leyburn, James G. *The Scotch-Irish: A Social History*. Chapel Hill: University of North Carolina Press, 1962.

Litwack, Leon F. *Been in the Storm So Long: The Aftermath of Slavery*. New York: Vintage Books, 1980.

Long, E. B., and Barbara Long. *The Civil War Day by Day: An Almanac 1861–1865*. New York: Da Capo Press, Inc., 1971.

Low, W. A., and Virgil A. Clift, eds. *Encyclopedia of Black America*. New York: McGraw-Hill, 1981.

Mandle, Jay R. *Not Slave, Not Free: The African American Economic Experience Since the Civil War*. Durham, NC, and London: Duke University Press, 1992.

Martinez, J. Michael. *Carpetbaggers, Cavalry, and the Ku Klux Klan: Exposing the Invisible Empire during Reconstruction*. London and Boulder: Rowman & Littlefield, 2007.

McDougall, Walter A. *Throes of Democracy: The American Civil War Era, 1829–1877*. New York and London: Harper Perennial, 2008.

McFeely, William S. *Grant: A Biography*. New York and London: W.W. Norton & Company, 1982.

McPherson, James M. *Battle Cry of Freedom: The Civil War Era*. New York and Oxford: Oxford University Press, 1988.

———. *Ordeal by Fire: The Civil War and Reconstruction*. New York: McGraw-Hill, 1992.

Mendenhall, Samuel Brooks. *Tales of York County*. Rock Hill, SC: Reynolds & Reynolds, 1989.

Miller, Orlo. *A Century of Western Ontario: The Story of London*. Toronto: Ryerson Press, 1949.

Morris, Norval, and David J. Rothman, eds. *The Oxford History of the Prison: The Practice of Punishment in Western Society*. New York and Oxford: Oxford University Press, 1995.

Neiman, Susan. *Learning from the Germans: Race and the Memory of Evil*. New York: Farrar, Straus and Giroux, 2019.

Oshinsky, David M. *Worse Than Slavery: Parchman Farm and the Ordeal of Jim Crow Justice*. New York: The Free Press, 1996.

Parsons, Elaine Frantz. *Ku-Klux: The Birth of the Klan during Reconstruction*. Chapel Hill: University of North Carolina Press, 2015.

Prince, K. Stephen. *Stories of the South: Race and the Reconstruction of Southern Identity, 1865–1915*. Chapel Hill: University of North Carolina Press, 2014.

Proceedings in the Ku Klux Trials, at Columbia, S.C., in the United States Circuit Court, November Term, 1871. London: Forgotten Books, 2015.

Reed, George Irving, ed. *Bench and Bar of Ohio: A Compendium of History and Biography*, Vol. 1. Chicago: Century Publishing, 1897.

Reid, Whitelaw. *After the War: A Tour of the Southern States, 1865–1866*. New York: Harper Torchbooks, 1965.

Report of the Joint Select Committee to Enquire into the Condition of Affairs in the Late Insurrectionary States, Vol. 3. Washington: Government Printing Office, 1872. (2018 reprint by Facsimile Publisher, Delhi, India)

Report of the Joint Select Committee to Enquire into the Condition of Affairs in the Late Insurrectionary States, Vol. 4. Washington: Government Printing Office, 1872. (2018 reprint by Facsimile Publisher, Delhi, India)

Report of the Joint Select Committee to Enquire into the Condition of Affairs in the Late Insurrectionary States, Vol. 5. Washington: Government Printing Office, 1872. (2018 reprint by Facsimile Publisher, Delhi, India)

Reynolds, John S. *Reconstruction in South Carolina, 1865–1877.* Columbia, SC: The State Co. Publishers, 1905.

Rolle, Andrew F. *The Lost Cause: The Confederate Exodus to Mexico.* Norman: University of Oklahoma Press, 1992.

Safire, William. *Safire's Political Dictionary.* New York and Oxford: Oxford University Press, 2008.

Schurz, Carl. *Report on the Condition of the South: 1865, Civil War Classic Library.* Middletown, DE: CreateSpace Independent Publishing Platform, 2012.

Scoggins, Michael C. *A Brief History of Historic Brattonsville.* Rock Hill, SC: York County Culture and Heritage Commission, 2014.

Scoggins, Michael C., and Nancy Sambets. *York: Images of America.* Charleston, SC, and Chicago: Arcadia Publishing, 2007.

Shapiro, Herbert. *White Violence and Black Response: From Reconstruction to Montgomery.* Amherst: University of Massachusetts Press, 1988.

Simon, John Y., ed. *The Papers of Ulysses S. Grant, Volume 27, January 1–October, 31, 1876.* Carbondale: Southern Illinois University Press, 2005.

Slide, Anthony. *American Racist: The Life and Films of Thomas Dixon.* Lexington: University of Kentucky Press, 2004.

Smith, Jean Edward. *Grant.* New York and London: Simon & Schuster, 2001.

Smith, John David. *We Ask Only for Even-Handed Justice: Black Voices from Reconstruction, 1865–1877.* Amherst and Boston: University of Massachusetts Press, 2014.

Sommerville, Diane Miller. *Rape and Race in the Nineteenth-Century South.* Chapel Hill: University of North Carolina Press, 2004.

Steiner, Bernard C. *The Life of Reverdy Johnson.* Baltimore: The Norman, Remington Company, 1914.

Taylor, Susie King. *Reminiscences of My Life in Camp With the 33rd United States Colored Troops.* San Bernardino, CA: CreateSpace Independent Publishing Platform, 2015.

Tindall, George Brown. *The Emergence of the New South, 1913–1945.* Baton Rouge: Louisiana State University Press, 1967.

———. *South Carolina Negroes: 1877–1900.* Columbia: University of South Carolina Press, 1952.

Trelease, Allen W. *White Terror: The Ku Klux Klan Conspiracy and Southern Reconstruction.* Baton Rouge and London: Louisiana State University Press, 1971.

Vile, John R., ed. *Great American Judges: An Encyclopedia, Volume One.* Santa Barbara, CA, Denver and Oxford: ABC CLIO, 2003.

Wang, Xi. *The Trial of Democracy: Black Suffrage and Northern Republicans, 1860–1910.* Athens: University of Georgia Press, 1997.

Webb, James. *Born Fighting: How the Scots-Irish Shaped America.* New York: Broadway Books, 2004.

Weiner, Mark S. *Black Trials: Citizenship from the Beginnings of Slavery to the End of Caste.* New York: Vintage Books, 2006.

West, Jerry L. *The Bloody South Carolina Election of 1876: Wade Hampton III, the Red Shirt Campaign for Governor and the End of Reconstruction.* Jefferson, NC: McFarland & Company, 2010.

———. *The Reconstruction Ku Klux Klan in York County, South Carolina, 1865–1877.* Jefferson, NC: McFarland & Company, Inc., 2002.

White, Richard. *The Republic for Which It Stands: The United States During Reconstruction and the Gilded Age, 1865–1896.* New York and Oxford: Oxford University Press, 2017.

White, Ronald C. *American Ulysses: A Life of Ulysses S. Grant.* New York: Random House, 2017.

Whitley, Hiram C. *In It.* Cambridge, MA: Riverside Press, 1894.

Wilkerson, Isabel. *The Warmth of Other Suns: The Epic Story of America's Great Migration.* New York: Vintage Books, 2010.

Williams, Lou Falkner. *The Great South Carolina Ku Klux Klan Trials, 1871–1872*. Athens and London: University of Georgia Press, 2004.

Williams, Robert C. *Horace Greeley: Champion of American Freedom*. New York and London: New York University Press, 2006.

Williamson, Joel. *After Slavery: The Negro in South Carolina during Reconstruction*. New York: W.W. Norton & Company, 1965.

Willoughby, Lynn. *The "Good Town" Does Well: Rock Hill, S.C., 1852–2002*. Orangeburg, SC: Written in Stone, 2002.

Wills, Garry. *Lincoln at Gettysburg: The Words That Remade America*. New York and London: Simon & Schuster, 1992.

Wineapple, Brenda. *Ecstatic Nation: Confidence, Crisis, and Compromise, 1848–1877*. New York: Harper, 2013.

———. *The Impeachers: The Trial of Andrew Johnson and the Dream of a Just Nation*. New York: Random House, 2019.

Winik, Jay. *April 1865: The Month That Saved America*. New York and London: Harper Perennial, 2001.

Winkler, Adam. *Gun Fight: The Battle Over the Right to Bear Arms in America*. New York and London: W.W. Norton & Company, 2013.

Witt, John Fabian. *Patriots and Cosmopolitans: Hidden Histories of American Law*. Cambridge, MA, and London: Harvard University Press, 2007.

Woodward, C. Vann. *Origins of the New South, 1877–1913*. Baton Rouge: Louisiana State University Press, 1971.

Zuczek, Richard. *State of Rebellion: Reconstruction in South Carolina*. Columbia: University of South Carolina Press, 1996.

Unpublished Works

Bratton, James Rufus, "For My Children in Future Life," undated, Bratton Family Papers, Louise Pettus Archives, Winthrop University.

Bratton, Virginia Mason, "Dr. J. R. Bratton," undated, Bratton Papers, York County Library, Rock Hill, SC.

Brattonsville Oral History Project, Historical Center of York County.

Crosswell, Ryan, "In the Shade of the Palmetto: Reconstruction, South Carolina, and David T. Corbin," senior honor's thesis, Vanderbilt University, 2003.

Hall, Marsha, "Dr. James Rufus Bratton," student research paper, Winthrop University, 1978, "Caroliniana," Louise Pettus Archives, Winthrop University.

Hamilton, Lois Neal, "Amos T. Akerman and His Role in American Politics," master's thesis, Columbia University, 1939.

Massy, Rebecca, "Dr. Bratton's Adventures as Ku-Klux Leader," undated, Bratton Papers, York County Library, Rock Hill, SC.

Miller to Mallaney letter, May 13, 1985, "Dr. James Rufus Bratton," Bratton Papers, York County Library, Rock Hill, SC.

Proctor, David Bradley, "The Reconstruction of White Supremacy: The Ku Klux Klan in Piedmont North Carolina, 1868 to 1872," master's thesis, University of North Carolina, Chapel Hill, 2009.

Proctor, David Bradley, "Whip, Pistol, and Hood: Ku-Klux Violence in the Carolinas During Reconstruction," doctoral dissertation, University of North Carolina, Chapel Hill, 2013.

Scoggins, Michael C., "Inventory of Slaves Belonging to the Estate of Dr. John Bratton, August 1843," undated, Michael C. Scoggins Collection, Historical Center of York County.

Swinney, Everett, "Suppressing the Ku Klux Klan: The Enforcement of the Reconstruction Amendments 1870–1877," doctoral dissertation, University of Texas–Austin, 1966.

Periodicals

Alschuler, Albert W., and Andrew G. Deiss, "A Brief History of the Criminal Jury in the United States," *University of Chicago Law Review*, Vol. 61 (1994).

Bond, James E., "The Original Understanding of the Fourteenth Amendment in Illinois, Ohio, and Pennsylvania," *Akron Law Review*, Vol. 18, no. 3 (1985).

Costa, Dora L., "Pensions and Retirement among Black Union Army Veterans," *Journal of Economic History*, Vol. 70, no. 3 (September 2010).

Curtis, Michael Kent, "The Curious History of Attempts to Suppress Antislavery Speech, Press, and Petition in 1835–37," *Northwestern University Law Review*, Vol. 89, no. 3.

"Departure of Our Fall Expedition," *African Repository*, Vol XLVII, no. 12 (December 1871).

Emberton, Carole, "The Limits of Incorporation: Violence, Gun Rights, and Gun Regulation in the Reconstruction South," *Stanford Law and Policy Review*, Vol. 17, no. 3 (2006)

Foner, Eric, "The Supreme Court and the History of Reconstruction—and Vice-Versa," *Columbia Law Review*, Vol. 112, no. 7 (November 2012).

Forman, James Jr., "Juries and Race in the Nineteenth Century," *Yale Law Journal*, Vol. 113 (2003).

Fowler, Wilton B., "A Carpetbagger's Conversion to White Supremacy," *North Carolina Historical Review*, Vol. 43, no. 3 (July 1966).

Fuke, Richard Paul, "Hugh Lennox Bond and the Radical Republican Ideology," *Journal of Southern History*, Vol. 45, no. 4 (November 1979).

Hansen, Susan, "The Racial History of the U.S. Military Academies," *Journal of Blacks in Higher Education*, Vol. 26, Winter, 1999-2000.

Landon, Fred, "The Kidnapping of Dr. Rufus Bratton," *Journal of Negro History*, Vol. 10, no. 3 (July 1925).

McNeil, John, "Retaliation in Missouri," *Century Illustrated Monthly Magazine*, Vol. 38 (1889).

Pearl, Matthew, "K Troop: The Untold Story of the Eradication of the Original Ku Klux Klan," *Slate Online Magazine*, March 4, 2016, www.slate.com/articles/news_and_politics/history/2016/03/how_a_detachment_of_u_s_army_soldiers_smoked_out_the_original_ku_klux_klan.html.

Pettus, Louise, "York County Men in Bloody Kansas," *York County Genealogical and Historical Society Quarterly*, Vol. X, no. 1 (June 1998).

Popper, Robert, "History and Development of the Accused's Right to Testify," *Washington University Law Review*, Vol. 1962, Issue 4 (January 1962).

Post, Louis F., "A Carpetbagger in South Carolina," *Journal of Negro History*, Vol. 10, no. 1, (January 1925).

"A Remarkable Man for Liberia," *African Repository*, Vol XLVII, no. 9 (September 1871).

Rothman, Joshua, "When Bigotry Paraded Through the Streets," *The Atlantic*, December 4, 2016, https://www.theatlantic.com/politics/archive/2016/12/second-klan/509468.

Schmidt, Benno C., Jr., "Principle and Prejudice: The Supreme Court and Race in the Progressive Era. Part 3: Black Disfranchisement from the KKK to the Grandfather Claus," *Columbia Law Review*, Vol. 82, no. 5 (June 1982).

Scoggins, Michael, "The Jim Williams Incident," *YC Magazine*, February 2009, York County Library, Rock Hill, SC.

Simkins, Francis B., "The Ku Klux Klan in South Carolina," *Journal of Negro History*, Vol. 12, no. 4 (October 1927).

Zuczek, Richard, "The Federal Government's Attack on the Ku Klux Klan: A Reassessment," *South Carolina Historical Magazine*, Vol. 97, no. 1 (January 1996).

Newspapers
Atlanta Constitution
Charleston (SC) *Daily Courier*
Charleston (SC) *Daily News*
London (ON) *Free Press*
New York Herald
New York Times
New York Tribune
Ottawa Daily Citizen
Rock Hill (SC) *Herald*
Yorkville (SC) *Enquirer*

Other Sources and Collections
Arkansas Confederate Pension Records, 1901–1929, Arkansas State Archives, Little Rock, AR.

Bratton Papers, York County Library, Rock Hill, SC.

Bratton Family Papers, Louise Pettus Archives, Winthrop University, Rock Hill, SC.

Bratton Family Papers, University of South Carolina Caroliniana Library, Columbia, SC.

Michael C. Scoggins Collection, Historical Center of York County, York, SC.

Letters Received by the Adjutant General, 1871–1880, Record Group 94, File 1432, National Archives and Records Administration, Washington, DC.

Letters Received by the Adjutant General, 1871–1880, File 2586—Terry, A. J., National Archives and Records Administration, Washington, DC.

Records of the District Courts of the United States, Fourth Circuit, Record Group 21.43, Rolls 95 and 97, National Archives and Records Administration, Atlanta, GA.

Widow's Application for Pension (Act of June 27, 1890), Applications Nos. 524175 (Rosa Williams, filed August 15, 1891) and 579537 (Delia Williams, filed January 9, 1892), National Archives and Records Administration, Washington, DC.

INDEX

About the Author

Scott Farris is the *New York Times* best-selling author of *Kennedy & Reagan: Why Their Legacies Endure*, the acclaimed *Inga: Kennedy's Great Love, Hitler's Perfect Beauty, and J. Edgar Hoover's Prime Suspect*, and *Almost President: The Men Who Lost the Race but Changed the Nation*. He is a former bureau chief for United Press International and political columnist who later worked in politics and government affairs, most recently on behalf of renewable energy. He has appeared multiple times on C-SPAN, MSNBC, CNN, and the BBC, and his work has been published in the *New York Times*, *Washington Post*, and *Wall Street Journal*.